PROCEEDINGS OF THE
XIITH INTERNATIONAL CONGRESS OF THE I.A.H.R.

STUDIES

IN THE HISTORY OF RELIGIONS

(SUPPLEMENTS TO *NUMEN*)

XXXI

PROCEEDINGS OF THE
XIITH INTERNATIONAL CONGRESS
OF THE I.A.H.R.

LEIDEN
E.J. BRILL
1975

PROCEEDINGS OF THE
XIITH INTERNATIONAL CONGRESS
OF THE INTERNATIONAL ASSOCIATION
FOR THE HISTORY OF RELIGIONS

HELD WITH THE SUPPORT OF UNESCO AND UNDER THE AUSPICES
OF THE INTERNATIONAL COUNCIL
FOR PHILOSOPHY AND HUMANISTIC STUDIES
AT STOCKHOLM, SWEDEN
August 16-22, 1970

EDITED BY

C. JOUCO BLEEKER — GEO WIDENGREN
ERIC J. SHARPE

LEIDEN
E.J. BRILL
1975

ISBN 90 04 04318 7

PRINTED IN THE NETHERLANDS

TABLE OF CONTENTS

PART FOUR

MINUTES, STATUTES AND MEMBERSHIP OF THE CONGRESS

PREFACE

The Editors regret that circumstances beyond their control have caused an unusually long period of time to elapse between the 1970 Congress of the International Association for the History of Religions and the publication of this volume of Proceedings. As usual a number of scholars have preferred to publish elsewhere the papers they presented to the Congress. This volume also contains a record of other proceedings in connection with the Congress.

The theme of the Congress was "Belief in God: High-God-belief; Pantheism; Polytheism; Monotheism", and the majority of the papers presented reflect one or other aspect of that theme. However, scholars were permitted to present papers outside this general area. The Organization Committee further decided that on this occasion no plenary addresses would be delivered; all papers were therefore read within their appropriate academic section.

The work of collecting papers and summaries, of supervising the typing of the manuscripts as well as of arranging the whole material was carried out by Widengren with the assistance of Dr. Hjärpe. Sharpe revised the manuscripts in English from the linguistic point of view, and checked the typewritten copies with the author's original manuscript. Bleeker finally, took charge of the whole material, seeing it through the press and doing the proof-reading.

C. Jouco Bleeker
Eric J. Sharpe
Geo Widengren

PART ONE

INTRODUCTION

ORGANIZATION OF THE CONGRESS

Honorary Committee

Dr. Helge Ljungberg, Bishop of Stockholm
Professor Dag Norberg, Rector of the University of Stockholm
Landshövding Allan Nordenstam, Stockholm
Professor H.S. Nyberg, Member of the Swedish Academy
Professor Torgny Segerstedt, Rector of the University of Uppsala

Organizing Committee

Professor Geo Widengren (President)
Professor Helmer Ringgren (Secretary)
Professor Carl-Martin Edsman
Professor Sven S. Hartman
Professor Åke Hultkrantz
Professor Hjalmar Sundén
Dr. Jan Hjärpe (Treasurer and Assistant Secretary)

Sections

I. The Ancient Near East and Egypt
   Chairman: Professor Åke Sjöberg
II. Israelite-Jewish Religion
   Chairman: Docent Agge Carlson
III. Christianity
   Chairman: Professor Eric Segelberg
IV. Islam
   Chairman: Professor Annemarie Schimmel
V. Greece and Rome, Hellenism
   Chairman: Professor Herman Ludin Jansen
VI. India and Iran
   Chairman: Professor Sven S. Hartman
VII. Buddhism and the Far East
   Chairman: Professor Joseph M. Kitagawa
VIII. The Religions of Illiterate Peoples, Social and Cultural Anthropology, Folklore
   Chairman: Professor Åke Hultkrantz

IX. Phenomenology and Sociology of Religion, Religious Language
Chairman: Professor Carl-Martin Edsman
X. Psychology of Religion
Chairman: Professor Hjalmar Sundén

PROGRAMME OF THE CONGRESS

August 16   Sunday
10.30   Meeting of the Executive Board
15.00   Meeting of the International Committee

August 17   Monday a.m.
10.00   Opening of the Congress in the Concert Hall (Konsert-huset, Lilla salen) at Hötorget.

Widengren: The Opening Address.

Monday p.m.
14.00   Meetings of sections:

Section I.
Gwyn Griffiths: Triune conceptions of Deity in Ancient Egypt.
Kàkosy: Die Weltanschauliche Krise des Neuen Reiches.
te Velde: Egyptian triads structured as one god with two goddesses.
Bergman: Ba als Gottesbezeichnung

Section III.
Mayeda: Monotheism in the New Testament.
Donini: Christmas and early Christianity.
de Savignac: L'Hymne à Dieu inséré dans les oeuvres de Grégoire de Nazianze, traduction et origine.
Magne: L'exégèse de Gen. 3:5 — 7 attestée par Lc 24:30 — 31 à l'origine du rabaissement, dans le gnosticisme, du dieu de l'Ancien Testament au rang de démiurge mauvais.

Section VI.
Parpola: The Religion of the Indus People.
Dandekar: God in Hinduism.
Bolle: Basic Changes in Indian Religious Conceptions and the Disappearance of Buddhism in India.
Keller: Shiva in Mānikkavācakar's Hymn PōTTi-Tiruvaka-val.

Section VIII.
Ström: Heutige Reste germanischer Götter.
Honko: Finno-Ugric Gods of Heaven.
Johansons: Die Schamanin der Abchazen.

Section IX.
Kippenberg: Gottesglaube und Ideologie.
Weckman: The Structure of Religious Fraternity.
W.C. Smith: Equivalents in various Languages for the term "God".
Raju: Monism and Monotheism.
Pentikäinen: Religio-Anthropological Depth Research.
Bourgault: Noms et structures du divin.

Section X.
Arnold: Moderne Methoden für die Religionspsychologie.
Krenn: Die Problematik des Monotheismus in der Religionspsychologie.

August 18   Tuesday a.m.
9.30   Meetings of sections:

Section I.
Zandee: Gott ist König. Königssymbolismus in den antiken Gottesvorstellungen, besonders in der Religion des alten Ägypten.
Sakellarakis: The Scene of the Bull-sacrifice on the Lamax from H. Triada.
Caquot: Le kathénotheisme sémitique.
Leibovici: Le dieu-ciel dans les civilisations du Proche-Orient.

Section III.
Nelson: Theology, Science, Machines, Faiths: Historic Encounters since the Middle Ages.
Saenz de Santa Maria: El Monoteismo en las Religiones Precristianos del Altiplano Guatemalteco y en sus formas actuales Cristianizadas.
Antweiler: Eine neue Deutung des Anselmischen Proslogion-Beweises.

Section V.
Chirassi-Colombo: The Sacrifice of the Divine Being in Greek Polytheism: some historical and cultural remarks on its origin, meaning and function.
Cold: Transitus Dei. Das Mysterium des Mithras.
H.L. Jansen: Das Gottesbild Plotins.
Betz: The Delphic Maxim "Know Yourself" in Hermetic Interpretation.

Section VII.
Ki-Yong: A New Interpretation of Buddhakāya (Body of Buddha).
Pezzali: The Mādhyamika Philosopher Nāgārjuna according to Chinese Sources.
Dumoulin: Theistic Trends in Japanese Buddhism.
Buri: Das Schicksal des Gottesgedankens in der Religionsphilosophie Keiji Nishitanis.

Section VIII.
Gaba: History of Religions Approach in Study of African Religions.
Sabbatucci: Origine di esseri sovrumani da pratiche divinatorie africane.
Dammann: Die Religion in afrikanischen Sprichwörtern und Rätseln.
Dupré: The God of "Primitive Religion". Some remarks on the idea of God among African Pygmies.

Section IX.
Edsman: Götteridentifikationen, Dämonisierung und Euhemerismus bei Religionsbegegnung.
Hidding: Der Hochgott und der mikrokosmische Mensch.
Colpe: Ideologische Gehalte in modernen Hochgott-Theorien.

Tuesday p.m.
13.30 Meetings of sections:

Section II. [+Section I.]
Heintz: Les lettres royales à la divinité en Mésopotamie et

en Israel antiques. (Esquisse d'un genre littéraire).

Haran: The Father's God and the God of the Fathers. Observations on certain traits of the pre-Mosaic religion.

Heinemann: The Premature Exodus of Ephraim and the Messiah of Ephraim.

Wagner: Zum Geschichtsverständnis des Deuterojesaja.

Section IV.

Montgomery Watt: The Belief in a High-God in Pre-Islamic Mecca.

Waardenburg: Faith and Reason in Koranic Argumentation.

Khoury: Le Dieu du Coran et le Dieu d'Abraham d'après les polémistes byzantins.

Antes: Der eine allmächtige Gott und das Böse, dargestellt an der frühen Ašᶜariya des Islam.

Section VI.

Hein: Monotheism in the Bhagavadgītā? A Stylistic Clue.

Eschmann: Der Avatārgedanke im neueren Hinduismus.

Martin: Variations on Tengalai Belief in a South Indian Village.

Organ: Hinduism as Sādhana.

Section VIII.

Boccassino: Die Seelenidee bei den Atscholi von Uganda.

Schlosser: Die illustrierte Zulu-Schöpfungsgeschichte Laduma Madela's, des Blitz-Zauberers und Gesandten des Schöpfergottes Mvelinqangi.

Krüger: Primitialopfer und Hochgott bei den philippinischen Negritos.

Cain: Die Entstehung von Obergöttern aus Ahnen in Polynesien am Beispiel des samoanischen Tagaloa.

Section IX.

Gerlitz: Pluralismus und Einheit. Universalreligiöse Aspekte in der gegenwärtigen Religionsgeschichte.

Fujimoto: A Contemplation on Religion and Religious Guidance.

Lewis: Phenomenology of Religious Experience and Belief.

Jurji: The Role of the History of Religions in College/University/Seminary Curricula.

Section X.
Kietzig: Möglichkeit und Grenze religionspsychologischer Interpretierung des Neuen Testaments.
Salman: Formes psychologiques des croyances relatives aux dieux.
Sundén: Mystische Gotteserfahrung. Alte Probleme in neuer Sicht.

August 19 Wednesday a.m.
9.30 Meetings of sections

Section II.
Elitzur: Theological Explanation of a Strange Revolt (To the riddle of Jer. 34:8 — 22).
Uffenheimer: Biblical Monotheism in the Light of Modern Research.
Schunck: Zentralheiligtum, Grenzheiligtum und Höhenheiligtum in Israel.

Section III./I. Nag Hammadi.
Robinson: The Nag Hammadi Library as a Collection of Holy Scriptures.
Ménard: L'"Evangile de Vérité" et le Dieu caché des littératures antiques.
Krause: Die Sakramente in der "Exegese über die Seele" in Codex II Nag Hammadi.
Pearson: The Heavenly World according to the First Tractate of the Coptic Gnostic Codex VII from Nag Hammadi.
Zandee: Gottesbegriff der vierten Schrift aus Codex VII von Nag Hammadi.

Section V.
Drijvers: Polytheismus und Monotheismus in der haträischen Religion.

Guépin: Gods do not exist.

Piccaluga: Il mito nel politeismo romano: Tradizioni relative alla fondazione del tempio capitolino.

L.F. Janssen: Die Di Indigetes und die Apotheose des Romulus.

Section VII.

Haglund: Religious Trends in Japan of to-day.

Kitagawa: Ainu Kamuy and Japanese Kami: Contrasts and Similarities.

Yoshida: Sur les problèmes de la mythologie du Japon.

Smart: Problems of the Application of Western Terminology to Theravada Buddhism, with special reference to the relationship between Buddha and the gods.

Section VIII.

Siiger: The Gods of the Lepchas of Sikkim.

Mariscotti: Die Stellung des Gewittergottes in den regionalen Pantheen der Zentral-Anden.

Hellbom: All Saints' Cult, esp. in Mexico.

Hultkrantz: The Structure of Theistic Beliefs among North American Indians.

Section IX.

Bianchi: Croyances en Dieu et dualisme.

Brelich: Comment se forme un dieu?

Brandon: Iconography as a Primary Source for the Conception of Deity.

Klimkeit: Joachim Wach's Hermeneutical Principles.

Szolc: Das Kunstwerk als Ausdruck des Gottesglaubens.

Wednesday p.m.

14.30   Meetings of sections:

Section II.

Mantel: The Dichotomy of Judaism during the Second Temple.

Erlandsson: The Wrath of YHWH.

Simon: L'angélolâtrie juive: mythe ou réalité?

Gaster: "Anoint thee, witch, anoint thee"; the Charm against Lilith.

Section IV.
Mohebbi: Etude comparative sur l'idée de Dieu en Islam Chiite.
Hjärpe: Un texte concernant les "Pseudo-sabéens de Harran".
Schimmel: Mir Dard, a Naqshbandi Mystic of Delhi in the 18th century.

Section VI.
Sharma: Pantheistic Monism.
Jain: Jainism and other Indian Religions. A comparative study.
H.D. Smith: Monthly Ancestral Offerings in Hinduism.
Stephenson: Wirklichkeit und Geschichte im Werk Vivekanandas.

Section VIII.
Sharpe: Andrew Lang and the Problem of Religion.
Parrinder: Monotheism and Pantheism in Africa.
Korvin-Krasinski: Gottheit und Idol.

Section IX.
Waardenburg: The Category of "Faith" in a Phenomenology of Religion.
Oxtoby: Is the Sacred the same as the Holy?
Takeuchi: Time, Space and the Absolute.

Section X.
Ståhlberg: Methods of Personality Studies in Psychology of Religion.
Papadimas: The Fire Walking of "Anasthenaria" in Langada as a Religious Phenomenon.
Gunn: God in Psychedelic Religion.

17.00 *Section IV. and section VI.*
Ghirshman: La Terasse sacrée de Masjid-i-Solaiman.

August 21   Friday a.m.
9.30   Meetings of sections:

Section II.
Philonenko: Shiur Komah: La mesure du corps de Dieu.
Hultgård: Messie et Sauveur dans les Test. XII Patr.
Shatz-Uffenheimer: The Dialectical Concept of God in Lucianic Kabbalah.
Rupp: Amarnaglaube und Jahwemonotheismus.

Section III.
Drynjeff: Réflexions sur l'homilie des Naassènes.
Posse: Isaac de Niniveh.
Klimov: Boehme et la langue adamique.

Section IV.
Makdisi: The Sufism of the Hanbali jurisconsult and theologian Taqi ad-Din Ibn Taimiya.
Bausani: An Islamic Echo of the "Trickster". The ᶜayyārs of Indo-Persian and Malay romances.

Section VI.
Wiessner: Iranisches Christentum und Zoroastrismus.
Kanus-Credé: Das Zarātušt-nāmä des Zartušt Bahrām Pašdū und sein Quellenwert.
Ries: La révélation dans le manichéisme.

Section VIII.
Turner: The Religious Reactions of Primal Societies to Higher Cultures: a new field in the history of religions and a centre for its study.
Bouritius: Jenseitsglauben vorschriftlicher Religionen in phänomenologischer Betrachtung.

Section IX.
Hemberger: Polytheistic Patterns of Thinking in Secret Religions and Secret Societies of Today in the middle of Europe. The Adonism of Dr. Musallam as modern or neo-polytheism.
Lanczkowski: Gotteshüter und verborgene Heilbringer.
Long: Symbols in the Religion of American Blacks.
Vesci: Qualis cultus talis deus. A note on the role of cult in shaping the "Divine".

Fabian: Sexual Fault and Original Sin in the teaching of an African charismatic movement.

Section X.
Keilbach: Zur Frage nach der Echtheit religiösen Er-lebens. Stellungsnahme zu Experiment und Droge.
Magni: Religion and Alcohol.

Friday p.m.
15.30   Meeting of the International Committee.

August 22   Saturday
13.00   Closing of the Congress. Concert Hall.
        Bleeker: "Looking backward and forward".

THE OPENING ADDRESS

BY

PROFESSOR GEO WIDENGREN

In the name of the Executive Board of the International Association for the History of Religions and of the Organizing Committee I declare the XIIth Congress of the I.A.H.R. open.

Since World War II congresses have been organized at Amsterdam (1950), Rome (1955), Tokyo (1958), Marburg (1960) and Claremont (1965). Including the present congress, this means that of the twelve international congresses held since 1900 not less than six have been held since the war. Is it too bold to see in this intensified activity an influence of the I.A.H.R., an organization having as one of its special aims the holding of international congresses? The first international congress was held as early as 1900, but between 1900 and 1940 only six congresses were organized, many of them on a rather small scale. This present congress has approximately 250 registered participants, 130 of whom have offered to read papers.

The biggest congress was that at Rome, counting about 500 participants. Marburg, too, with its 400 participants was a fairly large congress. Various reasons could be adduced to explain why Stockholm has not proved to be a very attractive city for a congress like ours. I do not wish to enter upon an analysis of these factors; I only state the fact.

Before World War II participants in congresses were free to speak on whatever theme they liked — generally, of course, preferring to deal with a subject connected with their own research work. At that time we still lived in a liberal age, and individual freedom was still a prerogative, even at congresses. It cannot be denied that this freedom led to a rather heterogeneous impression of what was offered. Since the second world war things have changed considerably. Special themes have been fixed for readers of papers. This method had the advantage that a certain character of unity was bestowed upon a congress. But above all, in that way a current problem of great interest could be treated from the point of view of various religions and various disciplines. No doubt the method in question brings great advantages. On the other hand it cannot be denied that it also carries with it certain disadvantages. The connection between the official theme and the actual paper could sometimes be rather loose. The chosen theme was a kind of Procrustean Bed, to which everything had to be adjusted — with the same result as in the case of the bed King Procrustes offered his guests.

The Organizing Committee at this congress has tried to be slightly more hospitable to our guests than was Procrustes. We have therefore on the one hand offered the participants a rather general theme — but one of central importance for the history of religions, a theme in which I confess a personal interest — but on the other hand we have given a free choice to delegates to read a paper on any subject within our discipline that is of special interest to an individual scholar. This opportunity has been utilized to a great extent.

The division of the sections at this congress is on the whole rather traditional. Of course there is again a marked difference between the first congress seventy years ago and the present congress. The congress held in Paris in 1900 had fixed the following sections:

I.   Religions of non-civilized peoples and of pre-Columbian America
II.   Religions of the Far East
III.   Religions of Egypt
IV.   Semitic religions: Assyrio-Babylonian, Judaism and Islam
V.   Indo-Iranian religions
VI.   Greco-Roman religions
VII.   Nordic-Teutonic, Celtic and Slavonic religions
VIII.   Christianity

The difference between this division and ours lies in the addition of sections IX and X, the phenomenology of religion and the psychology of religion. However, phenomenological and psychological problems were sometimes touched upon, sometimes actually analysed, already at this first congress. But obviously the predominantly *historical* character of our studies was emphasized at the congress, and expressed also in a letter by Max Müller to Albert Réville, the president of the congress. Gradually a new discipline, the phenomenology of religion, appears in the pro-

ceedings of the following congresses. At the first congress after
the war, that at Amsterdam in 1950, this section was firmly
established, and included papers by Professor Eliade, Professor
James and Professor Kerényi (to mention some outstanding
scholars). At the next congress, that at Rome in 1955, we find
the psychology of religion making its entrance in this section.
Here, at this present congress, we have devoted a special section
to this discipline. The sociology of religion, however, has been
weakly represented at our congresses and we felt there to be no
need to arrange for a special section.

I confess that it has caused some embarrassment that a few
sections have attracted so little interest. Quite especially it has
been felt a loss that the ancient Scandinavian-Teutonic religion
should be so poorly represented as far as quantity is concerned.
However, it may be a consolation that at the second congress in
Basle in 1904 this section had to be suppressed, and at the Paris
congress combined with the section devoted to the so-called
Primitive religions. Other sections poorly represented are those
for classical religions, especially Roman religion. This trend was
observable already in 1964 at the Study Conference in Strasbourg and remarked upon by me in the conference report. One
of our colleagues in Strasbourg told me afterwards that he found
my misgivings somewhat exaggerated, and that he found that
research work in the field of Roman religion was proceeding
satisfactorily. Unfortunately he is not present here to tell us
about the current situation in this field. It is also typical that
Mesopotamian and Near Eastern religion in general is one of the
less-represented fields at our congress. Egyptian religion on the
other hand seems to be better represented at our congresses and
conferences. Islam seemed at one time to be about to receive the
most qualified representation so far, but unfortunately some outstanding scholars have been compelled to withdraw. Nevertheless
the situation may be said to be more satisfactory now than it
used to be. Voices have been heard claiming that Islam is singu-
larly ill-suited to be associated with studies in our field. At the
Jerusalem conference in 1968 I took up for discussion this view
and do not want to repeat what I said then. To my mind there
should be more Islamic studies orientated from the viewpoint of
the History of Religions in general, and I gather that this attitude
is shared by many experts in this field. At the present we must

say that although there is a growing interest in Islam and other world religions among historians of religion, leading up to more concentration on these religions in both research and teaching, there still remains much to be done.

As far as our intimate cooperation with such branches as Islamology and Buddhology and the participation of experts in these fields at our congresses and conferences is concerned, we have really tried to keep in contact. But here we come across in an acute form a difficulty which we encounter in several fields, a difficulty arising out of the compartmentalization of scholarship in our day. Before the First World War, to a certain extent even up to the Second World War, it was natural for prominent scholars who were not holders of chairs in the History of Relgions, but representatives of Classical and Oriental languages as well as Germanic languages, to take an interest in the history of religions, to do excellent research work, and to be present at our congresses. The lists of participants are full of the names of such great philologists. Today the situation is vastly different. At Marburg in 1960 I complained about the absence of many outstanding scholars from our organization. Here I have to express regret at the fact that so many scholars, active in our field, but chiefly possessed of a philological education, do not even visit any congresses of the history of religions. At least a few factors having a bearing upon the situation may be mentioned here. First of all, a scholar who is an Assyriologist, an Egyptologist or a specialist in some other field is a member of an Association of Assyriologists, of Egyptologists, and so on. He goes not only to the vast congresses of Orientalists, *Orientalisten-Tagungen,* etc., but perhaps above all to the conferences and *rencontres* arranged by his own Association. Classical scholars belonging to a well-established discipline of course also have their own international union. And last year scholars concerned with Islamic studies organized themselves in a corresponding union. Congresses for Islamic and Arabic studies have moreover been arranged fairly frequently; one such congress will be held at Brussels in a few weeks' time — an unhappy coincidence. I need not dwell upon corresponding organizations in other fields.

It stands to reason that most workers in our field feel themselves more closely associated with colleagues in their special field of research and prefer to go to their conferences and congresses, reserving for them the communication of research work. Even the historian of religion, working in the field of — let us say — Islamic studies, may of course feel more interested in what is going on in this field than in the vast domains of the History of Religions in general, where one is more or less lost, and is often exposed to the accusation of dilettantism if one should try to keep in touch with what is going on outside one's own field.

But there is another remarkable trend, too. Even when a philologist works with religious texts, analyses them, presents his findings, does all the work we usually classify as appertaining to the History of Religions, he may still refuse to attend our congresses under the pretext that he is no "historian of religions". This tendency seems to be quite especially marked in German-speaking countries. "Ich bin doch kein Religionsgeschichtler", answered one outstanding specialist in Islamic mysticism, when I tried to enlist his cooperation for this congress. I asked him: "Whom would you then qualify as such? Perhaps only holders of chairs for the History of Religions?" He said: "Yes, perhaps". "Then", I replied, "some of the greatest names in the history of our discipline would be no historians of religions. To mention but a few names of a former generation: Cumont, Norden, Reitzenstein, Goldziher, Snouck Hurgronje, Oldenburg, Frazer would be no historians of religions? Is that not ridiculous?" He admitted that it was, adding: "I didn't think of that". But he did not give me his name for the congress.

It is as though the subject itself had lost its good name, its reputation, in some quarters — especially in Germany, where the number of chairs always was deplorably small and where there always was a resistance against our discipline, quite especially among theologians. It is highly regrettable that this aversion now also seems to have spread among orientalists and classical philologists in Germany. My above-mentioned colleague does not belong to this category; he is still active in the field, though refusing to be labelled a "historian of religions". But the trend is undoubtedly to turn away from our studies. Even scholars who in earlier years made excellent, or even pioneer, work in the History of Religions have left the field — at least officially. They refuse their cooperation, declining to be in any way classified as "historians of religion". Such was not the case in former years, as I have said. Before the I.A.H.R. was created in 1950 an International Committee with a permanent Secretary was responsible for the planning of congresses. The International Committee elected at Lund in 1929 counted among its seventeen members such scholars as two anthropologists, Boas and Lowie, two Old Testament and Semitic scholars, S.A. Cook and Eerdmans, four classical scholars, Cumont, von Jahr, Nilsson and Zielinski, one specialist in Arabic and Islamic studies, Sir Thomas Arnold, one specialist in Indo-Iranian philology, Sten Konow, and one scholar with Finno-Ugrian studies as his special subject, Uno Holmberg-Harva, all in all eleven, while at most six scholars, including the Secretary, could be classified as holders of chairs in the History of Religions: Alphandéry and Toutain at the Ecole Pratique des Hautes Etudes, Oltrameare at Geneva, Grønbech at Copenhagen and Pettazzoni at Rome. The Secretary, Professor Bertholet – unless I am mistaken – held a combined chair at Berlin University, representing Old Testament studies as well as the History of Religions. The situation has changed in forty years. Great sections are falling away because of lack of interest. Outstanding experts refuse their cooperation and seem shy of the label of "Religionshistoriker" [*Religionsgeschichtler*] which in Germany appears to have pejorative overtones, whereas *Religionswissenschaftler* sounds more respectable.

Moreover, even where research work is going on, and important results are published, the scholars concerned still do not go to our congresses. Thirty-seven German-speaking scholars have been asked to contribute to the well-known series *Die Religionen der Menschheit*; three of them are now deceased. Seven scholars will treat various aspects of Christian religion, the rest non-Christian religions. Now, of these thirty-seven scholars only three are present at this congress. One outstanding scholar, Professor von Grunebaum, was prevented from coming just a few weeks before the start. To the best of my knowledge no other contributor had announced his intention of coming, except the editor Dr. Schröder, who, however, withdrew after the second circular had been distributed. I abstain from further comment, except that I observe that the situation would seem to be typical of German conditions.

The sections exposed to the havoc already mentioned all fall within the history of religions in its proper sense of a *historical* discipline. The loss is to some extent compensated for by the

development and ever increasing extension of the phenomenology of religion. Already at the pre-war congresses this new discipline made its entrance, though not yet officially recognized as
an independent constituent of the History of Religions. Gradually it has been accepted and its position is long since firmly
established, even if some scholars would prefer to rebaptize it — I
cannot see to what advantage for this discipline. But at no congress has it been numerically so well represented as it is here.

I do not think that anyone would wish to accuse me of mini-
mizing the importance of the Phenomenology of Religion. But I
confess that I look upon this overwhelming domination of phenomenology with some misgivings. I see here, among other
things, a characteristic trait of our time, which as we all know is
extremely anti-historical — in marked contrast to the preceding
century and the period up to the First World War. Since then
there has been an ever growing hostility against all historical
research and against every historical interpretation of facts, except for those having to do with "modern" times (the term
"modern" being in general very vaguely defined).

I do not wish to enter upon a discussion of this trend. What I
want to put forward for your meditation are a few problems of
method. It has always been taken for granted (and how could it
be otherwise?) that the phenomenology of religion takes its material from the sister, or rather mother, discipline, the History of
Religions. Is it possible to understand the phenomenology of
religion, and especially the phenomena of a given religion, without knowing its history? I think the interesting colloquium arranged by our Italian colleagues in Rome in December last year,
with Professor Bianchi as the moving spirit, tended to emphasize
the role played by historical research. We cannot start our career
as workers in phenomenology if we do not know thoroughly the
history of a single religion. He who wants to interpret the religious phenomena must of course know extremely well these phenomena, including their history, which often give us the clue to
their understanding. And although we may think that we could
base our research exclusively on the *modern* history of the great
religions, how would it be possible to understand the problems of
modern times without the historical perspective? And on the
other hand what would a phenomenological study (or phenomenology in general) be like, if the ancient religions were left out of

consideration. Thus the historical study of religion is of continuing importance, not only for its own sake, but also for the study of the phenomenology, sociology and psychology of religion. Time prevents me from dwelling further on this topic.

For the reasons indicated, fewer big guns are to be fired at this congress as at earlier ones. Though I feel the absence of some outstanding scholars regrettable, especially in those cases in which I know that they really *wanted* to participate in the congress, their absence has led to a pleasant feature of this congress: here we meet more young scholars than before. In this regard the difference between 1970 and 1900 is simply fantastic. I am indeed very glad to see this week so many of the younger workers in the field. I have tried to encourage this trend as much as possible. Their presence here is a symptom of the progress of our studies. After all, a new generation of scholars enters the stage. I sincerely hope that they will find here something of the same inspiration and joy I felt 32 years ago when I visited the first congress of my life, the orientalists' congress at Brussels in the company of Professor Nyberg. I was rather young, and probably looked still younger, for when I was introduced to Professor Julian Morgenstern he looked at me and observed: "I suppose this is your first congress."

At this congress there is another characteristic as distinguished from earlier congresses. As you can see in the programme we have papers only in the sections, but no general lectures. Everyone wishing to read a paper has been given the chance to do so. I spoke just now about the big guns fired at a congress. According to my experiences from more than thirty years these big guns are sometimes loaded with blank ammunition. I hasten to add that I have no misgivings about any of our distinguished colleagues here present. I trust they will demonstrate their power in the sections. And I hope that at some social events we will all have the opportunity of listening to the voices of some famous men. Speaking of the sections, I would like to thank the heads of the sections who assumed this task, which can sometimes be rather delicate, as we all saw in Jerusalem two years ago. I thank quite especially the non-Scandinavians, Professor Annemarie Schimmel and Professor Kitagawa.

In many countries, including Sweden, religious studies have lost considerable ground. This fact makes itself felt in many ways. A week ago I visited the best-known supermarket in Stockholm and went to its bookstalls. They were marvellously equipped: you could find there everything from philosophy to crime, from travels to sex. Not even history was absent. But I looked in vain for some books belonging to the field of religious studies. Well, there are bookshops in Stockholm, too, where you can find such books — though decently tucked away in a corner. When one of our greatest publishers of pocket-books advertises these, he mentions all their titles, except those of the books dealing with religious subjects. My friend Professor Georges Dumézil had one of his books, *Les dieux des Germains*, published in a Swedish translation. This book has attracted much interest and has sold well. Yet there were no signs of it on the shelves. This was not an isolated phenomenon. It is extremely rare for a book within the field of the History of Religions to be reviewed in Swedish newspapers or journals. Here again we have lost much, for the situation 25 years ago was altogether different, as I know from my own experience.

Now we may take what attitude to religion we like, be it positive, negative or indifferent. But we cannot ignore its existence. In the history and life of mankind religion has always played a central role and so it does even today to a much greater extent than publishers and mass media in this country seem willing to admit. All honour to galaxies, but, to quote Alexander Pope "the proper study of mankind is man". I hope that this congress will contribute to the understanding of the fundamental role of religion in the history of mankind and on the whole give that contribution to the renaissance of historical studies that is much needed. The History of Religions has behind it a great history and we hope there will be a still greater future for it.

Expressing the hope that the work of the congress will be successful and your stay in Sweden not without its agreeable moments, I have the honour to declare the XIIth Congress of the International Association for the History of Religions open.

"LOOKING BACKWARD AND FORWARD"

BY

PROFESSOR C. JOUCO BLEEKER

Twenty years ago I read at the General Assembly of the congress in Amsterdam a short paper, entitled "Looking backward and forward". With the aid of the résumés of the lectures I made the bold attempt of picturing the main tendencies of the study of the history of religions, of assessing the results of this inquiry and of enumerating the problems which should be tackled in future. At that time I stood at the beginning of my career as Secretary General of the I.A.H.R. Now that I am about to resign my office, I take much pleasure in offering to you, at the request of the President, some afterthoughts on the past twenty years. Again my subject will be: "Looking backward and forward".

Having become wiser than I was twenty years ago, I shall not venture to present a survey of the results of this congress. My purpose is to put forward some ideas on the study of the history of religions with the intention of offering a general view of the research and of opening some kind of perspective. Thus my paper will contain an inventory of what has been achieved in the past twenty years under the aegis of the I.A.H.R., a summary of my experience as Secretary General, a record of the tendencies which in my opinion dominate the history of religions at present, and finally some tentative remarks on our future work.

It is with satisfaction that we can look back on the work which the Association has done in the past twenty years. Many members of this congress will remember with pleasure previous meetings. They will agree with me, when I say that these meetings, each in its own way, reached a high level both of organization and of scholarship. In general the attendance was not so overwhelming that one got lost in the masses of delegates. There was a sufficient opportunity to make acquaintance and to become friends with one another. Our happiest memories must surely include the hours spent with old or new friends, perhaps not in a lecture room, but in some pleasant restaurant. Our strongest impressions may well date from a symposium visited by fifty or sixty persons who met together day by day, and who were therefore able to discuss the main theme thoroughly and at leisure.

Our work started in Amsterdam in 1950 at a congress of modest size, devoted to the then burning issue of "The Mythical-Ritual Pattern". The next congress, in Rome in 1955, was on a larger scale, and its central theme, "The Sacral Kingship", attracted many scholars. Shortly thereafter, in 1958, our Japanese colleagues organized in Tokyo a congress that has become famous. It had several aspects: in the sections all kinds of subjects were treated; because the congress was part of UNESCO's major project on East-West relations, the problems of the relationship between Eastern and Western culture were discussed at a symposium; a series of public lectures was also held. In addition, delegates to the congress made excursions to quite a number of Shinto shrines and Buddhist temples. In 1960 the students of the history of religions assembled in Marburg in Germany, where the main theme was "Origins and Eschatology". There I attempted to start a discussion on the nature of our discipline with a lecture, delivered at the General Assembly and entitled "The Future of the History of Religions". In 1964 a successful symposium took place in Strasbourg, devoted to the theme of "Initiation". Far more ambitious was the congress held in Claremont, California, in 1965, which included, first, sections dealing with the subject of "Guilt or Pollution and Rites of Purification", secondly a symposium on "The Impact of Modern Culture on Traditional Religions", and thirdly, public lectures on "The Role of Historical Scholarship in Changing the Relations among Religions". In this connection may be mentioned also the well-prepared Messina symposium of 1966 on Gnosticism, though the honour or its success should of course be conferred upon the Italian organizers. Lastly, the symposium in Jerusalem in 1968 can be recorded: an interesting subject had been chosen, viz., "Types of Redemption". Moreover this meeting possessed a special significance. At the congress in Tokyo the idea had been mooted that the I.A.H.R., being a world-wide organization, should in future launch two series of congresses, one for the West and the other for the East. Consequently an Afro-Asian secretariat was set up in Tokyo. However, the project of organizing the second Oriental congress in India fell through. Under these circumstances the

I.A.H.R. owes a great debt of gratitude to the Israeli scholars who assumed the difficult task of preparing a symposium in Jerusalem.

Thus far the review of the meetings, and of the subjects which were discussed. The list shows that essential issues of the history of religions have been entered upon, an impression which is strengthened by reading the proceedings of these meetings. These have appeared either as modest collections of the resumes of the lectures, or in the form of the integral publication of all the lectures and discussions: examples of this include the volume on "The Sacral Kingship", the extensive proceedings of the congress in Tokyo and those of the Messina symposium, which is now the standard work on Gnosticism.

This leads to another field of I.A.H.R. activity, i.e. the publications which always appear in a well-produced form thanks to the excellent services of our publishers, E. J. Brill of Leiden. Particularly well-known is *Numen*, the international review for the history of religions, which was founded by Pettazzoni, and which now appears in its seventeenth volume. The Editor-in-chief may perhaps be allowed to express the hope that he has managed to raise its level steadily. But he is not content. He receives far too little support from those scholars who might be considered to belong to the "inner circle" of the I.A.H.R. Let everybody take this remark to heart. With the support of U.N.E.S.C.O. a bibliography is published, of which the twelfth volume will soon appear. If the Secretary General were not already grey-haired on account of his age, the difficulties attending the publication of this bibliography would have made him so. That is, however, in no way the fault of the present bibliographer, Dr. Alich, who is a capable and conscientious worker. After having fallen into arrears due to personal circumstances he has by a great effort completed the manuscripts of the bibliographies for 1965 and 1966, and the volumes for 1967 and 1968 will probably appear in the course of next year. To *Numen* two series of supplements are attached: seventeen "Studies in the History of Religions", an impressive series of monographs; and three "Dissertationes ad Historiam Religionum Pertinentes", incorporating studies by younger scholars. This last series deserves the attention of all colleagues who might wish to edit the researches of their pupils. Lastly, the new handbook for the history of religions, "Historia Religionum", edited by the President and Secretary-General of this Association, should be mentioned. This work differs from its predecessors in that all the articles are to a certain extent written according to the same scheme, thus facilitating religio- historical and phenomenological comparison.

What is the human aspect of all these activities? First, perhaps, there is the correspondence of the Secretary General, who also acts as Editor-in-chief of the publications, with scholars all over the world. If I were to write my memoirs — which I certainly do not intend to do — I could tell many interesting and piquant stories about my dealings with colleagues, and with the officers of U.N.E.S.C.O. Let me rather extend a word of cordial thanks to all those who have offered me their cooperation and their friendship. Their number has gradually increased. Up to this congress the I.A.H.R. consisted of fifteen national groups, those in Austria, Belgium, France, Germany, Great Britain, Hungary, India, Israel, Italy, the Netherlands, Norway, South Korea, Sweden and the United States of America. During this present congress five new groups have been affiliated, those of Canada and Poland, and a second group in Germany, Italy and the U.S.A. Further, the I.A.H.R. has established contact with scholars in countries in which no group has as yet been formed, for instance in Denmark, the Latin American countries and Switzerland. It has been decided to appoint in these countries correspondents whose task it will be to maintain contact with the secretariat.

However impressive these facts may be, we should clearly realize that the activities of the I.A.H.R. are not identical with the study of the history of religions as such, and that our organization does not include all historians of religions. Let us be realists and admit this fact. My teacher, the late W. Brede Kristensen of Leiden, a pioneer in the field of the study of the religions of Antiquity, for instance, always showed supreme contempt for congresses. He was and is not alone in this regard. We shall unfortunately never succeed in compiling a congress programme which brings together all the stars of the history of religions. Stating this fact must be a cause of modesty in the appraisal of the significance of our Association. We are in constant danger of either overrating or misinterpreting the nature and the aims of the I.A.H.R. It should be emphasized time and again that the I.A.H.R. is not a movement striving after a certain goal, and that

the officers of the I.A.H.R. do not follow a predetermined policy. The I.A.H.R. is merely an administrative apparatus, the aim
of which is to bring together students of the history of religions,
so that they can present the results of their inquiries, and by the
friendly criticism of their colleagues get a new stimulus for their
study. The really creative work is not performed at congresses,
but in the strenuous work of the study.

It would be a great source of satisfaction if we could get to
know the results the history of religions has reached in the past
twenty years, in which direction the study is moving and whether
there has been progress in our discipline. Unfortunately we have
no systematic surveys of the whole field of research. Moreover,
the type of scholar who is capable of surveying the total field of
the history of religions, or at least great parts of it, seems to be
slowly dying out. This is why it is impossible at present to satisfy
the desire which we all feel to know what has happened in this
branch of scholarship during the past twenty years.

However, I shall not dismiss you with empty hands. Although
I must refrain from presenting a survey, I shall try instead to
draw your attention to some tendencies which in my opinion
have come more and more to dominate the study of the history
of religions; and I shall try to formulate my wishes in regard to
the future pursuit of religio-historical studies.

1. It is evident, as I have already indicated, that the study is
steadily moving in the direction of an increasingly refined special-
ization. This means a loss in breadth of vision. It can also involve
a gain in precision of study procedure. Thus all kinds of general
theories, such as that of the "prelogical" thinking of primitive
people, animism, dynamism and totemism, are losing their fascination and importance. Historians of religions are becoming more
aware of what the phenomena have to tell them. In the meantime
a new problem is arising, concerning the ultimate aim of the
history of religions. Numerous studies are appearing which stick
fast in philological or historical researches, clever and illuminating though these may be. Philology and history are of course
indispensable auxiliaries of the history of religions. But they have
no higher value than maidservants. The actual object of the study
lies farther away and is more difficult of access. This object is, as
Kristensen put it, that of understanding the faith of the believer.
Let us be aware that so long as we have not clarified the religious

import of the phenomena, we have not achieved our aim.

2. A renewed discussion is going on around the object and the method of the phenomenology of religion, and even about its very right to exist. Half a century ago, when this discipline arose, the method already met with opposition. People thought that this was a hybrid science, an illegitimate blend of the philosophy of religion and the history of religions. However, the phenomenology of religion has gradually won an honourable position. Of late the magnum opus of our retiring President, Professor Widengren, his *Religionsphänomenologie*, has convincingly proved that this discipline is indispensable and that it is able to offer clarifying insight into the nature and structure of religion. And yet the critical voices have not been silenced. Pettazzoni once made the remark that phenomenology pays too little attention to the development of religious events, and shows as it were static pictures, but does not describe religious life in its movement. In order to meet this objection, I have myself introduced the idea of "the *entelecheia* of the phenomena", under which heading I have treated a series of relevant problems. However, a new question arises, viz., that of the allotment of the different tasks to the different disciplines which together form the science of religion. Where are we to place the treatment of these problems: in the care of the phenomenology of religion or in that of the general history of religions? A second crucial question is that of method: there is constant argument about the real or pretended unbiased character of the phenomenological method. Some of our colleagues advocate a radical solution. Together with the name, which in their opinion always will remain unpopular, they wish to abolish the science as such, claiming that the work could be done as well by what they call "the systematic science of religion". I doubt whether this would be an improvement, however. Phenomenology has many merits. One of them is that it forces scholars to inquire into the presuppositions of their work. Historians of religions do not as a rule worry greatly about this issue. This is not their task. But as real scholars they should realize that they are constantly handling concepts and presuppositions which now and then must be tested as to their reliability. Therefore phenomenological reflection cannot be dispensed with.

3. Though I am an enthusiastic student of the religions of antiquity, I must with great regret state that interest in this study

is decreasing. Many years ago Ortega y Gasset contended that the modern mass-man has no interest in history. That is still more true today. People believe that the past is gone, and that what is dead is dead. This attitude is extended to the religions of antiquity. The general public is primarily concerned with what is happening today. As far as religion is concerned — and there certainly is a widespread interest in religious literature — the predilection of this generation is clearly directed towards the religions of the present. In this connection we may put our finger on another weak spot. It is a fallacy to think, as people often do, that the study of religion ultimately aims at producing a definition of religion which can shed new light on the problem of religion in a secular age. But this is the concern of the philosophy of religion and of Christian theology. It is likewise erroneous to think that the history of religions can be used for practical purposes, such as the fostering of mutual understanding among the followers of different religions or the furthering of world peace. The history of religions is an exclusively scholarly business, aimed at discovering historical truth for the sake of truth itself. I hope therefore that there will continue to arise some strange fellows who will devote themselves to the study of the religions of antiquity. They may be the martyrs of science, but they will receive a rich reward in the unique fascination of their demanding study.

4. Two of the sciences which together constitute the science of religion deserve special mention: these are the psychology of religion and the sociology of religion. Both disciplines are sailing against an adverse wind. They find few supporters. In order to study these sciences effectively one should be trained in the respective methods of modern psychology and sociology. Otherwise it amounts to nothing but sheer amateurism. The fact is that the sciences in question are so rigidly bound to the statistical method and hence to the solid facts of human behaviour that religion, which is a unique phenomenon, easily disappears from the scientific horizon. It requires great courage and special capacities to pursue the psychology of religion and the sociology of religion in such a way that new, original conceptions of the psychological and sociological structure of religion may be created. We should encourage all those scholars who dare to take this course. For the application of the methods and the insights of these younger

disciplines would certainly at the same time enhance the popularity of the history of religions.

5. We are living in an age in which religion is passing through a
crisis; this is clear from the fact that many people are rejecting
the so-called vertical line, choosing what is called horizontalism,
and with regard to religion orientating themselves solely on man.
It is no wonder that so many scholars have such high expectations of anthropology. The anthropological approach is loudly
advocated. Without further explanation this slogan can only
create misunderstandings, however. We are bound to ask which
kind of anthropology is meant: a branch of medicine or psychi-
atry which describes the physical-psychological being in a factual
manner? Or a philosophical or religious anthropology which in-
troduces values and norms, and passes beyond empirical conceptions of man to an evaluation of man? Or cultural anthropology,
which draws its conclusions about man's cultural status mainly
from the data of primitive cultures? I must confess that I have
come to the conclusion — a rather heretical one — that anthropology is only relatively important for the history of religions.
Religion can never be totally understood on a basis of the empirical being of man. The object of the history of religions is not to
understand the believer as an anthropological phenomenon, but
to offer more insight into the conception of "the Holy", which
apparently can overwhelm people so strongly that their anthropological nature is fully transformed.

Looking backward and forward, it is natural that I should have
paid rather a lot of attention to the past and to the present. But
what about the future? Here I am going to be very brief. Pre-
dicting the future is a risky business. Let me limit myself to five
points which I recommend to your attention.

1. It is imperative that historians of religions should clearly
realize what the ultimate aim of their studies is, viz., insight into
the essence and the structure of religion in the manifold forms in
which it appears. This is the criterion for the value of their researches. The history of religions is an autonomous discipline. Its
very nature prescribes a critical, independent and yet congenial
study of the religious phenomena so that their inner religious
logic becomes transparent.

There is another reason why I emphasize this point. Society and culture are in a state of rapid transformation. Appreciations are changing. Personally I am not so sure that the history of religions in its traditional form will in the long run capture and retain the imagination of the present generation. We have to rethink the objectives and also the method of our study. The starting point of this reassessment will always be the principle of study which I have indicated.

2. We cannot avoid tackling anew the problems of methodology which are especially raised by the phenomenology of religion. There exists much confusion of tongues in the domain of these studies. There is sometimes a deplorable lack of clarity in the concepts which people use. In my opinion we should from time to time sit together to clarify the terminological apparatus with which we operate. The symposium in Messina has set a good example by defining what Gnosticism really is. A symposium could duly be devoted to such questions.

3. Historians of religions are individualists. Everybody chooses his own field of study, and has every right to do so. Often the results of solitary research are brilliant. Nevertheless it would be useful to consider how we could obtain surveys of what is being done in the different fields of the discipline. Secondly, we ought to find out how we might create more cooperation and a better division of labour between the scholars in question. Perhaps this too would be a good subject for a symposium.

4. Looking backward, we see that important aspects of religion have been dealt with at congresses and by scholars individually: for instance, the idea of God, the mythical-ritual pattern, sacral kingship, Gnosticism, guilt and rites of purification, types of redemption, the relation of the cultures of the West and of the East, and origins and eschatology. Two important subjects, religious anthropology and cult, are missing from this list. There is certainly a modest volume, *Anthropologie religieuse*, which was published on the occasion of the congress in Rome. But the subject is by no means exhausted and is favoured by our contemporaries. The second subject, cult, has received far too little attention. Yet cult plays a predominant part in the religions of the primitives and of antiquity, as it does in Eastern religions and in some forms of Christianity. Sacrifice, prayer, sacrament and the different types of cult should be chosen as topics of future congresses and of individual research.

5. Let us not forget that we are living in a period in which religion and cultural values are compelled to fight for their very existence. The question arises: What will be the future of religion and of our civilization? Science cannot corroborate, nor can it renew a faltering faith and a decaying culture. Nor can the history of religions. But it could make its contribution to the solution of the crisis by presenting a clear picture of the intrinsic value of religion. The history of religions, studied impartially and critically, shows that religion always has been one of the noblest possessions of humanity, and that it has for the most part served to spiritualize culture. This is a truth which might bring new hope to the present generation, a generation which is struggling for more spiritual certainty and for a culture permeated by the ideas of justice and peace.

PART TWO

ABSTRACTS OF COMMUNICATIONS

SECTION FOUR: ISLAM

Mir Dard, a Naqshbandi mystic of the 18th century in Delhi, by Annemarie Schimmel.
Faith and Reason in Koranic Argumentation, by Jacques Waardenburg.
An Islamic Echo of the "Trickster": the ayyārs of Indo-Persian and Malay Romances, by Alessandro Bausani.
Un texte concernant les "pseudo-sabéens de Harrān", by Jan Hjärpe.
Le Dieu du Coran et le Dieu d'Abraham d'après les polémistes byzantins, by A.-Th. Khoury.

SECTION FIVE: GREECE AND ROME, HELLENISM

Das Gottesbild Plotins, by H. Ludin Jansen.
The Delphic Maxim "Know Yourself" in Hermetic Interpretation, by H.D. Betz.
Gods do not exist, by J.P. Guépin.
Die di indigetes und die Apotheose des Romulus, by L.F. Janssen.

SECTION SIX: INDIA AND IRAN

The Madhyamaka philosopher Nāgārjuna according to the Chinese sources, by Amalia Pezzali. See under Section VII
Reconstructing the Harappan Hinduism — Sources and Methods (Summary of the preview of a forthcoming monograph), by Asko Parpola.
Monthly Ancestral Offerings in Hinduism, by H. Daniel Smith.
Wirklichkeit und Geschichte im Werk Vivekanandas, by Gunther Stephenson.
Iranisches Christentum und Zoroastrismus, by Gernot Wiessner.
Hinduism as Sādhana, by Troy Organ.
Variations on Tengalai Belief in a South Indian Village, by James L. Martin.
Der Avatāragedanke im neueren Hinduismus, by Anncharlott Eschmann.
Basic Changes in Indian Religious Conceptions and the Disappearance of Buddhism from India, by Kees W. Bolle.
Shiva in Mānikkavācakar's hymn Pōtti-Tiruvakaval, by Carl-A. Keller.
Pantheistic Monism or Absolute Advaita, by P. Sarveswara Sharma.
La révélation dans le manichéisme, by Julien Ries.

SECTION SEVEN: BUDDHISM AND THE FAR EAST

Sur les problèmes de la mythologie du Japon (La structure mythologique et l'idéologie politique), by Tomoo Yoshida.
The Madhyamaka Philosopher Nāgārjuna according to the Chinese Sources, by Amalia Pezzali.
Das Schicksal des Gottesgedankens in der Religionsphilosophie Keiji Nishitanis, by Fritz Buri.

The Role of the History of Religions in College/University/Seminary Curricula, by Edward J. Jurji.

The Structure of Religious Fraternity, by George Weckman.

Comment se forme un dieu?, by Angelo Brelich.

Croyance en Dieu et dualisme, by Ugo Bianchi.

Iconography as a Primary Source for the Conception of Deity, by S.G.F. Brandon.

Sexual Fault and Original Sin in the Teaching of an African Charismatic Movement, by Johannes Fabian.

Die hermeneutischen Prinzipien Joachim Wachs (Joachim Wach's Hermeneutical Principles), by Hans-Joachim Klimkeit.

SECTION TEN: PSYCHOLOGY OF RELIGION

Religion and Alcohol, by Klas G. Magni.

The bare-footed walking on burning charcoal of Anastenaria, as a religious phenomenon, by Stylianos Papadimas.

Methods of Personality Studies in Psychology of Religion, by Gustaf Ståhlberg.

Formes psychologiques des croyances relatives aux dieux, by D.H. Salman.

Möglichkeit und Grenze religionspsychologischer Interpretierung des Neuen Testaments, by Ottfried Kietzig.

Moderne Methoden für die Religionspsychologie, by W. Arnold.

God in Psychedelic Religion, by C. Douglas Gunn.

SECTION I

THE ANCIENT NEAR EAST AND EGYPT

B3 als Gottesbezeichnung im alten Ägypten

von Jan Bergman

Die von den Pyramidentexten ab bis in die christliche-koptische Literatur vorherrschende Gottesbezeichnung *nṯr* (NOYTE) ist in Bezug auf Ursprung und Grundbedeutung dunkel, in Hinsicht auf Gebrauch unbestimmt und vag. Mit Vorteil sollen deshalb andere, anscheinend sogar ältere Gottesbegriffe herangezogen werden, um die wichtigsten Wesenszüge der ägyptischen Gottesvorstellungen zu beleuchten. Unter den betreffenden Gottesbezeichnungen hebt sich vor allem *b3* hervor, womit besonders *šḥm* und *3ḥ* wichtige Berührungspunkte aufzeigen.

Wichtigste aktuelle Bibliographie: Elske Marie Wolf-Brinkmann, *Versuch einer Deutung des Begriffes "b3" anhand der Ueberlieferung der Frühzeit und des Alten Reiches* (Diss. Basel, angeregt durch S. Morenz). Freiburg i.Br. 1968. — Louis V. Žabkar, *A Study of the Ba Concept in Ancient Egyptian Texts* (SAOC, Band 34). Chicago 1968.

I. *b3(w)* wird in den Pyramidentexten parallel zu *nṯr(w)* gebraucht (Pyr. 478a-479a; 941c-942b; 1004c-1005c vgl. 1973 ff.; 153a, 155a, 157a und 159a) und stellt keine niedrigere Kategorie von Gottheiten dar. Das heliopolitanische Schlachtritual Pyr. 1543 ff. zeigt keine Abstufung im Rang zwischen *nṯrw* und *b3w* auf. *3ḥw* — nicht *b3w* — als νέκυες οἱ ἡμίθεοι Osiris als *b3 pw* in Nedit Pyr. 2108b; vgl. aber 754c.

II. *Hauptsächliche Wesenszüge des b3.*
1) *"Gestaltfähigkeit"* (so übersetzt W.-Br. geläufig *b3*). Diese ganz zentrale Eigenschaft der äg. Gottheiten kann auf verschiedene Weise beleuchtet werden: a) *Epigraphisch* (siehe z.B. die Deutezeichen in Parallelen zu Pyr. 1913c: Nt. 625 und Nt. 734 Vgl. auch 1027b); dieser Tatbestand ist auch für die Deutung der Mischgestalten mehrerer ägyptischen Gottheiten von Gewicht. b)

Grammatisch. Das Schwanken zwischen Singular und Plural *b3(w)* (Žabkar: "intensive plural"). (Von Pyr. 992c und 1472b bzw. 477a ab.) c) *Theologisch*. Gerade *b3* stellt den Begegnungspunkt zwischen verschiedenen Göttergestalten dar. Typische Beispiele sind *b3.wj dmd* (usw.) für die Einheit von Re und Osiris, *b3 b3w* als Summe der vier *b3*-Gestalten des Widders von Mendes usw. Somit verbindet *b3(w)* Einheit und Vielheit im Wesen der äg. Gottheit, indem *b3(w)* sowohl die Gestaltfähigkeit als die konkreten, durch diese realisierten Gestalten bezeichnet. Somit stellt *b3* einen Schlüsselbegriff zum Verständnis der ägyptischen Gottesvorstellung dar, die in der Spätzeit ihren authentischen Ausdruck im Anruf an Isis "una quae es omnia" gefunden hat.

2) *Aktivität*. a) *B3* als "Gestaltfähigkeit" drängt zur Gestaltung. *b3* stellt die Voraussetzung jeder konkreten Gottesoffenbarung dar. Gewöhnliche Verbindung mit *h^{c}j* "erscheinen" usw. (z.B. in theophoren Namen aus dem Alten Reich). Oft wird die *tremendum*-Seite hervorgehoben (vgl. *b3w* als "Gewalt", "Rache" usw. vor allem in Königsinschriften des Neuen Reiches und später). *b3* betont besonders die konkrete Gegenwart, kann aber auch als transzendent aufgefasste Universalgottheiten (wie vor allem Amun und Hathor in der Spätzeit) bezeichnen, b) Somit ist *b3* ein dynamischer und dramatischer Gottesbegriff (vgl. *b3* als Mittel der Verwandlungen in der Totenliteratur). c) Hiermit hängt der Zug der Freizügigkeit zusammen, die den Gott — und in seiner Folge dem Toten — eine Art von Ubiquität zusichert (*b3* wird zwar in einigen formelhaften Wendungen dem Himmel zugeschrieben, ist aber auch auf der Erde, am Kultort, wie in der Unterwelt zu Hause). d) Alle diese aktiven Züge können in der gewöhnlichen Bezeichnung *b3 ^{c}nh* "lebender Ba" zusammengefasst werden. Diese Lebenskraft des *b3* kann sehr konkrete Ausdrücke finden (die Verbindung von *b3* und Phallus z.B. CT II 67c-72c; TB Kap. 17; Reliefdarstellung auf dem Naos von Nektanebos).

So kann das Studium von *b3* und die Einfühlung in diesen wichtigen Gottesbegriff einen guten Dienst leisten, wenn es auf Fragen nach *abstractum — concretum*, nach Immanenz — Transzendenz, nach monotheistischen-polytheistischen-pantheistischen Tendenzen in den ägyptischen Gottesvorstellungen geht.

Le dieu-ciel dans les civilisations du Proche-Orient ancien

par Marcel Leibovici

Dès la haute époque sumérienne dans les plus anciennes listes divines l'idéogramme AN signifie ciel, dieu-ciel, et devient par la suite le déterminatif de toute divinité dans la tradition épigraphique mésopotamienne. Cette utilisation de l'idéogramme AN: DINGIR comme classificateur constitue le premier témoignage de l'origine céleste du concept de la divinité en Mésopotamie. Les plus anciens panthéons sumériens sont ordonnés par rapport à un dieu suprême qui est le dieu-ciel AN à Uruk, le dieu Elum à Fara, et le dieu Enki à Eridu. A côté du dieu AN, dès l'époque d'Agadé apparaît dans les noms propres akkadiens le dieu *Ilum*, mais à la différence de plus anciennes divinités sémitiques Sin, Šamaš, Ištar, le dieu *Ilum* ne figure pas dans les mythes et rites babyloniens. La présence de l'élément théophore IL dans l'onomastique amorite dès la troisième dynastie d'Ur, et dans les noms propres attestés dans les sources de Mari se rattache à la tradition occidentale du Dieu *EL,* chef du plus ancien panthéon à Ugarit. Précisons que dans les textes de Mari c'est l'idéogramme AN, qui est utilisé par les scribes pour exprimer le théophore IL/EL. Mais le dieu-ciel, qui figure dans le panthéon de Mari est rendu par l'expression: D.*UTU ša šame,* dieu du ciel, le dieu UTU étant ici synonyme du babylonien *ilu:* dieu (cf. G. Dossin, Studia Mariana I, p. 46). D'autre part, S. Smith a identifié la plus ancienne forme akkadisée du dieu-ciel, en écriture syllabique: d. *Ša-mu,* dans la formule de malédiction de la statue du roi Idrimi découverte à Alalakh. Cette divinité "syrienne" du ciel, doit être mise en rapport avec le dieu-ciel mésopotamien *Anu.* Toutefois la présence des divinités ouest-sémitiques dans l'onomastique d'Alakah n'exclue pas, en occurence, la possibilité d'une divinité du ciel du type occidental: *Ba'al-šamen,* seigneur du ciel. En effet cette divinité est invoquée dans une inscription araméenne du Ve siècle à côté de Sahar, dieu-lune et *Šamaš,* dieu-soleil. La triade dieu-ciel (Ba'al-šamem), dieu-lune (Aglibol) et dieu-soleil (Malakbel) est attestée à Palmyre. Le culte de *Ba'al-šamem,* dieu-ciel, dépasse les frontières de la Phénicie proprement dite. Il s'agit d'une version locale du dieu ciel devenu divinité suprême, en milieu ouest-sémitique.

Mais c'est le nom commun de dieu, babylonien *Ilu,* cananéen *'el,* sud-arabique *'il,* nord-arabique *'el* qui a été à l'origine le nom du dieu suprême des anciens Sémites. Cet appelatif *'el/'il* repose sur le protosémitique commun *'il (u).* Notons aussi la tendance d'utiliser le nom commun de dieu en Assyrie pour noter le dieu suprême d'un panthéon local dans la cité d'Assur.

Egyptian Triads structured as one god with two goddesses

by H. te Velde

Divine triads, found in various religions and also in the structure of theological thought in Egyptian religion, form an interesting minor problem in the complicated relations between polytheism and monotheism.

1. Two kinds of triads distinguished, one consisting of a single and a dual unit. We find that the latter may be subsumed in a unity. The two units then remaining are in such contrast (male-female) that they can only be unified in the divine child. In that case, however, the triadic structure of father, mother and son subsists, stressed or not, and plurality remains.

2. The other kind of triad, consisting of three male or three female units, has a clear trinitarian and monistic tendency; Ptah-Sokaris-Osiris is regarded not only as a plurality but also as one. On the other hand, the single sun-god may also be conceived as a triad: Khepri-Re-Atum (cf. Qodshu-Anat-Astarte and Hathor becoming 7 in three stages, 1 + 2 + 4). The Egyptian pantheon can also be explained as a male monistic triad: "The pantheon (*ntrw nbw*) is a triad: Amon, Re, Ptah" (pap. Leiden 7350, IV 21).

3. It is noteworthy that at certain temples the pantheon is called not a triad, but an ennead (3 x 3), which may be specified in 9, but also in 7, 11 or 15 gods and goddesses. Most Egyptian triads consist of father, mother and son: Osiris, Isis, Horus; Amon, Mut, Khonsu; Ptah, Sakhmet, Nefertem; etc. They are often a constrictive choice from the nome or city gods. Such triads cannot be reduced to unity because they contain the male – female opposition. Three is the first number to indicate the plural, as evidenced in Egyptian script.

4. In triads displaying the male – female contrast we find not only the male duality father – son with a female unit, but exceptionally a male god with two goddesses: Khnum with Satis and

Anukis; Montu with Iunyt and Tenenet; Atum with Iusaas and Nebet-hetepet. The Osirian cycle also displays such triads: Osiris with Isis and Nephthys or Horus with Isis and Nephthys. Horus as pharaoh can also form a triad with Nekhbet and Uto or with Hathor and another goddess.

5. When the male unit in such triads is not duplicated, either the father or the son being absent, we find a tendency not towards unification of the male-female poles, but instead towards reduplication of the female complex. Such couples are Mut-Sakhmet, Bastet-Sakhmet, Anat-Astarte, the two Maat, the two Meret, etc. The female duality, apart from a doubtful exception (Satis-Anukis), is not that of mother and daughter, analogous with father and son, but less simple: good and bad wife or mother; mother and lover; woman with some masculine characteristics and woman with striking female characteristics; especially she who bears and she who brings up. Often the duplication is symmetrical.

6. In short, woman and the male-female contrast prove too great a problem for Egyptian theology to arrive at universal monotheism. (Bi-sexual conceptions of the deity remain exceptional: the bisexual Atum is included in a triad with two goddesses Iusaas and Nebet-hetepet or he is "the one who became three" with Shu and Tefnut.)

Triune Conceptions of Deity in Ancient Egypt

by J. Gwyn Griffiths

TRIADIC systems came to be a common feature of Egyptian religion, and the late lamented Siegfrid Morenz assembled in his *Ägyptische Religion* a number of data which suggested that a triad was sometimes regarded as forming a unity, the concepts of three and one being interplayed.

The Ennead of Heliopolis is one of the earliest divine groups attested, and at first sight it is tempting to explain it as consisting of three triads. But the group is essentially a combination of four marital pairs, while Atum stands outside as the primal god who created without the aid of a spouse. Yet in Coffin Texts II, 39 b-e Atum, Shu and Tefenet are regarded as a triad, and it is said of Atum, *he was One and became Three*. The Christian formulation in the Council of Chalcedon, A.D. 451, is comparable in some ways.

The all-male triad in Memphis (Ptah, Sokar, Osiris) is often treated as a singular grammatically, and Morenz urged that the triad was therefore being treated conceptually as a unity. Something different, however, may be at work here — the fusion of three gods into a syncretistic unity. Cf. Amen-Rē'-Harakhty and Rē'-Harakhty-Osiris; each is now a single composite deity.

In the Demotic Chronicle V, 12-13 it is said that *Apis is Ptah, Apis is Rē', Apis is Harsiesis,* and in this case Morenz's interpretation is well founded, although one might add that here is a triune concept with loud overtones of theological supremacy in favour of Apis. Another text involving Apis (Mariette, *Sérapéum,* III, pl. 8) has been translated *Osiris-Apis, Atum, Horus, together the great god;* but it more probably means *Osiris-Apis, Atum, Horus of Nekhen, the great god,* in which case the concept of a unified triad disappears. A celebrated passage in the Leiden Hymn to Amûn (IV, 21-2) states that Rē' and Ptah are forms of Amûn, Rē' being his countenance and Ptah his body. The three gods are regarded as one, and the trinity based on Amûn involves a function of the other two gods in a modalistic sense. The first sentence in this passage is usually translated, *Three are all gods, Amûn, Rē', Ptah.* All gods, according to this, are reducible to three — a remarkable and unparalleled claim. *Nbw* in this sentence more probably means "lords". *Three are the gods (who are) lords:* here is a claim that suits the dominating position of these gods.

A text from the temple of Opet in Karnak (De Wit, *Opet,* 119 and 167) claims that Thoth is present in important functions — heart, tongue and throat — of three other eminent deities; this is hardly a triune concept. There are clear examples, however, of a modalistic interpretation of the three gods who form a unity in the sun-god; and in one of the early didactic names of Akhenaten a trinitarian formulation was rightly recognized by Morenz; here the divine father is identified with the son whom he has created.

Die weltanschauliche Krise des Neuen Reiches

von László Kákosy

Man begegnet in der ägyptischen Religion in der ersten Hälfte der 18. Dynastie auffallenden Änderungen. Sowohl die Jenseitsvorstellungen, wie auch andere Gebiete des religiösen Lebens wurden von gewissen Wandlungen getroffen. Im Besitz des Amduat-Textes haben die Könige für sich anscheinend besondere Privilegien im Jenseitsreich beansprucht. Der Vezir User liess die Amduat-Szenen und Texte wohl ohne Genehmigung des Königs an die Wände seines Grabes malen.

Nach der Verweltlichung der Thematik der privaten Grabbilder am Anfang des Neuen Reiches, ist eine entgegengesetzte Richtung schon in der Vor-Amarna-Zeit wahrnehmbar. (Vgl. J. Spiegel, *MDIK*, 14, s. 190 ff.) Es gibt auch andere Anzeichen für eine Richtung, die schon auf die charakteristischen Eigentümlichkeiten der ramessidischen Religion hinweisst. (Der Tierkult tritt in Vordergrund und der Volksglaube gewinnt im allgemeinen an Bedeutung.) Unter Amenhotep III. verschärfen sich die ideologischen Gegensätze. Die Reform des Echnaton bildet eigentlich keinen Höhepunkt einer langsamen Entwicklung, vielmehr ist sie ein kühner Versuch mit den Richtungen abzurechnen, die den Weg zu einer Theokratie bzw. Hierokratie ebneten, und die für ein weltlich eingestellte Herrscherschicht auch sonst recht widrig erscheinen mussten.

Es sei hervorgehoben, dass man unter den religiösen Richtungen, die nach Echnaton die Oberhand erhielten, mit wesentlichen Unterschieden rechnen muss. Die Theologie der Amunspriester strebte nach einer henotheistischen Theokratie, die sich zunächst nicht gegen den Polytheismus und gegen den Vorstoss der Volksreligion wandte, erst später mehr und mehr Anspruch auf die offizielle und allgemeine Anerkennung der Allmacht des Amun erhob. Das Eindringen der Volksreligion in die höheren Kreise und die steigende Verbreitung der Magie war natürlich ein Prozess ohne bewusste Zielsetzung. Die neuen Formen der Vergöttlichung der Könige (bes. Ramses II) sollten dagegen die weltliche Regierung gegen die Machtansprüche der Amunspriester ideologisch unterstützen. Damit hängt indirekt (intensive Verehrung verstorbener Könige) auch die für die Spätzeit so charakteristische, in die Vergangenheit blickende, archaisierende Richtung zusammen.

Unter den zahlreichen Faktoren der religiösen Wandlungen spielte das Priestertum von Memphis eine wichtige, bisher nicht genügend beachtete Rolle.

SECTION II

ISRAELITE-JEWISH RELIGION

Shiur Komah: la mesure du Corps de Dieu

par Marc Philonenko

La doctrine du *Shiur Komah* ou "mesure du Corps" de Dieu appartient aux spéculations les plus mystérieuses de la mystique juive.[1] La révélation est faite au visionnaire des mesures fantastiques du Corps de Dieu. La description de l'amant dans le *Cantique des cantiques* en fournit le plus souvent les matériaux.

Graetz a soutenu que ces spéculations sont apparues tardivement dans le judaïsme sous l'influence de l'Islam.[2] M. Gaster, au contraire, avait reconnu le caractère archaïque et juif de la doctrine, mais il n'avait pu alléguer en faveur de son hypothèse qu'un texte d'Irénée qui prête à un gnostique chrétien, Marc le Mage, une description du "Corps de Vérité" qui n'est pas sans rappeler les spéculations du *Shiur Komah*.[3] Plus récemment G. Scholem s'est efforcé de montrer à son tour que la doctrine est ancienne et qu'Origène y fait allusion dans l'introduction à son Commentaire du Cantique des cantiques.

On se propose ici de confirmer ces témoignages indirects par un passage passé inaperçu, mais parfaitement explicite du *Livre des Secrets d'Hénoch*.[4] Ce texte renvoie de façon certaine à la doctrine du *Shiur Komah* dont il établit ainsi l'authenticité juive et l'antiquité.

---

[1] Voir G. Scholem, *Les grands courants de la mystique juive*, Paris, 1950, p. 76-80, et "Age of Shiur Komah Speculation and Origen" in *Jewish Gnosticism, Markabah Mysticism, and Talmudic Tradition*, New York, 1960, p. 36-42.

[2] Graetz, "Die mystische Literatur in der gaonäischen Epoche", *Monatsschrift fur Geschichte und Wissenschaft des Judenthums*, 8, 1859, p. 103-118.

[3] M. Gaster, "Das Schiur Komah", *Monatsschrift für Geschichte und Wissenschaft des Judenthums*, 1893, p. 179-185 et 213-230.

[4] A. Vaillant, *Le Livre des Secrets d'Hénoch*, Paris, 1952.

Amarnaglaube und Jahwemonotheismus

von Alfred Rupp

Die Anklänge zwischen Ps. 104 und dem grossen Amarnahymnus werden verschieden beurteilt und lassen immer noch viele Fragen offen. Von besonderem Interesse ist religionsgeschichtlich das so frühe auftauchen eines reinen Monotheismus bzw. einer auf einen solchen hin gerichteten Entwicklung.

Die Besonderheiten stellt bereits der Vergleich der Konzeption der beiden genannten Texte heraus. Der Amarnahymnus ist eng verknüpft mit der Königstheologie. Motivisch stellt sich der Aufbau dar in der Reihung Gottheit-Königtum–Gottheit-Königtum. Künstlerisch ist der Hymnus sorgfältig durchgearbeitet, von einander entsprechenden Rahmenstücken umschlossen und von 4 zusammenfassenden hymnischen Liedern durchsetzt. Das ganze wird beherrscht von der durchgehenden Idee der Tag-Nacht-Folge. Demgegenüber ist Ps. 104 gekennzeichnet durch uneinheitliche Traditionen und durch den Mangel einer durchgehenden einheitlichen Idee, wenn man von der recht allgemeinen Vorstellung "Jahwes schöpferische Mächtigkeit" absieht.

Der Vergleich verwandter Motivgruppen in beiden Hymnen deckt ungleiche Reihenfolge und Sinnverschiebungen auf.

Engere Berührungen bestehen mit ugaritischen Traditionen wie der "Keret-Sage" und dem "Ba'al-Text". Nach allem wäre eine Vorstufe zum vorliegenden Ps. 104 denkbar, auf welcher möglicherweise bereits abgewandelte Motive des Amarnahymnus und kanaanäisches Gedankengut (um einer problematischen Konkretisierung auszuweichen) miteinander verbunden waren. Es spräche manches dafür, dass eine solche hypothetische Zwischenstufe vor Israels geschichtlicher Zeit gelegen hat, mindestens aber ohne seine Mitwirkung entstand.

Die Grundprinzipien der religiösen Konzepte im Amarnahymnus und in Ps. 104 sind gegenläufig. Ps. 104 ist synkretischer Art, angesichts des alttestamentlichen Monotheismus also das Ergebnis eines rezeptiven Prozesses. Dagegen liegt dem Amarnahymnus das Prinzip der Reduktion im Ausgang von einer polytheistischen Stufe zugrunde. Die Tendenz läuft durch die immer konsequenter durchgeführte "interpretierende Identifikation" im Grunde genommen auf einen Monotheismus hinaus, den Achanjati aller

Wahrscheinlichkeit mit voller Eindeutigkeit erreicht hätte, wenn
er nicht, im Verhältnis zu seinem religiösen Werk jedenfalls, zu
früh gestorben wäre.

Zentralheiligtum, Grenzheiligtum und
"Höhenheiligtum" in Israel

von Klaus-Dietrich Schunck

   Das Referat dient der Begründung der These, dass im vorexil-
ischen Israel drei grosse Gruppen von Heiligtümern zu unterscheiden sind, die durch die hebräischen Vokabeln: היכל,
בית יהוה (nebst Varianten) und במה bezeichnet werden. Das
Wort היכל , das vom Sumerischen E-KAL herkommt und im
Hebräischen ein Fremdwort ist, steht im Alten Testament sowohl
in der Bedeutung "Palast" als auch in der Bedeutung "Tempel".
In letzterem Verständnis begegnet es jedoch stets nur im Singular
und wird nur für den Tempel von Silo und den Tempel von
Jerusalem gebraucht. היכל ist somit im Alten Testament spe-
zielle Bezeichnung für ein Zentral — bzw. Hauptheiligtum.
   Demgegenüber werden weitere Heiligtümer, die ebenfalls aus
einem massiven Kultgebäude bestanden und nicht mit einer במה
identisch sind, nur allgemeiner als בית יהוה (vgl. Jer. 41,5),
בית האלהים (vgl. Ri. 1831) oder בית ממלכה (vgl. Am. 7,13) bezeichnet. In Verbindung mit der Ausgrabung eines derartigen
Kultgebäudes auf tell ᶜarād durch Y. Aharoni sowie unter Berücksichtigung der Lokalisierung dieser kultischen Gebäude in
den jeweiligen Grenzgebieten von Israel bzw. Juda führt dies zu
der Annahme, dass es sich bei diesen Heiligtümern um königliche
Grenzheiligtümer gehandelt hat. Sie entsprachen in ihrer Anlage
und Funktion weitgehend dem Zentralheiligtum (dieses konnte
ebenso wie die Grenzheiligtümer auch ganz allgemein בית יהוה
oder מקדש genannt werden); um jedoch den Unterschied zu dem
Zentralheiligtum und seiner speziellen Bezeichnung als היכל noch
deutlicher werden zu lassen, sollte man die Grenzheiligtümer
nicht als "Tempel", sondern besser nur als "Gotteshaus" bezeichnen und das Wort "Tempel" dann allein der Übersetzung der
Vokabel היכל vorbehalten.
   In eindeutigem Unterschied zu היכל und בית יהוה (= Tempel

und Gotteshaus) steht schliesslich die במה . Die Übersetzung dieses Wortes als "Höhenheiligtum" bzw. "Kulthöhe" ist ebenso missverständlich wie die von Th. Oestreicher gewählte Bezeichnung als "Ortsheiligtum" (vgl. die Bedeutung der grossen Bamah von Gibeon; l. Kg. 3,4). Es erscheint vielmehr am besten, hier von einem "offenen Kultplatz" zu sprechen. Die gelegentliche Erwähnung eines בית במות bezieht sich dabei auf eine Halle bzw. Hütte zur Einnahme von Opfermahlzeiten auf der Bamah (vgl. 1. Sam. 9,22).

L'angélolâtrie juive: mythe ou réalité?

par Marcel Simon

Plusieurs auteurs ecclésiastiques de l'antiquité, ainsi que le polémiste païen Celse, définissent le judaïsme comme un culte des anges. Nous savons que l'angélologie tenait une place importante dans l'enseignement des Pharisiens et des Esséniens. D'autre part, l'existence de pratiques angélolâtriques est sûrement attestée dans certaines formes de dévotion populaire juive et dans des sectes syncrétistes judéopaïennes (Epître aux Colossiens, papyrus magiques). En revanche, on n'en trouve pas trace dans le judaïsme rabbinique, qui tout au contraire répudie catégoriquement de telles déviations et semble s'être toujours cantonné, pour ce qui est des anges, sur le plan de la pure spéculation, sans lui donner de prolongement cultuel.

On peut dès lors se demander comment les auteurs en question en sont venus à assimiler judaïsme et angélolâtrie. Il est possible qu'ils aient arbitrairement transposé sur la Synagogue orthodoxe des pratiques particulières à des milieux sectaires marginaux. Mais il est également possible, et peut-être en définitive plus vraisemblable, que leurs affirmations traduisent non pas la constatation d'un fait réel, mais une interprétation tendancieuse du judaïsme. Leur point d'appui concret, c'est sans doute l'importance assignée par le judaïsme aux considérations astronomiques pour la fixation du calendrier (néoménies), les anges étant communément associés ou identifiés, dans la pensée antique, aux puissances astrales. Plus précisément, la racine d'une telle conception du judaïsme est à chercher en *Actes*, 7, 42, où il est dit que Dieu se détourna du peuple juif après l'épisode du veau d'or et le livra au culte de l'armée du ciel. L'accusation d'angélolâtrie formulée à l'endroit des Juifs serait ainsi d'origine essentiellement livresque, et ne correspondrait à aucune réalité cultuelle très voyante dans le judaïsme orthodoxe.

The Premature Exodus of Ephraim and the Messiah of Ephraim

by Joseph Heinemann

Many theories claiming to explain the origin of the legend about the Messiah of Ephraim (or Joseph), who is destined to fall in battle, have been suggested. The multiplicity of messianic figures as such must now be accepted as a fact, especially in view of the material from the DSS. As regards the strange motif of the Messiah's death, most scholars hold that it emerged in consequence of the defeat of Bar Kokhba; yet we know of no connection of the latter with the tribe of Ephraim. One decisive fact about this legend has been generally ignored, viz. that it has come down to us in two opposed versions, only one of which speaks of the death of the Messiah of Ephraim in battle, while the other glorifies him as the victor in the eschatological wars against the Roman empire. Obviously, the version which knows nothing of his death must be the earlier one; and any attempt to account for the genesis and evolution of the legend must take note of this radical change in its tendency, which took place at some time or other.

The legend of the premature Exodus of the tribe of Ephraim has reached us in a number of versions. According to some, the Ephraimites in their pride and arrogance presumed to redeem themselves without divine assistance or sanction; others speak of a tragic error, caused by a mistake in calculating the time of redemption. Yet another version expresses a highly complex and ambivalent attitude towards the attempt at self-redemption on the part of the Ephraimites: the account of their Exodus is followed by the surprising statement that the same Ephraimites, who had fallen in battle with the Philistines, were the dead resurrected by Ezekiel. It is more than likely, that this sequel to the legend was added in the period following the defeat of Bar Kokhba. The original legend must have seemed to Bar Kokhba's contemporaries and to the survivors of his revolt to mirror the events of their own time; hence the attempts to evaluate the tragic attempt at premature redemption less negatively and less harshly. In consequence of this association of Bar Kokhba with the Ephraimites he was also identified, eventually, with the Messiah of Ephraim, of whom tradition had it that he would defeat the Romans; by adding the motif that this militant Messiah would fall in battle, it became possible both to uphold the belief in Bar Kokhba as a true messianic figure and to explain his failure and death.

Lettres royales à la divinité en Mésopotamie et en Israël antiques: esquisse d'un genre littéraire

par J.G. Heintz

L'affirmation de la rélévation divine par l'histoire en tant que constante de l'historiographie de tout le Proche-Orient antique a été récemment soutenue par B. Albrektson, *History and the Gods*, (Lund, 1967), en opposition à la thèse généralement reçue, selon laquelle ce thème caractériserait uniquement la religion de l'antique Israël.

Parmi la documentation extrabiblique avancée par cet auteur figurent certains exemplaires de "lettres à la divinité" (*Gottesbriefe*); cependant, malgré une bibliographie déjà abondante/le sujet est le plus souvent abordé au cours d'ouvrages généraux: cf., par ex., J.J. Stamm et R. Labat (1939), C.J. Gadd (1948), E.A. Speiser (1955), A. Moortgat (1959), A.L. Oppenheim (1964), H. Hirsch (1965), etc./, il est difficile d'acquérir une vision d'ensemble des attestations, de la nature et de la fonction exactes de cet important genre littéraire.

Dans le cadre général des "lettres à la divinité", dont le plus grand nombre appartient aux périodes sumérienne et babylonienne ancienne et qui sont des "lettres-prières", des suppliques — réelles ou fictives (exercices de scribes) — à la divinité ou au roi (divinisé)/cf. A. Falkenstein, *Z.A.*, 44 (1938), pp. 1-25 et *An. Bibl.*, 12 (1959), pp. 69-77; W.W. Hallo, *J.A.O.S.*, 88 (1968), pp. 75-89; cp. J. Nougayrol, *Ugaritica V*, (1968), p. 24/, nous proposons — par hypothèse — de distinguer les "lettres royales à la divinité".

Cette catégorie particulière ne se distingue pas uniquement par la fonction royale de l'expéditeur, mais également par le contexte qui semble motiver l'envoi de la missive: l'assistance d'une divinité est invoquée par ce mode épistolaire à l'occasion d'une crise politique ou d'une campagne militaire, en vue d'assurer la sécurité du roi, la pérennité de la dynastie royale et le salut du peuple.

Sources
A) *Archives royales de Mari*:
    i)   *A.R.M., I/3*;
    ii-ind.) *A.R.M., IV/18, ll. 17-22*;
    iii)   *Syria, 19 (1938), p. 126*;
    iv-ind.) *R.A., 42 (1948), pp. 128-132, ll. 24-28 & 34-36*;
    v-ind.) *A.R.M., X/4, l.3*;
    vi-ind.) *A.4260, ll. 44-46* (Tr. lat.).
B) *Inscriptions royales assyriennes*:
    i)   Salmanasar IV (*B.L.*, Pl. LIII, n° 169 — fragment);
    ii)   Sargon II
        a) *T.C.L.*, vol. 3 + compléments: "8° campagne";
        b) *B.M. 81-3-23, 131*: "fragment d'Azeqah";
        c) *K.4471*: — fragment (?) — ;
    iii)   Assarhaddon (*Z.A.*, 40 (1931), pp. 255-259);
    iv)   Assurbanipal (*C.T.*, vol. XXXV, Pl. 44-45)
    Cp. "lettres divines":
    a) Šamši-Adad V (*K.A.H.*, vol. II, n° 142);
    b) Assurbanipal (?)
        i) *R.A.*, 36/1939, pp. 33-34;
        ii) *K. 14.676* — fragment.
C) *Ancien Testament*:
    · *II Rois 19/9*[b]*—19* (// Es. 37/9[b] —20) = récit B[2]
    /en parallèle à II Rois 19/1-7 (// Es. 37/1-7) = récit B[1].

Conclusions:
    A la suite de la longue tradition suméro-akkadienne des "lettres à la divinité", expression de la piété royale ou privée, un usage spécifique de ce genre littéraire fait son apparition en Mésopotamie du Nord, à Mari et en Assyrie: il appartient au roi, en temps de guerre, de soumettre au dieu de la cité/*A* — [d]Dagan à Mari et à Terqa; *B* — [d]Aššur en Assyrie; cp. *C* — Yahweh à Jérusalem/un compte rendu de la situation politique et militaire;

l'accomplissement de ce rite, par l'affirmation de la "royauté divine" qu'il implique, marque l'intervention du dieu souverain, pour la perte de l'ennemi et le salut de son peuple.

Les structures fondamentales du genre littéraire ainsi défini peuvent se résumer de la manière suivante:

—a) en cette civilisation de l'écriture et dans le cadre de l'épistolographie mésopotamienne, la "lettre à la divinité" fournit ce lien que recherche la piété pour abolir la distance qui sépare l'homme de son dieu/cf. *A*/ii-ind. et iii/, ... "du point de vue de la 'forme littéraire', bien entendu, car si on considère 'le fond', toutes les inscriptions historiques sont des messages aux dieux" (J. Nougayrol).

b) la relation littéraire, établie à la lumière de plusieurs sources, entre ce genre littéraire et l'apparition d'un phénomène prophétique/*A*/iv, v et vi-ind.; *C*/ou oraculaire/*B* — "lettres divines"/permet de mieux situer — par-delà les variations historiques, notamment à l'époque néo-assyrienne — le *Sitz im Kultus* de ces lettres royales à la divinité, dont l'initiative revient ainsi souvent à la divinité ellemême ... ou à son clergé!

Un passage historique de l'Ancien Testament/*C*/fournit à cet égard, en deux récits parallèles, un témoignage capital quant à l'interdépendance des deux phénomènes: au récit B², un parallèle de situation avec le rituel que présuppose le présent genre littéraire; au récit B¹, par contre, la prédominance de l'élément prophétique, de par l'intervention d'Esaïe, s'insère nettement dans la tradition religieuse d'Israël.

c) du point de vue religieux, la vision éminemment théocratique de l'histoire, telle qu'elle est présupposée par ce rituel, assignait au roi une fonction précise, celle d'agent de la souveraineté divine/*A*/i: avec anamnèse historique et vi-ind.; *B* et *C*/.

d) une parenté thématique indéniable, enfin, vient confirmer cette interdépendance entre nos documents et les oracles prophétiques: de part et d'autre apparaissent une série de formules stéréotypées, indices de cette idéologie prophétique de la guerre sainte que nous avons tenté — à la suite de G. von Rad — de décrire ailleurs/cf. *S.V.T.*, 17 (1969), pp. 112-138/et à laquelle les présents textes nous semblent apporter un témoignage non négligeable, quoique connexe.

La "lettre royale à la divinité", de par sa corrélation avec le phénomène "prophétique" ou oraculaire attestée aux divers stades de son histoire, apparaît comme un moment privilégié de l'expression religieuse de cette époque, une sorte de creuset littéraire du langage humain dans son dramatique dialogue avec la souveraineté de la parole divine.

N.B.: Le texte complet de la présente communication paraîtra dans la *Revue d'Histoire et de Philosophie Religieuses*, Strasbourg-Paris.

Two Items of Jewish Religious Folklore

by Theodor H. Gaster

(1) *"Anoint thee, witch, anoint thee!" The Charm against Lilith*

Until recent times, it was a well-known Jewish popular usage to hang up a charm against LILITH, the child-stealing witch, in the room where a birth was expected. The charm can be traced to Byzantine models, and a feature of it is a list of enigmatic names under which the beldam operates. These will now be identified as follows: (a) איילו אוקופדו = ᾿Αελλώ and ᾿Ωκυπέτη, the harpies mentioned in Hesiod's *Theogony*; (b) קלי בדוזה = κλέπτουσα ; (c) שטרינה = error for שטריגה = *strix, strygoi, strega*; (d) פטרותא = πτερωτή ; (e) אבו נקטה = ἐπινύκτιος . — It will be shown also that the Canaanite magical plague from Arslan Tash (8th cent. B.C.) is indeed an early form of this charm, and is not directed against demons in general, as has been recently suggested.

(2) *Pueri mantellati in the Service for the Rejoicing of the Law*

It is a custom of the synagogal service on the Feast of *Simḥath Torah* to call minors, not yet regarded as "children of the commandment" (ברי מצוה) to the rostrum at the public reading of the Law, while a prayer-shawl (*ṭallith*) is held or spread over them. It will be suggested that, in line with the whole service's being a skit on the wedding ceremony, this custom originated from the gentile usage whereby illegitimate children could be legitimized at the marriage of their parents by having the bride's veil or the pallium of the altar spread over them.

The Dichotomy of Judaism during the Second Temple

by Hugo Mantel

The various aspects of the generally accepted theory that Artaxerxes' mandate to Ezra was to make the Torah the law of the land are examined and found wanting. It is proposed therefore that Artaxerxes' rescript constituted a legalization of "the Community of the Exile" as an autonomous body, under the leadership of Ezra. The professional guilds in Old and New Babylonia, and even in the Assyrian Empire, were such autonomous bodies. The Zoroastrian communities, as well as the Greek colonies, no doubt had their own courts of justice. That the Jewish "Golah" in Babylon, under the leadership of its "elders", lived by the laws of the Torah, goes without saying. The subsequent history of the Jews in all countries leaves hardly any doubt that such was also the situation in the Persian Empire. Artaxerxes' rescript merely extended the same arrangement to the "communities of the Golah" on "the other side of the river", namely, the Euphrates.

The position of the high priest as the supreme authority of the hieropolis of Jerusalem was not affected by Artaxerxes' rescript; especially, as the concern of the "Sons of the Golah" was chiefly the private religious life of its members, whereas the high priests' main interest was the Temple and its cult.

The fundamental controversy between the high priests and the leaders of the Golah revolved around their conception of the Torah. The former had a static, the latter a dynamic, approach. This opposition, which had its source in the days of the first Temple between the prophets and the priests, persisted till the end of the second Temple in the form of the conflict between the Sadducees and the Pharisees.

SECTION III

CHRISTIANITY

L'Hymne à Dieu inséré dans les oeuvres de Grégoire de Nazianze, traduction et origine

par J.D. de Savignac

L'auteur donne une traduction personelle de cet hymne, différente au moins de celles qui ont été publiées en français, s'efforce de justifier cette traduction et montre du même coup que l'hymne est bien de Grégoire de Nazianze. Les thèmes de philosophie grecque sont cependant manifestes et certaines expressions demandent à être expliquées du point de vue de la foi chrétienne. Cet hymne constitue néanmoins une synthèse très parfaite de pensée juive et grecque. Finalement, cet hymne magnifique pose le problème de la connaissance intuitive de Dieu en dehors de la révélation chrétienne et de la valeur de la raison.

Monotheism in the New Testament

by Goro Mayeda

According to the Gospels, Jesus advocates the traditional monotheism of Israel, but His God is, different from the leaders of His times, a God who unconditionally forgives sinners.

Paul also follows Israelite tradition in the form, but, when he treats with monotheism at length, he stresses the unity of believers. Idolatry and polytheism are criticised, because they divide the community.

What Johannine thought characteristically is, is firstly, the unity of God the Father and His Son, and secondly, the eschatological hope for the unity of all men through Christ.

The New Testament takes a negative attitude towards angel worship which had some polytheistic tendency in Judaism.

Man as a sinner cannot perfectly obey the God of righteousness, because in his life he is serving another god, e.g. that of lust.

Man is a polytheist by nature. He can be monotheist only through faith in Jesus Christ the Redeemer. Sharing this redemptive act among each other, men can unite. In the New Testament, the idea of "God is one" means that God is the only Being who has the real power to unite.

The causative meaning of oneness is so manifest in the New Testament that it illustrates monotheism in the best way, which has its foundations prepared for in the Old Testament. Biblical semantics is a profitable way of interpretation especially in regard to monotheism.

Empirically, Biblical monotheism is one of the monotheisms in the history of religions. The more it is treated as such on a scientific basis, the clearer its characteristics become. E.g. the question of whether the God of the Bible is anthropomorphic or not can be readily understood if it is treated from the angle of monotheism.

Trinity is the form and unity is the content. The formation of Trinitarian doctrine shows the development of monotheism based upon its Biblical meaning.

Absoluteness of Christianity is inseparable from the problem of monotheism. The New Testament shows paradoxically the unique God of absolute tolerance given through His Only Son to those who, under the Law, can not be monotheists.

Theology, Science, Machines, Faiths: Historic Encounters since the Middle Ages

by Benjamin Nelson

Surprising as this may now seem, few theologians or other spokesmen for religion or high culture appear to have taken stands against technology or machines until the close of the 18th century. Entries for "machine", "industry", "technology", are not even to be found in the copious index of Andrew Dickson White's well-known treatise, the *History of the Warfare of Science with Theology in Christendom*. (2 vols. New York, 1896.)

Indeed, the Later Middle Ages and Early Modern eras witness a sequence of forward thrusts toward science and technology which need to be seen as expressions of profound religious impulses in the explication and in the enhancement of God's Word and World, rather than as secular attacks against the spirit of religion. The union of theology, science and magic arts is asserted again and again in the Promethean imagery of Renaissance engineers and artists.

When the earliest important attacks on technology and the shocking effects of new industrialism did come, they came not so much from theologians as from poets, cultural critics, and men of letters. The most critical figures are those who perceived that the new industrialism involved very important dangers to spiritual values of the past. Most important among these dangers were: the spread of "mechanization of spirit", of autonomization of instrumental functions, of the routinization of everyday life, of new forms of servile dependence and new forms of domination; the permeation of civil society by crassness and commercialism; the erosion of community bonds and inherited traditions of reciprocity.

The animus against technology and technoculture came to a head not very long after the emergence in Germany and elsewhere of what was to be perhaps one of the most fateful revolutions of the late 19th and 20th centuries, the "rationalization revolution". The new sensibility finds its fullest expression in writers of many lands and points of departure, including Max Weber, Henry Adams, and Evgenii Zamîatin, who were horrified by the threat of the total coordination of all resources in accordance with the principles of instrumental rationality. Their fear of a sort of "nightmare of entropy" has continued to echo strongly throughout the 20th century.

The ambiguous and ambivalent attitudes to science and technology in contemporary religious and social outlooks across the world suggest that we are at a new turn in the history of the relations of Western and Eastern civilizations. New fusions of "Westness" and "Eastness" are apparently in the making.

L'exégèse du récit du Paradis terrestre attestée par le récit des Pèlerins d'Emmaüs, à l'origine du rabaissement, dans le gnosticisme, du dieu de l'Ancien Testament au rang de démiurge mauvais

par Jean Magne

La citation implicite de *Gen.* 3,7: "Et *leurs yeux s'ouvrirent et ils connurent* qu'ils étaient nus" en Lc. 24,31: "Alors *leurs yeux s'ouvrirent et ils* le *reconnurent"* identifie le pain de l'euch-aristie au fruit de l'arbre de la connaissance et les définit l'un l'autre comme sacrement de la gnose.

En ce qui concerne l'eucharistie, j'ai montré dans ma communication au *Fourth Int. Congress on N.T. Studies,* Oxford, sept. 1969 (résumé à paraître dans *Studia Evangelica,* VI), que telle était bien sa signification originelle.

Je voudrais montrer ici que la citation implicite et l'étroite dépendance littéraire et structurale du récit d'Emmaüs par rapport à celui du Paradis attestent une exégèse de ce dernier dia-métralement opposée à celle qui s'exprime déjà en *Rom.* 5,12 et qui est devenue traditionnelle.

Selon cette exégèse, loin de conduire Adam et Ève à la dé-chéance et à la mort, leur transgression de l'ordre du créateur leur procure, par la vue de leur nudité, la révélation gnostique fonda-mentale: la connaissance de soi-même indispensable pour découvrir d'où l'on est venu et où l'on doit retourner.

Loin aussi d'avoir agi par cnvie (*Sag.* 2,24), le serpent, qui fait accéder Adam et Ève à cette connaissance de salut, est mu par la pitié, et fait figure de révélateur et de sauveur, comme dans la tradition des Naassènes, Ophites, Pérates, Séthiens, etc.

Le dieu créateur, au contraire, par sa jalousie et son mensonge dénoncés par le serpent (Adam et Ève ne meurent pas mais de-viennent comme des dieux), se révèle comme un dieu inférieur, ignorant, vantard, etc. — tel, d'ailleurs, qu'il devait apparaitre à un lecteur grec à peu près d'un bout à l'autre de l'A.T. — et qui veut maintenir l'homme sous sa domination.

A partir de cette exégèse, se poseront pour les gnostiques les trois grands problèmes que les écoles s'efforceront de résoudre:
— problème de l'émanation des êtres célestes et du créateur à partir de l'immutabilité du dieu suprême;
— problème du salut ou retour de l'homme au monde d'en — haut d'où il vient;
— problème du sauveur qui appartient lui aussi nécessairement au monde d'en-haut mais exerce son action dans le monde d'en-bas pour l'homme et contre le démiurge mauvais.

L'invention de solutions diverses à ces problèmes dans les différents milieux intellectuels et religieux grecs, syriens, égyptiens, iraniens, juifs, etc., et les réactions de ces solutions les unes sur les autres en vue de les perfectionner constituer-ont le grand mouvement religieux des Ier et IIème siècles.

En certains milieux grecs, en particulier, le sauveur céleste vaincra le prince de ce monde et ses archontes, les planètes de l'Heimarméné, dans l'acte même par lequel ils espéraient triompher de lui, sa crucifixion cosmique.

En milieu juif, le créateur et dieu de l'Alliance et de la Loi sera rétabli au rang de dieu suprême, son rôle pervers reporté sur Satan ayant pris les traits du serpent, et la transgression libératrice deviendra faute, mais dont on comprend mal désormais qu'elle puisse entraîner déchéance et nécessiter rédemption. Le sauveur céleste, devenu ennemi et vainqueur du serpent qui était lui-même (il restera cependant le serpent d'airain de Nom. 21, 8-9), sera progressivement redéfini, à coup de *testimonia* vétérotestamentaires, sous les traits du messie juif attendu, et humanisé jusqu'à pouvoir n'être plus considéré que comme un agitateur zélote quelconque exécuté par les Romains puis messianisé et incompréhensiblement divinisé par les siens. Faisant ainsi récupérer au gnosticisme tout l'A.T., les juifs ne parviendront cependant pas à faire pratiquer la Loi, ni même les préceptes noachiques aux chrétiens.

Ne pouvant apporter ici la justification de toutes ces affirmations qui, d'ailleurs, en tant qu'elles ne font qu'énoncer les thèses bien connues de la gnose, n'en ont guère besoin, je ne présenterai que quelques textes se rapportant au créateur mauvais et montrant, d'une part, sa réidentification au dieu suprême en tant que créateur, d'autre part, son identification à Satan en tant que mauvais.

Eine neue Deutung des Anselmischen Proslogionbeweises

von Anton Antweiler

1. Wie es vielen Menschen leicht fällt, an wenige oder viele oder unzählige Götter zu glauben, so fällt es wiederum vielen leicht, an einen einzigen Gott zu glauben.

Unter ihnen wieder fällt es manchen schwer, daß sie an diesen einen Gott sollen nur glauben können. Sie verlangen danach, wenigstens zu prüfen, ob sie ihn nicht auch wissen können.

Aus diesem Streben sind die Gottesbeweise entstanden. Sie beabsichtigen nicht, jemanden, der nicht an Gott glaubt, an diesen Gott gläubig zu machen. Sie wollen nur das, was sie glauben, auch wißbar machen, ganz oder teilweise. Solcher Beweise gibt es viele. Wohl der berühmteste und umstrittenste ist der Beweis, den Anselm von Canterburry (1033-1109) in seinem Proslogion vorgelegt hat.

2. Dieser Beweis, auf eine Kurzform gebracht, die nicht in dieser Form von Anselm stammt, aber sich seiner Worte bedient, lautet:

Man kann sich etwas denken, über das hinaus nichts Größeres gedacht werden kann.

Man kann sich dasselbe denken, aber jetzt nicht nur als gedacht, sondern auch als seiend.

Was ist, ist mehr als was nur gedacht wird. Also gibt es das Größte" auch in Wirklichkeit.

3. Gegen diesen Beweis kann man erstens einwenden, daß es nicht angeht, vom Gedachten auf Seiendes zu schließen, und zweitens, daß dieses "Größte" nicht der christliche Gott zu sein braucht. Alle Gegner des Beweises haben sich nur mit dem ersten Einwand befaßt: weder eine paradiesische Insel (Gaunilo) noch 100 Taler (Kant) brauchen deswegen zu sein, weil man sie denken kann.

4. Dieser Einwand setzt voraus, daß alle Eigenschaften, die für endliche Dinge gelten, auch für das Unendliche gelten. Zwar benutzt Anselm nie das Wort unendlich; was er aber meint, ist das Unendliche. Georg Cantor (1845-1918) hat gezeigt, daß neben dem Unendlichen, als Begriff und Bezeichung für Gott, auch andere Gegenstände, insbesondere Zahlen, als unendlich gedacht und als vorhanden betrachtet werden können und müssen. Er hat es auf einfache und einleuchtende Weise nachgewiesen, und nicht nur, daß es eine derartige unendliche Zahl gibt, sondern deren unendlich viele. Alle haben gemeinsam, daß, wenn man etwas hinzufügt oder wegnimmt, sie nicht größer oder kleiner werden müssen, und daß ein echter Teil von ihnen mit dem Ganzen gleich "groß" ist — beides ist bei endlichen Zahlen unmöglich.

Nimmt man diesen Grundgedanken, daß nämlich nicht alle Eigenschaften endlicher Zahlen auch für unendliche Zahlen gelten, so besagt er, angewandt auf den Anselmischen Gottesbeweis, daß es möglich und notwendig ist, bei allen endlichen Dingen zwischen Gedachtwerden und Wirklich-sein getrennt werden muß, daß das aber bei dem einen höchsten Wesen, Gott, nicht möglich ist und daß gerade dadurch Gott von allem Endlichen grundsätzlich verschieden ist.

Diesen Unterschied hat auch Anselm geahnt, wenn auch nicht grundsätzlich ausgesprochen, aber doch tatsächlich benutzt. "Ohne jedes Bedenken (fast könnte man übersetzen: mit Vergnügen) sage ich: wenn jemand etwas vorzuweisen vermag, das entweder in Wirklichkeit oder auch nur in Gedanken da wäre und auf das meine Überlegungen angewendet werden könnten, außer dem Einen, worüber hinaus Größeres nicht gedacht werden kann, so will ich diese verlorene Insel (von der Gaunilo spricht) finden und sie ihm geben, so daß sie nicht wieder verloren werden kann".

5. Die Belege für diese Deutung des Proslogionbeweises werden in Band 4 der "Analecta Anselmiana" vorgelegt werden.

SECTION III/I

NAG HAMMADI

The Nag Hammadi Library as a Collection of Holy Scriptures

by James M. Robinson

This paper will begin with an assessment of the present state of plans to translate and publish the Nag Hammadi Library. The international English language edition, to be published by Brill in Leiden in connection with a new monograph series, Nag Hammadi Studies, is in an advanced state of preparation. Now that the library is in draft translation, the preliminary general assessments by Doresse and others, based upon samplings, can in various respects be revised and supplemented. The syncretistic nature of the library, sensed since Doresse's division of the materials into four categories, can be further exemplified. E.g. the identified fragment of the Coptic version of the Sentences of Sextus in the fragmentary Codex XII indicates the presence of non-gnostic pagan wisdom literature (subjected no doubt in use to an interpretatio gnostica, which however, has not been interpolated into the written text itself). The close relation of this Codex to the rest of the gnostic library seems indicated by the identification within it of fragments of a Sahidic version of the Gospel of Truth known in Sub-Achmimic from Codex I (the Jung Codex). The association of some tractates with the philosophic gnosis opposed by Plotinus can be made more specific, in that the initial correlation of tractate names with those listed by Porphyry can be corrected and supplemented, as dialectic traits, vocabulary, and matters of content give more profile to this cluster of tractates.

Although this report, like its predecessors, remains quite preliminary and tentative, in that the study following upon translation has only begun, it will provide some orientation moving beyond what has been available thus far.

Boehme et la langue Adamique

par Alexis Klimov

Dans ses *Nouveaux Essais sur l'entendement humain,* Leibniz a soulevé le problème de savoir s'il y a possibilité de retrouver la langue adamique, c'est-à-dire "la langue radical et primitive". Pour Jacob Boehme, cette recherche de l'*adamique* est essentielle. Non pas pour des raisons linguistiques mais métaphysiques qu'il expose principalement dans les chapitres 35 et 36 de son oeuvre maîtresse: le *Mysterium magnum.*

Le grand mystère est celui de l'origine: celui de la création du monde spirituel comme étant l'*expression* du Verbe, de l'Un, de Dieu à la fois "Tout et Rien". Au centre de ce mystère du passage du non-être à l'être, il y a l'ignorance dans laquelle, au départ, si l'on peut s'exprimer ainsi, Dieu se trouve vis-à-vis de lui même. A rapprocher, par exemple, de Plotin, *Enn.,* V, 3, 13: "la réalité la plus simple de toutes n'a pas la pensée d'elle-même; si elle l'avait, elle serait une multiplicité."

Or Dieu ne peut, selon Boehme, que chercher à se connaître. Il prononce l'être à partir de lui-même et, par là, se découvre. Le monde créé est donc langage divin, langage qu'avant la chute, Adam, en communion avec la totalité du réel, comprenait. Retrouver dans sa pureté la langue adamique apparaît comme étant la voie royale de la gnose boehmienne, puisqu'elle conduit non seulement à une connaissance totale, mais encore au salut. En d'autres termes, saisir l'essence de notre langage équivaut à découvrir notamment les structures ou, mieux encore, les dynamismes fondamentaux du cosmos entier. Et cette découverte par laquelle se dévoile le sens de l'être, mène à Dieu, à l'Un, au Tout.

Par ailleurs, cette découverte n'est possible que si l'on parvient à se détacher de la lettre pour en retrouver l'esprit: "Nos savants se font appeler docteurs et maîtres et aucun ne comprend la langue de sa Mère. Ils n'entendent rien de plus de l'esprit que le paysan de l'outil qui lui sert à cultiver son champ; ils se servent tout simplement de la forme saisie des mots grossièrement formés et ne comprennent pas ce que le Verbe est dans son sens (...)." (*Mysterium magnum,* chap. 35, 61)

La conclusion de cette communication a été, quoique indirectement, inspirée par les thèmes esquissés ci-dessus.

L'historien des religions peut-il prétendre n'être qu'historien, alors que ses recherches s'inscrivent dans un domaine où tout renvoie à un réel qui ne se limite pas au monde spatio-temporel, à l'ordre phénoménal? Et s'il est vrai que ce réel ne se découvre que dans l'approfondissement de l'expérience intérieure, il importe que la démarche de l'historien des religions soit liée à une quête de sagesse. En l'éclairant notamment sur la complexité de la réalité humaine et sur l'indicible simplicité qui fonde cette dernière, elle l'aidera à comprendre la complémentarité des différentes approches qui forment ce que, avec plus au moins de bonheur, nous appelons les sciences de l'homme et, du même coup, elle l'empêchera de s'en tenir exclusivement à l'une d'entre elles. Pourquoi ne pas rappeler ce que tant de créateurs — Paul Claudel, Arthur Honegger, Robert Oppenheimer, etc. — ont constaté: "Les progrès les plus marquants ont été accomplis par des amateurs ou en tout cas, par des savants en dehors de leurs domaines spécialisés." Il y a là une grande leçon à retenir. A notre époque où prolifèrent les formes de contestation dissimulant une terrible angoisse quant au sens de l'existence, on ne devrait apporter aucune contribution à l'amoncellement d'une poussièreuse, étouffante et stérile érudition. N'est-ce pas dans la mesure où elle nous permet d'accéder avec plus de vérité, de compréhension et de connaissance au trésor spirituel de l'humanité, que l'histoire des religions acquiert véritablement ses lettres de noblesse?

SECTION IV

ISLAM

Mir Dard, a Naqshbandi mystic of the 18th century in Delhi

by Annemarie Schimmel

The Naqshbandi order is usually considered quite uninterested in artistic expression. However, in Delhi in the early 18th century the members of this order contributed a great deal to the development of Urdu poetry (Shāh Gulshan, Muḥammad Nāṣir ᶜAndalīb, Maẓhar Jānjānān). The finest representative of this school is Khwaja Mīr Dard (1719-1785) who, for the first time, wrote touching mystical poetry in Urdu. Besides, he left a large work in Persian, and the study of his persian prose works reveals a hitherto neglected aspect of his thought, e.g. his feeling of being the "first of the Muḥammadans", a mystical leader endowed with all qualities of the station of "annihilation in the Prophet". The analysis of his mystical thought throws light upon the ideas of the *ṭarīqa Muḥammadīya*, an offshot of the Naqshbandiya, and is interesting for the study of the psychology of a mystical leader and "inspired" poet.

(The ideas of the paper are discussed in two articles on Mir Dard, one in the Festgabe deutscher Iranisten zur 2500. Jahrfeier Irans, Stuttgart 1971, and one in the S.F.G. Brandon Memorial Volume, Manchester 1973).

Faith and reason in koranic argumentation

by Jacques Waardenburg

As a religious document, the Koran offers to the researcher the direct expression of a prophet's belief in God and of his appeal to others to come to the same belief, through the Koran as God's revelation. The present paper analyzes the way in which this appeal is made, and in particular the place which is given thereby to the reasoning capacities of man. Subject of inquiry is in the first place the Koranic notion of man's intelligence enabling him to see the signs of God, and in the second place the way in which the Koranic argument itself is structured in its appeal to man's reason. It is shown that there is a connection between the Koranic idea of reason and the reasoning process itself as it is found in Koranic argumentation. Belief in God, according to the Koran, has a reasonable evidence, and subsequent Islamic theology has not departed from this position.

An Islamic echo of the "trickster": the ᶜayyārs of Indo-Persian and Malay romances

by Alessandro Bausani

Indo-Persian *dāstāns* and Malay romances (*hikayat*) show the strange characters of the so called ᶜ*ayyār*, a sort of clownish but in the same time heroic figures that surround the Protagonist (generally a prince or famous warrior). Similar characters, called *panakawan*, are present in old Javanese romances (beginning with the XIIth century), in *wayang* plays and in the Javanese-Islamic romance of Amir Hamzah (*Ménak*). The A. tries to sketch a typology of these characters and to show that they may have a common origin, though in Iran they seem derived from the *adhyār*, sort of paladins in the feudal "Männerbünde", and in Java they seem an echo of the old wizard-exorcist of pre-Islamic and even pre-Hindu traditions.

Their origins is probably composite but the A. thinks that they ultimately derive from a mythical cycle somehow connected with the "trickster" type of ethnic religions.

(The Paper has been published in the Festschrift for Tucci).

Un texte concernant les "pseudo-sabéens de Ḥarrān"

par Jan Hjärpe

Il y a dans le 5ème chapitre du *Talbīs Iblīs*, "l'imposture du diable", d'Abu-l-Farağ ibn al-Gawzī (m. en 1201) deux petites sections qui sont très intéressantes:

1) Le paragraphe intitulé *Ḏikru talbīsihi ᶜalā aṣḥābi-l-hayākil*, "Son imposture quant aux adorateurs des Temples".

2) Le paragraphe intitulé *Ḏikru talbisihi ᶜala-ṣ-ṣabi'in*, "Son imposture quant aux sabéens".

Le premier de ces deux paragraphes est composé de deux parties dont la première contient le raisonnement suivant:

Les "Temples" sont les planètes ou plutôt les sphères planétaires et la sphère des étoiles fixes. Ces Temples sont les sièges des divinités appelées "les êtres spirituels" (*ar-rūḥānīyāt*). On fait des sacrifices, soit directement aux Temples, soit aux idoles qui les représentent. Chaque idole, ainsi que chaque sanctuaire, doit être conforme à la forme et à la substance de la planète en question.

Ce raisonnement est en concordance avec la base de la théologie des "sabéens de Ḥarrān" ainsi qu'on connait leurs doctrines selon les sources bien connues (an-Nadīm, aš-Šahrastānī, ad-Dimašqī, le Ġāyat-al-Ḥakīm).

La deuxième partie du paragraphe contient une description des sacrifices aux divinités planétaires. La source d'ibn al-Ġawzī est un nommé Yaḥyā ibn Bišr an-Nihāwandī. Dans une autre section du livre ibn al Ġawzī dit: "Cela est ce qu'a raconté an-Nihāwandī. Je l'ai copié d'un livre ... qui fut écrit il y a 220 ans." La source d'ibn al-Ġawzī date alors du 10ème siècle de notre ère.

Chaqu'une des sept descriptions des sacrifices est bâtie de la manière suivante:

1) Une description du rituel du sacrifice.

2) L'oraison qui l'accompagne.

Chaque sacrifice — ainsi que les oraisons — s'adapte à la nature de la planète.

On retrouve les traits de ce récit, avec des différences importantes, chez ad-Dimišqī (dans le Nuḫbat-ad-Dahr), où les donneés sont arrangées de la manière suivante: 1) Description du sanctuaire de la divinité en question, 2) Description de l'idole, 3) Description du rituel du sacrifice, 4) L'oraison.

Les descriptions des sanctuaires (qui manquent chez an-Nihāwandī) correspondent aux descriptions des sanctuaires sabéens chez al-Maṣᶜūdī et chez aš-Šahrastānī. C'est évident qu'ad-Dimašqī a eu deux sources, l'une contenant les dommées sur les sanctuaires, l'autre contenant les données sur les sacrifices.

C'est surtout les sacrifices à Saturne (un taureau) et à Mars (un homme blond couvert de taches de rousseur) qu'on doit remarquer. La tête de l'homme sacrifié à Mars est employée à des usages divinatoires. Ce rite divinatoire (avec ou sans rapport au culte d'une planète) est confirmé par d'autres textes concernant les "pseudo-sabéens". Le sacrifice d'un taureau semble être un fait historique attesté par plusieurs sources.

Le 2ème paragraphe contient 1) l'avis de l'auteur sur l'étymologie du mot "sabéens", 2) Les avis différents des anciens commentateurs du Coran sur les "sabéens", 3) Les avis des scolastiques (*al-mutakallimūn*).

Nous y trouvons des données intéressantes sur le rituel des prières et du jeûne des sabéens. Il s'agit de traditions dont les parallèles se trouvent aussi bien dans les textes du grand recueil de Chwolsohn ("Die Ssabier und der Ssabismus", 1856) que dans d'autres sources.

Le Dieu du Coran et le Dieu d'Abraham
d'après les polémistes byzantins

par A.-Th. Khoury

La figure d'Abraham occupe une place centrale dans l'histoire religieuse du Judaïsme, du Christianisme et de l'Islam. Bien que la majorité des polémistes chrétiens n'eût jamais exprimé de doutes sur l'identité du Dieu du Coran, un auteur intransigeant, Nicétas de Byzance, élabora néanmoins une thèse extrémiste qui connut un étonnant succès à Byzance du Xe au XIIe s. Nicétas prétend que, sous les dehors d'un monothéisme ostentatoire, Mahomet a en réalité prêché le culte des idoles, plus précisement l'adoration de Satan; le Dieu du Coran n'a donc rien à faire avec le Dieu d'Abraham.

Nicétas appuie sa thèse sur le fait que les rites du pèlarinage islamique à la Ka^{c}ba reprennent les cérémonies que les Arabes païens célébraient en l'honneur d'Aphrodite. En outre, le Coran contient des serments, où Dieu jure par les créatures. Donc le Coran prêche l'idolâtrie et le culte des démons.

Mais le Coran rapporte que le temple de la Ka^{c}ba fut bâti par Abraham et son fils Ismaël. Ce récit est contredit par les données de l'Ecriture sainte, réplique Nicétas. Quant à la déclaration coranique qui, d'après la tradition musulmane, place le sacrifice d'Isaac aux environs de la Mekke, elle n'a pas de consistance, comme Jean Damascène l'avait déjà montré.

On ne saurait alléguer que l'Islam a emprunté à Abraham la

circoncision et connaît des vérités partielles sur Dieu. Le Coran lui-même, en effet, rompt cette relation avec Abraham, en faisant agir son Dieu à l'encontre du Dieu d'Abraham: il prescrit d'adorer Aphrodite, il mêle aux vérités des erreurs essentielles, il fait jurer Dieu, non par lui-même, comme dans la Bible, mais par les créatures, enfin il fausse les desseins de Dieu, en déclarant par exemple que le passage merveilleux de la Mer Rouge est un signe de l'authenticité de la mission de Mahomet.

D'ailleurs l'Evangile affirme: "Qui n'honore pas le Fils, n'honore pas le Père" (*Jn* 5, 23), et: "Nul ne connaît le Fils si ce n'est le Père, comme nul ne connaît le Père si ce n'est le Fils, et celui à qui le Fils veut bien le révéler" (*Matth* 11, 27). L'Islam, qui rejette le Fils, ne connaît donc pas le Père, le Dieu d'Abraham, et ne saurait adorer le vrai Dieu.

Enfin Dieu déclare vouloir accorder son Alliance au seul Isaac, et il ne donne à Ismaël qu'une bénédiction matérielle: il lui promet une nombreuse postérité (*Gen.* 17, 19-21).

La thèse intransigeante de Nicétas, malgré son succès durable, appela au XIIe s. une révision. La décision officielle prise à Byzance reconnut que l'Islam prêche le monothéisme et adore le vrai Dieu commun aux juifs et aux chrétiens.

SECTION V

GREECE AND ROME, HELLENISM

Das Gottesbild Plotins

von H. Ludin Jansen

Plotin benutzt mit Vorliebe die Bezeichnung *to hen*, das Eine, von der Macht, die ihm im Moment des Erlebnisses begegnet ist. Nicht dass diese Bezeichnung dem, was er sagen will, völlig entspricht. Er meint aber augenscheinlich, dass sie mehr besagt als die andern Ausdrücke, deren er sich bedient. In Wirklichkeit ist das Eine unaussprechlich, jenseits von allem, so dass man ihm überhaupt keinen Namen geben kann. Darum wählt er am liebsten eine negative Charakterisierung: "Das Eine ist überhaupt nichts, nicht etwas von einer bestimmten Beschaffenheit oder Grösse, auch nicht Geist oder Seele, nicht etwas sich Bewegendes oder Stillstehendes, in Raum oder Zeit." Mit diesem und ähnlichen Ausdrücken will er betonen wie unmöglich es ist, eine brauchbare Bezeichnung zu finden. Das Eine ist kurzweg "etwas ganz anderes", ungleich allem was wir kennen. Er betont, dass wir es mit dem letzten Ursprung der Mannifaltigkeit im Dasein zu tun haben. Überall ist es nämlich so, sagt er, dass es hinter der Mehrheit eine unbedingte Einheit gibt. Alles scheint auf diesen Urgrund zurückzugehen, sowohl das Sichtbare als das, was man mit dem natürlichen Auge nicht sehen kann. Das Eine ist, als Quelle alles Seienden, eine unpersönliche Kraft, eine Urkraft, wenn man will.

Die Vorstellung von dem Einen besagt doch nicht alles, was das Gottesbild Plotins betrifft. Er rechnet auch mit einem persönlichen Gott, und dieser persönliche Gott ist identisch mit, oder vielleicht besser, ist eine eigene Form des Einen, nämlich so wie es in der Begegnung mit dem einzelnen Menschen hervortreten kann. Da kann man nicht mehr von einer sprudelnden Kraft reden, sondern von einem *theos,* einem Gott, einem persönlichen Gegenpol des einzelnen Individuums.

Es scheint sich so zu verhalten, dass Plotin vorzugsweise an der

Bezeichnung "Das Eine" festhält, wo der Gesichtspunkt kosmisch ist, während er am liebsten von Gott spricht, wenn es gilt, die Beziehung zwischen dem Einen und dem Menschen auszudrücken.

Diese zweifache Auffassung des Gottesbildes wird durch das Erlebnis erklärt. In der Entzückung kann das persönliche Moment bisweilen ausgewischt werden. "Die beiden werden eins", wie er sagt. In andern Fällen wird das Göttliche ganz natürlich als persönlich betrachtet. Das gilt vor allem Begegnungen, wo es von neuer Kunde oder von einem persönlichen Beruf die Rede ist.

The Delphic Maxim "Know Yourself" in Hermetic Interpretation

by H.D. Betz

It is the thesis of the paper that the sayings quoted as "holy word" in *Corpus Hermeticum* I (Poimandres) secs. 18 and 21 represent a Hermetic interpretation of the Delphic maxim "Know Yourself". The "holy word" in sec. 18 is a composition out of several elements, one of which reads "Let the one who has the 'Nous' recognize himself as immortal". Other versions of the saying are quoted in sec. 21: "He who has recognized himself departs into him(self)," and "If you learn that he is out of life and light and that you are constituted of the same substances, you will return into life," and finally "Let him who has the 'Nous' recognize himself". Clearly the Hermetic writer has taken these sayings from some source. The source can be determined with some degree of certainty, because we find similar sayings as interpretations of the Delphic maxim in the writings of Cicero, Seneca, Epictetus, Philo of Alexandria, and the Neoplatonist philosophers. These interpretations can be traced back to Plato. Thus the Hermetic sayings in secs. 18 and 21 follow one of the traditional interpretations of the Delphic maxim "Know Yourself". In the course of this history the maxim is not only interpreted but also reformulated, in order to directly express the meaning intended. The history of these transformations is, of course, simultaneously a reflection of the history of Greek theology, from the simple wisdom of the Delphic Apollo of the early period to the speculative systems and esoteric wisdom of late entiquity.

The paper of which only a summary can be given will appear in the Harvard Theological Review, in 1970 or 1971.

Gods do not exist

by J.P. Guépin

How can one prove that gods do not exist! It is a matter of charging one's opponent with the burden of proof. Is there any advantage to be derived of such an atheistic attitude for the study of religion? I think there is. We can now with an easy conscience put disbelief on an equal footing with belief, and better appreciate the influence of rational arguments on the development of religious phenomena, which always are partly determined by valid incredulous objections.

See J.P. Guépin, *The Tragic Paradox, myth and ritual in Greek tragedy,* Amsterdam, Hakkert, 1968, pp. 9-10.

Die di indigetes und die Apotheose des Romulus

von L.F. Janssen

Die Frage nach der Bedeutung der *di indigetes* war von jeher mit den in den Listen der *indigitamenta* verzeichneten Sondergötter aufs engste verknüpft, aber eine befriedigende Interpretation des Begriffes *indiges*, das auch als Beiname gewisser himmlischen Gottheiten begegnet, wurde schwerlich gefunden. Die Lösung der verworrenen Problems wurde wesentlich von Wissowa gefördert, indem er einen scharfen Trennungsstrich zog zwischen *di indigetes* und *indigitamenta*; statt dessen stellte er die Hypothese auf, das die *di indigetes* als die alten Götter sich zu den neu-eingebürgerten *di novensiles* verhielten als das Patriziat zum Plebs.

Es ist das Verdienst Carl Kochs, die Schwachheit dieser Wissowa'schen Konstruktion aufgewiesen zu haben; in seiner Studie über die "Gestirnverehrung im alten Italien" (1933), hat er sämtliche Daten über die als *Indiges* verehrten Götter, wie Sol, Juppiter und Aeneas zusammengestellt und er kan namentlich auf Grund der Verehrung von *Sol Indiges* durch die gens Aurelia zu dem Ergebnis, dass die *di indigetes* als eine Vielheit stammväterlicher Gottheiten zu betrachten seien; der Kult des *Sol Indiges* galt ihm vor allem als der einer urväterlicher Gottheit des latinischen Volkes. Das im römischen Kalender verzeichnete *sacrifi-*

cium publicum für *Sol* berechtigt zwar (mit Bömer) zu dem
Schluss, dass *Sol Indiges* in Rom als eine staatliche Schutzgott-
heit verehrt wurde, aber damit ist nicht bewiesen, dass die *di
indigetes* ihrem Gesamtcharakter nach staatliche Schutzgott-
heiten waren. Zudem soll man bei jedem Versuch zur Interpretation der *di indigetes* die Möglichkeit einer Relatierung mit den
indigitamenta-Listen nicht völlig ausser Betracht lassen; die meisten der darin verzeichneten Sondergötter überwachen Handlungen, welche im Dasein des primitiven Menschen immer wieder
aufs Neue zurückkehren, bei der Feldarbeit, bei Hochzeit und
Geburt. Dabei kommt es darauf an, den richtigen Weg zu einer
fruchtbringenden Integration menschlicher Handlungen und göttlicher Wirksamkeit; die Sondergötter bilden gleichsam die Arche-
typen des menschlichen Handelns; in diesen Kreis gehört *Sol* richtig hinein, nicht weil er Vorbild ist, sondern weil er Voraussetzung ist für jede das Leben fördernde Arbeit und Fürsorge. Der
manchmal mit *Sol Indiges* in Verbindung gebrachte *Aeneas Indiges* hat diese Qualität erhalten infolge seiner *pietas*, welche ihn
ganz besonders zum *Pater Indiges* ausgezeichnet hat; gleich wie
Sol griechischer Anschauung gemäss zum Urvater des lateinischen
Volkes geworden, so war es Aeneas, der die *gens Latina* zur
höchsten Stufe ihrer Entwicklung emporführte, indem er durch
seine exemplarische *pietas* die Einheit des Gentilverbandes begründete; so wurden die ethischen Grundlagen geschaffen, wor-
auf das später römische Volk sich ausbildete.

  Dann hat es nur noch eines Romulus bedurft um Rom und den
römischen Staat zu gründen, aber das gab diesem nicht die Möglichkeit zum *Indiges* zu werden, weil diese politische Form nicht
mehr dem Stammverband, sondern einer höheren Stufe des
menschlichen Gemeinschaftlebens angehörte.

SECTION VI

INDIA AND IRAN

The Madhyamaka Philosopher Nāgārjuna according to the Chinese Sources

by Amalia Pezzali

Years ago Max Walleser has treated the subject ("*The life of Nāgārjuna from Tibetan and Chinese sources*", Hirth Anniversary Volume, London 1922, p. 421-455), comparing the Chinese and the Tibetan sources, without reaching, after his accurate study, any definitive solution of the problem.

Prof. Etienne Lamotte, in his excellent translation of the *Vimalakīrtinirdeśa* (VKN, Louvain 1962, p. 70-77), gave some important suggestions in order to put the problem under a new light. Throughout some Chinese sources, interpreted in a very acceptable and quite illuminating way, he established some probable dates for the life of the madhyamaka philosopher Nāgārjuna.

For the study of Buddhism, from the historical point of view, such dates are not a mere curiosity. That is why, starting from the previously mentioned studies, I have examined all the Chinese texts dealing with such a problem. Comparing them, those that are the most ancient sources with all the other material at our disposal, I am trying to afford an answer to the following questions:

— Have there been one or more Nāgārjuna?
— In what period has the madhyamaka philosopher Nāgārjuna lived, and how long has been his life?
— Where has he had birth, and where has he spent his life?
— Has he had a master?
— Who have been his disciples?
— What have been his works?

The conclusions I reached will be published quite soon in a monograph on the philosopher Nāgārjuna on the type I have already done for Śāntideva (Firenze, Vallecchi, 1968).

Reconstructing the Harappan Hinduism
— Sources and Methods (Summary of the preview
of a forthcoming monograph)

by Asko Parpola

I. Introduction
   1. Previous studies of the Harappan religion — Sir John Marshall.
II. The starting point: The Indus script and iconography
   2. The main results of the decipherment of the Indus script.
   3. The identity of the planetary deities of the Indus inscriptions and of later Indian tradition with the main gods of Hinduism.
   4. The main theses:
      (A) The original language of Hinduism is Dravidian.
      (B) Hinduism is a very ancient religion, which was systematized and developed into a comprehensive world view by the Harappans.
      (C) Astronomy played a predominant role in the Harappan Hinduism and its formation.
III. Other, independent sources and methods
   (A) 5. The linguistic evidence for the Dravidian origin of Hinduism (cf. my paper at the Third conference of Tamil Studies, July 1970).
   (B) 6. The prevalent view according to which Hinduism has developed from Vedism is due to the distortion of perspectives caused by the supposed identity of the age of the tradition (ideas) and the age of the form (texts) in which it has been handed down.
        7. Conclusions cannot be drawn *ex silento,* because our sources are incomplete and often biased.
        8. Hinduism in the Rigveda and the Brahmana texts. Amalgamation.
        9. The Upaniṣads, Buddhism, Jainism and Classical Hinduism with its philosophic systems go back to the common archetype of Harappan Hinduism, which survived as a strong undercurrent during the Vedic period and came to the surface when the Veda lost its grip.
       10. The reconstruction of the archetype of these various traditions.

11. The internal structure of the archetype as a tool in the reconstruction: rediscovery of the original, rounded whole, the systematically constructed Hinduism where the same fundamental pattern is repeated in all the different conceptual categories, synchronized with each other.

(C) 12. The mathematical mind of the creators of the Harappan Hinduism: the systematization probably took place simultaneously with the fixing of the Hindu calendar system and the construction of the great cities, both dating about 2400 B.C.

13. The important role of the astronomy in the classical Hinduism and the Vedic sacrifices. The lunar marking stars (nakṣatras).

14. Early borrowings as an important source: especially the Chinese marking stars and animal cycle and the pre-Buddhist Yin-Yang wu-hsing doctrine, which are of harappan origin.

15. The intimate connection of the names etc. of the nakṣatras and of the zodiac with the Hindu mythology, e.g. the Indian deluge myth can be read from the stars when the stars are called by their original Dravidian names.

16. The specificly Indian flora, fauna and climate, and Dravidian puns, which have been among the main factors in the making of the Hindu mythology, definitely prove its Indian origin.

IV. Major results of the study

17. Basic facts about the language, religion, science, social structure, toponymy etc. of the Harappan people become known. In addition to many previously unclear myths, symbols and names, Hinduism can for the first time be understood as a coherent system, and its historical development can be followed from the neolithic times until the present day, including many branches both inside and outside India which have previously not been connected with it. The Indian civilization and its place in the history of mankind can now be better understood.

Monthly Ancestral Offerings in Hinduism

by H. Daniel Smith

Rarely do treatments of Hinduism available in the West give adequate emphasis to the concern for ancestors at various levels of Hindu custom and ritual. It is difficult to overestimate the degree to which the typical Hindu feels he lives in a vibrant and continuing relationship with his deceased forebearers. To those wandering spirits in the world beyond the funeral pyre their direct descendents feel an obligation to "satisfy" those departed ancestors' imposed restiveness with offerings of foodstuffs and prayers. *Tarpaṇa,* the formalized rites performed within ortho-prax brāhmaṇical circles in honor of the departed ancestors, is a word derived from a Sanskrit term meaning "satisfaction" — and reflects in its faithful performance a continued concern for the welfare of the *pitṛs* ("fathers"). Failure to maintain the regularity of these offerings, some feel, condemns the wandering ancestral spirits to rebirth and redeath again and again in a round of rein-carnation rather than to "suspended animation" and blessedness in the relatively stable and peaceful existence of the spirit world. To observe the rites as they are performed once a month on the New-Moon Day *(amāvāsya-tarpaṇa)* is to see how the all-pervasive concerns of brāhmaṇical ritualism inform and direct even escha-tological hope in Hinduism.

It is the (eldest married) son's function in a family to maintain these rites without interruption. Indeed, the Sanskrit word for son is *putra,* sometimes construed to mean "one who saves from the particular hell experienced by the childless after death"; hence the typical Hindu desire for a son springs, at least in part, from just such a context of ideas as here. For, it is one's direct male issue who through his ritual efforts — on Death Anniversa-ries, during the more important family rites known as *saṃskāras,* during the obligatory daily *pañcamahā-yajña* routines, while un-dertaking purificatory steps, on New Moon Days, at New Years, at the end of the half-Year, at eclipses, indeed whenever he seeks to define his identity as a concrete individual in the ongoing physical world — can stave off rebirth and redeath for the entire ancestral line. Although like other ritual concerns they are losing their hold even on the conservatives or are being streamlined

almost beyond recognition among large groups of progressive
Hindus, the formalized ancestral offerings, both monthly and
annual, continue to be celebrated in more or less elaborate form
among large segments of the Hindu population today.

The never-before filmed rite of *amāvāsya-tarpaṇa* is re-enacted
for the camera by a Tengalai brāhman of Madras City. It is performed on the New Moon Day, during the morning hours, under
the direction of the hereditary family Āchārya. The length of the
film — less than ten minutes — approximates the duration of time
it takes typically to perform these rites of "satisfaction". The
film depicts accurately the way ancestral offerings are made nowadays, and suggests the central place the worship of the *pitrs* still
enjoys in contemporary Hindu piety.

Wirklichkeit und Geschichte im Werk Vivekanandas

von Gunther Stephenson

Mit der Rückbesinnung des Neuhinduismus auf die nationale
Eigenständigkeit und geistige Substanz der Vergangenheit hält
eine vorher kaum gekannte Dimension des Denkens Einzug in die
indische Vorstellungswelt: die Geschichtlichkeit. Geschichtliches
Denken entfaltet sich durch die Auseinandersetzung mit der europäischen Kultur einerseits und durch die Erneuerung des
Vedanta seit Ramakrishna und Vivekananda andererseits.

Geschichtliches Denken artikuliert sich keineswegs allein in der
Geschichtsschreibung, sondern vielmehr im bewussten, zielge-
richteten Handeln der Gegenwart, im Willen zur Veränderung der
Welt, in der Besinnung auf die kontinuierliche Linie von Vergangenheit und Zukunft. Geschichtsbewusstsein betont das Individuelle und Einmalige der fortzeugenden schöpferischen Tat gegen
die Wiederkehr des Gleichen durch gesetzliche Abläufe. Ohne
Freiheit ist Geschichte zwar denkbar, aber nicht menschenwürdig
zu realisieren. Geschichtlichkeit bedingt das Herauswachsen des
Menschen aus der kosmischen Einheit der Natur. — Den Gegenpol zum geschichtlichen Denken bilden Begriffe wie Sein, ewige
Wahrheit, Idee, Natur, Gesetz.

Im Neuhinduismus ringt geschichtliches Denken mit der religiösen Tradition der ewigen Wiederkehr, mit der naturhaften Im-
personalität, den Daseinsgesetzen und weltflüchtiger Erlösungs-

sehnsucht. — Bei Vivekananda finden sich bereits interessante Ansätze zum Geschichtsverständnis, zur geschichtsphilosophischen Spekulation und zum eigenen geschichtlichen Verhalten.

Eine psychologische und biographische Voraussetzung liegt bereits in seiner Person. Er war ein Mann voller Tatkraft, Freiheitsdrang und Zielstrebigkeit, voller Leidenschaft und Ruhelosigkeit, ausgerüstet mit einem natürlichen Geschichtssinn un hohem Selbstbewusstsein. Seine zahlreichen Weltreisen öffneten ihm den Blick für die Probleme der Menschheit und die individuelle Eigenart einzelner Kulturen. — So sah er den "Volksgeist" seines Mutterlandes im religiösen Erbe der Upanishaden, deren geistige Erneuerung ihm zur missionarischen Aufgabe wurde. Die fruchtbaren Elemente der Vergangenheit sollten die Zukunft gestalten und die Welt verändern helfen. Ein idealisierter Advaita-Vedanta mit seinem spirituellen Monismus wurde zum Prinzip und Ziel seiner Reformation.

Eine entscheidende Bedeutung für das geschichtliche Denken kommt dem doppelten Aspekt der Wirklichkeit zu, die doch letztlich nur eine sein kann. Der maya-Begriff wird überwiegend realistisch gedeutet und damit Voraussetzung für geschichtliches Werden gegeben. Die Vielheitswelt ist Manifestation des Absoluten und damit werthaltig als Medium für die individuellen Wege der Menschheit zum letzten Ziel der Einheit. Dic Reinkarnation erscheint als positiver Faktor (Freiheit!) auf dem Stufenweg in die Zukunft. "Schöpfung" bedeutet Niedergang, Geschichte: Chance zum Aufstieg. Die Hoffnung erfüllt sich im Brahman als letzter Wirklichkeit, sie hebt die Geschichte wieder auf. So wurde die mystische Heilserfahrung in die geschichtliche Bewegung hineinprojiziert.

Iranisches Christentum und Zoroastrismus

von Gernot Wiessner

Im angekündigten Vortrag soll ein weiteres Zwischenergebnis der Bemühungen zur Diskussion gestellt werden, die besondere geistige Welt der christlich gewordenen Iraner in ihrem Unterschied zur aramäisch-christlichen und griechisch-christlichen Tradition innerhalb der Christen des Sassanidenreiches herauszuarbeiten.

Ansatzpunkt sind die Feststellungen, die G. Widengren jüngst hinsichtlich der iranischen Bedeutung und iranisch-indo-germanischen Verankerung des ausserfamiliären Erziehungsinstitutes vorgelegt hat (*Feudalismus*, Kp. III.IV). Die Kenntnis dieses Institutes bei den Christen Irans ist durch Widengren anhand von Beobachtungen am Yazdīn- und am Sīrīn-Roman nachgewiesen worden. Ausgangspunkt unserer Überlegungen ist wiederum die Analyse des Qardaḡ-Romans (BHO 555.556). Dabei kann festgestellt werden, dass auch in diesem Roman das Erziehungsinstitut vorausgesetzt wird und die Bedeutung hat, den Helden — ebenso wie im von Widengren analysierten Parallelmaterial — in die iranisch-feudal-ritterliche Tradition der Sassaniden mit ihrem besonderen Wertsystem ritterlicher Fähigkeiten und religiöser Kenntnis und Sinngebung einzufügen. Dieses Wertsystem iranischer Herkunft bleibt im christlichen Qardaḡ-Roman in den Grundzügen erhalten mit Ausnahme des, dem iranischen Erziehungsinstitut aber inhaerenten, religiösen Mass-stabes dualistisch-zoroatrischer Prägung.

Die Erhaltung des feudal-ritterlichen Wertsystems geschah der Erzählung des Qardaḡ-Romans zufolge dadurch, dass der iranische Feudalheld durch den Umgang mit dem Einsiedler ᶜAḅdišoᶜ eine neue ethisch-religiöse Begründung für das von ihm verkörperte iranische Erziehungs- und Menschen-ideal erfährt. Die Unterscheidung wird dabei dergestalt gegeben, dass ein echter Vollzug des iranischen Leistungssystems erst unter christlichem "Vorzeichen" ermöglicht wird. Zoroastrisch-iranisch begründete und christlich-iranisch begründete Leistung werden in der Darstellung bei Bestehenbleiben ihres gleichen Inhaltes in wertender Parallele jeweils einander gegenübergestellt. Durch eine christlich-religiöse Interpretation kann das iranisch-feudale Menschenbild de facto vollinhaltlich erhalten bleiben.

Die historische Verankerung dieser Art Konkurrenz-Institution zum iranischen Erziehungsinstitut in der Umwelt der iranischen Christen ist jedoch noch undurchsichtig. Die heidnisch-iranische Umwelt, aber auch die christliche Mönchstradition liefern u.W. keine Parallelen zur Rolle ᶜAḅdisoᶜs, da man von vergleichbaren indischen Phänomenen absehen muss. Die Häufigkeit des nach Art des Qardaḡ-Romans beschriebenen Eremiteninstituts in der christlichen Legendenliteratur iranischer Herkunft führt jedoch zu der Vermutung, dass es sich bei dieser Art von Anachoreten um ein genuin iranisch-christliches Phänomen handelt. Wenn dieses Erziehungsinstitut der Eremiten nicht auf historischer Wirklichkeit beruht, so ist es in seiner schriftstellerischen Fixierung doch Ausdruck des Bemühens, iranisch-feudales Menschenbild unter den christlich gewordenen Iranern zoroastrischer Herkunft zu erhalten (christlicher Ritter), das dualistisch-getragene iranische Menschenbild ins Christentum aufzunehmen und damit zugleich eine Umdeutung vorzunehmen, die christlichen Monotheismus und heidnische ritterliche Tradition bei den christlichen Iranern sind untereinander verbinden liess.

Hinduism as Sādhana

by Troy Organ

The analysis of Hinduism as either a philosophy or a religion is a form of cultural imperialism because Hinduism does not fit the pattern of either as they have developed in the West. This "imperialism" can be detected both in the works of Western students of Hinduism and in the attempts of Hindu intellectuals to interpret Hinduism to the West. To present Hinduism as a *philosophical* religion or as a *religious* philosophy compounds the issue by rooting Hinduism still more into Western patterns of life and thought. Hinduism must be studied on its own terms. It is a *sādhana,* a program of selfrealization. It sets before man the goal of perfection and the means for its attainment. The goal, however, is not a static one which can be attained; it is a direction of progress. Man is a being whose "being" is "becoming". Therefore, the ideal of the Perfected Man (*ātmansiddhi*) is the ideal of the Perfect*ing* Man. Four paths of perfecting (*mārgas*) are offered in Hinduism: the path of thought, the path of loving devotion, the path of action, and the path of physical-psychological discipline. The *mārga* of the Perfecting Man is a *pravrithi mārga* (a path of progress) which encompasses the values of all the paths.

Variations on Tengalai Belief in
a South Indian Village

by James L. Martin

Pillai Lokāchārya, the 13th century follower of Rāmānuja, formulated a system of Vaiṣṇava belief which came to be known as Teṅgalai. A contemporary, Vedānta Deśika, formulated a variant interpretation, known as Vaḍagalai. The Teṅgalai system was distinguished from the Vaḍagalai system chiefly by a greater stress on a doctrine of pure grace, which made irrelevant such matters as caste restrictions, sacred times and places, or individual merit. God's mercy alone was sufficient for forgiveness of sin. God's consort, Lakṣmī, though a created being, was so wholly at one with the Lord that she could act as a mediator between man and God, both leading man to God and influencing God to extend mercy.

The village of Tirukkurungudi in the Tirunelveli District of Tamil Nadu has a large and active Viṣṇu temple, which is controlled by a Teṅgalai math. The current status of Teṅgalai belief in this village was investigated in 1964, as part of a study of the role of the temple in community life. Since the village has a history of conflict between Teṅgalai and Vaḍagalai residents, the investigator anticipated that the differences between the teachings of the two sects would be well understood.

The survey indicated that, although the elements of Teṅgalai belief are expressed formally through purānas and temple festival presentations, adherents of the Teṅgalai sect were unfamiliar with distinctive teachings of the sect and were unable to define these beliefs clearly. Interviews with both Brahmins and non-Brahmins showed that the people modified the doctrine of grace by holding that pious acts such as visits to the temple were necessary before grace could be granted. There was no knowledge of the familiar distinction between Teṅgalai "cat-philosophy" and the Vaḍagalai "monkey-philosophy". The role of the consort was never emphasized. Differences between the two sects were always described in terms of superficial behavior.

The story of Viṣṇu's granting of salvation to a harijan and a demon, as related in the Kaishika Purāna, was often repeated, and was seen as an illustration of the free grace of God. However this was never cited as a specifically Teṅgalai doctrine. The story of the conversion of Tirumaṅgai Ālvār by the grace of Viṣṇu was seen as reflecting favorably on the Marava community, a backward tribe well represented in the village, rather than as specifically teaching divine grace. The presence of Śiva image in the Vaiṣṇava temple was explained through a story that Viṣṇu had once saved Śiva from the attack of a demon, and had ever since had Śiva under his protection; the interpretation generally given was that this indicated the greater power of Viṣṇu.

Although virtually all villagers expressed belief in monotheism, there was frequent unreflective assertion that one image was more powerful than others. In practice temple authorities and others accepted the possibility that local deities could interfere with the temple deity.

Der Avatāragedanke im neueren Hinduismus

von Anncharlott Eschmann

A. Der Begriff des Avatāra spielt im neueren hinduistischen Denken und seiner Auseinandersetzung mit dem Christentum eine entscheidende Rolle. Im heutigen Neohinduismus werden Avatāras meist als Inkarnationen der Gottheit beschrieben, deren aufsteigende Folge sich durch alle Religionen zieht und den religiösen und sittlichen Fortschritt der Menschheit bewirkt. Das vorliegende Referat will an ausgewählten Beispielen untersuchen, wie sich diese Auffassung entwickelte, in welcher Beziehung sie zu den verschiedenen geschichtstheologischen Entwürften und deren Wertung von Pantheismus und Monotheismus steht, und wie sie sich zu der traditionellen Avatārlehre verhält.

B. 1. Im traditionellen Hinduismus sind Avatāras verschiedenartige Inkarnationen der Gottheit, die eine zeitweilige "Lastabwälzung" für die Erde, bezw. eine "Wiederaufrichtung des Dharma" bringen und dem Einzelnen den Zugang zur Erlösung erleichtern. Dies geschieht im Rahmen eines cyklischen Geschichtsbildes: innerhalb des Weltalters eines Kalpas entspricht die sich intensivierende Offenbarung in der Folge der Avatāras dem unaufhaltsamen Verfall von Welt und Mensch, der schliesslich zum Weltuntergang und zum Beginn eines neuen Kalpas führt.

2. Für Ram Mohan Roy war "Avatarismus" gleichbedeutend mit Idolatrie: die "monotheistische" Offenbarung der Einheit und Einzigkeit Gottes, die allen Religionen zu Grunde liegt, im Vedānta aber ihren erhabensten Ausdruck gefunden hat, ist der Vernunft jederzeit unmittelbar zugänglich und bedarf keiner Mittler.

3. Bankim Chandra Chatterjee (1838-1894) nimmt den Avatāragedanken wieder auf und verbindet ihn mit dem Inkarnationsbegriff der liberalen evangelischen Theologie den er aus den Werken G.B. Seeleys (vor allem "Ecce homo", 1866) übernimmt:

Gott sorgt für die Schöpfung, Erhaltung und den Fortschritt
-unnati- (nicht wie im traditionellen Hinduismus die Zerstörung)
der Welt. Um diesen Fortschritt, der sich ohnehin durch die Na-
turgesetze vollzieht, noch zu beschleunigen hat Gott unmittelbar
in die Geschichte eingegriffen und durch seine Inkarnation in
Krishna ein vollkommenes Ideal der Humanität -manushyatva-
gesetzt. Die Verwirklichung dieses sittlichen Ideals ist das Ziel der
Menschheitsentwicklung.

4. Svāmi Vivekānanda weitet die evolutionistische Deutung
auf alle Religionen aus und relativiert sie gleichzeitig: jede
"grosse Seele, die um die Erhebung der Menschheit kämpft"
muss als Avatāra verehrt werden. Avatāras bringen zu verschiedenen Zeiten das ewige Gesetz des "tat tvam asi", das allen Religionen zu Grunde liegt, wieder zur Geltung und vermögen es,
dem Einzelnen unmittelbar zu dieser erlösenden Erkenntnis zu
verhelfen. Die "Erhebung der Menschheit" als allgemeiner Fortschritt ist nur eine Folge dieses Wirkens.

5. In den Werken von Srī Aurobindo Ghose ist der äusserste
Punkt in der universalen und evolutionistischen Interpretation
der Avatāralehre erreicht: Ziel der durch alle Religionen wirken-
den Folge von Avatāras ist es, das "himmlische Königreich" sowohl in jeder einzelnen Seele als auch auf Erden unter der Gesamtheit der Menschen zu errichten. "Avatāraschaft" ist ein dop-
peltes Geschehen, in dem sich der Herabstieg der Gottheit mit
dem Aufstieg der Menschheit trifft und eine fortschreitende Vergöttlichung der gesamten, auch der physischen, Natur des Menschen bewirkt.

C. Die Entwicklung der Avatāralehre im neueren Hinduismus
zeigt, wie die integrierende Kraft der traditionellen Lehre vom
Herabstieg der Gottheit, die sich z.B. in der Aufnahme Buddhas
unter die Avatāras ausdrückt, durch die Verbindung mit linear-
evolutionistischen Geschichtsentwürfen und dem Gedanken des
Aufstiegs der Menschheit wesentlich verstärkt wurde.

Basic Changes in Indian Religious Conceptions and the Disappearance of Buddhism from India

by Kees W. Bolle

Various suggestions have been made to explain the disappearance of Buddhism from India. Two explanations have often been

repeated: a supposed moral decay of Buddhism, and the Muslim invasion with the harm it did to Buddhist cult centers. Neither suggestion can stand up to serious criticism. The former rests on an inadequate understanding of Tantrism, which was as Hinduistic as it was Buddhist, and leaves the question untouched why only Buddhism disappeared, and why it did not disappear in Tibet. The second suggestion bypasses the fact that Buddhism faded gradually in the course of centuries, and again that Hinduism did not fade, although it was at least as much under attack. Without pretending to indicate the all-explaining cause of a complex historical development, it is possible to focus on historical facts that make the development in India understandable. The disappearance of Buddhism must be seen together with a resurgence of Brahmanic conceptions, particularly those concerning the class system. Of special importance are the hierarchic developments within Buddhism that made the resurgence of Brahmanic socio-religious conceptions and the rise of (later) Hinduism possible.

SHIVA in Mānikkavācakar's hymn PōTTi-Tiruvakaval

by Carl-A. Keller

The importance of Tamil Shaiva hymns in general, and of Mānikkavācakar's Tiruvācakam in particular, lies in the fact that they are not the result of theological speculation about God, but rather the expression of a personal encounter with Shiva. Shiva has revealed himself to the poet-saint, he has entered his life and turned him into his servant, and now the bhakta cannot but sing the praises of his God out of a heart touched and transformed by a real encounter with the divine. Mānikkavācakar is not primarily a theologian nor a philosopher, but a witness to the living God of the religious experience of Hinduism.

It is to be regretted that Tamil devotional literature has not as yet found the place it deserves in the scientific study of Hinduism. This is of course due to the general neglect of Tamil studies in European universities, and consequently to the lack of exegetical and philological work on the Tamil poet-saints (available translations of the Tiruvācakam are inadequate tools for penetrating analysis).

The hymn PōTTi-Tiruvakaval is chosen as the subject of this

paper because it offers a useful basis for the study of Mānik-kavācakar's conception of Shiva. It consists of two parts: first, a long sentence (lines 1-87) leading up to the exclamation "pōTTi, praise!" — praise to him who, unknowable to the gods but of easy access to the bhaktas, *rears* and saves those who in the midst of manifold errings and temptations firmly cling to the conviction that God exists and that he reveals himself, and who consequently lead a life of unfailing bhakti. In the second part (lines 88-225), this first exclamation is followed by 158 similar ones, each one of them preceded by one or two expressions or phrases describing Shiva. The whole provides an overall portrait of the god.

The classification of these names and epithets is not always easy, but the analysis which is proposed in the paper permits nevertheless to draw some conclusions. As is already suggested by the long elaboration of the first "pōTTi" (lines 1-87), Shiva is primarily a god who maintains a very positive relationship to the phenomenal world in that he "*rears*" his bhaktas, even if this "rearing" amounts finally to the cessation of karma. But it is not only cessation of karma; indeed we find in the hymn more than a hundred statements to the effect that Shiva is the creator and the life of the universe (as he is also the one who maintains and destroys), and in particular the king of the Tamil country and of its peoples (his residing in the temples of South India being of outstanding importance), and the loving saviour of animals (as shown in various myths) and of human beings. The poet himself proclaims him as his very personal god. — Over against this overwhelming praise of Shiva's graceful presence in the world, we find only some two dozen statements about his absolute transcendance: he is "beyond word and knowledge" (124) and even "beyond turiya" (195).

If Shiva is truly *aruvam* (without form), the poet knows him first of all as *uruvam* (manifesting himself) (193).

Pantheistic Monism or Absolute Advaita

by P. Sarveswara Sharma

Founder of this Pantheistic Monism or Absolute Advaita as it is called, was Śaṅkara who lived in later part of 8th century. The

central texts of this school are Śaṅkara's commentaries on the
principal Upaniṣads — the Chāndogya, the Bṛhadāranyaka, the
Taittirīya, the Kena, the Kaṭha, the Īśa, the Praśna, the Muṃ-
ḍaka, and Māṇḍūkya —, the Bhagavadgītā and the Vedānta Sūtra
of Bādarāyaṇa. Upadeśasahasrī and Vivekacūḍāmaṇi reflect his
general position. Śaṅkara insists on interpreting the Upaniṣads in
a single coherent manner. According to him, the knowledge of
Brahman which we gain from the Upaniṣads must be uniform
throughout and without contradiction. Śaṅkara attempts to har-
monise such of the assertions of the Upaniṣads as seem most
opposed. Metaphysics is a consideration of what is implied in the
fact of experience. In the introduction to his commentary on the
Vedāntasūtra, Śaṅkara asks whether there is anything in experience which may be regarded as foundational, and discusses the
claims of all the factors of experience to such a title. Our senses
may deceive us and our memory may be an illusion. The past and
the future may be abstractions. The forms of the world may be
pure fancy, and all our life may be a tragic illusion. Nothing
prevents us from regarding the waking tracts of experience as
analogous to dreamworlds, where also we visit places, handle
shadows and do battle with ghosts, and remember, too, all our
adventures in the fairy land. If dreams are facts, facts may well
be dreams. Though all objects of knowledge may be matters of
belief and so open to doubt, there seems to be still something
transcending it. If one finds within oneself something not made
by one's environment but making it and moulding it, if in the
very possibility of one's knowledge and evaluation of the sense-
world there is implied that which cannot be derived by the
sense-world, the logic requires that one should affirm the reality
of that transcendent presence within oneself. Everyone is conscious of the existence of his own self, and no one thinks "I am
not". If the existence of self were not known, then everyone
would think "I am not", which, however, is not true. All means
of knowledge exist only as dependent on self-experience, and
since such experience is its own proof, there is no necessity for
proving the existence of self. Each function and faculty the gross
body and vital breath, the senses and the internal organ, the
empirical "me" appear only on the basis of and in relation to the
Ātman. They all serve an end beyond themselves, and depend on
some deeper ground of existence. Ātman cannot be doubted,

"for it is the essential nature of him who denies it." (S.B., ii.3.7.) Śaṅkara argues that it is impossible for us to know the self by means of thought, since thought itself is a part of the flux belonging to the region of the not-self. Though it escapes our knowledge, it does not entirely escape us. It is the object of the notion of self (asmatpratyayaviṣaya) is known to exist on account of its immediate presentation (aparokṣatvāc ca pratyagātmaprasiddheḥ, S.B., i.1.1.). It cannot be proved since it is the basis of all proof and is established prior to all proof (ātmā tu pramāṇādivyavahārāśrayatvāt prāg eva pramāṇādivyavahārāt sidhyati/S.B. ii.3.7; S.B.G. xviii.50).

Śaṅkara tries to distinguish the true self from the object, and declares that subject and object are opposed like light and darkness, so that what is truely subject can never become an object. Metaphysically, the conception of self-existence involves the ideas of eternity, immutability and completeness. What is truly real is what has being in itself and for itself, so that to affirm the reality of Ātman or the permanent self is to affirm the reality of an eternal Brahman (Ātmā ca Brahma, S.B., i.1.1.). The proof of the reality of Brahman is that it is the ground of the self of everyone (sarvasyātmatvāc ca brahmāstitvaprasiddheḥ/S.B., i.1.1).

Though we know that the self is, we do not know what it is, whether finite or infinite, knowledge or bliss, one only or one among others like itself, a mere witness or an enjoyer, or neither. As there are conflicting opinions about the nature of the self, Śaṅkara says that it is both known and unknown. The "I" must be distinguished from the "not I", which includes not only the outer world, the body and its organs, but also the whole apparatus of understanding and the senses. In ordinary usage we regard mental states as subjective, and physical states as objective. But from the metaphysical point of view both orders of phenomena, material and mental, are equally objective. For instance as one is accustomed when it goes ill or well with his son or wife and the like to say, "it goes ill or well with me", and thus transfers the qualities of outer things to the self, in just the same way he transfers the qualities of the body when he says, "I am fat, I am thin, I am white, I stand, I go, I sleep", and similarly the qualities of the sense-organs when he says, "I am dumb, impotent, deaf, one-eyed, blind", and similarly the qualities of the internal organ (antaḥkaraṇa), desire, wish, doubt, resolution and the like. Thus also he transfers the subject presenting the "I" (ahaṃpratyayin) to the inner self present solely as witness (sākṣin) of the personal tendencies, and, conversely, the witness of all, the inner self to the internal organ and the rest (S.B., i.1.1.). The materialists identify self with the body or senses. But consciousness and matter represent different kinds of reality, and one cannot be reduced to the other. Nor can we identify the self with the senses. For then there would be as many selves as there are senses, and this would make the recognition of personal identity a problem. Besides, if the different senses constitute the self, there should be simultaneous enjoyment of sight, sound, taste, etc. The self cannot be identified with a series of impermanent mental states, as we cannot account for the facts of memory and recognition. Even if we declare the whole world to be void, this void presupposes the cogniser of itself (śūnyasyāpi svasākṣitvāt). Even in dreamless sleep there is the self, for when one rises from it one is aware that one had good sleep undisturbed by dreams. This he knows from memory. Since memory is of presentations, the bliss of sleep and the consciousness of nothing must have been presented during the sleeping state. If it is said that the absence during sleep of disquiet and knowledge is only inferred from the memory of the state before sleep and the perception of the after it, then it is replied that we cannot infer anything the like of which was not presented. If it is said that a negative concept cannot have any percept answering to it, and therefore the absence of knowledge and disquiet is only inferred, it is said in reply that absence of knowledge, etc., to be inferred must be conceivable, i.e. must have been directly perceived during their absence. So we have during dreamless sleep direct consciousness of the absence of knowledge and disquiet. In that state the empirical mind is inactive, and pure consciousness alone is present. The self is not to be identified with the inner feeling which accompanies the continual changes of our mental attitudes or the empirical "me", consisting of a number of mental contents developing in time. It is true that self-consciousness (ahaṃkāra) precedes activity, but it is not the self, since it is not antecedent to knowledge, as it is itself an object of knowledge (S.B., ii.3.40.). To equate the self with a flux of states, a presentation continuum, or a stream of consciousness, would be to confuse the principle of consciousness with portions of its contents. The felt-masses and conscious streams rise and fall, appear and vanish. If all these varying contents are to be connected, we require a universal consciousness which ever accompanies them. "When it is said, It is I who now know what at present exists, it is I who knew the past and what was before the past, it is I who shall know the future and what is after the future, it is implied in these words that, even when the object of knowledge alters, the knower does not alter, for he is in the past, present and future, as his essence is eternally present" (S.B., ii.3.7.).

We can know temporal series of events as a series only if the facts are held together through somethin present alike to each of them and itself therefore out of time. The self is not a creature of the natural world, for the simple reason that there would not be any natural world were not the principle of self presupposed. Śaṅkara holds that we get the notion of the ātman if we divest it of all that surrounds it, discriminate it from the bodily frame with which it is encompassed, strip it of all contents of experience. To our logical minds it may appear that we have reduced it to a bare potentiality of thought, if not mere nothing, but it is better to regard it this way than as a whole of parts or a thing with qualities or a substance with attributes. It is undifferenced consciousness alone (nirviśesacinmātram) which is unaffected even when the body is reduced to ashes and the mind perishes.

The crux of all philosophy is this, that the sense-organs and the neural process of the body, which is in space and time, seem to produce conciousness. Surely the non-conscious cannot be the cause of the conscious. If anything, the conscious must be the cause of the non-conscious. The senses, the mind and the understanding are not self-sufficient. "The activity of these organs demands in addition upalabdhi (presence in all times), which belongs to the Ātman ... whose very nature is eternal knowledge." (nityopalabdhisvarūpatvāt, S.B., ii.3.40.) But this consciousness, which is the cause of non-conscious, is not the finite consciousness but the ultimate one, for ever so many objects and events that do not exist in this or that finite consciousness still exist in reality. So we must assume an ultimate consciousness of which the finite is only a fragment. The fundamental consciousness, which is the basis of all reality, is not to be confused with the human consciousness, which appears rather late in the cosmic evolution. Presentations are subject to origin and decay, and are not self-luminous, and they are known only through the light of Ātman, whose essential nature is self-luminosity. It is pure consciousness (caitanyam) are mere awareness, the supreme principle in which there is no differentiation of knower, knowledge and known, infinite, transcendent, the essence of absolute knowledge (Vivekacūḍāmani, p. 239). It is of the nature of non-objective consciousness. "The Ātman is throughout nothing but intelligence; intelligence is its exclusive nature, as the salt-taste is of the lump of salt" (S.B., iii.2.16. See also S.B., i.3.19,22). Spirit cannot have an unspiritual nature. By the law of its being, it is ever shining. As the sun shines when there is nothing for it to shine on, so the Ātman has consciousness even when there is no object (S.B., ii.3.18). True existence and intelligence go together. Ātman cannot be existence without intelligence or intelligence without existence. It is also of the nature of bliss (ānanda). Ānanda is freedom from all suffering. Ātman has nothing to cast off and nothing acquire, nothing dark or disorderly. Śankara denies activity to Ātman, since activity by its nature is non-eternal. "The self cannot be the abode of any action, since an action cannot exist without modifying that in which it abides (S.B., i.1.4.). All activity presupposes the self-sense, and so far as we arc awarc, it is of thc form of pain (S.B., ii.3.40.) and motived by desire (Śankara's introduction to Tait. Up.). Activity and enjoyment are dependent on a dualistic vision, which is not the highest truth (S.B., ii.3.40). There can be no agency without the limitation of the Ātman by a body, etc., and every limitation is unreal. The Ātman by itself has no agency.

Commenting on the Brahmāsutra 11.1.4.: "It is argued that he who maintains the nature of the Brahman to be immutable contradicts the tenets of Iśvara being of the world; because the absolute unity of Brahman precludes the relation of the ruler and the ruled. To this, we reply, no, for omniscience and other qualities of Iśvara depend on the evolution of the germs of name and form, which are of the nature of nescience. Forming as it were the very soul of Iśvara, are name and form, produced by nescience, incapable of being described as *its* nature or as the nature any other that, which constitutes the germs of the phenominal universe. This is the wonder-working power (māyāśakti) of the omniscient Iśvara called Prakṛti as we learn from the holy books of Wisdom, *śrutis* and *smṛtis*. This omniscient-Iśvara is other than those two namely *name* and *form*. Thus, Iśvara is dependent upon the conditions of *name* and *form*, produced by nescience, just as space is dependent upon the conditioning objects, jars, pots, etc. From the stand-point of phenominal universe He is the sovereign of those who are jivas or individual souls, who are capable of perception and knowledge and who are his very self but depend on bodies that aggregates of organs of action produced by name and form based on nescience, resembling in this the space of a jar. Hence, Iśvara's lordship, omniscience and omnipotence depend on the limitation of the condition of the nature of nescience. From the standpoint of noumenon, the activities involved in being the ruler, ruled, omniscient, etc., cannot subsist in the self, cleared of all limiting adjuncts by right knowledge (vidyā)."

Again, commenting on the Brahmasūtra, 1.4.3., Śaṅkara says: "In the supreme Brahman there is no duality. This concept of Iśvara necessitates the concept of a causal fore-state (prāgavasthā) of the world, dependent on the Iśvara, but without which Iśvara cannot become a creator. This causal state of the world is called avidyā, nescience, for it is destroyed by vidyā, the true knowledge of Ātman, which secures for the mukta, the released one, once for all, the realisation of the absolute unity of all life. This nescience is also called *avyakta,* unmanifested, for before creation, it cannot be perceived; sometimes it is spoken of as *māyā* (illusion)."

La révélation dans le manichéisme

par Julien Ries

L'examen des deux verbes coptes, *kjôlĕb abal* et *ŏuônh abal* qui expriment la transmission de la gnose, nous donne une idée précise de la notion de révélation dans les textes coptes manichéens de Medinet Madi. Dans cette bibliothèque gnostique, les Kephalaia sont les documents les plus explicites pour notre recherche.

La révélation gnostique au sens strict s'exprime invariablement par le verbe *kjôlĕb abal*. Trois phénomènes bien distincts caractérisent cette révélation. Il s'agit en premier lieu de l'émanation

des éons sortis du Pére de la Grandeur et de l'essence du Royaume de la Lumière. Après cette révélation ontologique qui est
comme à l'origine du deuxième temps manichéen, celui de mélange, vient la communication aux hommes des secrets et des
mystères. Le Paraclet venu du Père les révèle à Mani qu'il charge
d'initier les hommes. Mani devenu à son tour paraclet et illuminateur, révèle les secrets, forme ses disciples dont chacun doit, à son
tour, actualise ces mystères dans sa vie et devient illuminateur
pour les autres. L'ultime étape de la révélation gnostique se fait
au cours du troisième temps, après la séparation définitive de la
Lumière et des Ténèbres. Alors, le Père révèlera son image
(*hikôn*) aux élus entrés dans le Royaume.

La gnose de Mani connaît une étape complémentaire de la
révélation. Celle-ci est exprimée par *ŏuônh abal*. Le verbe se
trouve dans les divers textes qui décrivent la manifestation visible
de la gnose, de ses acteurs comme de ses effets. Le Royaume de
la Lumière doit se montrer aux hommes. Il doit aussi se manifester aux Ténèbres. Le soleil constitue un élément typique de
ces diverses manifestations. Par ailleurs, le verbe *ŏuônh abal* est le
mot de l'herméneutique gnostique. Mani explique sa doctrine à
ses disciples. Il leur fait connaître les vertus et les signes caractéristiques. Cette exégèse constitue un élément important dans l'Eg-
lise de Mani: *ŏuônh abal* est un mot technique de la catéchèse
manichéenne. Enfin, il y a une manifestation particulière, celle
qui montre les diverses images (*hikôn*) gnostiques, notamment
l'image de Mani.

La gnose de Mani se présente comme la révélation ultime et
définitive de tous les mystères. En trois mots elle prétend tout
dire: le commencement, le milieu, la fin. Par deux mots les Kephalaia coptes déterminent le double processus de la révélation:
kjôlëb abal, initier; *ŏuônh abal,* manifester.

SECTION VII

BUDDHISM AND THE FAR EAST

Sur les Problèmes de la Mythologie du Japon
(La structure mythologique et l'idéologie politique)

par Tomoo Yoshida

Grosso modo, le monde mythologique est clairement séparé en deux: le monde du royaume céleste et le monde-de-la-terre, qui est géographiquement identifié avec une région qui se trouve au bord de la Mer du Japon. Cette idéologie de la division du monde vient de la conception de la distinction du mal et du bien. Philosophiquement parlant ces deux extrêmes sont toujours traités monistiquement. La mythologie du Japon est caractérisée par un compromis entre l'idéologie du monde et la conception théologiquement monistique du "mal-bien".

L'évolution de la conception du mal-bien se trouve aussi dans le développement de la mythologie. Il se présente ainsi: (1) le chaos, (2) la naissance des dieux, (3) le monde de la mort, (4) le royaume céleste, (5) le monde-de-la-terre, (6) la descente du fils de la tribu céleste; bien arrangé pour que le mal et le bien arrivent alternativement.

Le noyau de la mythologie, (4) et (6), constitue une mythologie explicative du rite solstice d'hiver. La justification de cette cérémonie du palais est en même temps la justification de l'héritage de la souveraineté. Mais pourquoi est-ce que (5) se place entre (4) et (6)? D'abord pour garder l'alternance des deux extrêmes et à cause de la conception dont j'ai parlé. On y voit la rivalité des deux mondes qui signifie l'opposition du mal et du bien. Cela a déjà commencé avec la naissance de la Déesse, la reine du monde céleste, et son Frère-pécheur, qui est le héros et le roi du monde-de-la-terre. De toute façon il faut finalement conquérir (purifier, d'après le texte) le monde appartenant à son descendant, avant que le fils du royaume céleste ne descende.

Pourquoi est-ce qu'une région au bord de la Mer du Japon est traitée particulièrement comme le monde rival du monde céleste? Même en se basant sur les études archéologiques, il est dificile de dire que c'etait un grand centre culturel ou politique. Et, donc, on essaie de l'expliquer par la correspondance entre la conception du monde de la mort et révolution du soleil, puisque cette région se place vers l'ouest de la région capitale. Et, en plus, elle se trouve derrière les montagnes quand on se place du côté de la région capitale. C'est là une explication géographique, mais ce n'est pas suffisant. Il faut attendre la réponse des historiens qui cherchent la relation entre la puissance religieuse de cette région et l'evolution historique de la construction du centralisme qui avait, pour fondement, le culte du soleil.

Quand on compare la mythologie du Japon à autres mythologies il faut tenir compte du fait qu'elle a été écrite par le gouvernement. Il s'y trouve donc, d'une part des éléments de cultures complexes des peuples-chasseurs (patriarcat), et des peuples agricoles (matriarcat), et d'autre part l'idéologie politique de l'Etat centraliste, basée sur le rite du soleil et s'efforçant de justifier l'ascendance divine du roi.

The Madhyamaka Philosopher Nāgārjuna according to the Chinese Sources

by Amalia Pezzali

Years ago Max Walleser has treated the subject (*"The life of Nāgārjuna from Tibetan and Chinese sources"*, Hirth Anniversary Volume, London 1922, p. 421-455), comparing the Chinese and the Tibetan sources, without reaching, after his accurate study, any definitive solution of the problem.

Prof. Etienne Lamotte, in his excellent translation of the *Vimalakīrtinirdeśa* (VKN, Louvain 1962, p. 70-77), gave some important suggestions in order to put the problem under a new light. Throughout some Chinese sources, interpreted in a very acceptable and quite illuminating way, he established some probable dates for the life of the madhyamaka philosopher Nāgārjuna.

For the study of Buddhism, from the historical point of view, such dates are not a mere curiosity. That is why, starting from the previously mentioned studies, I have examined all the Chinese texts dealing with such a problem. Comparing them, those that are the most ancient sources with all the other material at our disposal, I am trying to afford an answer to the following questions:

— Have there been one or more Nāgārjuna?
— In what period has the madhyamaka philosopher Nāgārjuna lived, and how long has been his life?
— Where has he had birth, and where has he spent his life?
— Has he had a master?
— Who have been his disciples?
— What have been his works?

The conclusions I reached will be published quite soon in a monograph on the philosopher Nāgārjuna on the type I have already done for Śāntideva (Firenze, Valecchi, 1968).

Das Schicksal des Gottesgedankens in der Religionsphilosophie Keiji Nishitanis

von Fritz Buri

Der Gottesgedanke taucht in der Religionsphilosophie Nishitanis sozusagen nur am Rande auf, um jeweils sogleich wieder zu verschwinden und dem absoluten Nichts und der völligen Leere Platz zu machen. Es geschieht dies aber in für westliche Religionsphilosophie und Theologie höchst bedeutsamen Zusammenhängen und in einer Weise, die uns an buddhistische Denker einige Fragen stellen lässt.

Nishitani sieht die Religion heute bedroht durch Saekularismus und Nihilismus als Folgen der modernen Wissenschaft und Technik und des dahinterstehenden Bewusstseinsdenkens. Wohl geht von diesen Grössen eine befreiende Wirkung aus, aber gleichzeitig reissen sie den Menschen aus seinem Geborgensein in naturhaften und geistigen Sinngefügen heraus und scheinen insbesondere das westliche Denken und die christliche Theologie in unlösbare Widersprüche zu verwickeln. Von dieser Problematik sieht Nishitani auch den existentialistischen Nihilismus betroffen.

Eine wirkliche Ueberwindung des Nihilismus kann für Nishitani nur in dessen Radikalisierung zum völligen Leerwerden im Sinne der Zenbuddhistischen Sunjata bestehen. Soweit er diesen Heilsweg philosophisch darlegt, sind für ihn charakteristisch: Beseitigung der Subjekt-Objekt-struktur des Bewusstseinsdenkens und der aristotelischen Logik sowie weltschöpferische Bedeutung des erleuchteten Selbst. Für alle drei Momente kann er auf gewisse — aber nach ihm unzulängliche — parallele Bestrebungen in westlicher Philosophie hinweisen. Vorstufen dazu glaubt er auch in christlicher Mystik — bei Meister Eckhart und Franz von Assisi — sogar im Neuen Testament und bei Luther feststellen zu können, wobei er freilich deren Bezugnahme auf den Gottesgedanken stillschweigend eliminiert.

Wesentlicher als eine Diskussion dieser Bezugnahme Nishitanis auf Ausformungen des westlichen Denkens bzw. christlichen Glaubens scheinen uns jedoch die Probleme zu sein, die sich für uns auf dem Boden von Nishitanis Religionsphilosophie ergeben — von denen wir die westlichen Parallelen allerdings nicht weniger betroffen sehen:

Erstens: Ein angeblich ungegenständliches Denken und Reden stellt als solches das Gegenteil von dem dar, was es zu sein behauptet, und noch die Behauptung, der Satz vom verbotenen Widerspruch komme hier nicht in Frage, stützt sich auf diesen.

Zweitens: Wie bei Heidegger unklar bleibt, ob es sich im Denken und Sprechen des Seins um einen Genetivus subjectivus oder objectivus handle, so weiss man nicht, wer in der "grossen Masse des Zweifels" bei Nishitani eigentlich noch zweifelt.

Drittens: Wird die besondere Sinnmöglichkeit der Einsicht in die Buddhaschaft durch ihre Ausweitung ins Kosmische nicht gerade ihrer Besonderheit beraubt bzw. ins Nichts aufgelöst — genau gleich wie dies im absoluten Idealismus des Westens geschieht?

Viertens: Stellt die Buddhologie wie die "Christologie ohne Gott" ungewollt nicht ein blosses Bruchstück einer Metaphysik dar — und zwar als Ausdruck menschlichen Selbstverständnisses in einer für den Dogmatismus beider gleich problematischen Weise?

Fünftens: Sind buddhistische und christliche Mystik und Gnadenreligionen in ihren ethischen Konsequenzen den sozialen Problemen und deren saekularistischen Lösungsversuchen, von denen sie sich bedroht sehen, gewachsen?

Als positive Ergänzung zu diesen kritischen Fragen, schlagen wir einen Gottesgedanken vor, der konstituiert ist durch die Unterscheidung einer allgemeinen Offenbarung als überall zu machende Erfahrung der Abgründigkeit des Seins, vor der wir nur verstummen können, und einer besonderen Offenbarung im Inne-werden verantwortlichen Personseins, zu dessen Verwirklichung in Gemeinschaft wir uns unausweichlich bestimmt erfahren, und auf das hin der Mensch schlechthin ansprechbar ist — wenn er sich nicht zu seinen Götzen wegschleicht.

Theistic Trends in Japanese Buddhism

by H. Dumoulin

Buddhism in all its forms and phases has never lacked theistic elements. It may be said, however, that the theistic tendencies which existed from the beginning reached their fullest development and gained a special emphasis in Japanese Buddhism.

The theistic tendencies in Japanese Buddhism seem to be connected with a characteristic trait of the Japanese character and are relevant to this day. Professor Nakamura explains: "The attitude of absolute devotion to a specific person manifests itself as a sublimated attitude of complete devotion to the Buddha as an ideal person, and thus faith in Buddha is emphasized."

The theistic elements of Japanese Buddhism, namely devotion to a person, faith and awareness of transcendence, appear in different variations. This can be shown by evaluating the theistic tendencies in the three main Buddhist currents of the Kamakura era, the Zen movement, the Amida devotion and Nichirenism.

Zen seems to be furthest removed from all theism, yet theistic tendency is not lacking. Significantly, it is most clearly apparent in the most typically Japanese form of Zen, namely in the Zen of Dôgen handed down by the Sôtô school. Although Dôgen adheres in his metaphysics to a strict monism, theistic tendencies crop up in his religions life. He emphasizes faith. His inclination towards transcendence appears especially in his preference for the negative way. The theistic tendency also appears in modern disciples of Dôgen, for example, in the contemporary Japanese Zen masters Harada Sogaku, Yasutani Hakuun, and Nagasawa Sozen.

Amidism is known as the theistic current in Buddhism. The theistic trait of the piety of Hônen, who practised Amida devotion in an exemplary way, is evident. His disciple Shinran is one of the most outstanding representatives of Japanese Buddhism. He emphasized faith in the Original Vow of Amida, in which the absolute efficacy of the "Other Power" is revealed. Otani Kôshô, the contemporary heir of the Eastern Honganji temple in Kyôto, gives an existential-anthropological interpretation of the *tariki*-faith in Jôdo Shinshû of Shinran, which uncovers the theistic tendency of the religious experience of Shinran and the Amida faithful.

The theistic trait in the religion of Nichiren is revealed chiefly in his prophetic consciousness and in his faith. The religion of Nichiren has seen in our days an unexpected renaissance in the modern popular religions of Japan. The theistic element is apparent in the writings of the leaders of the two most important modern religions, Risshô Kôseikai and Sôka Gakkai.

We may conclude this brief survey by noting that the theistic trends which characterized the development of Japanese Buddhism in the past may play an important role in the future as well.

Problems of the Application of Western Terminology to Theravāda Buddhism

by Ninian Smart

The paper concentrates on the Theravāda or the Pali canon, and may not be applicable therefore to all manifestations of the Theravāda in such countries as Ceylon and Burma at the present time. Since Western ways characterizing religions have tended to emphasize the questions of whether a given tradition is theistic, or polytheistic, or pantheistic, or incorporates belief in a high god, it is worth while examining the role of the gods in the Pali canon and their relation to the Buddha. We may note that:

1. The gods are not the object of a cultus, i.e. any cults that they may have had (e.g. Sakka) are not endorsed by the canon.
2. They are impermanent, so that their type of existence has as much to be transcended as man's, by the attainment of *nirodha*.
3. Worship of the gods does not conduce to liberation.
4. It is the normal condition of liberation that a god is reborn as a *man*.
5. The perception of gods is confined to *arhants*, typically in *samādhi*.

6. The Buddha transcends the gods — as *devātideva*, though strictly not a god.
7. Some gods seem to be specifically Buddhist creations via the idea of rebirth of prominent Buddhists in heaven.
8. Nibbana is superior to even the most refined states of *jhāna*, themselves coordinated to a cosmological scheme of heavenly realms, such as the *arūpadhātu*.

Because of this, the gods are admitted on strictly Buddhist conditions, and are peripheral. Hence it is misleading to say that the Theravāda is polytheistic (like saying that Catholicism is non-Nestorian). It is better to categorize it by its central style of behaviour, the life of meditation. The gods represent a bridge to popular religion, and are the Theravāda's version of *upāyakauśala*. If one *must* try and categorize the Theravāda by reference to traditional concerns in the Western history of religions, it is a transpolytheistic, non-theistic religion of contemplation.

THE RELIGIONS OF ILLITERATE PEOPLES, SOCIAL AND CULTURAL ANTHROPOLOGY, FOLKLORE

"Primitialopfer" und Hochgott bei den philippinischen Negritos

von Heino Krüger

Das "Primitialopfer" der Altkulturen, zuletzt dargestellt in der Arbeit von A. Vorbichler über das Opfer als eine Hingabe des Lebens an die Gottheit, wird anhand des Materials der philippinischen Negritos überprüft. Eine Durchsicht der Quellen ergab für das Primitialopfer bei den Negritos folgende Merkmale:

1. Die jagdbare Tierwelt ist verbunden mit jeweils einem höheren Wesen. Dieses ist in ausgeprägter Form ein Herr der Tiere, der bisweilen die Gestalt eines Tieres annehmen kann (Zambales), oder aber nicht mit bestimmter Gestalt beschrieben wird (Mindanao, Negros, Panay). Er hat betont ambivalente Eigenschaften. Während in Zambales, Mindanao, Negros und Panay keine Verbindung mit der jeweiligen Hochgottheit besteht, scheinen in Nord- und Ostluzon beide Aspekte in einer Person verbunden zu sein, allerdings sind hier die Quellen nicht sehr klar.

2. Die Jagd und die Tötung des Tieres erfordern eine bestimmte Verhaltensweise gegenüber dem Tier und der betreffenden Wesenheit, mit der das Tier in enger Verbundenheit gesehen wird. Diese erfolgt durch das Plazieren von kleinen Stücken des Fleisches, Teilen des Kopfes, der Leber, des Herzens oder des Fells, meist erhöht auf einem Felsstück oder einem Baum, verbunden mit einer Dedikation.

3. Beachtung verdient auch die weitere Behandlung der Jagdbeute. So heisst es immer wieder und für fast alle Gruppen, dass das Wild in einer bestimmten Weise zerlegt und aufgeteilt werden muss, da anderenfalls die künftige Jagd gefährdet ist. Oftmals wird betont, dass derjenige, der den Tod des Tieres herbeigeführt hat, den Kopf als "Trophäe" erhält. Der Kopf wird auf einem Pfosten vor der Behausung oder an den Bäumen in der Umgebung der Siedlung aufgehängt.

Der beschriebene Sachverhalt ergint klar, dass die Deutung P.W. Schmidts, das Primitialopfer sei als Lebensmittelgabe an die Gottheit zu verstehen, wodurch ihre ursächliche Eigentumsgewalt über diese dankend anerkannt werde, nicht zutreffend ist. Das gilt ebenfalls für Vorbichler, der Schmidts These dahingehend erweitert, dass die im Opfer dargebrachten Teile als Träger des Lebensprinzips angesehen werden und daher die Handlung als Rückgabe des Lebens selbst an die Gottheit zu begreifen ist. Sie ist vielmehr als ein Tiererneuerungsritus zu interpretieren, wie er in ausgeprägterer Form etwa auch von den nordasiatischen Jäger-kulturen bekannt ist.

Im Gegensatz zu Vorbichler, der darin eine aus dem Primitial-opfer hervorgegangene kulturhistorisch jüngere Tiervermehrungs-magie sieht und zu Meuli, der den Bezug auf eine übernatürliche Wesenheit ablehnt, ist in der Handlung ein eigentlich religiöser Vorgang zu sehen, in welchem der Mensch und die Gottheit, und zwar bei den Negritos der Herr der Tiere, der klar von der Hoch-gottheit, einem Gewitter- und Sturmgott, unterschieden wird, zu-sammenwirken. Der Mensch schafft die notwendigen Vorraus-setzungen — die rituelle Behandlung der getöteten Tiere —, die es dem numinosen Partner erlauben, seine schöpferische Kraft ein-zusetzen, das Leben des Tieres zu erneuern und damit dem rituel-len Handeln des Menschen einen Sinn zu geben. Da der Terminus "Primitialopfer" den beschriebenen Vorgang nicht umfassend be-schreibt, wird der Begriff "Renovationsritus" vorgeschlagen.

Die Stellung des Gewittergottes in den regionalen Pantheen der Zentralanden

von Ana Maria Mariscotti

Verschiedene regionale Pantheen präinkaischer Zeit überdauer-ten die Expansion der Inkas und hatten Bestand, bis die Spanier Anfang des 17. Jahrhunderts ihren Feldzug zur Ausrottung der "Abgötterei" unternahmen. Auf Grund ausführlicher Berichte, die damals die Visitadores dem Erzbischöflichen Ordinariat in Lima vorlegten, und an Hand mehrerer Chroniken aus derselben Zeit lassen sich einige der präinkaischen Regionalpantheen rekon-struieren.

Dank dieser Quellen kennen wir nicht nur die Namen verschie-

dener Gewittergötter vom Hinterlande Limas und anderer mittel-
peruanischer Regionen, sondern können auch wesentliche Züge
ihrer schillernden Gestalt skizzieren. Gemeinsame Charakteristika
dieser Götter sind der Aspekt regenspendender Fruchtbarkeits-
gottheiten und ihre Mehrgestaltigkeit, die vermutlich aus der Tatsache abzuleiten ist, dass sie Blitz, Donner, Regen, Hagel und
Schnee verkörpern. Sie sind zugleich als Personifikationen der
Kräfte gedacht, die die Indios den mächtigsten der schneebedeck-
ten Berggipfel zuschreiben. Wie die überlieferten Mythen zeigen,
handelt es sich um Numina mit so stark ausgeprägten Zügen von
Kulturheroen und Heilbringern, dass man religionsgeschichtlich
gesehen annehmen könnte, sie seien erst nachträglich zu dem
Range von Göttern aufgestiegen. Den Mythen zufolge stammen
sie von einem höchsten Gott und Schöpfer ab und sind ihm
untergeordnet. Gleichwohl stehen *sie*, nicht ihr Stammvater im
Mittelpunkt des religiösen Lebens und sind auf der regionalen
Ebene die bedeutendsten männlichen Gottheiten.

Unser Beitrag geht der Frage nach dem Grund für diese heraus-
gehobene Stellung des Gewittergottes in den lokalen präinkaischen Pantheen nach. (Bewusst wird also Illapa, der inkaische
Gewittergott, und seine Position im offiziellen Pantheon von
Cuzco ausser Betracht gelassen.) Hauptquelle sind dabei die bis jetzt
kaum beachteten, wegen ihrer Kompliziertheit schwer zu hand-
habenden, jedoch sehr wertvollen Berichte, die Lizentiat Rodrigo
Hernandez Principe, Pfarrer in einem Dorfe Mittelperus und guter
Kenner der einheimischen Sprache, in den Jahren 1621/22 ver-
fasste und die erst 1923 von Romero veröffentlicht wurden. Unsere Untersuchung kommt zu dem Ergebnis, dass die Gewittergötter als Erzeuger der Stammväter jener Geschlechter, welche
wahrscheinlich die obere, mit dem männlichen Prinzip identifi-
zierte "moiety" darstellen, gelten und dass sie aus dieser Eigenschaft ihre bevorzugte Stellung erhalten. Jene Stammväter sind
vermutlich nichts anderes als mythifizierte Anführer einer über-
lagernden Gruppe.

Monotheism and Pantheism in Africa

by E.G. Parrinder

It was formerly said that the religions of tropical Africa were
neither monotheistic nor pantheistic, and studies made in this

century have revealed a good deal of polytheism. However, African writers have affirmed the belief in and occasional worship of a Supreme Being, and a "Diffused Monotheism" has been described in which other gods are worshipped. Terms such as the "unity and plurality of God" indicate divine activities, both single and personified in other beings. Some African religion is "modalistic", being monotheistic and polytheistic at different levels, corresponding to different ways of thinking about the numinous and to various kinds of ritual.

The theory of Vital Force or Dynamism, in Central and East Africa, emphasizes the unity of world-views. This force comes from God and under him there is a hierarchy of powers which interact. A universal force is being itself, only known in manifestations, in which all beings coalesce. A model of this hierarchy of powers is a pyramid, with God at the apex, lesser powers at the sides and base, and man in the centre. The supreme power is divinity, not in a separate spirit-world but participating in human life.

Such a pyramid, or circle, in West Africa is coherent and in equilibrium, with the same energy circulating everywhere under the impulse of God. The hierarchy of powers is as unchangeable as the divine essence, and cosmic powers are quantitative variations of the supreme power. Man is central in this world, but God is supreme and uncreated, and all depend upon him. Such African philosophies go beyond polytheism and resemble Indian pantheism, but God is always supreme, and African thought is both theistic and unitary.

The religious reactions of primal societies to higher cultures:
A new field in the history of religion
and a centre for its study

by H.W. Turner

In the last two decades increasing attention has been given by many disciplines to the range of prophet-led or salvation-seeking movements surveyed on a world scale by Guariglia and Lanternari, and the University of Lancaster in England has plans for a special Centre for the Study of New Religious Movements. While this phrase applies to the early history of most religious traditions it is being used here to refer to a specific group of movements emerging from the primal societies in recent centuries, and the following provisional demarcation is suggested for the phenomena to be considered: a historically new religious movement arising in the encounter of a primal society and its religion with one or more of the higher cultures and their major religions, and involving some substantial departure from the classical traditions of all the cultures concerned, in order to find renewal through a different religious system.

This may prove to be a new field in the history of religions, depending on the answers to the many basic questions this working definition raises:

1. Is the *encounter* situation an essential milieu for such movements? How do they differ from the ordinary internal sects and schisms, folk religions and derivative religions within a single culture? And have the primal societies produced such movements in their own pre-contact history?

2. Must one of the participants in the encounter always be a *primal* religion, and the other a major religion? Is there any difference from movements originating in the encounter of two major religions?

3. Can *any* of the major religions serve as one party to the encounter? Hinduism and Buddhism have done so, but the position of Islam is unclear. Most movements involve Western culture and Christianity, which may have a special capacity for stimulating these reactions.

4. Is there any difference between *the major sections* of the Christian tradition in relation to such movements? There is some special connection with Protestantism, but Roman Catholicism has also been productive, and some are related to Orthodox Christianity.

5. Were similar movements produced in the *earlier* expansion of the Christian religion and Graeco-Roman culture into the tribes of northern Europe and north Africa? If not, why on this scale in modern times and with Western culture?

The Centre planned will emphasize the multi- and inter-disciplinary approach, from physiology where peyote cults are concerned, through history, psychology and the social sciences, to the phenomenology and history of religion and the theologies.

Die illustrierte Zulu-Schöpfungsgeschichte LADUMA
MADELA's, des Blitz-Zauberers und Gesandten des
Schöpfergottes Mvelinqangi

von Katesa Schlosser

Mit Hilfe von Farblichtbildern möchte ich Sie bekanntmachen
mit einem Genie des Zuluvolkes, LADUMA MADELA, und seinen Werken.

Madela lebt in der Südafrikanischen Republik, in den Bergen
des Zululandes. Er ist etwa 62 Jahre alt. Madela ist Schnied,
Blitz-Zauberer, Wahrsager, Gesandter des Schöpfergottes Mvelinqangi, Philosoph, darstellender Künstler und unermüdlicher
Schrifsteller.

Als Junge begleitete er seinen Vater als Träger von dessen Me-
dizinsack zu vielen fremden Kralen, in welche der Vater als Zau-
berdoktor gerufen wurde. Voller Interesse lauschte Madela dort
den Geschichten, welche die Grossmütter den Kindern erzählten
und die die Geschichten seiner eigenen Grossmütter ergänzten.
Besonders interessierten ihn die Berichte über die Erschaffung
der Welt durch den Schöpfergott Mvelinqangi.

Kurze Zeit gehörte Madela einer christlichen Bantukirche an.
Er nennt sie "Ohlangeni". Zweifellos haben manche Bibelstellen
ihn beeindruckt.

Als er älter wurde entwickelte Madela sich zu einem echten
Philosophen. Er kombinierte die Details, die er von der Schöp-
fungsgeschichte gehört hatte und schloss dabei logische Lücken.
Viele dieser Ergänzungen wurde ihm geoffenbart durch den
Schöpfergott selbst, der Madela in einem Walde erschien — und
der Madela darüber hinaus so zahlreiche Aufträge erteilte, dass
Madela sich als Gesandten Mvelinqangis bezeichnet. Derart schuf
Madela eine umfassende Kosmogonie einschliesslich der Erschaffung der Winde, der Himmel, der Festländer und des Erscheinens
der Menschen. In Madelas Kosmos stehen 5 Welten übereinander,
von denen unsere Welt die mittlere ist. Jede dieser 5 Welten hat
ihre eigene kleine Unterwelt.

Dramatisch ist Madelas Schilderung vom Niedergang unserer
Welt mit ursprünglich ewigem Leben durch den Tod. Unsere Un-
sterblichkeit ging uns verloren durch Neid und Gier! Der erste
Neidische war Mvelinqangis böser Bruder Sibi, der Mvelinqangi

dessen schöpferische Fähigkeiten missgönnte. Um Mvelinqangis Geschöpfe zu vernichten, suggerierte Sibi Mvelinqangis ältestem Sohn Sitha Neid auf das angeblich dessen jüngerem Bruder Zwilakho allein zufallende Erbe an Reichtümern aller Art. Neiderfüllt liess Sitha seinen Sohn Ntulo (d.h. Eidechse) bei Mvelinqangi für die Menschen den Tod erbitten. In Irrtümern befangen gewährte Mvelinqangi sie Bitte. Bald jedoch erkannte er, dass er einen Fehler gemacht hatte. Seine durch den Tod verdorbene Welt wird er gänzlich vernichten. Dann aber wird er sie neu erschaffen als eine Welt ewigen Lebens.

Madela hat nie eine Schule besucht, aber von Verwandten das Schreiben gelernt. Rechtschreiberegeln freilich sind ihm gleichgültig. Starke Impulse zu Niederschriften traditioneller Ueberlieferungen und eigener Weisheit in ganz grossem Umfange erhielt Madela durch das Interesse, das Dr. W. Bodenstein, Prof. Dr. O.F. Raum und auch ich selbst seiner Persöhnlichkeit, seinen Kenntnissen der Tradition, seiner Philosophie und seiner Kunst entgegenbringen. Seit 1957 hat Madela mehrere tausend Seiten Manuskripte verfasst. Ihre Uebersetzungen ins Englische übernahme Professor Nyembezi, Vincent Gitywa, B.A. hons., und Bingham Tembe, B.A. hons.

Seinen Manuskripten hat Madela viele hundert Illustrationen beigefügt. Darunter befinden sich Bilder von Mvelinqangi, wie Madela sie in verschiedenen Visionen erblickt hat. Niemals hat vor Madela ein Zulu ein Bildnis des Zulu-Schöpfergottes geschaffen.

The God of Primitive Religion
(Some remarks on the idea of God among African Pygmies)

by Wilhelm Dupré

Accepting the idea that religion is a cultural reality (i.e. the result of constitutive processes), a phenomenological analysis necessarily implies and presupposes the dimension of a "first". In this sense "primitive religion" has to be understood as the horizon within which the empirical phenomena gain transcendental significance. As such "primitive religion" is a theoretical necessity, whose clarification is dependent upon the empirically given as well as disclosing of its structure and meaning. Consequently

while aiming at a comprehensive understanding of religious phenomena we nonetheless have to search for empirical instances
which are, if not representative symbols, than at least of methodological import for (the transcendental) function and content of
"primitive religion". There can be no doubt that the idea of God
has to be approached from such an angle.

Yet, where do we find a cultural situation, which, by dint of
its typological structure, is particularly suited for an analysis under transcendental conditions and with transcendental intention? Is it the cultural situation of gatherers and hunters, for
instance, as represented by the African Pygmies? An attempt in
this direction certainly cannot hurt. On the contrary, even if it
should not be convincing, it at least will provide a critique of
historical positions (in particular of the theory of proto-mono-
theism), which allegedly relied heavily upon ethnoreligious data
taken from such and similar cultural situations.

First, if we analyze the ethno-religious data concerning the
Ituri-Pygmies (main sources: Paul Schebesta; Colin Turnbull), we
observe two features of their religious expressions: Whatever instances of prayer, ritual and cult we refer to, they are, either in
forms of momentary re-collection or temporary re-actualisation,
integrated into the accounted mythology. On the other hand the
mythological figures cannot be nominally fixated. In the context
of mythology they are transitional, thereby recalling the whole
correlation between consciousness, world and meaning. As such
they indicate a mythic structure which precedes actual mythology.

Secondly, in order to attune these features to the universality
of man (i.e. to the reality of consciousness under the condition
of language), we have to abandon that interpretation of religion
which is inherently dependent upon definite (or rationalized)
relations (e.g. God in the sense of a mono-theistic conception)
and/or categorizations (e.g. religion understood as man's encounter with the Sacred). As far as the African Pygmies are concerned, their "God" is primarily presence. It is a presence in
which the person prays (i.e. finds names together with personal
otherness and transcendence) and lives (i.e. experiences life-
power). In brief, the idea of God is that of the Divine which, in
mythological figures and structures, provides the ideational environment for personal existence.

Is there an indication that such may be the symbols that permit us to re-present the "God of Primitive Religion"? To the extent that these symbols are synthesized with the process of survival, they point to a coincidence of culture and religion within the constitutive process of world and consciousness. Since such a coincidence is transcendentally conclusive, the evidence is in favor of an affirmative answer.

Die Entstehung von Obergöttern aus Ahnen in Polynesien am Beispiel des samoanischen Tagaloa

von H. Cain

Das Studium der Aitu auf Grund der vorhandenen Literatur sowie in Samoa selbst hat erbracht, dass diese Vorstellungen, die eine grosse Rolle in der Mythologie spielen und die religiöse Praxis der Samoaner beherrschten, auf dem Seelenglauben beruhen und dass die religiöse Verehrung der Aitu im Wesentlichen ein Ahnenkult ist. Die Bedeutung der Aitu hängt ab von der sozialen und politischen Stellung der Familie, zu der sie gehören. Diese Erkenntnis fordert eine Überprüfung der von Stair aufgestellten Götterhierarchie Samoas an Hand der Häuptlingsgenealogien und der überlieferten Mythen. In der noch weitgehend akzeptierten Einteilung Stairs wird Tagaloa im Gegensatz zu den Aitu als Atua ("original god") bezeichnet, wodurch ein grundsätzlicher Unterschied zwischen ihm und den Aitu postuliert wird. Ob ein solcher Unterschied besteht, ist indessen sehr fraglich, denn Tagaloa könnte auch ein vergöttlichter menschlicher Vorfahre aus der Migrationszeit sein, wie schon Buck vermutete.

Da in Samoa keinerlei Erinnerung an die Einwanderung bewahrt ist, dürfte diese Gestalt relativ alt und mythologisch zum Schöpfergott umgedeutet worden sein. Diese Vermutung findet unserer Ansicht nach ihre Bestätigung durch die Genealogie der Tuimanu'a, die wahrscheinlich die ältesten Herrscher über ganz Samoa und die umliegenden Inselgruppen waren. Der politische Einfluss der Tuimanu'a hat dann zur Verbreitung des Ahnen dieser Familie, Tagaloa, geführt. Der sehr bald einsetzende Machtverfall minderte umgekehrt die Relevanz Tagaloas, so dass er otios wurde.

Der samoanische Schöpfungsbericht ist vermutlich nichts Anderes als die mythische Darstellung des Migrationserlebnisses, das für die Besiedler Samoas von vitaler Bedeutung war. Aus diesem Zusammenhang heraus würden sich auch andere Funktionen Tagaloas als Gott des Meeres, der Winde und des Wetters, der Fische usw. zwanglos erklären lassen.

Es kann als wahrscheinlich angesehen werden, dass Tagaloa seinen Ursprung in Manu'a hatte und sich von dort über das Einflussgebiet der Tuimanu'a verbreitete. Die unterschiedliche Stellung Tagaloas auf den verschiedenen Inselgruppen ergibt sich mit grosser Wahrscheinlichkeit einmal daraus, dass sein Bekannt-werden nicht überall gleichzeitig erfolgte und zum Anderen aus der Tatsache, dass er, besonders auf den Randgruppen Poly-nesiens, nicht direkt von Manu'a, sondern von anderen Gruppen eingeführt wurde.

Die Religion in afrikanischen Sprichwörtern und Rätseln

von Ernst Dammann

Auf den ersten Blick scheint die Religion, zu der im Rahmen dieses Themas auch die Magie gerechnet wird, in der didaktischen Dichtung (Sprichwort, Rätsel) keine grosse Rolle zu spielen. In diesen beiden Literaturgattungen findet vielmehr das alltägliche Leben mit seinen empirischen Realitäten einen Niederschlag.

Im Bereich der Naturreligionen Afrikas wird in Sprichwort und Rätsel der Hochgott selten erwähnt, etwas häufiger finden sich Bezüge auf Geister, Hexen, Medizinmänner und Zauberer. Auch wird auf magische Praktiken angespielt.

Religiöse Bezüge zeigen sich in verschiedenen Formen. In eini-gen Fällen findet man eine direkte religiöse Aussage. In anderen werden religiöse Wendungen oder Anführungen nur als Meta-phern für andere Aussagen benutzt. Bisweilen wird ein anschei-nend "säkulares" Sprichwort religiös interpretiert.

In den vom Islam beeinflussten afrikanischen Kulturen sind stärkere Anklänge an die muslimische Glaubenswelt zu verzeich-nen. Vereinzelt sind auch Einflüsse des Christentums nachzu-weisen.

Abgesehen von dem "literarischen" Niederschlag der Religion zeigen Tabuisierungen, die für Rätsel belegt sind, eine Verbin-dung der didaktischen Dichtung mit der religiös-magischen Welt.

In der homiletischen Praxis der Gegenwart sind Sprichwörter nicht selten ein beliebtes Mittel, die christliche Botschaft anschaulich darzustellen.

Heutige Reste germanischer Götter

von Åke V. Ström

Einige alten germanischen Götter leben ein verhülltes Leben in gewissen Festgebräuchen des Nordens und des deutschen Gebietes. Einige Beispiele zu Weihnachten:

1. *Lussi* oder Lusse als heutiger volkstümlicher Name des hl. Lucia in Schweden ist keine beliebige Dublette. Der Name ist vorchristlich als *luttu* im Finnischen entlehnt. Lussi als morgenfrühe, weissgekleidete Spenderin, mit Katzen, hat, wie L. Kretzenbacher gezeigt hat, teils mit einer freigiebigen Pudelmutter, teils mit einer gefährlichen Lutzelfrau vieles gemeinsam. Schwedische und norwegische Volkssagen sprechen von einem in der längsten Nacht des Jahres tätigen Zauberweib, das als Straferin, Todesvorbote und Totenherrin wirkt. K. McLennan hat auf eine "germanische weibliche Kultgestalt" gedeutet. Aber welche?

Von der gebenden aber gefährlichen Fruchtbarkeitsgöttin und Totenführerin Freya mit ihren Ziegen und wagenziehenden Katzen, eine Gestalt, die schon aber in der Edda auch böse genannt wird, geht die Linie über Baedas *modraneht* (Mutternacht) zu den heutigen Lussi-Sitten mit gegürtetem Totenhemd und "Lussi-Katzen" (lussekattor). Die Verknüpfung Freya — Lucia findet sich schon bei T. Arnkiel, 1691.

2. *Stephan* oder Staffan kommt noch in Volksliedern und Volkssitten vor. Er fährt mit fünf Fohlen, zwei von denen weiss, zwei rot und einer grau sind. Der Protomärtyrer Stephan (Apg. 6) und Stenphi, der Apostel Hälsinglands (Adam, *Gesta* III: 77, IV: 24) haben nichts spezielles mit Pferden zu tun. Frey aber war der Pferdegott (vgl. Phol der ersten altfränkischen Merseburger Beschwörung), fünf ist nicht eine christliche aber eine beliebte indogermanische Zahl (*Bṛhad-ar.-up.* 1: 4: 17), und die Farben sind die der drei alten Stände.

D. Strömbäck hat gefragt, auf welches vorchristliche Material man die Gleichsetzung Staffan — Frey stützen will. Antwort: Die Abbildungen im Grabmal in Kivik, Schonen, die Ortsnamen auf *leik-* und *-skeid* und literarische Beispiele (*Freys leik* = Wettreiten, *Haraldskv.* 6) bestätigen den heidnischen Ursprung. Die Jahreszeit entspricht dem vedischen Pferderitus *vājapeya* am Ende des Jahres.

3. *Knut* (dänisch Knud) "zeigt Weihnachten die Tür", sagt man in Schweden. Das Sprichwort oder sonst die Knut-Sitten haben nichts mit dem (dänischen) hl. Canutus zu tun. Die Knutzeit (Mitte Januar) wird mit Verkleidungen, Auftreten, Tierfellen, sondergeschlechtlichen Schmäusen, Hinauswerfen des Weihnachtsbaumes, Verspeisen der Weihnachtsreste und gewissen Feuerriten gefeiert.

Hinter der germanischen Götterwelt können ja oft, wie G. Dumézil dargelegt hat, Representanten des indogermanischen Pantheons wahrgenommen werden. Rudra-Śiva hat genau dieselben Eigenschaften wie Knut: er ist *paśupati* mit einem speziellen Fell, ist *vāstavya*, der die Reste verzehrt, ist der Gott der Schauspieler und Tänzer (*naṭarāja*) und der der Alters- und Geschlechtsklassen, ist mit Agni verknüpft und vor allem der grosse Abschliesser und Auffresser, durch dessen *tāṇḍava*-Tanz die Welt zerspringt.

Knut *knýja*, *knúda*, *knúinn*, "drücken", "bezwingen", ist ein recht passender Name einer nordischen Rudra-Gestalt. Das fehlende Zwischenglied zwischen Rudra-Śiva, als Yogin dargestellt, und dem mittelalterlichen und heutigen Knut ist der europäische "dieu dans la pose dite 'bouddique'", in *paryaṅka-āsana* sitzend, der nach P. Lambrechts in 33 Beispielen ikonographisch vorkommt, z.B. auf dem Gundestrup-Kessel und in dem Oseberg-Schiff.

4. Die Osterntiere heutzutage — Hasen und Hennen (mit Eiern) — sind Reste des Frühlingswechsels, am 17. März, zwischen einer Wintergottheit *Hreða-Skaði* (mit Hasenaussehen auf ein Felsenbild in Nord-Norwegen) und einer Frühlingsgöttin (*Uṣas-Eostra-Ostara*) mit Hühnern und Eiern.

Gottheit und Idol: Das Problem einer differenzierten und adaequaten religionswissenschaftlichen Terminologie - illustriert am archäologischen Material des stein- und bronzezeitlichen Europas

von Cyrill v. Korvin Krasinski OSB

Die Notwendigkeit einer Zusammenarbeit der Religionsgeschichte, der Ethnologie und der Archäologie wie der gegenseitigen Berücksichtigung ihrer neuen Erkenntnisse drängt nach einer einheitlichen Terminologie. Nicht selten gebrauchen Vertreter einer Disziplin, z.B. der Archäologie, bestimmte Termini — wie *Gottheit* und *Idol* — in einer Bedeutung, die andere Disziplinen, z.B. die Religionsgeschichte, heute auf eine viel differenziertere Weise — nur auf gewisse Fälle eingeschränkt — anwenden. Diese Zweideutigkeit gibt Anlass dazu, dass Forschungsergebnisse einer Disziplin in einem Sinne interpretiert werden, den die andere seit langem nicht uneingeschränkt annehmen kann.

Bevor man den Terminus IDOL im Sinne plastischer Darstellung einer Gottheit gebraucht, müsste eindeutig festgelegt werden, was man unter GOTTHEIT versteht. Religionsgeschichtliche Tatsachen lassen uns seit dem Ausgang der späteren Steinzeit folgende Wesen unterscheiden, die — je nach den Umständen — neben — oder nacheinander Gegenstand eines religiösen Kultes gewesen sind, ohne dadurch stets die Eigenschaften und die Würde einer Gottheit zu beanspruchen: *Verstorbene, Ahnen, heroisierte* Ahnen, *Heroen, divinisierte* Heroen, heroisierte *Gottheiten* (z.B. Olympische Gottheiten, auf welche der Kult lokaler Heroen samt derer Beinamen übertragen wurde), divinisierte *Geistwesen*, niedere und höhere Gottheiten, und endlich unter bzw. über den letztgenannten die *Hochgottheit* einer bestimmten Religion.

Gebraucht man nun den Terminus IDOL auf undifferenzierte Weise in der Bedeutung der stofflichen Darstellung gleichwelchen Vertreter der obengenannten Reihe übersinnlicher Wesen, so trägt man dadurch — oft in unbeabsichtigter, aber irreführender Weise — zur Verwischung derer spezifischen Eigenschaften bei, man verwechselt Ahnenkult mit Götterkult und setzt die Existenz mannigfaltiger *Gottheiten* in *nicht* polytheistischen Kulten voraus.

Gebraucht man dagegen den Terminus "Idol" bewusst im Sinne z.B. der Votivstatuetten, welche die Anbetenden rund um die Opferstätte im Kulte vertreten, oder im Sinne von Ahnenfiguren, dann stellen solche "Idole" keine Gottheiten dar, und der Terminus Idol darf dann nicht mehr oder zugleich für Darstellungen von Gottheiten und Hochgottheiten verwendet werden. Eine falsche Terminologie muss hier notwendig zu einer falschen Interpretation der Funde führen.

Versteht man aber unter Idol die Darstellung einer *Gottheit*, dann ist die Statuette der kleinasiatischen "Magna Mater" sicher ein Idol, weil sie eine Gottheit repräsentiert, die bewusst als Gegenstand der Anbetung der Gläubigen hingestellt wird. Sie steht ja im Zentrum der Anbetung und betet selbst niemanden an. Ihre Gesten weisen auf sie selbst hin. Dagegen stellen die unzähligen Votivstatuetten aus cykladischem Marmor, die in Kretischen Kultstätten aufgefunden worden sind, keine Gottheiten dar, sondern gläubige Anbeter, die mit erhobenen Händen der klassischen Oranten aller Zeiten — rund um die zentrale Kultstätte auf steinernen Kultbänken hingestellt — ihr Gesicht zur hl. Opferstätte wenden und selbst nicht angebetet zu werden "wünschen", sondern die anbetenden Gläubigen repräsentieren. Der Gebrauch des Terminus "Idol" in undifferenzierter Weise für die "Magna Mater", für die genannten Votivstatuetten wie für die unzähligen Orantendarstellungen der skandinavischen bronzezeitlichen Felszeichnungen ("hällristningar") und auf den analogen Zeichnungen im Hohen Atlas oder in Val Camonica setzt in all diesen Fällen eine Wesensgleichheit dort voraus, wo sie entweder gar nicht existiert oder erst eindeutig formuliert werden müsste, wobei die Bezeichnung "Idol" von "Gottheit" abzuheben sei, sollte sie ein brauchbares wissenschaftliches Verständigungsmittel bleiben.

Der Referent hat zur Klärung dieses Problems persönlich ein anschauliches Vergleichsmaterial auf vorindogermanischen Kultstätten gesammelt — von Norwegen und Irland bis Nordafrika und den Kanarischen Inseln, den Balearen u. Kreta — und veranschaulicht seine Darlegungen an der erstaunlichen Verbreitung des sogen. *Turnus Sacralis* und seinem Vorhandensein in den vorpolytheistischen Kulten des gesamten Eurasischen Kontinents: "Vom Dach der Welt zur Heimat Abrahams über den Skandinavischen Norden", wie sein noch im Manuskript liegendes Forschungsbericht lautet, dem das vorliegende Referat entnommen ist.

Die obigen Beispiele zeigen dass — je älter die archäologischen Funde sind — desto seltener sie sich einseitig als exklusiv "väterlich" oder "mütterlich" deuten lassen. Es scheint, dass wir heute alle allzu geneigt sind zu meinen, der göttliche Urgrund des Kosmos lasse sich nur in *materiellen* Idolen, d.h. auf statisch-*räumliche* Weise, verehren und kultisch vergegenwärtigen. Das *Sein* dieser Welt entfaltet sich jedoch ebenso im *Raum* wie in der *Zeit*. Das kosmische Symbol des "väterlichen" Himmelsgottes, der "*Himmel*", darf deswegen nicht bloss räumlich vorgestellt werden; die Bewegungen der Himmelskörper messen ja den Verlauf der *Zeit* u. regeln das *Leben* des Menschen, wie des Kosmos. Der göttliche Herr dieses Himmels, der "Grosse Geist", ist — im Gegensatz zur Grossen ruhenden Erde — die sich im Blitz und Donner äussernde himmlische Macht, die ihre Entfaltung und ihren Ausdruck nicht im statisch gedachten irdischen Raum findet, sondern dynamisch erfahren u. erlitten wird in den abwechselnden, am Himmel ablesbaren *Zeiten*, letztlich im festlich begangenen *Jahr*. Seine zwei astronomischen Höhepunkte sind die beiden Winter- und Sommersolstitien (21.XII. u. 21.VI.). Der *Ort* der ältesten Kulstätten ist offensichtlich aus *kalendarischen* Gründen gewählt, um — in einer schriftlosen Epoche — die jährlich sich wiederholende "hl. Zeit" zu markieren. (Almeria, Gozo, Pylos, Graubündener Schalensteine, Südtirol, Stonehenge.)

Mag dort oft die Grosse *Erdmutter* die plastischen *Idole* beherrschen, so beherrscht dortselbst zugleich der unsichtbare *Himmel* durch den an der Topographie des Horizontes ablesbaren, geregelten Aufgang der *Sonne* die hl. *Jahreszeiten* mit ihren Festen wie den Verlauf des menschlichen *Lebens* und *Sterbens*. Die wahre *Universalität* des kosmischen Hochgottes und seiner Symbole lässt sich weder exklusiv durch den *Vater* noch durch die *Mutter*, nicht ausschliesslich durch *räumlich*-statische oder *zeitlich*-dynamische Kategorien, nicht exklusiv durch Geist und Stoff erschliessen und ausdrücken, sondern stets durch *beide* zugleich, weil unser geschaffenes Universum grösser ist als seine Teile, und sein ungeschaffener *göttlicher Urgrund* uns höher, tiefer und ganzheitlicher begründet und trägt, als jedes *materiell*-weibliches *Idol* und jede *geistig*-männliche *Gottheit*.

Andrew Lang and the Problem of Religion

by Eric J. Sharpe

It is commonly recognised by scholars specialising in *Hochgottglaube* that the Scottish writer Andrew Lang (1844-1912) is to be counted among the pioneers of this approach. Yet Lang himself is surprisingly little known. His very versatility (as well as being an anthropologist, he was a poet, classicist, historian, journalist and literary critic) tends to arouse suspicion, while his interest in the problems of extra-sensory perception has caused some to dimiss him as an unreliable romantic. Yet his written work was of uniformly high quality, and often his instincts led him to correct conclusions, as against the theoretical constructions of the period.

Between about 1873 and 1887 Lang was a faithful disciple of E. B. Tylor, and the chief spokesman of the "anthropological school" in their running battle with the philological and nature-mythological school of Friedrich Max Müller. In a variety of contexts he dissected and ridiculed Müller's methods and conclusions, and ultimately brought about their downfall. His position was that the irrational elements in the classical myths is to be explained, not by a "disease of language", but by an understanding of primitive survivals in this material.

In his second period of anthropological writing, from 1897 to his death, he began to criticise the assumptions of the anthropologists, and particularly the assumption that religion had begun from something sub-religious. He pointed out that observers had already drawn attention to a belief in a moral creator-god among "primitive" peoples, and insisted that this was more consistent with the known facts than were the theories of the unilinear evolutionists. These findings he incorporated into the most important of his books, *The Making of Religion* (1898). He also insisted that we simply do not know what were the thought-processes of primitive men, and that to treat the growth of religion, as Tylor had done, in rational terms was self-defeating.

Although Lang probably believed privately in some form of *Urmonotheismus*, he was reticent in affirming this belief publicly. He did insist, however, that the evidence should be judged at its face value, and not on the basis of an *a priori* theory, however popular. Most of his contemporaries chose to ignore what he was saying, or to attempt to explain it away. But during the last four years of his life Lang found a powerful champion in Pater Wilhelm Schmidt, the first volume of whose *Der Ursprung der Gottesidee* appeared in the year of Lang's death. Schmidt went farther than Lang in his theory of primal monotheism, replacing Lang's tentative suggestions by more or less dogmatic (and theologically motivated) assertions. But as early as 1902 Nathan Söderblom had accepted Lang's position on Australian high gods, and had predicted that his views, if taken seriously, would ultimately bring about a revolution in the study of religion. We now know Söderblom's words to have been prophetic.

SECTION IX

PHENOMENOLOGY AND SOCIOLOGY OF RELIGION, RELIGIOUS LANGUAGE

*Pluralismus und Einheit: Universalreligiöse Aspekte
in der gegenwärtigen Religionsgeschichte*

von Peter Gerlitz

(1) Obgleich der Absolutheitsanspruch in den Religionen seit der europäischen Aufklärung fragwürdig geworden ist (Lessing, Troeltsch), haben die Weltreligionen in der ersten Hälfte dieses Jahrhunderts noch einmal versucht, ihr Sendungsbewusstsein mit den Mitteln eines exklusiven Offenbarungsbegriffs glaubhaft zu machen (die Dialektische Theologie im Protestantismus, die islamische Mission in Afrika, sogar die buddhistische Mission in Europa und Amerika). Nach dem Zweiten Weltkrieg allerdings haben Technik, Massenkommunikationsmittel, die Fluktuation in der Weltbevölkerung und vor allem die Säkularisation die Aufrechterhaltung von religiösen Absolutheitsansprüchen unmöglich gemacht und die äusseren Voraussetzungen für einen Dialog zwischen den Religionen geschaffen.

Diesem Trend zum Gespräch kommt von religionsphilosophischer Seite der frühchristliche Begriff des Logos spermatikos entgegen, welcher die Möglichkeit bietet, über ein Mutual Understanding hinaus sachliche Probleme zu diskutieren, die alle Religionen in gleicher Weise betreffen. Auf diese Weise tritt an die Stelle des Absolutheitsanspruchs der Begriff der Universalität (P. Tillich).

(2) Im einzelnen ergeben sich *vier Aspekte* für eine künftige interreligiöse Zusammenarbeit:

a) *Der gesellschaftsdiakonische Aspekt.* Er trägt im wesentlichen pragmatische und säkulare Züge und reicht von der sogenannten "Entwicklungshilfe" bis zur Begegnung der Religionen in den Schulen mit Schülern verschiedener Religionszugehörigkeit und in den Ehen, deren Partner verschiedenen Glaubens sind. Die Probleme, die hier auftauchen — und in Zukunft immer häufiger auftauchen werden — lassen sich nur mit Hilfe einer intensiven Information und Kommunikation bewältigen.

b) *Der sozialethische Aspekt.* Dabei handelt es sich um gemeinsame Aktionen, zu denen sich die Angehörigen verschiedener Religionen zusammenschliessen mit dem Ziel, gesellschaftliche Veränderungen herbeizuführen. Ein Beispiel dafür ist die Aktion gegen die Verstaatlichung des Yasukuni-Schreins in Tokyo, die von Christen, Buddhisten und den Angehörigen des Sekten-Shinto gemeinsam unternommen wurde.

c) *Der politische Aspekt.* Er schliesst sich an den sozialetischen Aspekt an bzw. erwächst aus diesem. Hier wird deutlich, dass die Religionen eine ihrer wichtigsten Aufgaben, nämlich Versöhnung bzw. Frieden zu stiften, ernst nehmen und mit ihren Traditionen neu zu begründen suchen (Christliche und Buddhistische Friedensbewegungen). Die feindlichen Auseinandersetzungen, wie sie sich überall in der Welt zwischen Angehörigen verschiedenen Glaubens ereignen, sprechen nicht gegen die Grundtendenz der Religionen und ihrer Stifter, "Frieden zu bringen".

d) *Der dogmatische Aspekt.* Damit wird das schwierigste Problem innerhalb eines Dialogs zwischen den Religionen angesprochen. Es ist nach wie vor unlösbar. Denn nach wie vor stehen sich hier völlig konträre Positionen gegenüber. Sie sind erwachsen aus den sakralen Traditionen und ihrer Geschichte und lassen sich darum aus keinem "Religionsgespräch" eliminieren. So steht beispielsweise das christliche Dogma von der Trinität bzw. das islamische Dogma von der Prädestination dem christlich-islamischen Gespräch im Wege, und so verhindert auch der personalistische Gottesbegriff in der jüdisch-christlichen Religion eine dogmatische Verständigung mit den a-personalistischen Religionen des Ostens.

Es ist aber andererseits auch Tatsache, dass die Diskussion von dogmatischen Problemen, wie sie beispielsweise Nicolaus von Cusa vorschwebte, keine Zukunft hat. Vielmehr schliesst der Begriff der Universalität die Möglichkeit von pluralistischen Antworten ein. Und es besteht kein Zweifel, dass sich gerade die dogmatische Vielfalt für die künftige Begegnung zwischen den Religionen sich als fruchtbar erweisen wird.

(3) Im übrigen muss man in der gegenwärtigen Religionsgeschichte mit Problemen rechnen, die für den säkularen Menschen in allen Religionen zunehmend Relevanz gewinnen: Es

sind dies die Fragen nach dem Sinn von Leben und Tod.

Damit kehren die Religionen wieder zum Ursprung ihrer Verkündigung zurück, indem sie die Frage nach Gott auf den Menschen anwenden.

Ideologische Gehalte in modernen Hochgott-Theorien

von Carsten Colpe

Für "Ideologie" wird nicht der positive Sinn des 18., sondern der negative Sinn vorausgesetzt, wie er sich seit dem Beginn des 19. Jahrhunderts entwickelt hat: *Ideologie* bezeichnet ein Verhältnis zur Wirklichkeit, das "nur" durch Ideen bestimmt und deshalb falsch ist. Die Bestimmung des Verhältnisses zwischen *Religion* und Wirklichkeit kann sich dann zwischen zwei Extremen bewegen: entweder ist Religion etwas gegenüber der Ideologie Eigenständiges, und wodurch jene sich von dieser unterscheidet, muss nun bestimmt werden; oder aber Religion wird als dasselbe bestimmt wie Ideologie und verfällt damit derselben Disqualifikation wie diese. Sowohl der Erweis des Unterschiedes als auch der Erweis der Identität von Religion und Ideologie nehmen für sich in Anspruch, Wissenschaft, hier also: Religionswissenschaft, zu sein. Damit ist gemeint, dass dieser Erweis selbst keine Ideologie sein, also die lautere Wahrheit enthalten will, die nicht als Verkleidung von irgendetwas anderem entlarvt werden kann. Es haben aber namentlich marxistische und bürgerliche Wissenschaft dennoch den Ideologieverdacht gegeneinander erhoben. Aus dem Kreis dieser Vorwürfe kann man nur herauskommen, wenn man die eigene Theorie auf ideologische Gehalte hin untersucht. In der Religionswissenschaft ist dies bei der Mythentheorie am ergiebisten, bei Theorien über den Hochgottglauben und seinen Spezialfall, den Urmonotheismus, aber am wichtigsten, weil hier die Wirklichkeit der Religion selbst in Frage steht.

Vier ideologische Gehalte scheinen sich in Hochgott-Theorien nachweisen zu lassen. Der *erste* besteht in der Verwendung des Ausdrucks "Hochgott" als Äquivokation, die auch "Gottheit", "Höchstes Wesen", "Ein-" und "Urgott" deckt und damit so verschiedene Phänomene wie lebendigen Glauben, religiöse Gleichgültigkeit, bloss theoretische Anerkennung und Umwandlung des Mythos von einer lebensbestimmenden Tatsache zu blosser Erzählung zusammenschliesst. Der *zweite* Gehalt liegt in der

mit der Theorie vom Urmonotheismus vorgenommenen Monogenisierung nicht nur aller späteren Glaubensweisen, sondern
auch aller sonstigen Geistesverfassungen. Der *dritte* Gehalt besteht in der Signierung von Kulturkreisen mit dem Hochgott, die
sich bis zur Abgrenzung von Kulturkreisen von anderen nach dem
Kennzeichen des Hochgottglaubens verkehren kann. Der *vierte*
Gehalt ist der Kurzschluss zwischen einer modernen Hochgott-
Theorie und demjenigen Bereich ihrer historischen Quellenbasis,
der selbst schon eine theologische Ausbildung von Mono- und
Henotheismus darstellt.

Zur Hochgott-Äquivokation ist zu sagen, dass es auch sonst
Ideologie ist, wenn die Idee der Einheit, die nur ein heuristisches
Prinzip sein darf, Übermacht über die Vielfalt der Tatsachen gewinnt; zur Monogenisierung, dass es auch sonst Ideologie ist,
wenn man für möglichst Vieles nur eine Ursache sucht, oder
wenn man in der Geschichte nichts weiter als die Entfaltung eines
Urprinzips sieht; zur Abgrenzung von Kulturkreisen nach dem
Kriterium des Hochgottglaubens, dass es auch sonst Ideologie ist,
wenn Kulturen bis hin zu Nationen wie ein naturwüchsiger Or-
ganismus gesehen werden, zu dem eine bestimmte Idee gehört;
zur Repetition theologischen Denkens in den Religionen durch
moderne Hochgott-Theorien, dass es auch sonst ein Wesensmerk-
mal des Ideologischen ist, wenn Lehrgebäude und geschlossene
Systeme hergestellt werden, in denen man sich gegen unvermu-
tete Überfälle aus der Wirklichkeit absichern kann.

Die Eliminierung ideologischer Gehalte ist am ehesten durch
Anwendung metalogischer bzw. semiotischer Methodik in der
Religionswissenschaft zu erreichen. Sie ermöglicht die Trennung
zwischen und Durchführung von Untersuchungen der Beziehungen zwischen den Hochgott-Begriffen untereinander, von Untersuchungen der Beziehungen zwischen dem Hochgott-Begriff
und dem, was er bezeichnen soll, und von Untersuchungen zwischen dem Hochgott-Begriff und seinen Benutzern. Eine Notwendigkeit a priori, semiotisch zu arbeiten, gibt es nicht, und
deshalb lässt sich diese Methode auch nicht in den Dienst irgend-
einer Apologetik nehmen. Aber es lässt sich mit ihr die Möglichkeit offenhalten, dass der Gottesglaube etwas anderes ist als die
Nachvalutierung eines Einheitsbedürfnisses oder die in grauer
Vorzeit geschehene entlastendbelastende Transzendierung des
Vaterkomplexes o.ä.

Gottesglaube und Ideologie: Desintegration traditionaler
Gesellschaften als Thema einer
kritischen Religionsgeschichte

von Hans G. Kippenberg

Das Objekt religionsgeschichtlicher Forschung ist abhängig von dem Erkenntnisinteresse des Forschers. Dieses besteht bei Marx darin, Religion nicht einfach zu denunzieren, sondern als notwendigen Ausdruck bestimmter gesellschatlicher Verhältnisse geschichtlich zu betrachten. Eine solche Betrachtung öffnet den Blick für die von der Religion vorausgesetzten Produktionsverhältnisse. Kritik der Religion ist daher Kritik der gesellschaftlichen Verhältnisse, die sich im Bewusstsein der Menschen als unveränderbar darstellen. Weber bringt das Wesen des Kapitalismus auf den Begriff "Rationalisierung aller Lebensbereiche", betrachtet diese als übermächtig gewordenes Residuum protestantischer Askese und befragt von hier aus die Weltreligionen nach ihrer Wirtschaftsethik und deren Rationalisierungsgraden. Rationalisierung im Sinne Webers impliziert — wie Habermas gezeigt hat — die Legitimation bestehender Produktionsverhältnisse, stellt mithin Ideologie dar. Zugleich aber markiert der Begriff jene Differenz, die die neuzeitliche Gesellschaft von der traditionalen unterscheidet. In dieser beruht die Legitimation von Herrschaft auf religiösen Überlieferungen, während die neuzeitliche Gesellschaft ihre Legitimation aus dem Anwachsen der Produktivkräfte bezieht. Dass religiöse Traditionen in traditionalen Gesellschaften Instrumente und Form politischen Handelns abgeben, zeigt sich immer wieder.

So wurde der erste sizilische Sklavenkrieg (136/5 — 132 vChr) von einem syrischen Wahrsager geleitet, dem die syrische Göttin Atargatis im Traum verkündet hatte, er werde König werden. In den drei Jahren, die sich das von Sklaven gegründete Staatswesen hielt, bildete sich auf Sizilien eine Ordnung heraus, die dem seleukidischen Königtum nachgebildet war.

An dem sizilischen Sklavenkrieg kann man erkennen, wie in traditionalen Gesellschaften der vorausgesetzte soziale Konflikt durch Rückgriff auf unterschiedliche religiöse Traditionen ausgetragen wird:
— eine Gruppe, die in ihrer Geschichte spezifische Gesellschafts-

modelle entwickelt hat, bringt die Voraussetzung zur Organisierung politischer Macht mit sich;
— die Götter autorisieren bestimmte soziale Ordnungen;
— Konflikte werden durch Wahrsager benannt und gelöst;
— der Kampf zwischen etablierter Ordnung und alternativem Gesellschaftsmodell ist ein Kampf um die Legitimität dieser Verkündiger.

Ökonomische Ausbeutung stellt sich in vorkapitalistischen Gesellschaften nicht als das Problem der Unterdrückung einer Klasse, weil der Widerspruch zwischen Produktivkraft und Produktionsverhältnis noch nicht jene Evidenz erlangt hatte wie in der Neuzeit. Soziale Konflikte treten als Konflikte zwischen verschiedenen religiösen Legitimationsrahmen auf. Die alten konfliktlösenden Instanzen dieser Gesellschaften werden die Stelle, von der aus eine Veränderung des institutionellen Rahmens vorgenommen werden kann. Die Religion ist Instrument und Form politischen Handelns.

A Contemplation on Religion and Religious Guidance

by Kazuo Fujimoto

I have been interested in religious education since my youth. In the course of my various endeavors in this field, I have conceived a theory related to the workings of a religious mind and have attempted to express it in the form of a graph derived from an analysis of the human mind.

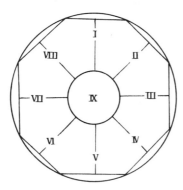

1. Fear (uneasiness)
2. Prudence
3. Piety
4. Reliance and being relied on
5. Thinking things through
6. Responsibility (thanking and gratitude)
7. All-embracing love or mercy
8. Faith
9. Religious mind

Every mind has these eight elements, i.e., fear (uneasiness), prudence, piety, reverence for what one believes to be Almighty, thinking things through, gratitude, love or mercy, faith, reliance and being relied on and responsibility or sense of duty. These are likened to bowstrings. The lines (workings of the mind), which divide the bowstrings into eight equal parts when drawn at right angle to the bowstrings, are certain to find the center of the circle, and when the tangents are made infinitely smaller and the number thereof is increased, they soon become points or entire perimeter.

Similarly, if the eight are increased to ten or a hundred, they are translated into daily behavior or individual feelings and ultimately will control the whole life of an individual, thus further elevating individual values. I believe that no matter what the religion may be, if it is the right religious belief, it should and must be attended by such functions of the mind. When actual functioning of a man's mind in his daily life is carefully observed and studied, we cannot fail to recognize these elements appearing more or less in every person if he is in possession of a normal mind. And this fact, without exception, proves that every person has a religious nature.

Consequently, denial of religious nature is tantamount to a denial of human nature. This is the most important point, and the publication of this theory has no other objective than to contribute towards realization of character or moral education on the basis of this principle.

I also tried to formulate some means of transmitting this idea to others. Of course, religious education is not an instruction in religion. However, to merely say that it is a method will probably be acceptable even in anti-religious nations like the Soviet Union. When a man is absolutely constant in all-embracing love, he does not become subject to anger. Even when some mischievous students try to make the teacher angry, the teacher, who is studing religious education, should never be prey to any emotion even appearing as anger.

A free educator, A. S. Neill, the master of Summer Hill School of Great Britain is an authority on religious education. In his school there is no formal chapel or worship service, but he publicly states, "In my school we have a religion of the school itself." He is well aware of the fact that anger is pregnant with the danger of leading a man to brutality. Anger changes love into hatred. Therefore, he is never angered. He looks upon all mischief as play. At one time a girl student tried to make him angry. For upward of an hour, though Mr. Neill told me on April 4, 1968 in his school that it was for three hours, she inflicted all sorts of indignities upon him, such as kicking his legs, spitting in his face, stepping on his feet and pulling at his hair, but he kept a smile on his lips all the while. The girl herself was tired out from all that mischief, and since that day, she became a gentle and obedient student. Neill said she had graduated from playing.

Neill declares, "It will be well to collect all the mischievous people of the world in my school, because there are no delinquents here." He says that he will convert them all into good students. He has converted till today already over five thousand mischievous students to good ones.

I believe this is one form of religious education, and the most difficult one. However, this difficult work is necessary for this study.

Religio-Anthropological Depth Research

by Juha Pentikäinen

The religio-anthropological approach is "man-orientated" in its problematics: religion is considered on the basis of the conceptions and behaviours of individuals and societies. This method is anthropological also in that it strives to describe religion *holistically* as a part of the cultural totality to which it belongs. Culture is a central concept in cultural and social anthropology, often defined as "man's social inheritance". The transmission of oral tradition in non-literate cultures and that of both oral and written tradition in literate cultures is the basic process by means of which the teaching, learning and "social transmission" of culture takes place. In the religio-anthropological approach, religion is studied as a part of the "learned social tradition of man". The central problem concerns religious *communication*, i.e. the transmission of religious tradition. The object of study is the interaction between the individual and society. This means that in spite of the fact that culture may be regarded superorganic — an individual born into a society does not form his culture, but culture forms him — it may be investigated in practice only on the basis of the conceptions and behaviour of the individual bearers of that culture. Religio-anthropological study is also *ecological* in that it concerns itself with the interdependence between religion and habitate (natural environment). Religio-ecological study may also attempt to determine whether an economic system has any influence upon religion. Ecological factors may also affect religious tradition and the behaviour or the development of a homo religiosus type within a certain culture.

Religion has psychological, sociological and cultural functions and in a religio-anthropological study, as it seems to me, it is useful to distinguish three levels: individual, social and cultural. Three aspects of experience, cognition, affection and conation, are distinguished in observation psychology and these are useful in the study of the individual. In the study of religion *cognition* includes, for example, the world view, the system of values, beliefs, dogmas, individual knowledge of religion, concepts of the universe, supra-normal beings; under the aspect of *affection* we may note the problematics of religious feeling and experience (a religious experience involves reciprocity between man and the supra-normal in which homo religiosus or the religious tradition familiar to him actualizes an encounter with a supra-normal being, with a god for example); *conation* concerns ritual behaviour by means of which an individual or a society seeks union with a supra-normal being. The *social* level deals with a religion as an institution; study here is principally of religious groups, reciprocity between religious and secular groupings, religious leadership as well as qualifications for membership of a religious group. With the *cultural* level we are dealing with the ecological environment in space and time. Is there a correlation between economic structure and religion? Is the fact that shamanism is a dominant form of religion in arctic and sub-arctic hunting and fishing cultures connected with habitate or economic structure? Or is acculturation the reason for the wide religious similarity? etc.

Religio-anthropological *depth research* is empirical in that it has as its basis primary material collected in intensive field work. The problems of the holistic study of culture, religious interaction systems, religious communication and ecological questions, for example, make such great demands vis-à-vis the material under study that depth collecting in any field is central to research. *Depth collecting* must be programmed in advance, but the study also allows for hypotheses actualized during field work and for this reason is different from the sociological method of collecting. Religio-anthropological depth research is inevitably inter-disciplinary because problems and methods of comparative religion, folkloristics, cultural and social anthropology and sociology are involved.

The possible fields of study are numerous. The smallest unit for such research is the individual, homo religiosus. The study may also concern itself with a group — for example a family, a village, an age or professional group. Religious groupings are another possibility. The idea behind depth research is to select a very narrow but representative field and to study it intensively. When a larger group or area is concerned, the so-called "point" or "case" study is useful. If for example we wish to make a comparative religio-anthropological study of Lappish religion, we omit general collection, and make a selection of Lappish villages representing various linguistic or ethnic groups. The same programming principles are observed in depth research in these villages, which is followed by a comparative analysis.

The paper deals with the theoretical and methodological problems of religio-anthropological depth research. The results of two depth research projects in progress in Lapland and Karelia are also given. This method is dealt with more thoroughly in the *Handbook of Social and Cultural Anthropology*, in the article "Depth Research" written by the author.

Is the sacred the same as the holy?

by Willard G. Oxtoby

Some twentieth-century discussions of the nature of religion have relied heavily on the interpretation which Rudolf Otto gave to the term "the holy". In the English-speaking world, the meaning of "the holy" has often been taken as equivalent in function to that of "the sacred". Otto's description of religion, where "the holy" is talked about, and the enterprise known as the phenomenology of religion, discussing "the sacred", have been seen as discussions of one and the same thing.

The paper begins with an attempt to distinguish the range of meanings of the two English words "sacred" and "holy", locating the circumstances under which one would choose to use one of these words rather than the other.

The difference is then tested against historical instances of such usage, both in the biblical religions of the West and in the critical tradition of Western philosophy external to them. The contrast becomes clearly focused when one examines the great nineteenth-century theories of the origin and nature of religion and twentieth-century theological reactions to these theories.

Rudolf Otto's attempt in his own theological theory of religion was to state a biblical religion's conception of itself in terms drawn in part from the external theories of religion. Some other influential theories of religion have, since Otto, made similar attempts. The concluding portion of the paper discusses the extent to which a theological theory, once its assumptions are identified as such, can prove useful to present needs in the description of religion.

Das Kunstwerk als Ausdruck des Gottesglaubens

von Piotr Otto Szolc (Scholz)

1) Die Betrachtungsweise des Kunstwerks im religionsphänomenologischen Sinne war nicht einer derartigen Veränderung unterworfen wie die der sog. heiligen Schriften. Es ist deshalb notwendig, sich für ein intensiveres Interesse an Kunst einzusetzen und sie in die religionswissenschaftliche Forschung einzubeziehen. Dies soll natürlich nicht besagen, dass man das Kunstwerk bisher in der Forschung vollkommen ignoriert hätte (z.B. Arbeiten von van der Leeuw, Volp, Bahr und solche von orthodoxen Theologen beschäftigen sich mit dieser Problematik). Der Umfang dieser Forschung ist jedoch im Vergleich zu der über religiöse Schriftquellen äusserst minimal. Es ist allgemein bekannt, dass sich die Völker in den Anfängen des geistigen Lebens des Kunstwerks als Mittel des Ausdrucks bedienten (paläolitische Kunst und die Kunst der Naturvölker). Die Kunst wurde zum Spiegelbild der religiösen und geistigen Haltung der ersten Menschen.

2) In den ersten grossen Kulturen der orientalischen und altamerikanischen Welt entstanden erste künstlerische Kanone als Vektoren des Gottesglaubens. D.h. dieser Glaube entspricht den durch die Priesterschaft geprägten Tendenzen, was jedoch nicht

heissen soll, dass sich nicht ausserhalb der religiösen Zentren religiöse Kunst entwickelt hätte. Repräsentiert wurde er durch die Formulierung entsprechender theologischer Doktrinen ((Ägypten, Mesopotamien, Syrien, Indien, Anatolien, Mexiko, Peru).

3) Eng verbunden mit dieser Thematik ist das Problem der religiösen Symbolik. (Semiotische Bedeutung der Zeichen in der religiösen Kunst: Wesen und Sinn). Die Symbolik ist eines der wesentlichen Momente der religiösen Sprache (wozu die theologischen Untersuchungen Paul Tillichs anzuführen sind). Die religiöse Symbolik, die in die Kunst einbezogen ist, wird als einzige Ausdrucksform der Unbegrenztheit theologischer Begriffe (z.B. Inkarnation, Offenbarung) durch Kontemplation gerecht (Probleme der Mystik in der Kunst).

4) Das Christentum war in seinen kanonischen Darstellungen in einem formalistischen Sinne abhängig von Ausdruckformen, die aus vorchristlichen Kulturen bekannt waren. Von ihrem Wesen her zeigen sie jedoch, falls sie noch mit dem Wort verbunden waren, (analog zur altägyptischen Kunst) eine unbegrenzte theologische Funktion, und zwar auch noch für die heutige christliche Orthodoxie.

5) Die Auflösung des religiös-künstlerischen Kanons ist Ausdruck für die Entstehung eines unreligiösen Systems (Säkularisation, Dechristianisierung, Atheismus), so z.B. in der Renaissance. Im Grunde besitzt jedoch die neue Kunst dem Urbild gegenüber einen sekundären Charakter (Urbild hat immer religiösen Charakter), dem immer ein schöpferischer Charakter innewohnte (Gauguin).

Time, space and the absolute

by Yoshinori Takeuchi

Time as it is explained by the "myth of eternal return" (prof. M. Eliade) can be recognized by means of ritual dance and procession. When performing a ritual dance the members of a group tend to make a circle, and through the repetition of the performance the dance becomes rhythmic (J. Harrison). Expressed in this round dance, cyclic time is hierophany and kratophany, since it is the primordial form of the projection of the sacred through one's *dromenon*. Every cyclic year is received with a ceremony. For example, the ceremony of "bringing in summer" and "carrying away winter". Further by means of performance of the cyclic dance, sacred space within the circle is cut off from the profane realm which is outside of it. Here the distinction between the sacred and the profane is made even before reflection. As ritual dance is the prototype of cyclic time, so the procession is that of rectilinear one.

Procession may be considered as a section of the sacred precinct which participants can actually cover, when they march along it, or as a ceremony entering into or retiring from the sacred place, or as a pilgrimage from one sacred place to another. In any case, here the sacred is contrasted and juxtaposed to the profane more definitely. The procession is symbolic of *Festzeit* (Van der Leeuw) and time tends to unwind its circular form into a straight line. Thus ritual dance and procession are presentations of our time-consciousness prior to reflection.

It is through the combination of these two types that the mythical reflection (re-presentation) of the beginning of the world, large year, eschatological ideas, etc., come to our mind. The primordial Sacred-Profane, as is expressed in a time-space category in *dromenon* is basic to the understanding of the personification of the absolute, and of singular and plural deities. Only through participation in this primordial category of time and space in the Sacred-Profane, and by no means through the qualitatively different (secular) time-and-space-category of the modern scientific mind which investigates objectively the nature and number of personal deities, can we come near to the primordial recognition of "the one and the many" concerning the problems of Pantheism, Polytheism and Monotheism.

Religious Experience and Belief

by H.D. Lewis

Religious Experience is not to be invoked to establish the existence of God. That is known independently of any particular kind of experience other than having the insight by which we grasp the inevitability of the being of God in everything. But all further claims about God must be justified eventually in terms of specific experiences. In these the individual will assimilate into his own experience the corpus of the insights and experience of others before him, and this will be much conditioned by his own culture. The validity of experience turns upon two main factors, namely the lively renewal of the sense of God's inescapable existence and the particular patterning of the experiences so determined in the course of history. All this is in some ways closely analogous to our knowledge of other finite persons, where pattern is again a central condition of objective references. Illustrations of this theme will be given from experiences of moral illumination, guilt and reconciliation. The linkage of it with particular historical processes will also be noted and a comment will be made on the relevance of these considerations to central doctrines like the idea of incarnation and the reflection of this in art and literature as well as in strictly religious scriptures.

Der Hochgott und der mikrokosmische Mensch

von K.A.H. Hidding

1. Im Glauben bekennt sich der Mensch zum Mysterium als dem Apriori von allem, was besteht. Man kann das Mysterium auf direktem Wege nicht erkennen. Der Mensch wird sich aber indirekt durch die Wahrnehmung der Wirklichkeit davon bewusst, dadurch dass er Bilder sieht und Worte hört, die beide als Offenbarungsmedia dienen können.

2. Der Gläubige sieht den Hochgott im Bild vom Himmel mit seiner alles bestimmenden und umfassenden Ordnung, die im Gegensatz zum Chaos das Bestehen des Kosmos ermöglicht und das Vorbild für das Denken — besonders des klassifizierende Denken — und Tun des Menschen ist.

3. Mit Preusz und Pettazzoni liegt alles Gewicht auf dem totalitären und naturalistischen Charakter des Hochgottes. Damit ist zugleich die These von Pater Schmidt verworfen, der ihn geistlich-transzendent versteht. Er macht damit den prinzipiellen Unterschied mit dem Gott des strengen Monotheismus unmöglich, der Gott, der die Welt als ein vergängliches Sein schöpft, alle Bilder und Mythen verwirft und sich durch das Wort offenbart.

4. Der Hochgott ist totalitär, allwissend und schiksalbestimmend und schöpft und umfasst alles und ist mit allem wesenseins. Man bekennt ihn als Einheit, die sich auch als Zwei-, Dreiheit

oder Mehrfaltigkeit offenbaren kann, z.B. als die Einheit von
Himmel und Erde, vom Tag- und Nachthimmel, als Gott mit
seinen Hypostasen etc. Er ist zugleich *deus otiosus* und *deus
movens,* wobei entweder das eine oder andere Moment vor-
herrscht.

5. Wo der Hochgott das Wesen der Erscheinungswelt ist, ist
jede Erscheinung im Wesen totalitär. So kennt man überall heilige
Bäume, Städte, Tempel, Paläste, Städte, Dörfer, Völker und Ge-
meinschaften etc. Alle diese sind als Mikrokosmos und Bild des
Hochgottes, d.h. des Allwesens totalitär und bekommen daraus
ihre göttliche Macht.

6. Auch der Mensch ist als Erscheinung ein Mikrokosmos. Die
kosmischen Faktoren konstituiren seinen Körper und er kann sie
erkennen, weil er selber im Wesen mit ihnen identisch ist. Sein
totalitärer Charakter tritt auch in Erscheinung in der sog. doppelten Seele, d.h. dem vergänglichen Lebensgeist und der Bildseele,
die nach dem Tode entweder im Totenreich oder in einer neuen
Inkarnation fortlebt, so dass der Mensch auch zeitlich eine unver-
gängliche Einheit ist.

7. Dem Glauben an den Hochgott liegt "die Anschauung des
Universums" zu Grunde. Der Mensch nimmt die Wirklichkeit und
sich selbst als Totalitäten wahr, in denen sich ganz verschiedene
Faktoren unterscheiden lassen. Die Totalität ist das Apriori so-
wohl von der Wirklichkeit als auch von der Erkenntnis davon.
Diese Erkenntnis ist das Produkt von Prozessen, die sich in be-
stimmten Organen vollziehen. Der Mensch erkennt im sichtbaren
Bild von jeder Erscheinung sein verborgenes, unsichtbares Wesen,
das sein Dasein bestimmt, wieder. Die intuitive Einsicht ist der
Grund dieses Glaubens.

8. Der objektive Grund der totalitären Art der Wirklichkeit ist
die Einheit von Zeit und Raum, die jede Erscheinung konstituiert
und am Leben hält, d.h. die Einheit von seiner räumlichen Aus-
dehnung und den sich darin vollziehenden Prozessen. Davon ist
Gott der unergründliche Grund und Horizont, woraus und worin
jede zeitlich-räumliche Erscheinung zum Vorschein kommt. Gott
offenbart sich entweder im primär räumlichen Bild der Erscheinungen und in den hiervon zeugenden Mythen und Riten oder im
ebenso primär temporellen Wort, besonders in Befehl und Begriff, die im Monotheismus eine zentrale Stellung einnehmen und
im heiligen Buch festgelegt sind.

The Role of the History of Religions
In College/University/Seminary Curricula

by Edward J. Jurji

This paper incorporates the findings of ten scholars who found themselves caught up during all of 1968 in investigating the above subject. The focus throughout fell on the theme of religion in the context of day to day experience and in relations of persons in societies. The experiment was geared to a definable objective: the development of a broad-guaged educational program steeped in the critical, analytical standards of the history of religions, and commensurate with the bold expectations of curricular architects.

Three distinct, though not altogether unrelated, dimensions of the problem began to shape up: attitudinal, revisionist, and programmatic.

A. *The Attitudinal Pathway*

It was the consensus that the world religions can scarcely ever hope to deal adequately with issues of alienation and fear/hatred/violence unless they take seriously their own irenic potential and an ultimate concern endowing them with a capability of articulating in unison, despite variations of creed and multiplicity of traditions. A key question to be raised is this: What are the prospects for opening windows from within each religion permitting believers to look positively on other world religious systems?

B. *The Revisionist Format*

Antiquarian no less than contemporaneous components constitute the genuine fabric of the history of religions. The inescapable urgency for the scholar in the history of religions is to prescribe that the teacher in the field must be constructive. There is to be room, however, in society for destructiveness. The meaning of an ancient document is important. The inevitable question must never disappear: What can the document mean to living men? And that is the preliminary requirement in any purposeful revisionist procedure.

C. *The Programmatic Design*

Vigorous research programs are requisite. At stake is the reappraisal of data available in non-Western as well as Western fields of inquiry. Envisioned is an academic and hermeneutic — both theoretical — design for action. Professional manpower is built through training of scholars competent to show their responsibilities of teaching and research planning and organization. The precise objective would be to evaluate the status of religion within various societies, bearing in mind the exigency of dominant ideologies.

The Structure of Religious Fraternity

by George Weckman

The role of social relationships or structures in religious phenomena has been brought to the attention of historians of religions most prominently in the works of Georges Dumézil and Claude Lévi-Strauss. The method which is common to these men emphasizes the relationships between elements of religious situations in contrast with their individual, inherent meanings.

It is my current concern to apply this method at a general level to the widespread phenomenon of the religious fraternity. Included in this category are monastic communities, orders, and even primitive secret societies (see my forthcoming article in *Numen*). In this project structural analysis is applied to an aspect of the so-called high or historical religions where doctrine (as well as myth and symbol) is seen in a new light.

The primary factor in the structure of religious fraternity is the group's existence within and recognition by a larger religious community. The expectations of the larger group plus the fraternity's consciousness of special significance illuminate certain practices and ideas in the total situation. Among the special characteristics of this situation is the development of initiation ritual, the notion of a kinship with the realm of the dead or the spirits, and the attempt to sacralize the entire course of a member's life. By recognizing the implications of the fraternity's place in a larger tradition its effects on that tradition and its peculiarities in any instance can be clarified.

Comment se forme un dieu?

par Angelo Brelich

Dans cette communication seront développées et soutenues les thèses suivantes:

1. L'historien des religions, en tant que tel — c'est-à-dire indépendamment de sa propre position religieuse — considère tout être surhumain, quel qu'il soit, conçu par les diverses religions, comme un produit humain: aussi recherche-t-il les raisons historiques de la formation de chacun d'eux.

2. Une comparaison étendue sans limitation de temps, d'espace, de niveau culturel, de couche sociale, etc., est en mesure de montrer que la formation de nombreux *types* d'êtres surhumains remonte à une époque antérieure à la naissance des plus anciennes civilisations supérieures.

3. Parmi ces types d'êtres il faut compter celui de l'Être Suprême encore que cela ne signifie naturellement pas que les Êtres Suprêmes concrètement observés dans les croyances de peuples primitifs actuels remontent à la préhistoire.

4. L'unicité n'est pas un caractère nécessaire ou nécessairement important de L'Être Suprême, aussi bien parce que la présence de ce dernier n'exclut pas celle d'autres types d'êtres surhumains dans la même religion, que parce que l'Être Suprême peut aussi n'être que le plus important parmi d'autres êtres typologiquement semblables (exemples: Kwot et les kut des Nuers, Biliku et les biliks des Andamaniens, etc.).

5. Une idée préhistorique de l'Être Suprême peut constituer un facteur de la formation aussi bien d'un dieu de conception monothéiste que d'un ou plusieurs dieux d'une religion polythéiste.

6. La formation des religions monothéistes aussi bien que celle des religions polythéistes se produit dans la phase — différente selon les époques et selon les conditions concrètes du processus —, dans laquelle une société accède au niveau de civilisation supérieur. Les conditions de ce passage sont largement déterminantes pour la formation des divinités; mais également déterminantes sont les conceptions religieuses préhistoriques qui entrent en jeu dans cette formation.

7. Aussi bien aux origines historiques du dieu unique du

monothéisme hébraique qu'à celles des divinités polythéistes
dont le nom est issu de la racine indo-européenne *dyeus* — entre
autre Iuppiter — on entrevoit la figure d'un Être Suprême de type
primitif.

8. Le contact des Hébreux avec les civilisations voisines (à
religions polythéistes) et la nécèssité d'une sanction religieuse de
l'unité d'une notion en formation et en lutte figurent parmi les
facteurs principaux de la transformation d'un Être Suprême en
un dieu national unique. La diversité des conditions du passage
des différentes sociétés de langue indo-européenne à la civilisation supérieure explique les différences entre les caractères et la
position, par exemple, de Dyaus pitar dans le panthéon védique
et celles de Zeus dans le panthéon grec et de Iuppiter dans le
panthéon romain.

9. L'histoire d'un dieu ne consiste pas seulement en sa genèse.
Des conditions historiques particulières ont fait du dieu unique
national des Hébreux un dieu universel, tandis que des conditions
historiques non moins particullières ont conduit le Iuppiter italique à sa forme "capitoline" à Rome.

Croyance en Dieu et dualisme

par Ugo Bianchi

Il est peut-être intéressant de soumettre à la discussion d'un
congrès ayant pour thème "Croyances en Dieu: croyance en un
dieu suprème, panthéisme, polythéisme, monothéisme" un type
de croyance non moins diffus dans le monde des religions et des
philosophies: le dualisme.

La question se pose avant tout de savoir si le dualisme, avec
toutes ses ramifications ou possibilités, qui sont multiples et var-
iées, mais qui n'en reviennent pas moins à un type suffisamment
caractérisé, est un phénomène à ranger à côté des autres évoqués
par le thème du congrès, ou si, au contraire, il doit s'inscrire dans
l'une ou dans l'autre des spécifications fondamentales de la croyance en Dieu ou en les dieux.

Il faut pour cela s'expliquer sur la nature du dualisme, que
nous définissons comme la doctrine des deux principes, ou, plus
explicitement, comme une doctrine admettant que deux principes — coéternals ou non — *fondent l'existence*, réelle ou appa-

rente, de ce qui existe et se fait sentir dans le monde. Dès lors, il y a lieu à se demander si des doctrines dualistes peuvent ou non coexister avec une religion monothéiste (ou de tendance mono-théiste, comme c'est souvent le cas pour la religion zoroastri-enne), ou avec une religion à type moniste, comme c'est le cas pour les religious indiennes de tradition védantique et pour l'or-phisme en Grèce, ou, encore, avec une doctrine et une mytholo-gie admettant une *arché* unique de type plus ou moins imper-sonnel, qui ne revient pourtant pas à un véritable monisme, comme c'est le cas pour le zurvanisme.

Si l'hypothèse de l'existence de formes dualistes au sein de doctrines monothéistes, monistes ou polythéistes devait être con-statés, et nous croyons qu'il en est ainsi, au moins dans certaines limites (pour la combinaison monisme-dualisme dans l'orphisme et le Vedanta la chose est claire), on se demandera alors si le dualisme existe en tant que forme spécifique pouvant se juxta-poser aux autres indiquées par le théme du congrès.

Tout en tenant compte de la valeur relative de toute classifica-tion phénoménologique (valeur qui est rehaussée si on aura tenu compte des résultats de la recherche historique: concept de typo-logie historique des religions), il faut reconnaître que le dualisme, d'une part, semble rentrer dans la problématique relative au "nombre" des divinités ou des principes admis par le croyant (un, deux, plusieurs, un-tout);[1] mais il suscite d'autre part des per-plexités à ce meme propos, étant donné sa facilité à s'accrocher à des formes différentes de croyance.

Puisque les formes du dualisme, tel que nous l'avons défini ci-dessus, semblent indiquer un type de conception religieuse assez caractérisé, bien que polyvalent, il faudra en conclure que le dualisme en tant que catégorie religieuse exprime une option particulière qui a pu se manifester dans des situations et au sein de conceptions différentes, qui sont celles évoquées par le thème du congrès. Mais si on poursuit l'enquête jusqu'aux différentes spécifications du dualisme, on en arrivera à identifier une con-nexion intime entre la forme la plus radicale du dualisme (le dualisme dialectique qui admet la coeternité des deux principes, ontologiquement irréductibles et indestructibles),[2] d'une part, et

---

[1] Il est évident que l'aspect "numérique" renvoie au sens religieux profond des conceptions relatives.

[2] Cette forme plus radicale du dualisme ne se réalise donc pas dans le dualisme

le monisme d'autre part (connexion moniste-dualiste des doctrines du type orphique-empédocléen et du type upanishadique-
védantique). Il en dérive la conclusion quelque peu paradoxale
que la doctrine de l'*advaita*, radicalement moniste dans la tradition védantique, est du même coup radicalement dualiste.

Iconography as a Primary Source for the Conception of Deity

by S.G.F. Brandon

Man drew pictures of his gods long before he learned to write
about them. The first depiction of deity was probably made in
the Upper Palaeolithic era; the first written texts in Sumer and
Egypt which mention deities date for about the middle of the
third millennium B.C. This chronological priority of iconography
is matched by the vivid immediacy of the visual image. Religious
texts rarely convey a clear impression of the form in which deities were imagined to exist by those who worshipped them.
Indeed, our conception of the gods of any specific religion de-
rives from our acquaintance with the related iconography.

In view of the obvious importance of iconography as evidence
of the conception of deity, its study has been strangely neglected
or underestimated in the history and comparative study of religions. The reason for this lack of attention is probably twofold.
Historians of religions are trained on the study of texts, and
consequently acquire the disposition to regard written evidence
as alone having primary value. They are suspicious and uneasy
about iconographical data when unaccompanied by texts; the
interpretation of such material seems inevitably to involve speculation based on emotive impressions. This neglect of iconography
should not, however, be permitted to continue, since it deprives
our discipline of a very rich source of insight and information.
Attention should be given to developing a technique of icono-
graphic research, possibly in collaboration with historians of art.

---

zoroastrien, qui, comme celui des gnostiques, se résout en perspective eschatologique.
De ce point de vue, la cosmologie de Platon, avec sa théorie dualiste-harmoniste du
monde, dérivant de l'*idea* et de la *chora* (qui revient à l'*ananké*), est plus radicalement
dualiste que l'anticosmisme des gnostiques. Ce n'empêche pourtant que le dualisme
gnostique, du point de vue existentiel, développe la visée dualiste bien au delà de son
modèle platonicien, en récupérant dans toutes ses implications métaphysiques et théo-
logiques l'antisomatisme orphique, dont Platon avait aussi hérité.

The rest of the paper will be devoted to illustrating, with slide material, how the iconography of deity expresses the quintessence of a religion with a subtlety of nuance impossible to written sources. The examples selected are from the iconographical traditions of Egypt, Greece, India, Christianity and the Aztecs.

The lecture was illustrated by slides.

Sexual fault and original sin in the teaching of an African charismatic movement

by Johannes Fabian

The Jamaa is a large charismatic movement which originated in Katanga (Congo Republic) as a response to the ideas and teachings of Placid Temples, a Belgian Franciscan missionary known as the author of *Philosophie bantoue* (Elizabethwille, 1945). Attracting large numbers of followers, especially in the urban industrial centers of the copper mining area, the Jamaa professes a vision of humanism (*umuntu*) centered on three basic values, life/force, fecundity/filiation, unity/love, realized, above all, in a total husband-wife communion.

It may be surmised that Jamaa teaching provides a solution to the problems of change and modernization in Katanga, that is, change from rural to urban environment, from kinship group to nuclear family. More interesting, however, than these social-structural implications are the actual content and form of the charismatic message which might prove to be of great importance for the historian of religion. To illustrate this, a text dealing with the temptation and fall of Eve in the paradise was chosen and submitted to analysis with emphasis on the following points:

(1) Establishment of the literary genre of the text (including a brief introduction to the history of the corpus of Jamaa doctrine);

(2) Location of key concepts in lexical-structural terms (a brief sketch of the main features of Jamaa language);

(3) Comment on the social-cultural context of the account (cultural definitions of husband-wife relationships in traditional and Jamaa teaching, the Christian elements);

(4) Comment on the meaning of a "sexual" interpretation of original sin.

— in terms of the African cultural context
— in terms of Jamaa doctrine
— in a historical comparative perspective: a possibility of a new understanding of "sexual" interpretations in the Western tradition.

The last point will receive special attention in continuation of an argument for the gnostic character of Jamaa teaching (cf Fabian 1969b).

Related publications:

1966   "Dream and Charisma — 'Theories of Dreams' in the Jamaa Movement (Congo)," *Anthropos*, 61: 544-560.

1967   "Tod dem Propheten — Ein Dokument zu einer prophetischen Situation (Death to the Prophet — A document on a prophetic situation)," *Sociologus*, 17: 131-146.

1969a   "Charisma and Cultural Change: The case of the Jamaa Movement in Katanga (Congo Republic)," *Comparative Studies in Society and History*, 11: 155-173.

1969b   "An African Gnosis — For a Reconsideration of an Authoritative Definition," *History of Religions*, 9: 42-58.

1969c   "Le Charisme et l'Evolution Culturelle: le Cas du Mouvement Jamaa au Katanga," *Etudes Congolaises*, XII (4): 92-116.

In Press "Religion and Change." In Paden and Soja (eds.), *The African Experience*. Evanston: Northwestern University Press.

In Press "Placide Tempels — His Work in an Historical Perspective." Bulletin CRISP, Brussels (in French).

In Prep. *Charisma and Cultural Change*. Northwestern University Press.

Die hermeneutischen Prinzipien Joachim Wachs
(Joachim Wach's hermeneutical principles)

von Hans-Joachim Klimkeit

In seinem Streben nach methodischer Klarheit um die Möglichkeiten, Voraussetzungen und Bedingungen sinnvoller religionswissenschaftlicher Arbeit wird Wach immer wieder auf das Problem der Hermeneutik zurückgeworfen. Seine gesamte Lebensarbeit ist gleichsam eine Suche nach dem rechten wissenschaftlichen Ort, der ein Verstehen fremder Religionen und ihrer Erscheinungen begründet und ermöglicht. Selbst in seiner späteren Zuwendung zur religionssoziologischen und sogar religionspsychologischen Typologie werden die früher liegengebliebenen hermeneutischen Fäden wiederaufgenommen. Es besteht für Wach eine enge Verbindung zwischen Hermeneutik und Typologie. So wird man auf

Grund einer Analyse seines Gesamtwirkens feststellen müssen, dass der Bruch, der zweifellos zwischen seinen deutschen und englischen Schriften liegt, das Verstehensproblem nicht in dem Masse berührt, wie es zunächst äusserlich erscheint. Für unser Thema bedeutet das fortgesetzte Bemühen Wachs um die Verstehensfrage, dass wir uns dem Kern seines Denkens von zwei Sprachen her nähern können. Dieser Umstand gestattet uns nicht unwichtige Rückschlüsse auf die Problematik.

Wachs Antwort auf die Frage nach den Bedingungen der Möglichkeit religionswissenschaftlichen Verstehens ist zunächst keine Lehre, erst recht kein System, sondern ein umfassendes Programm. Zu diesem Programm gehört in erster Linie die von ihm selbst in Angriff genommene Untersuchung hermeneutischer Theorien in verschiedenen Geisteswissenschaften. Die aus der Geschichte der Hermeneutik zu gewinnende Verstehenslehre soll in diesem Programm ergänzt werden durch eine Theorie der religiösen Ausdrucksarten. Ferner fordert Wach eine Erschliessung all jener Kategorien, die den Bezug zwischen Subjekt und Objekt im Verstehensprozess tangieren. Schliesslich verlangt er als vierten theoretischen Bezugsrahmen für ein angemessenes Verstehen fremdreligiöser Erscheinungen eine "formale Religionssystematik", die über eine Religionsmorphologie und -phänomenologie abstraktionsmässig noch weit hinausgeht. Es ist dies ein Gerüst von religionswissenschaftlichen Oberbegriffen, die aus dem Gemeinsamen aller Theologien, nicht aller Religionen, gewonnen ist.

Über diesen Entwurf hinaus formuliert Wach aber auch konkrete hermeneutische Leitlinien und Grundsätze, die für das religionswissenschaftliche Verstehen richtungsweisend sein wollen und Gültigkeit beanspruchen. Diese Prinzipien ergeben sich nicht als systematische Konsequenzen aus der grossangelegten hermeneutikgeschichtlichen Untersuchung, sondern als Nebenprodukte verschiedenster historischer und phänomenologischer Arbeiten. So finden wir sie auch in seinem gesamten Schrifttum verstreut, und es gilt hier, diese recht disparaten und z.T. fragmentarischen Gedanken zu einem einigermassen kohärenten Bild zusammenzufassen.

Die Tatsache, dass die heutige hermeneutische Diskussion in den Geisteswissenschaften weit über die Dilthey-Wachschen Ansätze hinausgegangen ist, dürfte die Religionswissenschaft nicht hindern, immer wieder Entscheidendes von Wach zu lernen.

SECTION X

PSYCHOLOGY OF RELIGION

Religion and Alcohol

by Klas G. Magni

In difficult times and in times of need, human beings turn to religion. They learn to use their faith, to get support and consolation from it, and to soothe their fears. Research has indicated that alcoholic drinks can also soothe fears temporarily and that people learn to use them in approximately the same way as religion. Should it not be possible then to replace alcohol by religion?

This was the starting point for an investigation, carried out at the request of the Swedish Society for Temperance and Popular Education.

Now, if the soothing of fears acted as reward for drinking, and if soothing of fears also acted as a reward for attending religious meetings, and these behaviours could be explained, at least in part by reference to well-known laws of learning, how could the "switching" of behaviour, "from one track to the other", be explained?

Religious *conversion* is postulated to take place here. In contrast to earlier treatments of conversion, mostly on an *ex post facto* basis, the structure and phasing of conversion was here postulated in advance. Thus, more or less operational hypotheses could be put to empirical tests.

The tests did give empirical support to the hypotheses in question, and further research was also indicated.

This investigation is the first of its kind in Scandinavia, and so far no direct parallell has been found anywhere else. The original Swedish report was soon out of print, but a new one is planned, and a short English version as well.

The bare-footed walking on burning charcoal
of Anastenaria, as a religious phenomenon[1]

by Stylianos Papadimas

In Langada, which is a town near Thessaloniki, there takes place a festival of Anastenaria, which is the bare-footed walking and dance on burning charcoal on May 21st of each year. There are about 20 to 30 persons who walk on a fire, which has been lit in the afternoon of the feast day of Saint Constantin and Helen. The dance on it continues until the fire is put out.

The persons who are going to walk and dance on the burning charcoal gather together in the house of the chief of Anastenaria and there they say their prayer and prepare themselves. There is a hard preparation of fast, prayer and dance until they are exhausted. On the day of the feast they all gather together again in the house of the chief of Anastenaria and repeat their prayer and dance, this time holding the holy Images of Saint Constantin and Helen and the Virgin Mary, coming in and out the house and courtyard. Some of them seem to reach a point of ecstasy. On the same day the chief of Anastenaria kills a calf, which he offers at dinner to his dancers and to the rest of those who are going to take part in the bare-footed walking on the burning charcoal and to their relatives. At the same time wood comes that is sufficient for the fire and seems to be especially chosen, somewhat thin wood for this purpose, so that it may not leave much thick coal. This wood is carried early to the place of walking. The lighting of the fire begins at 5 o'clock and after two hours' burning it becomes charcoal (ember) at 7 o'clock. At this time exactly, the bare-footed walking on the ember begins. The procession of the bare-footed walkers on ember starts from the house of the Chief of Anastenaria just a few minutes before the beginning of the walk on ember. The band of the folk-musical instruments is ahead the procession. They arrive at the place of dancing on ember, where crowds of people wait for them. The members of the dance — we call them anastenarides — take off their shoes and socks and give them to an old woman who is sitting near the ember and holding two lit wax-candles in her hands. The chief of Anastenaria makes three rounds around the ember and then

---

[1] The word Anastenaria is derived from the Greek one meaning: sigh, groan.

crosses it cross-shaped. The same is repeated by the other anastenarides (dancers) and then they dance for a long time on the
ember until they put it out. Then, they return with the escort of
musical instruments to the house of the chief of Anastenaria.
They repeat the same proceedings an hour later the following day
and the same again the day after, for still an hour later. They
begin fasting three days before the day of the ceremony and
finish it on the day of the ceremony. There is a suffocating
atmosphere in the house of the chief of Anastenaria on the day
of dancing and walking on the ember. The dance is a simple one,
the steps of which follow the vigorous gestures of the hands and
sometimes the motion of the whole body which scarcely goes
along with the rhythm of music. Firstly, the holy images belong
to Saint Constantin and Helen. There may also be used images of
the Virgin Mary as well and of others, etc. All the images have
been brought by them from their native country Thrace. Here we
are mainly interested in the preparation which leads to the bare-
footed walking on the ember. The preparation includes the following elements: Prayer, fasting, solemnization, self-concentra-
tion, and ecstasy. All of them do not step on the ember, but only
those who are chosen and those who have made a vow, a conse-
cration to step on the ember. The bare-footed walking on ember
as a religious phenomenon is explained by: a) The religious elements of or rudiments of preparation and b) the walking on the
ember as an individual, personal sacrifice to God and a kind or
means of adoration of God. It is to be noted that there is no
internal touch among the organ-players and the dancers-walkers of
Anastenaria.

Summary: The feast of Anastenaria is an exceptional religious
ceremony, once a year, and it may be a remnant of Orphean and
the rest of Thracian mysteries under a Christian goan. By the
intensive preparation of three days and the sensation of doing an
act of devotion to God, they walk on the ember after a variety of
religious ceremonies and dances.

Methods of Personality Studies in Psychology of Religion

by Gustaf Ståhlberg

The first part of this communication will be a short summary
of Samuel Z. Klausner's (1964) investigation of which methods

of data collection, according to 130 articles on empirical studies in the psychology and sociology of religion published in journals in the United States between 1950 and 1960, have been choosen, and which factors, especially of the nonrational type, have influenced the choice.

As an important rational factor, Dr. Klausner examines the nature of the variables to be studied. In doing so he has concentrated on the "system level" of the object of study and has classified the dependent variables into four groups. Those variables referring to personality constitute one group. As nonrational factors he has identified professional affiliation, time when training was completed, metaphor used in terms referring to dependent variable and the researcher's evaluation of his object of research.

The second part of this communication will give an account of my own investigation about the choice of methods used in studies published between 1960 and 1970 and reported in *Psychological Abstracts*. Contrary to Dr. Klausner, my investigation is limited to that "system level", where the dependent variables refer to personality, i.e. studies relating religious experiences and behavior to personality variables. The choice of methods will be reported in tabular form, and the data will be compared with Dr. Klausner's. The comparison will be made only on a gross scale because of the differences in the sampling of the articles.

In the third part of this communication the question, why researchers have chosen those methods which they have chosen, will be discussed. As a basis of the discussion the concept "paradigm" will be used, which was developed by Thomas S. Kuhn (1968). "Paradigm" refers to a model which provides the researcher with a view of the world and man, theories, concepts, methodological rules and empirical results. Paradigms, as a rule, give rise to a research tradition which the individual researcher assimilates at the same time as his education. In other words, the choice of methods is a paradigm-determined activity, and in a certain method there is a theory about the result already enclosed.

In the communication an attempt will be made to outline paradigms or parts of paradigms of personality studies in psychology of religion from the methods and the characteristics of the methods chosen by the researchers. Among other things the question will be raised, as to why the researchers didn't make more extensive use of interview methods but employed of questionnaires much more than was necessary.

At last we will touch upon the important problem that researchers have possibly chosen methods which have the consequence that a deeper understanding of the relations between religion and personality will be compromised.

Formes Psychologiques des Croyances Relatives aux Dieux

par D.H. Salman

La diversité des croyances en la divinité a traditionellement été discutée du point de vue de leurs objects possibles: Dieu unique transcendant des grandes religions monothéistes, dieu suprême de l'hénothéisme ou du kathénothéisme, dieux multiples des polythéismes, etc. Et l'on explicitait ensuite des croyances en décrivant l'organisation plus ou moins complexe des panthéons correspondants. Cette façon d'aborder le problème dégage sûrement un aspect valide de ces diverses modalités du fait religieux. Elle ne tient cependant compte que de l'aspect cognitif des attitudes, et donc des différences dans les manières de penser le divin. La croyance est pourtant une attitude psychologique beaucoup plus complexe, qui comprend bien d'autres composantes. Et c'est en explicitant l'ensemble de ces facteurs que nous voudrions reformuler ici le problème des croyances relatives aux dieux en des termes qui nous semblent mieux rendre compte des attitudes religieuses en jeu.

Nous interprèterons la croyance par la notion, classique en psychologie, d'attitude, en laquelle on reconnait communément trois composantes: l'une cognitive, la deuxième affective, la dernière opératoire. Cette attitude est ici celle du croyant à l'égard de ses dieux, et relève donc d'un style en général interpersonnel; et toujours elle en conservera quelques aspects puisqu'elle engage la personne du croyant à l'égard de l'Ultime et de l'Absolu.

Une première composante concernera donc le contenu cognitif de la croyance: dieu créateur ou organisateur, tout-puissant ou non, omniscient ou non, unique ou partageant son règne avec d'autres, personnel ou impersonnel, etc. Une deuxième composante concernera les facteurs affectifs de l'attitude, et donc la dévotion plus ou moins personnelle et plus ou moins exclusive du croyant. Outre la foi des grandes religions monothéistes, la *bhakti* hindouiste et la foi salvatrice de l'Amidisme en seraient des exemples, aussi bien que la confiance dans le dieu familier des cultes de possession de l'Ouest Africain. La troisième composante concerne le culte rendu et la prière. Et ces pratiques permettent elles aussi de définir l'attitude du croyant à l'égard du dieu, selon qu'on estime que ce dieu transcende ce culte ou qu'il est seul digne de latrie, ou encore que l'on distribue de manière calculée les oblations et les sacrifices entre de multiples divinités.

Les croyances particulières correspondront à l'intégration des modalités spécifiques des trois composantes signalées. Pour en achever l'analyse, il faudra toutefois tenir compte encore d'un quatrième facteur significatif, qui concerne les exigences du dieu, telles qu'elles apparaissent au croyant. Les obligations ainsi ressenties, qui son typiques d'une relation interpersonnelle, demeurent pourtant compatibles avec un ordre du monde impersonnel, comme dans le Bouddhisme Théravada, le Samkhya médiéval ou le stoïcisme d'un Marc-Aurèle. Selon les cas cependant, le dieu peut être indifférent à l'égard de la morale individuelle ou sociale, il en règle des aspects particuliers, ou il en contrôle l'ensemble. Quand des dieux multiples sont reconnus, ils peuvent jouer en ces matières des rôles différents. Et cette dimension aussi est caractéristique de l'attitude psychologique à l'égard du divin. La croyance relative aux dieux comporte donc quatre dimensions, dont il faudra tenir compte si l'on veut adéquatement en expliciter le complexe contenu.

Un dernier aspect du problème doit encore être signalé, qui concerne la distribution sociale des croyances. En bien des cultures, les croyances de la grande tradition des spécialistes du sacré seront fort différentes de celles de la petite tradition de la religion populaire. Et ces différences seront plus manifestes encore si l'on tient compte de leurs composantes culturelles, dévotionnelles et morales, en même temps que de leur dimension proprement cognitive.

Möglichkeit und Grenze religionspsychologischer
Interpretierung des Neuen Testaments

von Ottfried Kietzig

Einleitung: Der Charakter der Texte.

Barth unterscheidet an der Offenbarung die objektive und subjektive Offenbarungswirklichkeit. Die objektive Offenbarung *kommt*, sagt K. Barth, zum Menschen. Sie wird vom Menschen erkannt und anerkannt. Mit dieser Menschwerdung verwandelt sich die Offenbarung in eine Erlebniswirklichkeit, die dem Exegeten sachgemäss ein dieser Wirklichkeit entsprechendes Verständnis, d.h. auch eine religionspsychologische Betrachtungsweise abnötigt. Solche Überlegungen berechtigen uns zu unserer Themastellung. Wir wollen dabei den Ausdruck "religionspsychologisch" zunächst nicht schulmässig einengen. Wir gehen ganz allgemein davon aus, dass mit Religionspsychologie eine Frömmigkeitssicht gemeint ist, die sich auf den Zeugnischarakter der Texte erstreckt. Als solche kommt sie schon seit jeher in der Auslegung vor.

Die Anwendung religionspsychologischer, an der Frömmigkeit interessierter Gesichtspunkte in der neutestamentlichen Exegese wird festgestellt:

1. in der Exegese der Reformatoren

a) in der Auslegung des *Magnificat* durch Luther Lk. 1, 46-51, wo die auf den Frömmigkeitsgehalt gerichtete Textauslegung sich äussert α) in der stilistichen Kontrastierung, β) in der Auflockerung des Textes durch den Gebrauch von Beispielen, γ) in der persönlichen Zuspitzung der Textaussage.

b) Es schliesst sich eine ähnliche Untersuchung der Auslegung Melanchthons (Römer, 1. u. 2. Korinther) an. Diese bei der Auslegung herrschende psychologische Intention wird weiter verfolgt

2. in der Erfahrungstheologie bei J. Chr. R. v. Hofmann.

Hier begegnet uns die religionspsychologische Betrachtungsweise in der Bewertung der *Verschiedenheit* der evangelischen Berichterstattung trotz des gleichen heilsgeschichtlichen Themas (Jesus) und in dem Verständnis für die Verschiedenartigkeit der jeweiligen religiösen Lage, nach der sich die religiöse Aussage richtet. Es verschwinden in dieser Sicht die Lehrbegrifflichen Abgrenzungen von *pistis* bei Paulus, Hebräer und Jakobus.

3. Einen bewussten Vertreter und Förderer findet die psychologischreligionspsychologische Textinterpretierung erst an A. Deissmann, dem in diesem Zusammenhang ein dritter Abschnitt gewidnet ist.

4. Ein vierter Abschnitt fragt nach dem Beitrag der sogenannten "Biblischen Psychologie" zum Thema religionspsychologischer Interpretierung: Friedrich Roos, *Fundamenta Psychologiäe ex sacra scriptura collecta*, 1769; I. T. Beck, *Umriss der biblischen Seelenlehre*, 1862; und Franz Delitzsch, *Biblische Psychologie*, Leipzig 1861 (2. Aufl.).

Charakteristisch für die sog. Biblische Psychologie ist ein dreifaches:

a) man kann sie als *nacherlebende* und die neutestamentlichen Erlebnisweisen nachbildende Psychologie bezeichnen;

b) sie zeigt, dass die psychologische Beschäftigung mit den neutestamentlichen Texten nicht auf eine Psychologisierung und Modernisierung hinauswill und die Offenbarungswerte in keiner Weise abschwächt;

c) sie bleibt an die philologische Exegese gebunden, macht aber andrerseits auf neue Probleme wie etwa die Frage der Bekehrung des Paulus, die der Glossolalie u.ä.m. aufmerksam.

5. Die Möglichkeit der religionspsychologischen Interpretierung heute wird aufgezeigt: an Luk. 1, 26-35 mit der Reduzierung des Jungfrauenmythus auf das entsprechende Jüngererlebnis der göttlichen Präsenz Jesu, etwa nach Luk. 5, 8. Ferner an Joh. 2, 1-11 mit der Auflösung des Weingoldmythus in ein hintergründiges Christuserlebnis, etwa nach Phil. 4, 4. Schlieszlich an den Ostergeschichten mit der auf Grund religionspsychologischer Beobachtung festgestellten objektiven Gewiszheit von der Auferstehung Jesu, die in den Jüngererlebnissen aller Zeiten enthalten ist.

6. Die *Erprobung* der religionspsychologischen Interpretierung wird an zwei Beispielen aus den Schriftzeugnissen bei Johannes und Paulus andrerseits durchgeführt: Carl Schneider, *Die Erlebnisechtheit der Apokalypse Johannes*, 1930; O. Kietzig, *Die Bekehrung des Paulus, religionsgeschichtlich und religionspsychologisch neu untersucht*, 1932.

7. Die Grenzen der Anwendung religionspsychologischer Methoden auf die neutestamentlichen Texte ergeben sich

a) vom Text her (Beschränkung auf Erlebnisbereiche, Respektierung der Transcendenz),

b) von der Psychologie her (Ablehnung einer nivellierenden Psychologie, z.B. Psychoanalyse).

Moderne Methoden für die Religionspsychologie

von W. Arnold

Für die Zukunft wird die religionspsychologische Forschung im Rahmen der wissenschaftlichen Psychologie und die religions-psychologische Praxis im Rahmen der Seelsorge eine stärkere Beachtung finden, ja finden müssen.

Der Hauptgrund für diesen Anstoss ist das Bedürfnis der Menschen, in der seelsorgerischen Betreuung auch psychologische und psychagogische Hilfen zu erhalten. Deshalb müssen die Seelsorger aller Religionen und Konfessionen mehr als bisher den Fortschritt in den für sie bedeutsamen Grenzgebieten der Wissenschaften, insbesondere auf den Gebieten der Psychologie und der Didaktik, zur Kenntnis nehmen und danach seelsorgerlich praktizieren. Drei Themenbereiche treten in Anbetracht dieser Zukunftsaufgabe in den Vordergrund:

1. Die sozialpsychologische Erhebung mit den statistischen Sicherungen.

2. Die individual-psychologische Diagnose unter Berücksichtigung moderner diagnostischer Möglichkeiten (operationale und phänomenologisch-anthropologische).

3. Die Gruppen- oder Einzel-Erziehung und -Therapie. Hier ist besonders das persönliche Gespräch (die Exploration in ihren verschiedenen Applikationsmöglichkeiten) zu pflegen.

In allen drei Bereichen stehen sich phänomenologische und operationale Methoden als komplementäre Möglichkeiten, also in gegenseitiger Ergänzung, einander gegenüber; sie müssen sich für die Zukunft miteinander verbinden, wenn die Religionspsychologie fruchtbar werden soll.

God in Psychedelic Religion

by C. Douglas Gunn

The outlines of psychedelic religion formed around the drug experience of youth in the United States are beginning to become clear. There are several psychedelic churches committed to mind-expanding sacraments. We also have much personal testimony in books on the drug experience, underground newspapers, and from interviews with students. I offer the following generalizations about the place and nature of God in these cults as they appear today.

Three main emphases or views of the deity may be elaborated:

I. The first is a radical acceptance on the part of many "turned-on" people of an immanent deity. They — the "turned-on" people — *are* God. This kind of talk takes two main forms:

a) Those who talk in overtly mystical, mostly Eastern terms. These people have adopted Hindu or Buddhist terminology to speak of themselves as God. They claim that for them, the drug experience was some sort of enlightenment, analogous (or identical?) with Zen satori, Hindu samadhi, etc. Most who talk like this have read popular books on Eastern religions — Hesse, Suzuki, Watts, etc. In this sense, the self-god seems to be directly imported from such popular writings; the drug seems to have acted as a catalyst triggering belief.

b) The most interesting group of psychedelic gods are those people who now take seriously the practical implications of the claim, and try to be the best gods possible. Half in jest, half in seriousness, the ecologically minded, "turned-on" set take up the challenge to be gods or supermen, and are trying through invention, technological innovation, and Yankee ingenuity to re-make society.

II. The second emphasis is a rediscovery of gods of nature. The classics of the hippies illustrate this trend: The Martian-raised hero of Robert Heinlein's *Stranger in a Strange Land* confronts even blades of grass as sentient beings; Carlos Castaneda's *Teachings of Don Juan* pictures Mescalito, the god of peyote, as a mischievous sprite, playing with whomever he favors. The point is not merely the trend in such literature, but in the direction taken by the community which finds spiritual nourishment in these writings: the nature mysticism that finds gods in all natural phenomena (and particularly in psychedelic plants) is very strong. This is a most romantic notion of deity, and a direct challenge to prevailing forms of Western monotheism.

III. A third emphasis is only now appearing. There seems to be growing a reaction to the psychedelic movement from the

Christian side. So far, this has come only fringe fundamentalist groups — those with enough of a tradition of enthusiasm to relate to psychedelic turning-on. The more staid Protestant and Catholic churches have been notably silent in relating to the new claims of the drug-mystics. But just within the last year we are seeing bands of fundamentalist reformed drug-takers who claim that they "get a better high with Jesus", and that they gave up drugs for Christ because he turns them on better. The process of assimilation (or attempted assimilation) of the new religion by the old has begun; whether or not the Christian church can indeed convince the psychedelic world that Jesus will turn them on better than drugs remains to be seen. What this development implies for Christian notions of God is not worked out by the new brand of turned-on fundamentalist youths. It appears, however, that God again remains on the periphery of this religious tradition — eclipsed by the turn-on experience itself.

I conclude that psychedelic religion offers evidence that the monotheistic God of history is fast becoming a *deus otiosus* among the American counter culture.

PART THREE

PAPERS PRESENTED AT THE CONGRESS

LE KATHÉNOTHÉISME DES SÉMITES DE L'OUEST
D'APRÉS LEURS NOMS DE PERSONNE

ANDRÉ CAQUOT

En esquissant une classification des noms propres de personne, Cléarque de Soli, disciple d'Aristote, a distingué "les noms athées tels que Kléonymos et les noms théophores tels que Dionysios".[1] L'étude des noms théophores, ou onomastique religieuse, mérite de retenir l'attention des historiens des religions, car ces anthroponymes sont dérivés ou composés de noms divins dont quelquesuns peuvent être absents des documents laissés par les religions mortes. Même si les divinités ainsi attestées paraissent ne plus recevoir de culte au moment historique où ces religions commencent à être entrevues, leur souvenir persiste dans les anthroponymes, en vertu du caractère conservateur de l'onomastique. On sait le parti qu'ont tiré de l'onomastique religieuse Herrmann Usener dans ses *Götternamen,* pour certains secteurs du domaine indo-européen, et Julius Wellhausen dans ses *Reste arabischen Heidentums* (1887), pour reconstituer le monde divin de l'Arabie préislamique. Ces deux livres illustres se donnaient pour tâche de dresser des listes de dieux complétant celles que fournissent les autres sources, littéraires ou épigraphiques. Ils constituent des contributions à ce qu'on peut appeler l'histoire des cultes dans des polythéismes caractérisés. Mais l'examen de l'onomastique religieuse permet de satisfaire d'autres curiosités, si l'on consent à ne pas restreindre l'histoire des religions antiques à des inventaires de noms divins abolis.

L'historien des religions sémitiques occidentales ne manque pas d'instruments de travail lui permettant d'aborder cette étude. S'il ne dispose pas d'un relevé aussi ample que les *Ägyptische Personennamen* d'Herrmann Ranke (1935-1952), il peut utiliser plusieurs monographies et répertoires onomastiques établis pour divers secteurs d'un domaine très morcelé dans l'espace et dans le temps. Le matériel est sans cesse enrichi par de nouvelles découvertes, mais il ne semble pas que celles-ci doivent modifier les

---

[1] Athénée, *Deipnosophiste*, éd. Kaibel, X, 448 *e.*

conclusions qu'on peut retirer de la consultation des répertoires déjà élaborés. Sans prétendre être exhaustif, je crois devoir rappeler les titres de quelquesuns de ces ouvrages de référence, inventaires de noms propres accompagnés de leur interprétation, qui constituent des sources non négligeables pour l'histoire des religions.

Pour les Sémites occidentaux du second millénaire avant J.C., on dispose de deux compilations récentes: les noms propres attestés par les textes de Mari ont été recueillis en 1965 dans les *Amorite Personal Names in the Mari Texts* de Herbert B. Huffmon, qui n'a malheureusement pas pu intégrer le riche matériel onomastique apporté par le tome XIII des *Archives royales de Mari*, publié en 1964 par Georges Dossin; les tablettes syllabiques et alphabétiques de Ras Shamra-Ougarit constituent la seconde mine de noms de personne, rassemblés en 1967 par Frauke Grøndahl dans ses *Personennamen der Texte aus Ugarit*. D'autres listes de noms propres amorites ont été dressées, ainsi par Giorgio Buccellati (*The Amorites of the Ur III Period*, 1966) et I. Gelb ("An Old Babylonian List of Amorites", *J.A.O.S.*, 88, 1968, p. 39-46). Pour les Sémites du Nord-Ouest au premier millénaire avant J.C., les découvertes d'inscriptions ont considérablement accru ce que Mark Lidzbarski avait pu faire figurer dans l'index du *Handbuch der nordsemitischen Epigraphik* (1897) et des trois volumes de l'*Ephemeris für semitische Epigraphik* (1900-1915). L'onomastique n'a été jusqu'à présent étudiée systématiquement que pour deux secteurs: Palmyre (Jürgen K. Stark, *Personal Names in Palmyrene Inscriptions*, 1971) et l'aire phénico-punique (Frank L. Benz, *Personal Names in the Phoenician and Punic Inscriptions*, 1972). Pour les autres secteurs, on est encore contraint de recourir soit à des index accompagnant les recueils de documents (pour l'onomastique d'Eléphantine, par exemple, on peut utiliser l'excellent index onomastique joint par P. Grelot à ses *Documents araméens d'Égypte*, 1972), soit à des lexiques spécialisés comme celui du *Nabatéen* de J. Cantineau, paru en 1932 et très incomplet aujourd'hui. Il n'existe pas encore de répertoire complet des noms de personne révélés par les inscriptions sigillaires alphabétiques, bien qu'un abondant matériel ait été recueilli par Kurt Galling ("Beschriftete Bildsiegel des ersten Jahrtausends", *Z.D.P.V.*, 64, 1941, p. 121-202) et, pour le secteur hébraïque par D. Diringer (*Le iscrizioni antico-ebraiche palestinesi*, 1934), S. Moscati (*L'epigrafia ebraica antica*, 1951) et F. Vattioni ("I sigilli ebraici", *Biblica*, 50, 1969, p. 357-388); le dernier auteur a également rassemblé les données onomastiques des petites épigraphes araméennes ("I sigilli, le monete e gli avori aramaici", *Augustinianum*, 11, 1971, p. 47-87). On ne doit pas négliger les inscriptions grecques et latines de Syrie, où abondent les noms propres sémitiques, et il faut tenir à jour le répertoire composé en 1930 par H. Wuthnow (*Die semitischen Menschen-*

namen in griechischen Inschriften und Papyri des vorderen Orients);
pour cela, il est commode de compulser les index des sept volumes
parus des *Inscriptions grecques et latines de la Syrie* rédigés par
L. Jalabert et R. Mouterde, puis par C. Mondésert et J.P. Rey-Coquais.
Un inventaire complet des noms propres connus à Doura-Europos est
vivement souhaité. Les données onomastiques de l'Arabie sont maintenant plus aisément accessibles grâce au volumineux *Index and Concordance of Pre-islamic Arabian Names and Inscriptions* de G. Lankester Harding qui reprend, en les corrigeant et en les complétant, *Les
noms propres sud-sémitiques* de Gonzague Ryckmans (1934), ainsi
que les apports des grands recueils d'épigraphie thamoudéenne (travaux d'A. van den Branden et F.V. Winnett) et safaïtique (*Pars quinta*
du *Corpus inscriptionum semiticarum*, publications d'E. Littmann,
F.V. Winnett et G. Lankester Harding).

Les listes de noms propres ne représentent qu'un matériau brut
qu'il convient d'élaborer pour en dégager l'intérêt historico-linguis-
tique et historico-religieux, grâce en particulier à la comparaison qui
fait ressortir les constantes et les variables de l'onomastique dans l'aire
considérée. Le livre de Martin Noth, *Die israelitischen Personennamen
im Rahmen der gemeinsemitischen Namengebung* (1928), est bien
plus que l'inventaire des noms israélites connus par la Bible et par
d'autres documents. C'est l'exemple même d'une étude onomastique
totale qu'il serait utile de reprendre et d'élargir en tenant compte de
toutes les informations nouvelles fournies par l'épigraphie sémitique.

Toutes les onomastiques sémitiques occidentales montrent la
coexistence d'anthroponymes théophores et d'anthroponymes
athées, ces derniers consistant, comme ailleurs, en noms dérivés
de toponymes, en noms de métiers et surtout en sobriquets (des
particularités physiques ou morales). Il ne semble pas que la distinction établie par Cléarque de Soli corresponde à quelque différence de niveau social des porteurs de noms: à Palmyre, des
aristocrates peuvent porter des noms athées et des affranchis recevoir des noms théophores. La proportion de noms athées et de
noms théophores dans un secteur donné est révélatrice à un autre
titre. L'ancien arabe, épigraphique et littéraire, montre que les
noms athées ont été beaucoup plus nombreux dans l'Arabie centrale préislamique que les noms théophores et que ces derniers
sont du type le plus rudimentaire: un syntagme génitival expri-
mant que le porteur du nom est le "serviteur" (ᶜ *abd, taym*) de la
divinité. En revanche, les inscriptions de l'Arabie méridionale,
sabéennes, minéennes, qatabanites etc. révèlent une proportion
plus considérable de noms théophores, ayant souvent la structure
d'une petite phrase où le nom divin est accompagné d'un prédicat

nominal ou verbal qui indique une manière d'être ou d'agir de la divinité. Les anthroponymes présentant cette structure sont également fréquents chez les Sémites du Nord-Ouest, Amorites, Hébreux, Phéniciens, Araméens etc. Le contraste entre l'onomastique arabe et l'onomastique sud-arabe a inspiré des considérations d'ordre génétique: selon M. Noth,[2] les "noms-phrases", qui sont les plus chargés de signification religieuse, apparaissent au terme d'une évolution enrichissante; selon H.H. Bräu,[3] au contraire, la prédominance des anthroponymes athées et des théophores de structure rudimentaire en Arabie septentrionale et centrale manifeste un appauvrissement du patrimoine primitif. Ces considérations, inspirées par des hypothèses sur la diffusion et la diversification des cultures sémitiques, ne sont guère vérifiables. On préférera se borner à une constatation: la religion tenait plus de place chez les Arabes méridionaux que chez leurs congénères du Nord, fait peu surprenant si l'on pense à la différence radicale de leurs organisations sociales, différence qui se reflète dans leurs systèmes divergents du sacrifice, par exemple.[4]

L'onomastique religieuse, si développée chez les Arabes méridionaux et les Sémites du Nord-Ouest, apporte des renseignements sur la manière dont était conçu le rapport de l'homme à la divinité. Pour reprendre le titre d'un chapitre du livre de M. Noth, elle permet d'étudier "die Personennnamen als Äusserungen der Frömmigkeit". La démarche est légitime parce que les noms propres sémitiques sont la plupart du temps intelligibles, transparents, sans qu'il faille exclure la possibilité de réinterprétations (ainsi pour les noms composés avec le verbe ᶜqb). Les noms propres avaient un sens pour ceux qui les donnaient et les portaient, et ce sens nous demeure le plus souvent perceptible. L'adage d'Hérodien, "on ne doit pas considérer les étymologies des noms propres", ne peut être pris au pied de la lettre par les sémitisants qui n'hésitent pas à traduire les noms de personne, tout comme les Babyloniens traduisaient les anthroponymes cassites, ainsi qu'en fait foi un de leurs vocabulaires bilingues.[5]

---

[2] *Die israelitischen Personennamen*, p. 52 sq.
[3] "Die altarabischen kultischen Personennamen", *W.Z.K.M.*, 33 (1925), p. 31-59 et 85-115, en particulier p. 107.
[4] Voir J. Henninger, "Das Opfer in den altsüdarabischen Hochkulturen", *Anthropos*, 37-40 (1942-45), p. 779-810.
[5] Voir K. Balkan, *Kassitenstudien I. Die Sprache der Kassiten* (1954), p. 2 sq.

James Barr,[6] dont on connaît la méfiance à l'endroit des étymologies, a rappelé que les noms propres sémitiques étaient intelligibles, à la différence des nôtres, qui ont très rarement une signification intrinsèque, parceque en surtout à une onomastique de référence, à des noms qui ne signifient plus rien et n'ont d'autre titre à la survie que d'avoir été portés par des personnages du passé, saints du calendrier ou autres. Quand le fils posthume du duc de Berry reçut en 1820 les noms de Henri-Charles-Ferdinand-Marie-Dieudonné, seul le dernier a un contenu religieux précis et pertinent, les autres ne sont que des références à des personnages du passé, références entretenues par des traditions familiales (le prince porte, en particulier, le nom de chacun de ses grands pères, Charles et Ferdinand). Les Sémites ont pratiqué la dénomination par référence au grand père, ou papponymie, mais c'est pratiquement le seul principe de référence. Si grande que fût la place d'Abraham, de Moïse ou de David dans la tradition nationale, on ne connaît pas dans l'Antiquité d'Israélites qui aient repris leurs noms (la situation change dans le judaïsme, devenu une "religion du Livre"). On ne connaît que trois individus, à Eléphantine, aux environs de 300 avant J.C., appelés du nom, archaïque et devenu opaque, de Juda.[7] Rien ne permet de croire que la renommée d'Odeinat à Palmyre ait mis son nom à la mode.[8]

Papponymes ou non, traditionnels ou non au sein d'une famille, les anthroponymes sémitiques conservaient presque tous le même sens pour ceux qui les portaient que pour leurs ancêtres. Dans la mesure où ils ont un contenu religieux, celui-ci ne peut donc être tenu pour un témoignage sur une religiosité depuis longtemps éteinte. Les noms ne survivaient pas comme des reliquats vidés de leur sens, ils demeuraient comme des témoins d'une piété vivante, et leur témoignage ne s'est tu que lors du grand changement introduit dans la région par le triomphe du christianisme, puis par celui de l'Islam, qui ont imposé les noms faisant référence à leurs saints.

C'est le contenu religieux des noms propres significatifs qu'il

---

[6] "The Symbolism of the Names in the O.T.", *B.J.R.L.*, 52 (1969-70), p. 11-29.

[7] A. E. Cowley, *Aramaic Papyri of the Fifth Century B.C.*, 1923, n° 81, lignes 78, 96 et 132.

[8] Contrairement à l'opinion d'Enno Littmann (*Thamūd und Ṣafā*, 1940, p. 104), il est douteux que le nom d'Odeinat, attesté environ quatre-vingt fois dans les graffiti safaïtiques, ait été attribué en hommage à la gloire du prince palmyrénien.

faut maintenant analyser brièvement. Les théophores sémitiques se présentent sous deux formes. Les uns consistent en syntagmes génitivaux qualifiant la personne comme appartenant au dieu, comme son serviteur, ou son client, ou son fils, ou sa fille. Il n'est pas toujours facile de préciser l'intention religieuse sous-jacente dans les noms de cette catégorie. O. Eissfeldt[9] a suggéré que dans les noms du type *bn ᶜnt, br hdd*, le composant divin ne représente pas la personne divine, mais une qualité qui est par excellence celle de la divinité. Autrement dit, *bn ᶜnt* ne signifierait pas "fils de ᶜAnat", mais "guerrier aussi valeureux que la déesse ᶜAnat". On objectera qu'il est difficile de distinguer le contenu religieux des noms signifiant "fils du dieu X" et celui des innombrables anthroponymes qu'il faut traduire "le dieu X est un/mon père", de même qu'on ne peut séparer le nom propre phénicien *mtnbᶜl*, "don de Baᶜal", de *bᶜlytn*, "Baᶜal a donné", Si un homme est appelé "fils d'un dieu X", ce pourrait être pour exprimer la croyance que le dieu est responsable de l'existence de l'individu, qu'il le fait naître (cf. le nom hébreu *bᵉrå'yåh*, "YHWH a crée"). Mais la relation de filiation impliquée par ces anthroponymes risque d'être une simple métaphore pour la protection constante accordée à l'homme par la divinité. Ce qui invite à écarter l'idée de génération physique est qu'un dieu — un dieu mâle, et non une déesse — peut être qualifié de "mère" aussi bien que de "père": on rencontre à Ougarit *ᶜṯtr'um*, "ᶜAthtar est mère", à côté de *ᶜṯtr'ab*, "ᶜAthtar est père",[10] et le nom palmyrénien *bwlm'*, transcrit en grec *Bôlemmês*, s'interprète "(le dieu) Bôl est mère"[11]. Ce genre de nom propre cristallise une expression de piété connue dans la Bible où YHWH est plusieurs fois désigné comme "père" d'Israël, mais où l'épithète *mᵉholᵉ-lékå*, "qui t'a enfanté", de *Deutéronome* 32, 18, indique que les Israélites concevaient aussi leur relation avec la divinité sous l'image du lien de fils à mère.

La seconde catégorie de théophores, ceux qui ont la forme d'une petite phrase nominale ou verbale, présente des contenus religieux plus faciles à dégager. Je n'exploiterai pour cela que des

---

[9] "Gottesnamen in Personennamen als Symbole menschlicher Qualität", *Festschrift Walter Baetke* (1966), p. 110-117.

[10] Voir F. Grøndahl, *Die Personennamen der Texte aus Ugarit* (1967), p. 113.

[11] Voir sur ce nom H. Ingholt et J. Starcky dans J. Schlumberger, *La Palmyrène du Nord-Ouest* (1951), p. 150.

noms propres qui nous sont encore aussi intelligibles qu'à ceux qui les ont portés il y a des millénaires. Le répertoire des prédicats accompagnant les noms divins n'est pas illimité et se signale par son homogénéité et sa constance, depuis les plus anciens anthroponymes occidentaux connus par des documents accadiens depuis la fin du IIIe millénaire jusqu'aux noms sémitiques de Palmyre, Doura-Europos et Hatra, au début de notre ère. Le répertoire est limité, car il s'agit toujours de célébrer la providence manifestée par le dieu à celui qui porte ou qui donne le nom. Ce sont des expressions de reconnaissance, de confiance ou de prière, parfois très concrètes: le dieu est rendu responsable de la vie de l'homme, il le fait, le fait être, le crée, l'établit, le prend dans ses mains. Certains semblent insister sur la faveur divine que constitue pour les parents la venue de l'enfant: le dieu donne, accroît, accorde en échange. Tel doit être aussi le sens précis des noms signifiant que le dieu bénit ou guérit. D'autres anthroponymes célèbrent le bienfait divin, reçu ou espéré, de manière plus vague, de sorte qu'on ignore s'il s'agit d'une manifestation ponctuelle ou constante de la providence. Ainsi les noms qu'il faut traduire "le dieu connaît, se souvient, voit, écoute, favorise, sauve, garde, rachète, aime, rétribue, rend justice, est avec le fidèle etc." Cette catégorie, très riche, de noms théophores manifeste en tout cas le caractère subjectif, ou anthropocentrique, de la piété sémitique.

A côté de ces noms "subjectifs", il existe des noms définissables comme "objectifs" en ce sens qu'ils paraissent énoncer sur la divinité autre chose que ce qu'elle est par rapport à l'homme ou ce qu'elle fait pour lui. L'existence de ces noms est bien connue en Égypte, où l'on trouve des anthroponymes consistant en une assertion d'ordre général sur le dieu, ou rappelant des moments de la vie cultuelle (noms de personne du type "Horus est né"). Chez les Sumériens de la IIIe dynastie d'Our, comme chez les Égyptiens, on rencontre des noms propres qui définissent une relation entre le dieu et le roi, et non entre le dieu et le simple fidèle. [12] Faut-il tenir pour des noms "objectifs" les anthroponymes sémitiques signifiant que le dieu est grand, puissant, élevé, qu'il est "le seigneur", "le roi", ou simplement "le dieu"? Ou bien, ces noms disent-ils la grandeur du dieu parce que le fidèle l'a éprouvée ou espère l'éprouver dans sa vie? Il paraît cer-

---

[12] Voir H. Limet, *L'anthroponymie sumérienne dans les documents de la 3e dynastie d'Ur* (1968), p. 173.

tain que le titre de "roi", souvent donné dans les noms de personne, n'implique pas que le dieu qui le reçoit soit un souverain de l'univers ou des autres dieux selon le système religieux. L'onomastique ougaritique confère le titre de "roi" à une divinité insignifiante dans le panthéon comme ʿAthtar, et au dieu Rashap inconnu dans la mythologie. Si un dieu est appelé "lumière", ce n'est pas parce qu'il est de nature solaire ou astrale. Certes on trouve à Eléphantine *šmšnwry*, "Shamash (le dieu solaire) est ma lumière", mais le palmyrénien *nwrbl* ne signifie pas que le grand dieu Bêl soit une divinité solaire, et les noms israélites *ʾuryåh* ou *néryåh* ne confèrent pas davantage ce caractère au YHWH biblique. La lumière n'est pas un attribut physique de la divinité. C'est une image concrète dont Sverre Ålen[13] a montré la signification dans la littérature israélite et juive: il s'agit d'une métaphore pour le salut dont l'homme bénéficie. Les noms de personne donnant à un dieu le qualificatif "lumière" peuvent être rangés avec ceux qu'il faut traduire "le dieu X est un rocher" ou "un rempart", noms qui évoquent à leur tour d'autres expressions de la piété des *Psaumes*.

Ces considérations invitent à ne pas solliciter le témoignage des noms de personne pour compléter ce qu'enseigne la mythologie, quand il y en a une, ou pour suppléer à l'absence de mythologie (comme ont voulu le faire plusieurs historiens des religions de l'Arabie méridionale). Elles mettent aussi en garde contre les tentatives d'expliquer un théophore d'interprétation difficile par ce que la mythologie apprend sur le dieu figurant dans le nom.[14] Elles suggèrent enfin que l'existence de noms théophores "objectifs" n'est pas assurée chez les Sémites de l'Ouest. Ceux-là même qui en ont l'apparence doivent exprimer, en réalité, une relation du dieu à l'homme, relation indépendante de toute mythologie. Ce que M. Noth a écrit des noms de personne israélites, "es handelt sich hier um den breiten Strom der Volksfrömmigkeit, der immer da ist und seit alter Zeit da war, den auch Erlebnisse, wie sie Israel am Sinai hatte, nicht beseitigten",[15] vaut pour d'autres points de notre domaine: le Baʿal des noms propres ougaritiques

---

[13] *Die Begriffe "Licht" und "Finsternis" im A.T., im Spätjudentum und im Rabbinismus* (1951).

[14] J'ai présenté quelques remarques à ce sujet en recensant l'ouvrage de F. Grøndahl (*Syria*, 46, 1969, p. 254-262).

[15] *Die israelitischen Personennamen*, p. 218.

n'est pas le combattant au destin pathétique qui meurt et revient à la vie; le Bêl des noms propres palmyréniens n'est pas le
dieu cosmique trônant entre les deux grands astres. Baᶜal et Bêl
sont ici les seigneurs de leur fidèle et sa providence. Quant à
l'élément ʾl, qui apparaît partout, il ne désigne pas comme dans la
mythologie ougaritique le chef du panthéon; quand il est sujet, ce
peut être l'appellatif se substituant au nom propre d'un dieu,
quand il est prédicat d'un nom divin, c'est vraisemblablement le
dieu personnel.

Selon les noms théophores, chaque dieu peut être un père ou
un roi, chaque dieu bénit, guérit, voit, entend, sauve, donne etc.
Aucun théophore ne permet de soupçonner la place qu'occupait
dans le panthéon le dieu qu'il mentionne (le seul indice révélant
la prééminence locale d'une divinité est la fréquence de son nom
dans les anthroponymes: YHWH en Israël, Qaws chez les Édomi-
tes etc.). Ce que l'onomastique manifeste, c'est la constance
d'une expression de piété chez les Sémites de l'Ouest à travers
leur longue histoire et dans leurs différents rameaux. Le "breite
Strom der Volksfrömmigkeit" dont parle M. Noth prend-il sa
source dans un "monothéisme primitif" que le polythéisme et la
mythologie auraient éclipsé dans les religions constituées? Je l'ignore. Nous ne connaissons la plupart des religions sémitiques que
sous la forme de polythéismes différenciés (en raison de la disper-
sion et du particularisme des groupes sémitiques) et probablement structurés, comme l'était le polythéisme ougaritique, le seul
qui présente une mythologie. Mais il apparaît que derrière une
diversité foisonnante de cultes se trouve une attitude religieuse
simple et constante, celle que reflètent les anthroponymes théophores. Là, on se tourne vers un dieu quelconque s'il était le dieu
par excellence, le dieu qui agit pour le bien de son fidèle. C'est
l'attitude kathénothéiste.

Un article suggestif de Morton Smith [16] a proposé de retrouver
ce qu'il appelle "the common theology of the ancient Near East"
dans les formules "orientales" (égyptiennes, mésopotamiennes,
hittites) de l'hymne et de la prière, formules qui ne varient guère,
quelle que soit la divinité à laquelle on s'adresse, et il voit là le
substrat de la "théologie" biblique, trop souvent ramenée à une
monolâtrie, ou hénothéisme, dont l'inspiration nationaliste ne

---

[16] "The Common Theology of the Ancient Near East", *J.B.L.*, 71 (1952),
p. 135-147.

doit pas être mésestimée. Morton Smith rejoint, sans trop y penser, certaines des conclusions fameuses auxquelles l'étude des hymnes védiques avaient conduit F. Max Müller et pour lesquelles il avait forgé le terme "kathénothéisme". Alfred Bertholet avait déjà évoqué la position de Max Müller en traitant des hymnes assyro-babyloniens. [17] Mais le kathénothéisme des prières et des hymnes, dont la forme est savamment élaborée, pourrait passer pour la création de penseurs religieux, de "philosophes primitifs" en train de découvrir le monothéisme, sinon pour une pure convention littéraire. L'humble témoignage des noms de personne invite à considérér que, chez les Sémites au moins, ce kathénothéisme se situe à un niveau beaucoup plus ancien, beaucoup plus profond, et que c'est l'un des éléments de base de leur culture spirituelle. On pressent qu'à ce niveau fondamental de la religion, la divinité n'a pas été conçue à partir d'objets, fussent-ils célestes, mais qu'elle a été découverte dans les contingences de l'expérience individuelle.

---

[17]   *Die Religion in Geschichte und Gegenwart* [2], II (1928), col. 1803.

GOTT IST KÖNIG

Königssymbolismus in den antiken Gottesvorstellungen,
besonders in der Religion des alten Ägypten

J. ZANDEE

Die Anwendung des Prädikats "König" auf Gott ist vom Alten Testament her bekannt. Sie findet sich besonders in den Thron-besteigungsliedern, zum Beispiel in Psalm 47:

> "Unter Jauchzen stieg Gott empor,
> der Herr beim Schall der Posaune.
> Singt zu "unserem Gott", ja singt,
> singt zu unserem König, ja singt!
> Denn König aller Welt ist Gott,
> singt ihm ein machtvolles Lied!
> Ein König ward Gott über Völker,
> er thront auf seinem Heiligen Thron."

Bei den Propheten und nach dem Exil beschränkt sich die Herrschaft Jahwehs nicht auf Israel, sondern erstreckt sich über die ganze Welt. Alle Völker der Erde werden zum Herrn in Zion pilgern (Jes. 60). Die Vorstellung von Jahweh als König entwickelte sich erst als Israel in Kanaan sesshaft und mit der Satzung des Königtums in den Nachbarländern bekannt geworden war. Wenn das Volk einen irdischen König erheischt, wird man sich bewusst, dass Jahweh Israels wirklicher König ist (I Sam. 8).

In Israels Umwelt kannte man schon lange vorher die Königsprädikation in Bezug auf die Welt der Götter. In Ugarit ist El König der Götter und Vorsitzender der Götterversammlung. El war König von Ewigkeit her, und er genehmigte, dass auch Baᶜal nach dem Sieg über den Meergott Jam, die Königstitulatur annahm. Baᶜals Herrschaft war nicht nur zeitlich sondern auch räumlich beschränkt: Er herrschte nur über die Erde und über die Menschen.

Babylonien und Assyrien hatten schon von alters her ein fest gegründetes Königtum. Der himmlische Hofstaat wurde analog dem irdischen konzipiert. Der Hauptgott ist ein König, der von subalternen Göttern umgeben ist, die als seine Beamte, Minister oder sonstige Diener fungieren von Grosswesir bis Stallknecht (J. Bottéro, La religion Babylonienne, Paris, 1952, S. 64). Dem monarchischen Prinzip gemäss könnte nur ein einziger Gott König sein. Im mesopotamischen Pantheon aber empfangen viele Götter diesen Titel. Die erste Dreizahl sind die kosmischen Götter Anu, Enlil und Ea. Jeder bekommt das Königsprädikat. Anu heisst "König des Himmels", *šar šame*. Wie der irdische Fürst verfügt auch er über die Insignien, Zepter und Hirtenstab. Enlil wird schon in den ältesten sumerischen Texten "König der Länder", *luu-gal kur-kur-ra*, assyrisch *šar matâti*, genannt. Der sumerische Name des Ea ist En-ki, was "Herr der Erde" bedeutet, auf assyrisch *bêl erṣeti*. In den ältesten Texten heisst En-ki schon "König des Apsû" (Wassertiefe). Auch die astrale Dreizahl Šamaš, Sin und Ištar wird mit dem Königssymbolismus verbunden. So heisst zum Beispiel Šamaš "König der Gerechtigkeit", *šar mešari*. Der regelmässige Sonnenlauf festigt die kosmische Ordnung. Diese drückt sich in den festen Naturgesetzen und auch in den ethischen Normen aus. Deshalb ist Šamaš als König höchster Richter, *dajânu*, bei dem der Unterdrückte Hilfe sucht.

Ausser den kosmischen und den astralen Gottheiten gibt es in Mesopotamien noch die Lokalgötter, wie Marduk und Aššur. Sie sind die himmlischen Oberherren der Hauptstädte. Anu und Enlil übertragen ihre Autorität dem Marduk. Die vierte Tafel des Schöpfungsepos *Enuma eliš* beschreibt wie die Götter dem Marduk die Würdenzeichen bringen.

> "Marduk, du bist unser Rächer,
> Wir geben dir hiermit das Königtum über die Gesammtheit des ganzen Alls.
> Nimm Platz in der Versammlung, dein Wort sei da hoch erhaben."
> Dazu gaben sie ihm Zepter, Krone und Ornat,
> gaben ihm eine unbesiegliche Waffe, die die Feinde niederstösst.'

Freilich sollte hier untersucht werden, worüber sich die Königsherrschaft des Gottes erstreckt: Über die Menschen, über Babylonien, über die ganze Welt oder über den ganzen Kosmos, über Himmel und Erde. Auch ist Marduk König der Götter im Himmel. Oder sollen wir bei verschiedenen Göttern nur an eine himmlische Herrschaft über die Götter denken, und sind sie ein tranzendentes Analogon zum irdischen König, dessen Machtbereich unter den Menschen ist? Wir haben hier weder den Raum noch die Zeit, diese Fragen weiter zu erörtern, können sie nur andeuten.

Die ersten Zeilen der vierten Tafel von *Enuma cliš* lauten: "Sie stifteten für ihn einen fürstlichen Thron, damit er sich niedersetze vor seinen Vätern für die Ratschläge", *ana malikutum*. Die Wurzel *malaku* bedeutet im Akkadischen "beschliessen", "zu Rate gehen". Man fragt sich, ob die umstrittene Bedeutung des semitischen *malku, mèlèk*, König, "Berater" sein könnte. Der König hat Autorität, erhält das Land am Leben durch seine wunderbare Einsicht, seine Erkenntnis des Lebensweges.

Was Griechenland anbelangt denkt man zuerst an Zeus Basileus und an die ganze homerische Göttergesellschaft, die den Olymp bewohnt wie eine Idealpolis. Natürlich thront Zeus auf dem Gipfel des Berges wie auf einer Akropolis. Ganz unten treibt der Hephästos sein trübes Wesen wie ein schmutziger Schmidt. Schon im mykenisch-minoischen Zeitalter hatte jedes lokale Königsgeschlecht seinen eigenen Schutzgott der später als Zeus Polieus oder Athena Polias die gleiche Rolle im republikanischen Stadtstaat spielte. Die Vorstellung vom Himmelskönig muss also aus der Zeit der mykenischen Königsherrschaft stammen.

Da in Rom das Königtum ursprünglich nicht eine lateinische sondern eine etruskische Satzung war, ist es selbstverständlich, dass in der Religion der Römer das Gotteskönigtum niemals wichtig gewesen ist. Wenn Juppiter Optimus Maximus bisweilen als Himmelskönig betrachtet wird, so soll das auch von den Etruskern herrühren. Die Vorstellung von Gott als König passt zu einem personalistischen Gottesbild und dieses ist nicht original römisch. Die Römer stellten sich ihre Götter nicht als Personen vor sondern als unmittelbare Naturvorgänge. Juppiter war der klare Himmel zu dem man in direkter Weise betete und an dem man opferte. Selbst bei den späteren Tempelbauten sparte man ein Loch im Tempeldach, um den Kontakt mit dem Himmel draussen zu bewahren. So ein räumliches Gebilde wie der Himmel kann beschwerlich als König betrachtet werden.

Die auf die Gottheit angewendete Königsprädikation ist hauptsächlich aus Ägypten bekannt. Schon in den Pyramidentexten heisst es (Par. 814.c) "König Pepi hat die beiden Länder in Besitz genommen wie der König der Götter (*nsw ntrw*)". Sethe sagt in seinem Kommentar (IV, S. 53), dass an dieser Stelle der Gott Min von Koptos gemeint ist. Später ist *nsw ntrw* der bekannteste Titel des Amun-Re. Einer der heliopolitanischen Tempel hiess "Haus des Fürsten" (*ḥt sr*). Der Name ist sehr alt und Re-Atum soll also schon früh als Himmelsherrscher betrachtet worden sein. Wenn ein Ägypter sagen will, dass etwas sehr alt ist, dass es zurückge-führt werden kann zu den Urprinzipien der Welt, so sagt er, dass es schon da war "seit der Zeit des Re". In dieser Urzeit soll der Sonnengott persönlich die Königsherrschaft auf Erden geführt haben. Später hat der Pharao seine Stelle eingenommen. In den Pyramidentexten wird den Göttern befohlen sich um den verstor-benen und zum Himmel gefahrenen König zu sammeln, wie sie es für Atum tun: "O, alle ihr Götter, kommt zusammen, wie ihr versammelt und beisammen seit für Atum in Heliopolis" (Par. 1647). Die Vorstellung war also, dass der heliopolitanische Son-nengott einen Hofstaat um sich hatte, der ihm untertan war. So wird in den Sargtexten gesprochen vom "Hofstaat der um die Kapelle des Re herum ist" (C.T. I.391.b), gemeint ist die Kajüte im Sonnenschiff. Der Terminus "Hofstaat", *šnwt*, gehört zum Palastvokabular. Als sein "Hofstaat" sind die anderen Götter dem Re untergeben. Sein Königsname weist auf sein Primat hin. Wenn der Hauptgott als "König" qualifiziert wird, so ist das ein erster Schritt auf dem Wege zum Monotheismus.

Ein anderer Gott, dem ein urzeitliches Königtum zugeschrie-ben wird, ist Osiris. Bekannt ist der Rechtsstreit in Heliopolis um das Erbe des Geb. Die Frage ist: Wer sollte König sein, der feind-liche Bruder Seth, oder Horus, der Sohn des Osiris? Nach seinem Tode wurde Osiris König der Toten im unterirdischen Reich.

Während der einundzwanzigsten Dynastie (1070-945), der Zeit da in Israel das Königtum entstand, war in Theben der Gottes-staat des Amun, vielleicht die reinste Theokratie, die die Welt jemals gesehen hat. Der schwache Pharao residierte im Norden, im Delta, während im Süden die Hohepriester des Amun durch eine Militärdiktatur regierten. Gemäss dem Dogma aber war Amun selber König in Theben. Die Hohepriesterin hatte den Titel "Gottesweib des Amun" inne. So war es wenigstens seit der drei-undzwanzigsten Dynastie. Diese Königsherrschaft des Amun funktionierte auch praktisch. Durch Orakel gab der göttliche König seinen Ratschluss kund und erteilte Anweisungen für die Rechtsprechung. Exil und Amnestie, Ernennung hoher Beamter, usw. alles geschah gemäss den Entscheidungen des Königs Amun. Er war also nicht nur Götterkönig im Himmel sondern auch fak-

tisch König über die Thebaner auf Erden. Es sei hier aber bemerkt, dass es keinen grossen Unterschied zwischen dem Kosmos
und dem Lande Ägypten gab.

Die Anwendung der Königsprädikation auf den Gott Amun-Re
findet sich auch in einem unpublizierten Papyrus aus der Rames-
sidenzeit, der zur Sammlung des Reichsmuseums von Altertümer
in Leiden gehört. Die Registrationsnummer ist I 344. Die Vorder-
seite umfasst die berühmte "Mahnworte eines Propheten", 1909
von Gardiner herausgegeben unter dem Titel "Admonitions of an
Egyptian sage". Auf der Rückseite sind Hymnen an Amun-Re
geschrieben, von denen zwölf Kolumnen teilweise erhalten geblie-
ben sind. Diese Hymnen erwähnen den Gott oftmals in der
Sprache des Königssymbolismus. Am Ende der sechsten Kolumne
beginnt eine neue Strophe, die durch ein Rubrum angedeutet
wird: "Heil dir, Horus der Horusgötter, Herrscher der Herrscher,
Macht der Mächte, Älteste der Ältesten, Fürst der Ewigkeit, Herr
der Herren, Gott der Götter, König der Könige von Nieder-
Ägypten, König von Ober-Ägypten, Souverän der Ewigkeit"
(VI.9-VII.1). Es gibt hier die Superlativ-Bildung durch den Plural
im Genitiv, wie im Hebräischen "Lied der Lieder" (šīr haššīrim).
Der Horusname gehört zur Königstitulatur. Amun-Re ist der
höchste unter den Göttern, ihr König. In dieser Weise wird das
Primat des Amun unter den Göttern zum Ausdruck gebracht.
Dieselbe Ausdrucksweise findet sich mehrmals in den ägyptischen
Texten, zum Beispiel in den Inschriften des Edfu-Tempels, die
zwar ptolemäisch sind aber auf eine alte Überlieferung zurück-
gehen. Der Horus von Edfu übernimmt viele Prädikate vom Son-
nengott wie Amun. Er heisst: "König der Könige von Ober-
Ägypten, König der Könige von Nieder-Ägypten, wirksamer Herr-
scher, Herrscher der Herrscher, der als König den Thron seines
Vaters besteigt, Raubvogel der Raubvögel, in Ewigkeit" (Edfu
VI. 273.8, 9). Die Terminologie ist dem Horusfalken angepasst.
Der Horus von Edfu erstreckt seine Herrschaft über Götter und
Menschen (VIII. 133. 1, 2). In einer Inschrift der achtzehnten
Dynastie (Urk IV. 1217) heisst es von Amun-Re: "Souverän,
Herr der zwei grossen Federn, einziger, der am Anfang war. Älte-
ste der Ältesten, Urgott ohne seines Gleichen". Mit der Königsidee
ist der Gedanke eines Urgottes verbunden, der der Erste war. Alle
anderen Götter entstanden nach ihm. Deshalb sind sie ihm unterstellt. Schon in einem alten Sargtext empfängt der Sonnengott

Re den Titel "Herr der Herren" (C.T. VII. 100. j). Dieselbe Art Titel wird auch dem Pharao gegeben. Ein Pyramidentext sagt vom König:"'Er ist ein Fürst aller Fürsten' — so sagen sie, nachdem sie den König auf den Thron gesetzt haben inmitten der grossen Neunheit" (Pyr. 1127. b).

Wir vergleichen mit den oben genannten Ausdrücken was in Mesopotamien von Enlil gesagt wird: "Herr der Herren, König der Könige, leiblicher Vater der grossen Götter" (Falkenstein-von Soden, Sum. und Akk. Hymnen und Gebete, S. 296, Nr. 41).

Im Alten Testament ist Jahweh "Herr der Herren und Gott der Götter" ('adone ha 'adonim, 'elohe ha 'elohim) (Dt. 10: 17; 11: 36; Ps. 136: 3). Im Neuen Testament heisst der Messias "König der Könige und Herr der Herren" (I Tim. 6: 15; Apok. 19: 16).

Im Leidener Papyrus hat Amun die Herrschaft über die anderen Götter inne. Sein bekanntestes Prädikat ist "König der Götter" (X. 3; XI. 4) (nsw ntrw), das die Griechen als Amonrasônther verstanden haben. Der Ausdruck hat verschiedene Äquivalente: "Herr der Götter" (nb ntrw) (VI. 3; XI. 10); "mehr unterschieden als die anderen Götter" (tnw r ntrw)(VII. 1); "Oberhaupt der Götter" (ḥrj ntrw) (V. 8). Alle diese Titel bringen zum Ausdruck dass Amun-Re ein Primat unter den Göttern hat.

In einem sumerischen Hymnus an En-ki wird der Himmelsgott An "König der Götter" genannt (Sum. und Akk. Hymnen und Gebete, S. 110, Nr. 22). Das semitische Melek, König, ist vielleicht in Götternamen wie Molech oder Melquart aufgenommen worden. In einem Thronbesteigungslied, Psalm 96, wird Jahweh als Götterkönig beschrieben:

> "Denn gross ist der Herr und gar preiswürdig,
> furchtbar und hehr über allem, was Gott heisst!....
> Sprechet: Der Herr ward König! Fest steht der Erdkreis ohne Wanken!
> Er hält gerechtes Gericht in der Welt!"

Dem höchsten Gott wird wie einem König *Huldigung* dargebracht. In Papyrus Leiden I 344 heisst es von den Göttern im Gefolge des Amun: "Sie berühren den Boden mit der Stirn. Sie kommen ihm jauchzend entgegen" (I. 9, 10). Das "Berühren der Erde" gilt als ein Ehrenbeweis für einen Gott oder einen König (Wörterbuch V. 479. 1, 2). Ein Passus aus einem Hymnus an Re lautet: "Du bist erschienen als König der Götter. Die Himmelsgöttin macht eine Gebärde der Begrüssung für dich. Die Göttin

der Gerechtigkeit (*Ma'at*) umarmt dich zu aller Zeit. Die in deinem Gefolge sind jauchzen für dich. Sie berühren die Erde mit
der Stirn, während sie dir entgegen kommen, Herr des Himmels,
Herr der Erde, König der Gerechtigkeit, Herr der Ewigkeit, Herrscher der Unendlichkeit" (Book of the Dead, Budge, Introduc-
tory Hymn to Ra 11, 15). In ägyptischen Wandmalereien aus
dem Neunen Reich sieht man oft tributbringende Fremdvölker,
die die Proskynese vollbringen, wobei sie knieend mit der Stirn
die Erde berühren, wie es sich vor dem Pharao geziemt. Auf dem
schwarzen Salmanassarobelisk verbeugt sich der israelitische
König Jehu in derselben Weise vor dem assyrischen Fürsten.

Das Wort *Majestät* (*ḥm*), schon vom Alten Reich her ein Kö-
nigstitel, wird auch mit der Gottheit verbunden. Der Leidener
Papyrus erwähnt diejenigen, "die sehen durch die Kraft seiner
Majestät" (I. 10). Diesem Titel ist der übliche Wunsch beigefügt
worden: "Möge er leben, glücklich und gesund sein", wie er immer für den Pharao gebraucht wird. Wörter wie *rabutu* oder *nar-
bu*, Grösse, Majestät, werden im Assyrischen auch auf Götter
angewandt. Psalm 93, ein Lied auf die Hoheit Gottes, sagt:

> "Der Herr war König, umkleidet von Majestät" (*ge'ut labeš*).

Im Leidener Hymnus heisst Amun-Re "ein Herr der *Lobprei-
sung* unter der Neunheit der Götter" (I. 11). Sie umgeben ihn als
sein Hofstaat und huldigen ihm. So sind auch die Götter um
Jahweh versammelt um ihn zu ehren (Psalm 29):

> "Gebt Ehre dem Herrn, ihr göttlichen Wesen,
> gebt Ehre dem Herrn und rühmt seine Macht!
> Gebt Ehre dem Herrn und preist seinen Namen,
> vor dem Herrn fallt nieder in heiligen Schmuck!
> Die Stimme des Herrn erschallt überm Meer,
> es donnert der herrliche Gott,
> der Herr überm mächtigen Meer ....
> Es thronte der Herr ob der Flut,
> so thronet der Herr, in Ewigkeit König."

Jahweh trägt hier die Züge des kanaanitischen Donnergottes
Ba'al.

Amun-Re wird als König unterschieden durch den Besitz der
Regalien, Palast, Thron, Kronen und Zepter. Leiden I 344, VII. 9
sagt: "Der Palast (*stp s3*), möge er leben, glücklich und gesund

sein, ist dieses sein Heiligtum". Der Pharao wird genannt: "Deine wahre Gestalt, die im Palast ist, möge sie leben, glücklich und gesund sein" (IX. 7). Im König, seinem lebendigen Bild (*twtꜥ nh*) auf Erden, bewohnt Amun den Palast. Der Tempel des Marduk in Babylon, E-sag-il, wird ihm von den Göttern gebaut als das Ebenbild des Apsu, des Urozeans und Wasserreiches seines Vaters Ea. Das Gebäude ist Tempel und Palast, wo er die anderen Götter als Gäste empfängt. Das assyrische *egallu*, vom sumerischen *e-gal*, "grosses Haus", bedeutet Tempel und Palast. Das gleiche ist mit dem hebräischen hekal der Fall. In Psalm 29 bewohnt Jahweh wie ein König einen Palast: "Doch alles in seinem Palast (*be hekalo*) ruft: 'Herrlichkeit' ".

Im Leidener Hymnus wird Amun mit dem alten heliopolitanischen Sonnengott Atum gleichgesetzt (V. 6); er ist "Atum, der sich auf dem *Thron* befindet" (*ḫntj st wrt*). So wird auch Re in Edfu "herrlicher Gott auf seinem grossen Thron" genannt (V. 56. 10). Es ist kein Zufall, dass es hier den Sonnengott betrifft, dessen Tempel in Heliopolis "Haus des Fürsten" heisst. Jesaja sagt von seiner Berufung als Propheten: "Da sah ich den Herrn sitzend auf einem Thron, einem hohen und ragenden. Und der Saum seines Mantels erfüllte den Tempel" (Jes. 6: 1).

Von Amun heisst es weiter im Leidener Hymnus: "Du erhebst denjenigen, der auf deinem herrlichen Thron ist" (X. 2). Der Pharao sitzt also auf dem Thron des Gottes, der der eigentliche König Ägyptens ist. Amenhotep III ist es, "den Amun auf seinen Thron gesetzt hat als Herrscher dessen, was die Sonnenscheibe umzirkelt und (dem er gegeben hat) den Thron des Geb, das Amt des Atum und das Königtum des Re-Chepri" (Urk. IV 1667. 7). Es gibt eine gewisse Reziprozität: Der Gott ist König im Lande Ägypten; der Pharao sitzt auf dem Throne des Gottes und die Verwaltung des irdischen Fürsten tendiert zum Kosmischen. Auch der israelitische König sitzt auf dem Thron Jahweh's (*kisse Jhwh*) (II Chron. 9:8).

Im Leidener Papyrus werden mehrmals die verschiedenen *Kronen* des Amun erwähnt. Er ist es "dessen *Wrrt*-Kronfedern hoch sind" (VII. 1), "der Herr der Atef-Krone" (VII. 2), "der die Kronen aufsetzt" (*wṯs hꜥ w*)" (III. 3), "der die süd- und nord-ägyptischen Kronen vereint" (VII. 6). Im Amunritual wird von diesem Gott gesagt (Papyrus Berlin P. 3055 XV. 3, 4): "Du bist erschienen als Herr der Krone, du hast alle Länder in Besitz genommen.

Du bist mächtig im Süden, du bist mächtig im Norden. Du hast den Kranz und den Kopftuch vereinigt". Die Kronen verleihen dem Gott-König Macht. Wenn er sie trägt kann er die Herrschaft über die Länder ausüben. Die Tiara der assyrischen Götter ist mit Hörnern versehen wie die ägyptische Atef-Krone. Die Hörner sind Symbole der Zeugungskraft des Stieres.

Im Leidener Papyrus ist auch von den *Zeptern* die Rede (VII. 10). Amun heisst: "Herr des *Mks*-Zepters; er hat den *Ḥk3*-Zepter und den *W3s*-Zepter ergriffen, sodass sie vereinigt sind in seiner Faust. (Er ist derjenige, dessen) Königtum immer währt". Für den Pharao ist der *Mks*-Zepter das Würdenzeichen, das besagt, dass er das Land als Erbe des Gottes empfangen hat. *Ḥk3* bedeutet "Herrschaft" und *W3s* ist "Wohlergehen". Wenn ein Gott diese Zepter in den Händen hält, bedeutet das, dass er über diese Kräfte und Qualitäten verfügt. Auch die Zeichen *ḏd*, Dauer, *w3s*, Wohlergehen, und *ᶜnḫ*. Leben, sind oft als Zepter in den Händen der Götter abgebildet. Sie sind die Merkmale ihrer Herrschaft.

Genau so wie es mit dem Pharao der Fall ist, wird vom Gotte gesagt, dass seine Verwaltung *ewig* ist: "Was seine Annalen anbelangt, ihr Ende besteht nicht. (Er ist es, der) mit zahlreichen Jubiläen in unzählbaren Jahren (versehen ist). Er herrscht ewiglich" (Leiden I 344, Verso VIII. 1). Amun heisst auch "König der Ewigkeit" (III. 9, 10). Den Texten aus Ugarit gemäss schmiedet der göttliche Handwerksman Košer wa Chassis die Zepter des Baᶜal und verspricht ihm: "Du wirst dein ewig Königtum empfangen, deine Herrschaft auf Geschlecht und Geschlecht" (W. Schmidt, *Königtum Gottes in Ugarit und Israel*, Berlin, 1961, S. 43). So heisst es auch von der Königsherrschaft Jahwehs (Psalm 145: 13): "Dein Reich ist ein ewiges Reich und deine Herrschaft währt auf Geschlecht und Geschlecht".

Amun-Re regiert als ein guter und rechtfertiger König, der sich besonders der Hilflosen annimmt. Er ist der *Barmherzige*, der *Recht* tut. Leiden I 344, Verso V. 1-4 sagt: Er ist der, "der sich nähert, er, der erhört, der freundlich ist, wenn man zu ihm ruft ... der kommt auf der Stimme dessen, der zu ihm spricht, der den Schwachen rettet vor den Gewalttätigen, der das Kind, das ohne Vater und Mutter ist, aufzieht ... Er verabscheut das Böse, er der Rechtfertige, der die Übeltäter vernichtet in diesem seinen Namen 'Herr der Gerechtigkeit'". Wir haben schon gesehen, dass der

Sonnengott Ma‛at, die komische Ordnung und Gerechtigkeit, gründet. In Mesopotamien tretet Šamaš für den Unterdrückten ein, weil er der Herr der Wahrheit und der Gerechtigkeit, *kittu* und *mešaru*, und als solcher gerechter Richter ist. Mit denselben Wortstämmen sagt auch Psalm 99 von Jahweh als König: "Du hast Rechtmässigkeit gegründet, *konanta mešarim*.

Es werden im Papyrus Leiden I 344 Verso noch verschiedene Themen behandelt, die den Gott-König betreffen, und die wir der Zeit wegen nur kurz andeuten können. I. 8: "Seine Erscheinung entstand als Re". Diese *Erscheinung* (*ḫ‛w*) wird noch mehrmals erwähnt (I, 10, 11: II. 5; III. 11; VII. 1; IX. 9). Derselbe Terminus wird angewendet für den Sonnenaufgang und für die Epiphanie des irdischen Königs, wenn er sich bei seiner Thronbesteigung dem Volke zeigt. Der Gott erscheint also und wird inthronisiert als König und der Pharao erscheint wie Re bei seinem Aufgang. Wir begegnen hier wieder der oben erwähnte Reziprozität zwischen Gott und König: Der Gott ist König und der König ist Gott. Amun-Re offenbart seinen *"Schrecken"* (*šfšft*), wie der Pharao seinen Feinden gegenüber (I. 10). Die anderen Götter sind von ihm abhängig wie seine Untertanen. Er ist es, "der *Sorge trägt* für jeden Gott" (II. 2). Auch wird von ihm gesagt: "Du hast Tempel gebaut, sodass sie gegründet sind unter deinen Kindern (den Göttern) (VI. 1). So rühmt sich auch der Pharao in seinen Inschriften, dass er den Göttern Tempel errichtet hat. Er beschenkt sie mit Gaben für den Kult.

Amun ist "der *Hirte*, wachsam über das was er geschaffen hat" (I. 4). Im ganzen Nahen Osten werden Gott und König beschrieben als "guter Hirte", dem die Schafen der Herde ihr Leben verdanken. In Mesopotamien ist der König "der legitime Hirte", *reum kenum.* Wie ein guter Fürst "tut Amun nützliche Dinge für das was er erschaffen hat" (VIII. 7, 8). Er lässt das wachsen von dem die Länder leben "in seinem Namen 'Nilflut'".

Es ist Amun, "der zurückkehrt nachdem er gesiegt hat" (IX. 1). Solches wird oft vom irdischen König gesagt, wenn er in seinen Annalen erwähnt, wie er die Feinde Ägyptens besiegt hat. Im Leidener Hymnus steht es in einem Kontext, wo Amun mit der Überschwemmung des Nils gleichgesetzt wird. So hat er die Mächte des Chaos und der Unfruchtbarkeit vertrieben und über sie gesiegt. Die Überschwemmung des Nils ist also wesensgleich mit dem Triumph des Pharao über die Feinde Ägyptens. In beiden Fällen handelt es sich um einen Sieg über die Chaosmächte, die das Leben Ägyptens bedrohen. Phänomenologisch lässt dieses sich mit dem römischen Vegetationsgott Mars vergleichen, der auch den Sieg im Krieg schenkt.

Amun-Re verfügt über das *Schöpferwort*. Durch seinen königlichen Befehl schafft er Überfluss. Der terminus technicus für Schöpferwort lautet im Ägyptischen Hu, und weil das Wort Nahrung schafft, bedeutet es auch Nahrung. Von Amun-Re sagt der Leidener Hymnus (IX, 4, 5): "Hu ist sein Ausspruch. Nahrung geht hervor". Es wird in unserem Hymnus vom König gesagt (IX. 10-X. 1): "Er spricht gemäss dem, was du befohlen hast". Wie königlichen Erlässen gehorcht werden muss und sie sich als massgebende Aussprüche verwirklichen, realisiert sich das autorative Wort Gottes. Von Amun-Re sagt der Leidener Papyrus: "Du bist einzigartig. All dieses (d.h. die ganze Schöpfung) ist deinem Befehl unterstellt. Wer ist dir heute gleich?" (X. 8). Und wenige Zeilen weiter verfolgt der Text: "Dein Schrecken lässt unter dir die Königsherrschaft grossartig werden. Was du bestimmt hast wird geschehen" (XI. 2). Diese Stelle verdeutlicht, dass man beim Schöpferwort des Gottes an das Befehlswort des Königs gedacht hat.

Fragen wir zum Schluss noch nach der religionsgeschichtlichen Bedeutung des Königssymbolismus in der Gottesidee. Wenn wir feststellen würden: Man hat die Figur des irdischen Königs auf den Gott projiziert, so ist damit nichts gesagt und nichts erklärt. Denn dann bleibt noch die Frage: Warum hatte man das Bedürfnis, sich neben dem irdischen König auch noch einen himmlischen anzumessen? Wir sollten von der Gottesidee als etwas sui generis ausgehen. Man hatte im Gottesverhältnis die Erfahrung einer "Hoheit" gegenüberzustehen, wobei man sich als Menschen eine niedrige Stelle zuteilte. Es handelt sich um den Aspekt des Heiligen, das Rudolph Otto mit dem Worte "Majestas" beschrieb. Es ist "das Moment des übermächtigen" demgegenüber beim Menschen das Kreaturgefühl steht (Das Heilige, 1932, S. 23). Gott ist der Mächtige schlechthin. Ein gleiches Gefühl hatte man dem König gegenüber. Er ist zwar nicht der Mächtige schlechthin, aber im Verhältnis zum Durchschnittsmenschen ist er doch der Mächtige. Er kann das Wohlergehen der Gemeinschaft verwirklichen wie es der Untertan nicht kann. Er verfügt über eine besondere Einsicht, wodurch er Pläne bedenken kann, die das

Land am Leben erhalten. Statt zu reden von einer Projektion des Königsgedankens auf die Gottheit, kann man besser sagen, dass man mit dem irdischen König numinose Gedanken verbunden hat. Der König war ein sakraler König und eben darum war seine Figur fähig als Symbol für die Gottheit zu dienen. Neben dem Königtum Gottes redet der Leidener Papyrus auch vom sakralen Königtum, und bisweilen ist es schwierig zu unterscheiden ob der Hymnus vom königlichen Gott oder vom göttlichen König redet. Es heisst von Amun-Re (IX. 6-X. 2): Du bist "in deiner lebendigen Gestalt als Horus, der über die Menschen gestellt ist. Dein wahres Bild, das im Palast ist, es lebe, sei glücklich und gesund, der sorgt für das ganze Land ... Du trittst hinein in dieses Land. Du bist erschienen als Falke auf der Palastfaçade. Du vereinigst dich mit deinem Sessel der Lebenden. Deine *k3*-Seele, die im Palast ist, wird zufriedengestellt ... Es ist dein Wesen (*dt*), das im Herzen des Königs ist. Er stellt seine Macht gegen deine Feinde. Du sitzest auf dem Munde des Königs von Nieder-Ägypten. Er spricht gemäss dem was du befohlen hast. Dein Heiligtum sind die beiden Lippen des Herrn, er lebe, sei glücklich und gesund. Deine Majestät, sie lebe, sei glücklich und gesund, ist in ihm. Er spricht auf Erden aus was du festgestellt hast. Du bist bleibend als Horus. Der auf dem königlichen Thron ist ist auf deinem Thron". Da sie wesensgleich sind nennen die Texte den König "den Stellvertreter" (*ʾidnw*) des Gottes. Das ist zwar keine Identität aber Gott und König sind doch verwandte Figuren. Es sei hier bemerkt, dass auch in Mesopotamien die Könige *pa-te-si* oder *išakku*, das heisst Stellvertreter des Gottes sind.

Man hatte beim König nicht nur den Eindruck von Übermächtigkeit, sondern auch das Erlebnis der Geborgenheit. Man fühlte sich bei ihm sicher wie das Schaf bei dem guten Hirten. Der König soll das Recht handhaben und den Schwachen vor dem Starken beschützen. Dieselbe Erwartungen hegt der Mensch seinem Gott gegenüber. So kann es einen nicht verwundern, dass man in dem Glauben an die Majestät und die Güte Gottes die Figur des Königs gewählt hat, um seine Empfindungen dem Gott gegenüber symbolhaft zum Ausdruck zu bringen.

DIE SAKRAMENTE IN DER "EXEGESE ÜBER DIE SEELE" IN CODEX II VON NAG HAMMADI[1]

MARTIN KRAUSE

Obwohl der Gnostiker keine Sakramente nötig hat, sind in späten gnostischen Schriften Sakramente bezeugt. Hier liegen offensichtlich Einflüsse anderer Religionen vor, der Mysterienreligionen oder des christlichen Kultus. Hans-Georg Gaffron hat diesem Fragenkomplex zuletzt ausführlich in seiner Dissertation "Studien zum koptischen Philippusevangelium unter Berücksichtigung der Sakramente" erörtert.[2] Er konnte dabei leider nur die bisher veröffentlichten Texte aus Nag Hammadi bzw. Angaben über unveröffentlichte Schriften aus diesem Handschriftenfund berücksichtigen[3] und daher eine weitere Schrift, die bisher unveröffentlichte[4] "Exegese über die Seele" in Codex II von Nag Hammadi, in der ebenfalls Sakramente bezeugt sind, nicht in seine Untersuchung einbeziehen.

Die "Exegese über die Seele" zählt m.E. zu. Gruppe der christlich-gnostischen Schriften.[5] Sie enthält neben gnostischem sehr viel christliches Gedankengut, wie wir noch sehen werden. Wie bei allen Texten dieser Gruppe muß daher untersucht werden, ob eine ursprünglich nichtchristlich-gnostische Schrift durch Hinzufügung christlichen Materials verchristlicht wurde, was bei einer Reihe christlich-gnostischer Schriften, z.B. dem "Evangelium der Maria", der "Sophia Jesu Christi" und dem "Apokryphon des

---

[1] Im Folgenden wird der Text des am 19.8.1970 gehaltenen Referates unverändert wiedergegeben. Inzwischen erschienene Quellen und Literatur werden in den Anmerkungen nachgetragen.

[2] H.-G. Gaffron, *Studien zum koptischen Philippusevangelium unter besonderer Berücksichtigung der Sakramente* (Theol. Diss. Bonn 1969).

[3] Gaffron, aO. 71-76 (*Gnosis und Kultus.* Überblick über den Befund in den Nag Hammadi Schriften).

[4] Inzwischen veröffentlicht in: M. Krause u. P. Labib, *Gnostische und hermetische Schriften aus Codex II und VI* (Glückstadt 1971 = Abh. d. Deut. Archäol. Inst. Kairo, Kopt. Reihe Bd. 2), 68-87; deutsche Übersetzung auch in: *Die Gnosis.* Zweiter Band Koptische und mandäische Quellen eingeleitet, übersetzt und erläutert v. M. Krause u. K. Rudolph, mit Registern zu Bd. I und II versehen und herausgegeben von W. Foerster (Zürich und Stuttgart 1971), 127-135.

[5] M. Krause, "Der Stand der Veröffentlichung der Nag Hammadi-Texte", in *Le origini dello gnosticismo*: Colloquio di Messina 13-18 Aprile 1966 (Leiden 1967). 72.

Johannes" nachweisbar ist.[6] J. Doresse[7] scheint dieser Meinung
zu sein, denn er rechnet den Text zu den Offenbarungsschriften
der Propheten der Gnosis von Seth bis Zoroaster, also reinen
gnostischen Schriften. Die christlichen Elemente sind nach seiner
Ansicht wohl Zusätze eines Redaktors. Auch William C. Robinson will in einem demnächst[8] in Novum Testamentum erschei-
nenden Aufsatz, dessen Manuskript er mir freundlicherweise zur
Einsicht sandte, eine heidnische[9] Erzählung herausschälen, deren
genauen Umfang er zu bestimmen versuchte.[10] Diese sei durch
Stichwortzitate aus dem biblischen Schrifttum und Paränesen an-
gereichert worden.[11] Diese Erzählung ist aber — wie er selbst
zugestehen muß — nicht fortlaufend, sondern die verschieden
langen Teile enthalten Wiederholungen.[12] Außerdem unter-
schätzten sowohl Doresse[13] als auch Robinson[14] die feste Ver-
zahnung von Erzählung und Zitaten[15] und die Tatsache, daß
auch die Zitate den Fortgang der Handlung und Erzählung beeinflussen. Dieselbe Art der Exegese, die in diesem Text durchgeführt wird, hat Alv Kragerud[16] kürzlich bei der Untersuchung
der "Pistis Sophia" festgestellt.

---

[6] Krause, aO. 74 f.

[7] J. Doresse, *The Secret Books of the Egyptian Gnostics* (London 1960), 190 f.

[8] Inzwischen erschienen: W.C. Robinson, Jr., "The Exegesis on the Soul", in: *NT* 12 (1970), 102-117.

[9] Robinson, aO. 104-110 (Composition), 117: "The narrative seems to be pagan".

[10] Robinson, aO. 106: "narrative (127,22-129,5; 131,13-134,32; 137,4-11)" und 107-110: auch der erste Teil der Paränese gehöre noch zur Erzählung. Aus der Erzäh-lung müßten noch alle Zitate ausgeschlossen werden.

[11] Robinson, aO. 105: "The exegetical composition seems therefore to be a redac-tional insertion into the narrative *Vorlage*". Zu den Paränesen (hortary I und II) vgl. a.O. 107: in die erste Paränese, die "integral with the narrative" sei (aO. 107), seien noch Zitate eingearbeitet worden, die zweite sei von dem Redaktor, der die Zitate in die erste Paränese einarbeitete, angefügt worden. Ebenso seien alle Zitate sekundär. Diese Zufügungen müßten aber nicht auf einen einzigen Redaktor zurückgeführt wer-den: "the tractate's literary history may have been more complex".

[12] Robinson, aO. 107.

[13] Doresse (aO. 190 f.) vertritt die Ansicht, der "compiler of the manuscript" habe various eclectic glosses and references" in den Traktat eingearbeitet.

[14] Robinson, aO. 105 ff., vgl. A. 11.

[15] Vgl. M. Krause, "Aussagen über das Alte Testament in z.T. bisher unveröffent-lichten gnostischen Texten aus Nag Hammadi", in *Ex orbe religionum*: Studia G. Wi-dengren oblata I (Leiden 1972 = Studies in the History of Religions XXI), 449-456, 453 ff.

[16] A. Kragerud, *Die Hymnen der Pistis Sophia* (Oslo 1967), 212 f.; vgl. dazu G. Widengren, "Die Hymnen der Pistis Sophia und die gnostische Schriftauslegung", in *Liber Amicorum*. Studies in Honour of Prof. Dr. C.J. Bleeker (Leiden 1969), 269-281;

Ich bin daher der Überzeugung, daß keine literarische Überarbeitung einer ursprünglich gnostischen Schrift vorliegt, sondern daß der Verfasser, ein christlicher Gnostiker, bei der Ausarbeitung seiner Abhandlung versucht hat, die verschiedensten Gedanken, vor allem gnostische und christliche, miteinander zu verbinden,[17] wie wir das z.B. bei Philo[18] und im frühchristlichen Schrifttum finden.[19] Dazu bediente sich der Verfasser des Traktates der exegetischen Methode, was auch bereits der Titel, die "Exegese über die Seele",[20] aussagt. Inwieweit ihm das von ihm benutzte gnostische Material schriftlich vorlag, werden wir nicht mit Sicherheit erschließen können.

Der Verfasser zeigt seine gute Allgemeinbildung durch Zitate bzw. Anklänge an das Schrifttum Homers.[21] Er weiß, daß die "Weisen" der Seele einen weiblichen Namen gegeben haben[22] und die Seele sogar eine μήτρα besitzt,[23] was auch Philo[24] bezeugt usw.

Zu den gnostischen Lehren rechne ich vor allem die Aussage von der (erschlossenen) Spaltung[25] der mannweiblichen Seele in zwei Teile, deren weiblicher Teil in den Körper fällt,[26] den Herabstieg des männlichen Teiles,[27] seine Wiederverbindung mit dem weiblichen Teil im Sakrament des Brautgemaches[28] zur Er-

---

H.L. Jansen, "Gnostic Interpretation in the Pistis Sophia", in *Proceedings of the IXth International Congress for the History of Religions*, Tokyo and Kyoto 1958 (1960), 106-111; K. Rudolph, "Gnosis und Gnostizismus. Ein Forschungsbericht", in: *ThR* 34 (1969), 225-231; H.L. Jansen, Rez. von Kragerud in: *Temenos* 3 (1968), 180-183 (dazu Rudolph, aO. 231).

[17] Krause, Aussagen, aO. 455.

[18] J. Christiansen, *Die Technik der allegorischen Auslegungswissenschaft bei Philon von Alexandrien* (Tübingen 1969) (= Beitr. z. Gesch. d. bibl. Hermeneutik 7).

[19] Belege bei Widengren, aO. 275 ff.

[20] II 127, 18 und 137, 27.

[21] II 136, 28 ff.; vgl. Krause u. Labib, aO. 86.

[22] II 127, 19 f.; vgl. auch H. Jonas, *Gnosis und spätantiker Geist* I (Göttingen ²1954), 192 f.

[23] II 127, 22.

[24] Leg all. III 180; vgl. Jonas aO. II, 1, 39 A. 1.

[25] Der Terminus ⲡⲱⲣⲋ 'spalten" wird nicht verwendet. Der Text spricht davon, daß der weibliche Teil den männlichen *verlor* (II 133, 5) bzw. daß die Seele ihren Gatten *verläßt* (II 137, 6).

[26] II 127, 24 ff.

[27] II 132, 8 ff.

[28] II 132, 13 ff.

lösung des gefallenen Teiles und damit die Wiederherstellung des Anfangszustandes.[29]

Das christliche Gedankengut ist nicht nur bei weitem umfangreicher als das gnostische, sondern auf ihm ruht auch der Nachdruck der Aussagen. Dazu gehören neben den Zitaten aus dem biblischen Schrifttum,[30] die etwa ein Drittel des Textes ausmachen, innerhalb der Erzählung folgende Aussagen: entsprechend dem Handlungsablauf muß an erster Stelle die *Buße* genannt werden. Nicht nur die Seele tut Buße,[31] sondern auch die Menschen müssen Buße tun, um von Gott gerettet zu werden:[32] "Der Anfang des Heils ist die Buße. Daher kam Johannes vor der Parusie Christi, indem er die Taufe der Buße verkündete".[33] Die Rettung erfolgt dann, weil *Gott sich erbarmt.*[34] Gott wird beschrieben als "der des großen Erbarmens",[35] als "guter Menschenfreund, der die Seele, die zu ihm ruft, erhört und ihr das Licht zur Rettung schickt".[36] Der männliche Teil der Seele kommt nicht von selbst zur Rettung der Seele, sondern wird *von Gott* gesandt.[37] Auch die Reinigung der Seele wird *von Gott* vorgenommen.[38] Christlich ist ebenfalls die Terminologie der Reinigung: die Taufe.[39] Auch die Vereinigung der beiden Teile versucht der Verfasser aus dem biblischen Schrifttum zu belegen. Der Same, den die Seele im Brautgemach empfängt, wird in neutestamentlicher Ausdrucksweise als "Geist, der lebendig macht" beschrieben.[40] Dazu gehören auch die Bezeichnung der Erneuerung der Seele als "Wiedergeburt"[41] und ihre Rückkehr als "Auferstehung".[42] Die Wiedergeburt wird außerdem eine

---

[29] II 133, 6 ff.; 134, 6 ff.; vgl. C. Colpe, "Die 'Himmelsreise der Seele' außerhalb und innerhalb der Gnosis", in: *Colloquio di Messina,* aO. 429-447, 439.

[30] Krause in: *Colloquio di Messina*, aO. 72 u. A. 10 ff. und Krause u. Labib, aO. 71 ff.

[31] μετανοεῖν II 128, 7.30; 131, 18-19; 137, 10.

[32] II 135, 8; 137, 23.

[33] II 135, 21 f.

[34] ⲛⲁ : II 129, 4; 131, 19.

[35] II 135, 18; vgl. auch II 135, 14: "damit er (Gott) sich unser erbarme" und die Zitate, in denen vom Erbarmen die Rede ist: II 129 32; 134, 23; 135, 18; 136, 10.

[36] II 135, 26 ff.

[37] II 132, 7.

[38] II 131, 19 f.

[39] II 132, 2.

[40] Joh. 6, 63; 2. Kor. 3, 6: II 134, 1 f.

[41] II 134, 29.

[42] II 134, 12.

Gnade und ein Geschenk Gottes genannt. [43]

Die Abhandlung gipfelt — wie im Philippusevangelium [44] — in Aufrufen an die Leser oder Hörer, eingeleitet durch ϣϣⲉ "es ziemt sich". Es finden sich drei solcher Aufforderungen. Sie gelten der Wiedergeburt der Seele [45] und zweimal dem Gebet. [46]

Nicht als Kriterien für literarische Überarbeitungen des Textes dürfen verschiedene Aussagen angesehen werden, z.B. die Tatsache, daß am Anfang der Schrift die Rede vom Fall der Seele ist, [47] später vom Fall aus dem Hause ihres Vaters, [48] von der Flucht der Seele aus dem Jungfrauengemach, [49] vom Verlust de. männlichen Teiles durch den weiblichen, [50] davon, daß Aphrodite die Seele aus ihrer Stadt [51] gebracht habe. Diese verschiedenen Ausdrucksweisen sind das Ergebnis der Exegese des Verfassers, sind abhängig von gnostischen Lehrsätzen, an die sich Zitate als Belege und Erklärungen anschließen, [52] die angeführt werden, um den Fall der Seele zu illustrieren.

Die gnostische Lehre vom Fall der Seele und ihre Selbsterlösung durch ihren männlichen Teil ist also in unserem Text wesentlich verändert: jetzt rettet *Gott* die Seele mit Hilfe von Sakramenten.

Das zuerst genannte Sakrament ist die *Taufe*. Sie ist notwendig, um den in den Körper gefallenen weiblichen Teil der Seele von den erlittenen Verunreinigungen zu säubern. Sehr drastisch wird die Nahrungsaufnahme als Hurerei bezeichnet. [53] Als die Seele Buße tut und nachdem sich Gott ihrer erbarmt hat, wendet er ihre Gebärmutter, die sich — wohl infolge ihres Falles — außerhalb des Körpers befindet wie die männlichen Geschlechtsorgane, wieder nach innen. [54] Dadurch erhält die Seele ihre Individualität

---

[43] II 134, 32 f.

[44] II 52 (= Taf. 100), 28; 66 (= 114), 17; 67 (= 115), 13.16.17.19; 69 (= 117), 12; 70 (= 118), 3; 71 (= 119), 3.14; 72 (= 120), 3; 75 (= 123), 22; 76 (= 124), 18; 80 (= 128), 8; 82 (= 130), 29.

[45] II 134, 6 ff.

[46] II 135, 4 ff. u. 136, 16 ff.

[47] II 127, 25 ff.

[48] II 132, 20 f.

[49] II 129, 1 ff.

[50] II 133, 5 f.

[51] II 137, 2 ff.

[52] Vgl. Krause, Aussagen, aO. 453 (mit Lit.) und die in A. 16 genannte Literatur.

[53] II 130, 23 ff.

[54] II 131, 16 ff.

(μερικόν), wird getauft und reinigt sich von der Befleckung der
Außenseite, die man auf sie gepreßt hatte. Dieser Vorgang wird
veranschaulicht durch das Bild schmutziger Gewänder, die durch
Waschen wieder sauber werden. [55] Dieses Reinigen der Seele wird
beschrieben als "Empfangen ihrer Neuheit ihrer früheren physischen Beschaffenheit". [56] Die Seele wendet sich dann wieder.
"Das ist die Taufe". [57] Die Taufe wird also als eine Waschung, als
Reinigung der Seele von erlittener Befleckung, als Rückwendung
der μήτρα von außen nach innen verstanden. Wie im Philippusevangelium wird das Äußere negativ, das Innere positiv bewer-
tet. [58]

Damit ist die Seele aber noch nicht gerettet. Die Rettung findet erst im Brautgemach statt — wie wir noch sehen werden, —
wenn durch die Vereinigung der beiden Teile miteinander der
Zustand vor dem Fall der Seele wieder erreicht wird. Die Taufe
hat also nur eine vorbereitende Wirkung und damit denselben
geringen Wert wie im Philippusevangelium.[59] Dort wird bekanntlich die Salbung als wertvoller als die Taufe beschrieben[60] und vor
ihrer Überbewertung gewarnt.[61] Aus dem Kontext kann nicht er-
schlossen werden, ob die Taufe für die christlichen Gnostiker, die
die "Exegese über die Seele" lasen, ein *Sakrament* darstellte oder
nur eine Waschung als Vorbereitung auf das Sakrament des Brautgemaches war. Unklar ist auch, ob und wie sie vollzogen wurde.
Bezeugt ist aber der Ort der Handlung. Aus der Aussage: "sie
(nämlich die Seele) reinigte sich im Brautgemach"[62] möchte ich
schließen, daß sie im Brautgemach stattfand.

Ob die Formulierung: "sie (die Seele) füllte es (das Brautgemach) mit Wohlgeruch"[63] als Hinweis auf eine anschließende
Salbung — wie sie im Philippusevangelium[64] bezeugt ist — ge-

---

[55]   II 131, 31 ff.
[56]   II 135, 35 f.
[57]   II 132, 2.
[58]   Vgl. II 68 (= Taf. 116), 4 ff.; 79 (= 127), 8 ff.; 84 (= 132), 26; 85 (= 133), 4;
ebenso z.B. im Thomasevangelium log. 22 u. 89; vgl. dazu W. Schrage, *Das Verhältnis
des Thomasevangeliums zur synoptischen Tradition und zu den koptischen Bibelüber-
setzungen*, (Berlin 1964) (= BZNW 29), 171.
[59]   Gaffron, aO. 117-140, 221.
[60]   II 74 (= Taf. 122), 12 ff.
[61]   II 73 (= Taf. 121), 5 ff.
[62]   II 123, 13.
[63]   II 123, 13 f.
[64]   Gaffron, aO. 140-171, 221.

deutet werden kann, ist mir dagegen zweifelhaft.

Die Rettung der Seele findet dann im *Brautgemach* statt. Den männlichen Teil der Seele, der auch als "Erstgeborener" [65] und "ihr Bruder" [66] bezeichnet wird, sendet Gott vom Himmel zu ihr ins Brautgemach. Seit ihrem Fall kennt sie zwar nicht mehr sein Aussehen, doch sie träumt von ihm nach dem Willen des Vaters. Durch die Vereinigung der beiden Teile werden sie "ein einziges Leben", [67] was nach Ansicht des Verfassers bereits der "Prophet" [68] über den ersten Mann (= Adam) und die erste Frau (= Eva) in Genesis 2, 24 b gesagt hat: "sie werden ein einziges Fleisch werden". [69] Damit wird die anfängliche Vereinigung der beiden Seelenteile bei Gott vor dem Fall des weiblichen Teiles wieder hergestellt. [70] Der männliche Teil wird als "physischer Herr" [71] des weiblichen bezeichnet, was der Verfasser bereits in Genesis 3, 16 b und Psalm 44, 11-12 vorhergesagt findet, wo vom "Herrn" die Rede ist.

Wie dieses Sakrament, die Vereinigung im Brautgemach, vollzogen wird, bleibt unklar. Es wird nur betont, jene Hochzeit sei "nicht so wie die fleischliche Hochzeit, bei der die, die miteinander geschlechtlichen Umgang haben, sich an diesem Umgang zu erfreuen pflegen." [72] Ähnliche Aussagen finden wir im Philippusevangelium. [73] Es wird ferner betont, das sei die "große, vollkommene Wundergeburt, daß diese Hochzeit sich nach dem Willen des Vaters vollziehe". [74]

Es heißt zwar, die "Seele habe bei der Vereinigung den Samen empfangen, [75] dieser wird aber als "Geist, der lebendig macht" [76] gedeutet. Daraus möchte ich schließen, daß die Feier des Sakramentes des Brautgemaches der gnostischen Gruppe, die die "Exegese über die Seele" benutzte, die Verleihung des lebendigmach-

---

[65] II 132, 9.
[66] II 132, 8.
[67] II 132, 35.
[68] II 133, 1.
[69] II 133, 3.
[70] II 133, 3 ff.
[71] II 133, 9.
[72] II 132, 27 ff.
[73] II 129 (= Taf. 81), 34 ff.
[74] II 134, 4 ff.
[75] II 133, 35 f.
[76] Joh. 6, 63; 2. Kor. 3, 6: II 134, 1 f.

enden Geistes bedeutete. In welcher Form dies vollzogen wurde, bleibt ungesagt.

Auch im Philippusevangelium, in dem das Sakrament des Brautgemaches bekanntlich bezeugt ist, [77] bleibt unklar, wie wir uns die Feier dieses Sakramentes vorstellen müssen. Daß es sich um einen Kuß handelte, den der Myste vom Mystagogen erhielt — wie H.-M. Schenke [78] meinte — wird von Gaffron [79] m.E. zu Recht bestritten. Aber auch für die Deutung des Sakramentes des Brautgemaches als Sterbesakrament, als Salbung des Sterbenden durch Gaffron [80] bietet der Text keine Stütze. Die Aufforderung an den Gnostiker, daß sich seine "Seele wieder gebären soll", [81] was eine Folge des Vollzuges des Sakramentes des Brautgemaches ist, verbietet eine solche Deutung dieses Sakramentes, sie legt vielmehr die Auffassung nahe, daß das Sakrament sofort nach der Bekehrung, der Buße des Gnostikers und zusammen mit der "Taufe" vollzogen wurde, da ja die Taufe im Brautgemach stattfand.

Die Seele soll sich selbst wiedergebären, so daß sie wieder wie vor ihrem Fall wird, wieder zu dem Ort zurückkehrt, an dem sie früher war. Das wird als "Auferstehung von den Toten, die Erlösung aus der Gefangenschaft, das Hinaufsteigen zum Himmel, der Weg hinauf zum Vater" [82] beschrieben.

Diese Aussage erhellt eine Reihe von Aussagen des Philippusevangeliums: Hier wird bekanntlich die Meinung der Großkirche bekämpft, daß der Herr zuerst gestorben und dann auferstanden sei. Er ist "zuerst auferstanden und starb (dann)". [83] Daher — so wird gefolgert — wird jemand, der nicht zuerst die Auferstehung erwirbt, sterben. [84] Dieser Ausspruch kehrt ähnlich wieder: "Wenn man nicht die Auferstehung bei Lebzeiten erhält, wird

---

[77]   Gaffron, aO. 191-219, 222.

[78]   H.-M. Schenke in: Leipoldt-Schenke, *Koptisch-gnostische Schriften aus den Papyrus-Codices von Nag Hamadi* (Hamburg-Bergstedt 1960) (= Theologische Forschungen 20), 38.

[79]   Gaffron, aO. 212 ff.

[80]   Gaffron, aO. 218.

[81]   II 134, 6 ff.

[82]   II 134, 11 ff.

[83]   II 56 (= Taf. 104), 16 f.

[84]   Eine andere Übersetzung vertreten W.C. Till, *Das Evangelium nach Philippos* (Berlin 1963) (= PTS 2), 17; und J.E. Ménard, *L'Evangile selon Philippe* (Paris 1967), 57.

man nichts erhalten, wenn man stirbt."[85] Daraus wird gefolgert: "Solange wir in der Welt sind, ziemt es sich für uns, uns die Auferstehung zu erwerben, damit, wenn wir das Fleisch ablegen, wir in der Ruhe gefunden werden ..."[86] Auch aus II 74 (= 122), 12 ff. ergibt sich, daß die Auferstehung eine Folge des Sakramentes des Brautgemaches ist.

Wir müssen noch einmal zurückkehren zu der Aussage, die Rückkehr der Seele zu Gott sei "die Auferstehung von den Toten"[87] und "die Erlösung aus der Gefangenschaft".[88] Mit "Erlösung" ist koptisches ϲⲱⲧⲉ übersetzt worden, das griechischem ἀπολύτρωσις entspricht. Die Apolytrosis ist bekanntlich bei manchen Gnostikern als Sakrament gefeiert worden und begegnet auch im Philippusevangelium als 4. Sakrament.[89] Es wird dort in Beziehung zum Sakrament des Brautgemaches gebracht.[90] in der "Exegese über die Seele" ist die Apolytrosis kein Sakrament, sondern die Folge des Sakramentes des Brautgemaches. Dieselbe Bedeutung hat sie m.E. auch im Philippusevangelium und ist nicht "als Einleitung zum Sakrament des Brautgemaches" zu verstehen, wie Gaffron[91] meint.

Diese Erlösung findet der Verfasser wieder im Alten Testament vorausgesagt. Er zitiert daher Psalm 102, 1-5, wo nach Vers 4 Gott das Leben aus dem Tode "errettet" hat. Diese Rettung der Seele wird auch noch als "Wiedergeburt" bezeichnet.[92] Sie begegnet auch im Philippusevangelium.[93] Die Wiedergeburt wird als Gnade und Geschenk Gottes bezeichnet.[94]

Zusammenfassend läßt sich sagen, daß von den fünf Sakramenten des Philippusevangeliums zwar drei namentlich oder indirekt genannt werden, aber nur bei einem, dem Sakrament des Braut-

---

[85] II 73 (= Taf. 121), 3 ff.
[86] II 66 (= Taf. 114), 16 ff.
[87] II 134, 11 ff.
[88] II 134, 13.
[89] Gaffron, aO. 185-191, 222.
[90] II 69 (= Taf. 117), 23.26 f. (Krause in: ZKG 75, 1964, 177); diese Lesung ist inzwischen auch von H.-M. Schenke in ThLZ 90 (1965), 329 f. und J.E. Ménard, aO. 82 übernommen worden.
[91] Gaffron, aO. 191.
[92] II 134, 29.
[93] II 67 (= Taf. 115), 12 f.
[94] II 134, 32 f.

gemaches, ein Vollzug feststellbar ist, während bei der Taufe Un-
klarheit besteht, ob sie als Sakrament galt. Das Wie des Vollzuges
des Sakraments des Brautgemaches bleibt im Dunkeln. Dafür
wird deutlich, welche wichtige Rolle die Sakramente bei der Rettung der Seele spielen.

L'ÉPÎTRE À RHÈGINOS ET LA RÉSURRECTION

J.É. MÉNARD

Les textes gnostiques ont toujours besoin d'être interprétés à deux niveaux différents, soit qu'ils dépendent d'une *Vorlage* qu'ils relisent dans une perspective gnostique, soit qu'ils veulent donner l'impression d'orthodoxie. Dans un article publié dans la *Festschrift Pahor Labib* nous avons montré que l'auteur de l'*Epître à Rhèginos* pourrait se tenir bien près de la notion orthodoxe juive de résurrection et voudrait par le fait même se faire l'interprète de la notion paulinienne de σῶμα πνευματικόν

En effet, l'eschatologie de *Rhéginos*, bien que plus individualisée que celle de Paul ou de l'iranisme, en a retenu des traits essentiels qu'il est bon de rappeler ici, avant de souligner que ce ne peut être toutefois le seul aspect sous lequel il faille étudier la notion de résurrection de ce traité qui côtoie dans le Codex Jung (Codex I) l'*Evangile de Vérité* dont la symbolique de la résurrection est celle d'un éveil à la conscience claire. Déjà dans *Rhèginos* la résurrection est d'ailleurs une reprise en main de ce que l'on est. C'est là une idée chère aux gnostiques.

1. *Une première notion de résurrection dans l'Epître à Rhèginos*

Tout comme *Rhèginos*, l'Apôtre Paul admettait en 1 *Cor.* 15, 39ss la pluralité des chairs. La sentence 23 de l'*Evangile selon Philippe* blâme également aussi bien ceux qui nient la résurrection de la chair que ceux qui la proclament:[1]

Il y en a

qui craignent de (μήπως) ressusciter nus.
C'est pourquoi ils veulent ressusciter
dans la chair (σάρξ) et ils ne savent pas que ceux qui portent (φορεῖν) la [chair (σάρξ), ceux-là] sont nus.
Pour ceux qui se [dépouilleront] au point de se

---

[1] Cf. J.-É. Ménard, *L'Evangile selon Philippe*: Introduction, texte, traduction et commentaire, (Paris, 1967) [Commentaire, p. 142-143]. Nous avons mis en italique le passage important.

mettre nus, [ceux-là] ne sont pas nus. Il n'y a ni chair (σάρξ)
[ni sang qui peut] hériter (κληρονομεῖν)
[du Royaume de] Dieu. Quelle est celle qui n'héritera (κληρονομεῖν)
pas? Celle que nous avons revêtue. Mais(δέ) quelle
est celle qui héritera(κληρονομεῖν)? Celle du Christ
et son sang. C'est pourquoi (διὰ τοῦτο) il a dit:
"Celui qui ne mangera pas ma chair (σάρξ) et ne boira pas
mon sang n'a pas la vie en lui." Qu'est-ce
que sa chair (σάρξ)? Sa chair (σάρξ) est le Logos (λόγος), et son sang,
l'Esprit (πνεῦμα)-Saint. Celui qui a reçu ceux-là a
une nourriture (τροφή) et une boisson et un vêtement.
Moi, je blâme les autres, ceux qui disent
qu'elle ne ressuscitera pas. Or (εἶτα), ils sont tous les deux
dans la déchéance. Tu dis que
la chair (σάρξ) ne ressuscitera pas. Mais (ἀλλά) dis-moi
qui ressuscitera, pour que (ἵνα) nous te
vénérions? *Tu dis que l'esprit (πνεῦμα) est dans la chair (σάρξ),*
et il y a aussi cette lumière dans la chair (σάρξ). Car ce que tu
diras, tu ne dis rien en dehors de la chair (σάρξ).
Il faut ressusciter dans cette chair (σάρξ), parce que tout
est en elle.

Et l'auteur de l'*Epître à Rhéginos* enseigne de la même manière
(p. 47, 2-12):[2]

... ne doute (διστάζειν) pas de la
résurrection (ἀνάστασις), mon fils Rhèginos.
Car (γάρ) si tu n'existais pas
dans la chair (σάρξ), tu as reçu la chair (σάρξ) quand
tu es entré en ce monde (κόσμος). Pourquoi (alors)
ne recevras-tu pas la chair (σάρξ), si
tu montes dans l'Eon (αἰών)?
Ce qui est supérieur à la chair (σάρξ) est
pour elle cause (αἴτιος) de la Vie.
Ce qui existe à cause de toi, n'est-il pas (μή) ce
qui est tien?

Aussi bien dans l'esprit de *Rhèginos* que dans celui de l'auteur de
l'*Evangile selon Philippe* il est supposé à l'intérieur de l'homme
un esprit, une chair qui est supraterrestre, ou mieux, une lumière,
un peu comme cette lumière, dans l'iranisme, qui laisse l'élément

---

[2] Notre traduction est sensiblement la même que celle des éditeurs de l'*editio
princeps*, M. Malinine, H.-Ch. Puech, G. Quispel, W. Till (R. McL. Wilson, J. Zandee),
De resurrectione (Epistula ad Rheginum), Codex Jung F. XXII^r - F. XXV^v (p. 43-50),
Zurich-Stuttgart, 1963.

terrestre (*gêtik*) se fondre ou se transfigurer immédiatement après la mort en un élément céleste (*mênok*).[3] Tel est l'enseignement d'un autre passage de *Rhèginos* (p. 45, 24-46, 2):

Alors (τότε) donc, comme l'Apôtre (ἀπόστολος)
l'a dit, nous avons souffert
avec lui, et nous sommes ressuscités
avec lui, et nous sommes montés au ciel
avec lui. Mais (δέ), si nous
sommes manifestés dans
ce monde (κόσμος), le revêtant (φορεῖν),
nous sommes ses rayons (ἀκτίς)
et nous sommes
entourés par
lui jusqu'à notre couchant, ce qui
est notre mort en cette
vie (βίος); nous sommes attirés au ciel
par lui comme les rayons (ἀκτίς)
par le soleil sans que rien ne nous fasse
obstacle. Telle est
la résurrection (ἀνάστασις) spirituelle (πνευματική)
qui engloutit la psychique (ψυχική)
tout aussi bien (ὁμοίως) que la charnelle (σαρκική).

Ces dernières lignes laissent entendre que si la chair est sauvée, c'est d'une chair spirituelle qu'il s'agit, tout comme à la p. 46, 24 il sera dit que c'est l'esprit (νοῦς) qui sera sauvé. Et pourtant, un peu plus loin dans son traité (p. 47, 26-48, 12), notre auteur invoquera le témoignage de *Mc.* 9, 14ss sur la scène de la Transfiguration pour prouver que la résurrection de la chair n'est pas une illusion.

Il semble donc que l'*Epître* tenterait une synthèse de deux courants de pensée auxquels elle était confrontée: le courant judéo-chrétien ou iranien d'une résurrection de l'homme entier et celui, grec cette fois, d'une survie unique de l'esprit. Pour notre auteur, s'il y a discontinuité entre les deux états, terrestre

---

[3] Cf. H. Corbin, *Le temps cyclique dans le mazdéisme*, dans *Eranos Jahrbuch* 20 (1951), p. 149-183; J. Duchesne-Guillemin, *Espace et temps dans l'Iran ancien*, dans *Revue de Synthèse* 55-56 [XC] (1969), p. 259-280. Comme dans l'iranisme, le temps terrestre est dans la *Lettre d'Eugnoste* de Nag Hammadi une contrefaçon du temps céleste: les 360 jours de l'année sont une réplique des 360 Puissances célestes, cf. p. 14, 4ss et M. Krause, *Eugnostosbrief*, dans W. Foerster, M. Krause, K. Rudolph, *Die Gnosis*, II: *Koptische und mandäische Quellen (Die Bibliothek der Alten Welt)*, Zurich Stuttgart, 1971, p. 43.

et céleste, de la chair, il y a toutefois continuité, grâce à l'homme intérieur et à la chair spirituelle qui conserve des caractéristiques personnelles identifiables. Semblable interprétation se rapproche de la doctrine paulinienne, — bien que la résurrection survienne ici immédiatement après la mort —, et aussi de l'idée iranienne de la transfiguration du juste en sa *daēna* au moment de la traversée du pont Činvat. Mais, d'autre part, l'auteur de notre traité tient tout aussi fermement à l'idée que l'homme ressuscité est celui qui redécouvre ce qui est sien, — ce qui veut dire dans le langage gnostique son "moi" essentiel, ontologique et transcendantal (p. 47, 11-12) —, ou encore, que l'homme ressuscité est celui qui se libère de ce monde et se ressaisit lui-même (p. 49, 32-36):

> ... et il
> sera délivré de cet élément (στοιχεῖον)
> afin qu'il ne soit pas dans l'erreur (πλανᾶν), mais (ἀλλά)
> se saisisse lui-même de
> nouveau tel qu'il était d'abord.

Le maître de Rhéginos tente donc une synthèse entre deux courants de pensée aussi diamétralement opposés que le judéo-christianisme, d'une part, et l'hellénisme, d'autre part. Sa tentative de synthèse est par conséquent à étudier à deux niveaux, et cette synthèse est plutôt du syncrétisme. Ainsi que nous l'avons à maintes reprises répété, la gnose est née dans des milieux populaires. Elle sait faire flèche de tout bois. Elle tente de rassembler en un tout homogène des éléments épars empruntés à des contextes différents et à des doctrines qui n'avaient été jusque là que le bien propre des Ecoles et des Académies. Le difficile problème des origines de la gnose demeure entier, si l'on ne tient pas compte du syncrétisme d'une époque (II-III siècles) qui coïncide avec l'éclosion et la diffusion des manuels scolaires s'adressant aux couches sociales de petite et de moyenne culture.

2. *La notion juive et iranienne de résurrection*

Les deux conditions corporelles de σῶμα ψυχικόν et de σῶμα πνευματικόν que Paul oppose l'une à l'autre reflètent l'idée qu'on se faisait de la résurrection dans les milieux rabbiniques. Ces derniers mettent expressément en rapport l'esprit et la résurrection des morts "aux jours du Messie". De tous les textes rabbiniques celui qui éclaire de manière décisive l'adamologie dont dépend Paul et qui est renfermée dans l'expression πνεῦμα ζωοποιοῦν est le *Genesis Rabba* 14 (10c):[4]

> *Et il insuffla dans ses narines* (*Gn.* 2, 7b). Ceci enseigne qu'Il l'(Adam) a façonné comme une masse sans vie s'étendant de la terre jusqu'au ciel pour lui insuffler ensuite une âme. Car en cet éon la vie lui est accordée par le moyen de la respiration, tandis que dans l'éon à venir il la recevra comme un don ainsi qu'il est écrit: *Et je mettrai* mon esprit en vous (*Ez.* 37, 14).

L'auteur rabbinique oppose comme Paul la condition première de l'homme à celle des temps messianiques obtenue lors de la résurrection et due à une nouvelle effusion de l'Esprit divin. Pareille interprétation d'*Ez.* 37, 1-14 est courante chez les rabbins;[5] l'oracle fait même l'objet de la lecture liturgique au temps de la Pâque.[6] La *Règle de la Communauté* de Qumrân (I *QS* IV, 20-23), pour ne citer que ce témoignage entre bien d'autres,[7] établit également un lien essentiel entre l'homme eschatologique et l'esprit de sainteté. Il y est dit qu'au moment "de sa visite" ou "du jugement" Dieu nettoiera les oeuvres de chacun et qu'il épurera le coeur de l'homme

> en arrachant tout l'esprit de perversité de ses membres charnels et le *purifiant* par l'esprit de sainteté de tous les actes d'impiété; et il l'aspergera de l'esprit de fidélité comme d'une eau lustrale.
> (Ainsi seront enlevées) toutes les abominations mensongères (où) il s'était vautré par l'esprit de souillure.

---

[4] Cf. J. Theodor, *Bereshit Rabba mit kritischem Apparat und Kommentar* (Berlin, 1912), p. 132. Les dimensions immenses d'Adam sont celles de l'Adam-macrocosme de la littérature rabbinique, cf. *Tanch.B.* תזריע , 19a: "Dieu créa l'homme à son image" (*Gn.* 1, 27). Et il le créa dans des dimensions qui s'étendaient d'un bout à l'autre du monde"; aussi *Gen. R.* 8 (6a). 19 (13a); *Pesiqta R.* 46 (187b); *Sanh.* 38b, 18; H.-M. Schenke, *Der Gott "Mensch" in der Gnosis. Ein religionsgeschichtlicher Beitrag zur Diskussion über die paulinische Anschauung von der Kirche als Leib Christi*, Göttingen, 1962, p. 127-130. Cette ressemblance de l'homme à l'image de Dieu a été influencée par la représentation répandue en Orient d'un Roi paradisiaque doué de propriétés divines, mais aussi par l'idée encore plus répandue d'un géant primordial, tel le Purusha védique, dont les dimensions rejoignaient celles du *cosmos* dans lequel il s'étendait, cf. *Rg Veda* X, 90; K. Rudolph, art. *Urmensch*, dans *RGG*[3], (1962), VI, col. 1195-1197.

[5] Cf. *Pesiqta* 76a; *Pesiqta R.*, Supplément 1 (192b); *Gen. R.* 77 (49c); *Lev. R.* 27 (125c); *Midr. Qoh.* III, 15 (20b).

[6] Cf. *T. B. Megilla* 31a.

[7] Cf. R. Morisette, *L'antithèse entre le "psychique" et le "pneumatique" en I Corinthiens, XV, 44-46*, dans *RevScRel* 46 (1972), p. 97-143.

> Il fera comprendre aux justes la connaissance du Très-Haut et
> enseignera la sagesse des Fils du ciel (les anges) aux parfaits de con-
> duite.
> Car eux, Dieu les a choisis en vue de l'Alliance éternelle et toute
> la gloire d'Adam leur (appartiendra).

L'auteur qumrânien se rapproche de 1 *Cor.* 15, lorsqu'il mentionne la transformation radicale de l'homme dans les termes
d'une purification de ce qui est "charnel" au moyen de l'effusion
de l'Esprit. Il n'y avait qu'un pas à franchir pour faire la mention
d'un corps purifié par l'esprit, c'est à dire d'un σῶμα πνευματικόν

Mais par delà Qumrân, où s'est exercée l'influence du dualisme
iranien, Paul et l'*Epître à Rhèginos* rejoignent certaines idées
chères à l'Avesta récent sur la résurrection, celles, entre autres,
du *Yesht* 22, 7-12. Le texte décrit la rencontre de l'âme du juste
et de sa *daēna*, représentée sous les traits d'une jolie jeune fille se
tenant dans un beau jardin. A l'admiration du juste devant une
telle apparition la *daēna* répond, comme le fait le vêtement du
jeune prince du *Chant de la Perle* des *Actes* syriaques *de Thomas*[8], qu'elle est la nature de son propre corps et que, si elle est
belle, c'est parce que le juste l'a rendue ainsi grâce à ses bonnes
oeuvres et ses bonnes pensées (vv. 11-12):[9]

> 11. Alors *sa propre nature* lui répond. Je suis, ô jeune homme, *tes
> bonnes pensées, tes bonnes paroles et tes bonnes actions, la nature
> même de ton propre corps.* Qui t'a faite de cette grandeur (de deman-
> der le jeune homme), de cette excellence, de cette beauté, avec une
> odeur si parfumée, ainsi triomphante, dominant tes ennemis, telle
> que tu te présentes à moi?
> 12. C'est toi, ô jeune homme, qui m'a faite ainsi (formée de) ton bon
> penser, (de) ton bon parler, (de) ton bon agir, *la nature de ton propre
> corps* avec cette grandeur, cette excellence, cette odeur parfumée,
> cette force victorieuse triomphant des ennemis.

La tradition iranienne qui s'est cristallisée dans ce texte du *Yesht*
a pu facilement servir de substrat à l'eschatologie qumrânienne et
paulinienne, et elle expliquerait partiellement la notion qu'a
Rhèginos de la résurrection. Son idée de chair spirituelle, renfer-
mant une lumière, rejoint celle des iraniens prônant que l'être

---

[8]   Cf. J.-É. Ménard, *Le "Chant de la Perle"*, dans *RevScRel* 42 (1968), p. 289-325.

[9]   Nous empruntons la traduction de C. de Harlez, *Avesta.* Livre sacré de Zoroastre
traduit du texte zend (*Bibliothèque Orientale*, V, Paris, 1881), p. 570-571. C'est nous
qui soulignons.

matériel et terrestre (*gêtik*) et l'être spirituel et céleste (*mênok*) sont remplis de la même lumière qui les unit l'un à l'autre.

Néanmoins, il ne faudrait pas s'y méprendre. La résurrection est bel et bien actualisée pour le gnostique de l'*Epître à Rhèginos* (p. 49, 9-16):

> ... ne va pas
> comprendre (νοεῖν) partiellement (μερικῶς), ô (ὦ) Rhèginos, ni
> (οὔτε) te conduire (πολιτεύεσθαι)
> selon (κατά) cette chair (σάρξ), à cause de
> l'Unité —, mais (ἀλλά) dégage-toi
> des divisions (μερισμός) et des
> liens, et déjà (ἤδη) tu possèdes
> la résurrection (ἀνάστασις).

Et si cette possibilité existe pour le gnostique de remonter d'une multiplicité à une Unité, dont la résurrection est en somme le symbole, c'est parce que celle-ci ne fait que lui restituer ce qui est sien (p. 47, 2-12). Or, c'est là toute la notion centrale d'un autre traité du Codex Jung à la lumière duquel il faut aussi interpréter le *De resurrectione*. Et ce traité est l'*Evangile de Vérité*.

3. La "connaissance de soi" et la résurrection dans l'Evangile de Vérité

La connaissance exposée par l'*Evangile de Vérité* est une connaissance de soi-même, c'est-à-dire une re-connaissance par le spirituel de son origine divine (p. 27, 11-15):

> Tous les espaces sont Ses émanations(?) (du Père). [10] Ils
> ont connu que c'est de Lui qu'ils
> sont sortis, comme des enfants
> d'un Homme
> parfait.

ou encore (p. 22, 13-19):

> Celui qui possédera ainsi
> la Gnose connaît d'où il est
> venu et où il va.
> Il sait, comme quelqu'un

---

[10] L'expression copte † signifie originellement "don"; vu le contexte, elle pourrait signifier ici "émanation".

qui, ayant été ivre, s'est désenivré et qui, revenu à lui-
même, a rétabli ce qui lui est propre.

Cette prise de conscience et cette reconnaissance de ses origines
est le moyen de remonter vers le Père (p. 21, 11-22):

> Alors (τότε), si quelqu'un
> possède la Gnose, il prend ce qui
> lui est propre et il le ramène
> à soi. Car (γάρ) celui qui est
> ignorant est déficient, et c'est
> beaucoup qui lui manque, puisque (ἐπειδή)
> c'est ce qui doit le perfectionner
> qui lui manque. Puisque (ἐπειδή) la perfection du
> Tout est dans le Père
> et (δέ) qu'il est nécessaire (ἀνάγκη) que le Tout remonte
> vers Lui (et) que chacun
> prenne ce qui lui est propre.

Et c'est ainsi que le spirituel atteint à l'immortalité et aussi à la
résurrection.

En effet, si cette prise de conscience de soi-même est décrite
comme une sortie de l'enivrement causé par l'oubli (ⲃ̄ϣⲉ
λήθη), [11] elle est comparée à la fin du songe dont se réveille celui
qui possède la connaissance ou, encore, à la résurrection elle-
même (p. 30, 2-23):

> Mais (ἀλλά) ils (les gnostiques)
> les (les fictions du sommeil) abandonnent comme un
> rêve de la nuit, et, la Gnose
> du Père, ils l'apprécient à la mesure de
> la Lumière. C'est ainsi que
> chacun a agi, — comme s'il était endormi —,
> à l'époque où
> il était ignorant,
> et c'est ainsi qu'il
> se redresse, comme (κατά) s'il
> s'éveillait.
> Bonheur à l'homme qui est revenu à lui
> et s'est réveillé. Et
> bienheureux (μακάριος) Celui qui a ouvert
> les yeux des aveugles. Et
> l'Esprit (πνεῦμα), avec empressement, est venu à lui

---

[11]   Cf. p. 17, 14.33.36; 18, 1.6.8.11.18; 20, 38; 21, 36 et J.-É. Ménard, *L'Evangile
de Vérité (Nag Hammadi Studies, 2, Leyde, 1972).*

quand il le
ressuscitait. Venu à l'aide de
celui qui était étendu par
terre, il l'a dressé
sur ses pieds, car, aussi bien (δέ),
il n'avait pas encore ressurgi.

La grande remarque qui s'impose à la lecture de ces lignes, c'est que nous avons affaire ici à une "pensée dominée par la nostalgie d'une situation initiale qui commande toute actualité, par un mythe de la *Urzeit* et de l'*Ursprung*."[12] C'est dans la mesure où elle remontera au Plérôme-Olympe que l'âme se reconnaîtra elle-même et qu'elle sera délivrée de toutes ces Puissances et de toutes ces passions qui la retenaient à la matière et à l'erreur. Et elle en sera délivrée par le νοῦς, le λόγος, le πνεῦμα. Aussi les grands événements historiques comme celui du Christ, par exemple, deviennent-ils ici de l'atemporel et du mythique.[13] Le Christ en croix n'est que le symbole de l'homme crucifié à la matière,[14] et la résurrection elle-même est devenue le symbole du passage de l'inconscient ou du subconscient à l'état de conscience pure.

La notion de "connaissance" dans l'*Evangile de Vérité* se rapproche beaucoup de celle des milieux gnostiques ou gnosticisants.[15] Si on voulait tenter maintenant de donner une définition de la gnose en partant de ce que nous venons de dire et en apportant quelques autres témoignages émanant des idéologies gnostiques les plus diverses, on pourrait dire que la principale caractéristique de cette mystique est avant tout d'être, pour l'homme et par l'homme, une connaissance de son "moi" véritable, sans laquelle la connaissance de tout ce monde et de Tout ne saurait être ni totale ni universelle. Cette connaissance du "moi" est essentielle dans les gnoses.[16] A travers son "moi", le

---

[12] Cf. H.-Ch. Puech, *La gnose et le temps,* p. 110; K. Kerényi, *Mythologie und Gnosis,* dans *Eranos Jahrbuch* 8(1940-1941), p. 157-229.

[13] Cf. H.-Ch. Puech, *art. cit.*, p. 110.

[14] Cf. G. Quispel, *Der gnostische Anthropos und die jüdische Tradition,* dans *Eranos Jahrbuch* 22 (1953), p. 221s.

[15] Cf. J.-É. Ménard, *La notion de "Connaissance" dans l'Evangile de Vérité,* dans *RevScRel* 41 (1967), p. 1-28; *Die Erkenntnis im Evangelium der Wahrheit,* dans *Christentum und Gnosis* (= *BzZNW,* 37, Berlin, 1969), p. 59-64.

[16] H.-Ch. Puech a démontré dans ses cours du Collège de France que le phénomène de la gnose est sensiblement le même partout, cf. *Annuaire du Collège de France* 58

gnostique voit Dieu. C'est de l'immanentisme grec ou oriental, ce n'est plus du créationisme biblique. [17] L'Homme primordial est cette parcelle de divinité que nous devons reconnaître en nous-mêmes. [18] Et, puisque notre destin se joue dans l'Olympe pléromatique où les anges [19] sont notre "moi" transcendantal, il faut que toutes les semences de divinité que nous portons en nous-mêmes se rassemblent et se regroupent autour du Sauveur, afin de pouvoir entrer au Plérôme. [20] C'est alors que l'homme, n'ou-

---

(1957-1958), p. 233-239; 62 (1961-1962), p. 195-203; 63 (1962-1963), p. 199-213; 64 (1963-1964), p. 209-226. Pour le manichéisme, cf. C.-R.-C. Allberry, *A Manichaean Psalmbook*, Part II (*Manichaean Manuscripts in the Chester Beatty Collection*, II) (Stuttgart, 1938), p. 219, 19-20; dans le mandéisme, cf. *Livre de Jean*, p. 170, 17-18 Lidzbarski; p. 171, 16-19; *Ginzā* de gauche III, 4, p. 513, 5-10 Lidzbarski; chez les Grecs et les Latins, cf. Platon, I *Al.* 133b.d; Cicéron, *Tuscul.* V, 70; Sénèque, *Ep.* LXXXII, 6, p. 302, 6-12 Hense; Plotin, *Enn.* V, 1, 1; VI, 9, 1.7; Augustin, *Contre Fortunat* XX, p. 99, 21-23 Zycha: *qua scientia admonita anima et memoriae pristinae reddita recognoscet ex qua originem trahat*. "Comme dans toutes les gnoses ... (la) connaissance de soi et de Dieu contient en elle-même la certitude du Salut. Se connaître, c'est, en effet, se reconnaître, retrouver et récupérer son vrai "moi", auparavant obnubilé par l'ignorance où nous plongeait notre mélange avec le corps et la matière; la *gnôsis* est *épignôsis* ... Il y a consubstantialité entre Dieu et les âmes; les âmes ne sont que des fragments de la substance divine. Ce qui revient à dire que c'est une partie de Dieu qui est ici-bas déchue, liée au corps et à la matière, mêlée au Mal. Mais, du même coup, nous sommes assurés que Dieu ne saurait se désintéresser du Salut de ses membres ainsi engloutis et souffrants, qu'il les ressaisira et les réintégrera à lui. En somme, à travers nous c'est Dieu qui se sauvera lui-même: Dieu sera à la fois sauveur et sauvé; il sera le "Sauveur-sauvé", figure centrale de tout gnosticisme. Et nous-mêmes, nous sommes aussi des "sauveurs-sauvés". L'élément à sauver est notre âme; l'élément sauveur, l'esprit ou l'intelligence (en grec, le *noûs*; dans les textes nord-iraniens, le *manûhmed*), la partie supérieure de nous-mêmes dont émane l'acte de connaissance et qui nous est restituée par cet acte même", cf. H.-Ch. Puech, *Le manichéisme*. Son fondateur, sa doctrine (*Bibliothèque de diffusion*, LXV, Paris, 1949), p. 71-72.

[17] Cf. *C.H.* XIII, 22.

[18] Cf. Hippolyte, *Elench.* V, 6, 6, p. 80, 5-9 Wendland; V, 8, 38, p. 96, 7-9; X, 9, 2, p. 268, 15-16.

[19] Cf. *Evangile de Vérité*, p. 19, 27-33. Le terme copte ⲘⲞⲨⲚⲦ ⲚϨⲞ signifie littéralement "création, ouvrage, disposition, formation de la face". Semblable interprétation de *Mt.* 18, 10 est communément alexandrine. De plus, certaines théories marcosiennes prétendaient que les anges contemplent la face du Père, qu'ils en sont "les formes" ou qu'ils tirent en haut "les formes", c'est-à-dire les "spirituels" ou les "gnostiques" qui sont les images ou les reflets des anges, cf. Irénée, *Adv. Haer.* I, 13, 3: I, p. 118, 6-7 Harvey; I, 13, 6: I, p. 125; I, 14, 1: I, p. 131, 13; H.-Ch. Puech, dans *Evangelium Veritatis* (*Studien aus dem C.-G. Jung-Institut*, VI, Zurich, 1956), p. 52; W. Voelker, *Der wahre Gnostiker nach Clemens Alexandrinus* (*TU*, 57, Berlin, 1952), p. 403s. La réunion de l'image et de l'ange constitue le thème central de l'*Evangile selon Philippe* de Nag Hammadi.

[20] Cf. *Extraits de Théodote* 26, 3, p. 112 Sagnard; 34, 2, p. 134; 42, 2, p. 150; 49, 1, p. 162.

bliant plus sa racine,[21] devient Fils d'Homme et Fils du Père. Les ouvrages gnostiques préfèrent le mot "Père" à celui de Dieu, pour mieux souligner la filiation divine de l'Homme parfait. C'est le cas de l'*Evangile de Vérité* où "Dieu" n'apparaît que deux fois, alors que "Père" y revient plus de quatre vingts fois.

Ainsi qu'on peut le constater, l'*Epître à Rhèginos* et sa notion de résurrection sont à interpréter à deux niveaux.[22] Si l'écrit est redevable à un milieu judéo-chrétien et iranien de sa notion de chair spirituelle, il l'est tout autant, sinon davantage, à un milieu hellénistique pour qui l'immortalité est exclusivement celle du voῦς. *Rhèginos* n'est pas un chef-d'oeuvre, mais une oeuvre de petite ou de moyenne littérature qui tente une synthèse et n'y réussit pas. Le traité demeure marqué de syncrétisme dans son amalgame d'éléments hétéroclites qu'il essaie de fondre en un tout consistant. De plus, dans ces milieux de petite et de moyenne culture les distinctions trop nettes que l'on voudrait établir entre l'hellénisme de l'immortalité de l'âme et le judaïsme de la résurrection des corps ne valent pas. Notre auteur tient avant et pardessus tout à une retrouvaille par l'homme lui-même de ses origines divines, et sur ce point il se sépare du don paulinien d'un σῶμα πνευματικόν . L'homme est pour lui une émanation de Dieu, il n'est pas sa créature. En ressuscitant, il se ressuscite lui-même.

---

[21] Cf. *Ginzā* de droite XV, 20, p. 379, 19-34 Lidzbarski; *Ginzā* de gauche III, 4, p. 513, 5-17; J.-É. Ménard, *L'Evangile de Vérité*. Rétroversion grecque et commentaire (Paris, 1962), Index, s.v. ῥίζα, p. 214. L'emploi de ῥίζα pour désigner l'origine divine du voῦς est fréquent dans la littérature hermétique, cf. A.-J. Festugière, *La révélation d'Hermès Trismégiste*, IV: *Le Dieu inconnu et la gnose (EB)*, (Paris, 1954), p. 187, note 4; Oppien, *Halieutica* I, 409 Meir: Ζεῦ πάτερ εἰς δὲ σὲ πάντα καὶ ἐκ σέθεν ἐρρίσωνται.

[22] Cf. J.-É. Ménard, *Das Evangelium nach Philippus und der Gnostizismus,* dans *Christentum und Gnosis*, p. 46-58.

THE FIGURE OF MELCHIZEDEK IN THE FIRST TRACTATE OF THE UNPUBLISHED COPTIC-GNOSTIC CODEX IX FROM NAG HAMMADI

BIRGER A. PEARSON

The first tractate of Codex IX of the Nag Hammadi library[1] is clearly a very important document of "Christian" Gnosticism. Would that it were complete! As it is, not a single page from this document is completely preserved. Of the approximately 745 lines which this text comprised (1, 1-27, 10) only 130 are either completely extant or have been conjecturally restored. An additional 318 lines are partially extant or restored. Thus it is impossible to understand fully the contents of this tractate, or even the meaning and context of some obviously important sections.

Nevertheless it is possible to ascertain generally the position of this document in the development of Gnosticism as we know it from other texts. In thought-world, and particularly in its reference to key aeonic figures of the gnostic heavenly population, it resembles such other gnostic documents as the *Apocryphon of John*,[2] the *Gospel of the Egyptians*,[3] the *Three Steles of Seth*,[4]

---

* This article is an abbreviated version of the paper read at the Congress in Stockholm. It has also been partially revised to take into account advances made over the past three years in the study of the text with which it is concerned. Pagination and placement of the major fragments of this text have been ascertained, and additional conjectural restorations have been made, largely on the basis of study of the original manuscript in the Coptic Museum, Cairo.

[1] The thirteen codices from Nag Hammadi now carry the designation "CG" (= Cairensis Gnosticus); cf. "BG" (= Berolinensis Gnosticus 8502, ed. W. Till and H.-M. Schenke, TU 60[2], Berlin, 1972). See J. M. Robinson, "The Coptic Gnostic Library Today," *New Testament Studies* 14 (1968), 356-401. The Nag Hammadi Codices are currently being published in a multi-volume Facsimile Edition (Leiden, 1972-), and a complete English edition is in preparation under the auspices of the Institute for Antiquity and Christianity, Claremont Graduate School, Claremont, California, under the general editorship of J.M. Robinson. This edition will be published in the series, "Nag Hammadi Studies" by Brill in Leiden. CG IX will be published in a volume edited by the writer of this article. For a complete bibliography on the Nag Hammadi library, see D. Scholer, *Nag Hammadi Bibliography 1948-1969* (Leiden, 1971), annually supplemented in *Novum Testamentum* by Scholer.

[2] BG, 2; CG II, 1; III, 1; IV, 1. Ed. Till-Schenke, *op. cit.*, and M. Krause, *Die drei Versionen des Apokryphon des Johannes im Koptischen Museum zu Alt-Kairo* (Wiesbaden, 1962).

Zostrianos,[5] the *Apocalypse of Adam,*[6] and the *Discourses on the Three Appearances.*[7] In one aspect, however, it is unique amongst the Nag Hammadi documents, for it features as the key personage none other than the ancient Canaanite priest-king Melchizedek, of course in a highly mutated form! The title of the tractate itself (extant on a small fragment from page 1) is "Melchizedek."[8] It is also noteworthy that Jesus Christ is prominent in this document, apparently standing alongside of Melchizedek as a redeemer figure. It is clear that the roles of Jesus Christ and of Melchizedek are closely intertwined in this text. In fact it is not out of the question that the two are actually identified with one another. Certainty on this question is, unfortunately, not possible.

The *incipit* occurs on the same small fragment as the title, and reads, "Jesus Christ, the Son [of God ...]." In the fragments that follow reference is made to the ministry and sufferings of Jesus, and in a remarkable passage from a relatively complete page (p. 5) an "anti-docetic" polemic is directed at those (other gnostics?) who deny the reality of the incarnation, suffering, death, and resurrection of Jesus. A "liturgical" passage follows which consists of an invocation of the divine hierarchy, of which Jesus Christ is now a part. In a subsequent passage, very fragmentary, it is apparently affirmed that the gnosis concerning heavenly secrets is reserved for "the race of the High Priest" (6, 17), presumably the same group as the "congregation of [the Children] of Seth" mentioned on the previous page (5, 19 f.). Since the "High Priest" in our document is Melchizedek, we can conclude that the treatise arose in a "Melchizedekian" branch of "Sethian" Gnosticism.

The figure of Melchizedek occurs in contexts having to do

---

[3]   CG III, 2 and IV, 2. The version in CG III has been published by J. Doresse, "'Le Livre sacré du grand Esprit invisible' ou 'L'évangile des Égyptiens': Texte copte édité, traduit et commenté d'après la Codex I de Nag'a-Hammadi/Khénoboskion," *Journal Asiatique* 254 (1966), 317-435. (Doresse's numbering system for the codices is different from that which has become standard).

[4]   CG VII, 5, published thus far only in *The Facsimile Edition of the Nag Hammadi Codices* (Leiden, 1972).

[5]   CG VIII, 1, unpublished.

[6]   CG V, 5. Ed. A. Böhlig, *Koptisch-gnostische Apokalypsen aus Codex V von Nag Hammadi im Koptischen Museum zu Alt-Kairo* (Halle-Wittenberg, 1963).

[7]   CG XIII, 1, published thus far only in the *Facsimile Edition* (Leiden, 1973).

[8]   [.ⲙⲉⲗⲭⲓⲥ[ⲉⲁⲉⲕ]], with title decorations.

with the offering of sacrifices and baptism, and in contexts dealing with warfare against cosmic powers. He is referred to as "the
Holy One of God Most High" (15, 9 f., possibly 12, 10 f.) and
"the true High Priest" (15, 12; cf. "great [High Priest] of God
[Most High], 26, 2 f.), designations which reflect a developed
speculation on two key biblical texts, Genesis 14, 18 and Psalm
110.4. The following two passages, fragmentary of course, are
representative of the contexts in which Melchizedek functions:

Sacrifice-baptism: "I (presumably Melchizedek, or a cultic representative) have offered up myself to you as an offering
(προσφορά), together with those (things or persons) which are
mine, to you yourself, O Father of the All, and (to) those whom
you love, who came forth from you who are holy (and) [living], and
the [perfect] laws, I shall recite [my] name as I receive baptism
[now] (and) forever among the living (and) holy [names], and
in the [waters], Amen. [Holy are you,] Holy are [you], Holy are
you, O [Father ... ." (16, 7-17. There follows a series of blessings,
with the thrice-holy invocation, of the heavenly hierarchy).

Holy-war: "greeted[9] [me ...]. They said to me, "Be [strong, O]
Melchizedek, great [High Priest] of God [Most High. ...] us who
[   ] made war; you have [   ]. They did not prevail
over you [and you] endured, and [you] destroyed your enemies."
(26, 1-9)

As I have already indicated, it is difficult to make much sense
of this document because of the great loss of text it has suffered.
Yet what is there is tantalizing enough for close study, and one
fruitful way of studying the material is to look for possible parallels elsewhere. On the passages involving Melchizedek in our document, a number of interesting texts can be adduced that may
shed further light.

In the *Second Book of Jeu*, from the Codex Brucianus, [10] the
figure of Melchizedek occurs in a ritual baptismal context. Jesus
is revealing to his disciples the secrets of the Treasury of Light.
He describes how the soul is borne out of the body by the
"Receivers" of the Treasury of Light, is released from its sins,
and is brought into the world of light and is sealed with the

---

[9]   The preceding lines are completely missing. Lines 10-15 are so fragmentary as to
be incapable of restoration, and lines 16ff. are missing.

[10]   Carl Schmidt, ed., *Gnostische Schriften in Koptischer Sprache aus dem Codex
Brucianus* (TU 8, Leipzig, 1892).

mysteries. He then invites them to receive the three baptisms, baptisms of water, fire, and the Spirit. The disciples are sent to Galilee for the necessary ritual paraphernalia, wine, vine-branches, herbs, and oils. The disciples are clothed in linen, and they hold various ritual objects in their hands. Jesus then offers up a prayer, consisting of *verba barbara*, or "glossolalia,"[11] with Amens, and calls upon the Father to send the fifteen "Assistants" (παραστάται), who are named in order, to administer the baptism of the living water to the disciples:

"May they come and baptize my disciples with the water of light of the 7 virgins of light[12] and forgive their sins, cleanse their transgressions, and number them with the inheritance of the Kingdom of Light ... . May a sign take place and may Zorokothora come and bring the water of the baptism of light into one of the wine-vessels."[13]

Then the wine in the vessel changes into water. The disciples are baptized by Jesus, are given some of the "offering" (προσφορά), and are sealed with a special seal. Then Jesus calls for vine-branches, for the baptism of fire. In a rite similar to the previous one Jesus prays again to the Father, that the disciples might be worthy of the baptism of fire, and calls again for the coming of Zorokothora, here also named Melchizedek:

"May you cleanse all of them and cause to come forth secretly Zorokothora Melchizedek,[14] that he might bring forth the water of the baptism of the fire of the Virgin of light,.the Judge."[15]

After the prayer the miracle occurs; the disciples are baptized with fire, and are given some of the "offering" (bread and wine). Similarly, the baptism of the Holy Spirit is conferred.

The most interesting aspect of these texts for our purposes is the role of Zorokothora Melchizedek. He is a heavenly figure who plays a kind of priestly role in guaranteeing the efficacy of the baptisms. We have already seen that in the fragmentary first

---

[11]   Such "glossolalia" occur also in CG IX, I, in the "liturgical" sections, 5, 24 and (possibly) 16, 23.

[12]   "Light" is rendered here in the Coptic text with a symbol, a circle within a circle, ◎

[13]   Codex Brucianus 61, Schmidt ed., p. 107f., my translation.

[14]   In the text "Melchizedek" is abbreviated,.ϻⲉⲗ. That "Melchizedek" is meant is clear from the occurrence of the name "Zorokothora Melchizedek" in *Pistis Sophia*. See below.

[15]   Codex Br. 63, Schmidt ed. p. 110, my translation.

tractate of Codex IX, the figure of Melchizedek occurs in ritual baptismal contexts. Indeed he seems to be the chief mediator of the sacrament of baptism. The *Second Book of Jeu* offers us a parallel, therefore, to this function of Melchizedek in our tractate.

Melchizedek is also an important figure in the books included in the Codex Askewianus, [16] which for convenience we shall designate simply as *Pistis Sophia* (though there are a number of documents in that codex). In *Pistis Sophia* Melchizedek is also referred to as Zorokothora Melchizedek (*Pistis Sophia* 365, 369). [17] He is the "great Receiver (παραλήμπτης) of Light" (34, 193, 292, 338, etc.), the Envoy (πρεσβεύτης) of all the lights (365), who emanated from the Fifth Tree of the Treasury of Light (193). Melchizedek stands next in importance to the Great Jeu. His chief function is illustrated in the following passage (wherein Jesus responds to a question put to him by Mary):

"Before I preached to all of the archons of the aeons, and with all the archons of Destiny (εἱμαρμένη) and the Sphere, they were all bound in their bonds, and in their spheres and seals, just as Jeu, the Overseer of the Light had bound them from the beginning. And each of them was continuing in his order, and each was moving according to his course, just as Jeu the Overseer of the Light had placed them. And when the time of the number of Melchizedek should come, the great Receiver of Light would come into the midst of the aeons and all of the archons bound in the Sphere and in Destiny. And he takes away the purity of the Light from all the archons of the aeons and from all the archons of Destiny and those of the Sphere. For he was taking away from them what disturbed them. ....And Melchizedek the Receiver of Light purifies those powers, and carries their light into the Treasury of Light. [18]

The text goes on to say that the baser material of these archons was set down into the lower world. Thus Melchizedek has the function in *Pistis Sophia* of separating out the light, and restoring it to the Treasury of Light. In other texts in *Pistis Sophia* Melchizedek, as Receiver of Light, also functions in the salvation of

---

[16]   Carl Schmidt, ed., *Pistis Sophia, neu herausgegeben* (Coptica II, Inst. Rask Oersted, Hauniae, 1925).

[17]   Schmidt ed. p. 360 and 364.

[18]   *Pistis Sophia* 34-35, Schmidt ed., p. 34-35, my translation.

individual souls, sealing the saved souls and restoring them to the Treasury of Light. [19]

Thus, in *Pistis Sophia*, Melchizedek is a heavenly figure who performs crucial functions in the redemptive process. *Pistis Sophia* and the *Second Book of Jeu* show that very involved speculations had grown up in gnostic circles around the figure of Melchizedek. [20] Far from the ancient Jebusite fortress, he is enrolled in heaven as a prominent figure in the heavenly hierarchy, and performs redemptive functions in behalf of (gnostic) mankind. Our tractate from Codex IX now provides further evidence of this development, except that the speculations in IX, 1 are much more closely tied to the biblical texts (Gen. 14 and Ps. 110) than those of the other documents here treated.

If one looks at non-gnostic materials from an earlier period, one can see that speculation on the figure of Melchizedek was already far advanced even before Christian times. Psalm 110.4 already illustrates a stage in the process, dependent as it is on the traditions in Genesis 14. Jewish speculations on Melchizedek preserved in rabbinic, pseudepigraphic, and other literatures are often quite involved. For example, Melchizedek was sometimes identified with Shem, both in Judaism [21] and in Samaritanism. [22] According to one tradition Melchizedek had a miraculous conception and birth, and immediately after his birth spoke and blessed the Lord. [23] He was said to have been born circumcised. [24] When he died he was buried in the center of the earth,

---

[19]   Cf. *Pistis Sophia* 291, Schmidt ed., p. 290.

[20]   Cf. further, on the gnostic use of Melchizedek, C. Schmidt in his edition of Codex Brucianus, p. 372 ff., 403 f.; also G. Wuttke, *Melchisedech der Priesterkönig von Salem* (*ZNW* Beih. 5, Giessen, 1927), p. 28 f.

[21]   E.g. *Nedarim* 32b; *Genesis Rabba* 26.4; *Targum Ps.-Jonathan* and *Targum Neophyti* on Gen. 14.18. For an especially good treatment of the rabbinic speculations on Melchizedek see V. Aptowitzer, "Malkizedek. Zu den Sagen der Agada," *Monatschrift für Geschichte und Wissenschaft des Judentums* 70 (1926), 93-113. Cf. also other literature cited below.

[22]   Epiphanius *Panarion* 55.6.

[23]   Cf. the Appendix to *The Book of the Secrets of Enoch* (2 Enoch, Slavonic) translated by W. Morfill and ed. by R. H. Charles (Oxford, 1896), III. 17 f. (p. 89 f.). On the Jewish character of this legend see M. Delcor, "Melchizedek from Genesis to the Qumran Texts and the Epistle to the Hebrews," *Journal for the Study of Judaism* 2 (1971), 127-130. See also Ithamar Gruenwald, "The Messianic Image of Melchizedek" (in Hebrew), *Mahanayim* 124 (1970), 88-98, esp. 90-92.

[24]   *Aboth de R. Nathan* 2.2.

where Adam was created. [25] Philo of Alexandria allegorizes Melchizedek as a type of the Logos. [26] Yet in none of these various Jewish traditions mentioned so far is Melchizedek a heavenly being who performs crucial redemptive functions in man's behalf. Whence comes such an idea? Was it invented by the gnostics?

The Dead Sea Scrolls now supply an answer to this question. From a group of thirteen fragments from Qumran Cave 11 (11 QMelch), published first by van der Woude, [27] it is clear that Melchizedek was understood by the Qumran sectarians as a heavenly redeemer figure, [28] who is to come in the end of days for the salvation of the elect. Melchizedek is described as standing in the midst of the angelic hosts around the throne of judgment, and indeed participating in the judgment. He is described as exacting the vengeance of God from the hand of Belial and his fellow-spirits, and is thus also a heavenly warrior figure in the final battle against the wicked forces. Van der Woude suggests that Melchizedek is to be identified with the archangel Michael in these texts. However that may be, we now see that in a Jewish sectarian environment in the first century of our era, Melchizedek was already seen as enrolled in the hierarchy of heaven, and expected to function as a redeemer figure in the events of the last days. Indeed these fragments from Qumran provide the best parallel to those passages in CG IX, 1 which describe Melchizedek as doing battle with the hostile forces of wickedness, and emerging in the end victorious.

---

[25]   2 Enoch, Appendix III.35 (Morfill-Charles, p. 91).

[26]   Leg. All. III.82. Cf. also 2 Enoch, Appendix III.34: "Melchizedek shall be the head over all, (being) the great high priest, the Word of God, and the power to work great and glorious marvels above all that have been" (Morfill-Charles, p. 91).

[27]   A. S. van der Woude, "Melchisedek als Himmlische Erlösergestalt in den neugefundenen eschatologischen Midraschim aus Qumran Höhle XI," Oudtestamentliche Studien XIV, ed. P. A. H. de Boer (Leiden, 1965), 354-373. Cf. also J. A. Fitzmyer, "Further Light on Melchizedek from Qumran Cave 11," Journal of Biblical Literature 86 (1967), 25-41.

[28]   This is disputed by J. Carmignac, "Le document de Qumran sur Melkisédeq," Revue de Qumran 7 (1970/1), 343-378, but his views have not gained general acceptance. Cf. e.g. M. Delcor, op. cit. (n. 22), p. 133 f.; also F. du T. Laubscher, "God's Angel of Truth and Melchizedek. A Note on 11 Q Melch 13b," Journal for the Study of Judaism 3 (1972), 46-51. Indeed J. T. Milik sees in Melchizedek, as he appears in these Qumran fragments, nothing less than "une hypostase de Dieu, autrement dit le Dieu transcendant lorsqu'il agit dans le monde, Dieu lui-même sous la forme visible où il apparaît aux hommes." See J. T. Milik, "Milkî-sedeq et Milkî-reša 'dans la anciens écrits juifs et chrétiens," Journal of Jewish Studies 23 (1972), 95-144, esp. p. 125.

Overall, it appears to me that the figure of Melchizedek in CG IX, 1 is derived directly from *Jewish* traditions, without the mediation of Christianity. This is the case whether Melchizedek and Jesus Christ are regarded as separate figures or as identical. If the latter is the case, we simply have a re-interpretation of Jesus Christ in terms of a prior Melchizedek speculation. [29]

The question of the specific milieu of our document is, of course, an important one, and has been touched on already. But in that connection we cannot overlook what Epiphanius tells us in his *Panarion*, section 55, concerning a group of heretics whom he calls "Melchizedekians":

"They glorify the Melchizedek who is spoken of in the scriptures, and think that he is a great power of some kind. In their error they also say that he dwells in ineffable regions above, and that he is not only some sort of power but also superior to Christ. (1.2)

"They also deceive themselves by creating for themselves spurious books. (1.5)

"The aforementioned sect offer up their offerings in the name of this Melchizedek and say that he is their access to God, and that offerings to God must be offered through him, for he is an archon of righteousness, having been designated in heaven by God for this very purpose, a kind of spiritual being who has been appointed to God's priesthood. They also say that we must make offerings to him in order that they might be offered by him on our behalf, and that we might find life through him." (8.1-2) [30]

What is said by Epiphanius regarding this sect has a number of interesting parallels to CG IX, 1: Melchizedek in both is a redeemer figure, who stands alongside of Christ. Epiphanius refers to the offering of sacrifices (προσφοραί) in the name of Melchizedek, and reference is made in our document to offering of sacrifices (the word used is προσφορά). Perhaps, though this is not stated by Epiphanius, the sacrament of baptism is one of these ritual acts. Melchizedek, according to Epiphanius' sectarians, was appointed by God to God's priesthood; so is he also in

---

[29]   The Epistle to the Hebrews is an analogous case, but I see no evidence in CG IX, 1 of any dependence on the Epistle to the Hebrews.
[30]   My translation. Text ed. Holl (GCS).

CG IX, 1.[31] That Melchizedek is a heavenly warrior figure, too, is not explicitly stated by Epiphanius, but need not be ruled out for the sectarians described by him. And, of course, Epiphanius states that they wrote spurious books.

Nevertheless there is no clear subordination of Jesus Christ to Melchizedek in CG IX, 1, something which Epiphanius (perhaps wrongly) attributes to the sectarians he is describing. Also, the sect he describes apparently knows and uses the Epistle to the Hebrews.

In any case, the parallels are such that one can at least say that it is probable that CG IX, 1 arose in a sect similar to that described by Epiphanius, if not the very same group. They were a gnostic sect, who had taken over and expanded old Jewish traditions concerning Melchizedek, borrowed key ideas from other groups, and created a new synthesis: a new cultus and a new literature, centered around Melchizedek on the one hand, and Jesus Christ on the other. Which of the two came first in the evolution of their religion, Melchizedek or Jesus Christ, is at this point impossible to determine.

---

[31]   The word ἱερωσύνη used in *Pan.* 55.8.1. also (probably) occurs in CG IX, 1 at 20, 10 f.: [ΘΙΕΡѠ]ⲤⲨⲚⲎ

GOD AND MAN IN "THE TEACHINGS OF SILVANUS"
(Nag Hammadi Codex VII, 4)

J. ZANDEE

Introduction — The fourth treatise of Codex VII from the so called "Coptic Gnostic Library" from Nag Hammadi in Upper Egypt has been ascribed to a man called "Silvanus". Perhaps the heading was intended as a pseudepigraphic title under the name of Silvanus (or Silas), the companion of Paul (Silvanus II Cor. 1, 19; I Thess. 1, 1; II Thess. 1, 1; I Petr. 5, 12; Silas Acts 15, 22, etc.). The literary form is that of a Book of Wisdom, comparable to the Book of Proverbs from the Old Testament. The author addresses his pupil as "My son" (85, 1-2; cf. Prov. 1, 10). He admonishes him to accept his teaching or counsel (85, 29-30; 87, 5, etc.; cf. Prov. 1, 23; 2, 1). The wise man and the fool are opposed to one another (97, 7-10; cf. Prov. 3, 35). Wisdom is personified (89, 7-12; cf. Prov. 9, 5) and is equated with Christ (107, 4-13; cf. I Cor. 1, 25-27; 3, 18). The warning against sleep, in order to be saved as a gazelle or a bird from a trap (113, 34-114, 1), is a literal quotation from Prov. 6, 4-5.

Although the form is that of O.T. Wisdom, our treatise nevertheless aspires to be a Christian writing. This is especially true of the second part wherein Christ is depicted as the one who reveals the Father and descends into the hell of this world in order to rescue man. Our writing is certainly not gnostic. God himself is the demiurge, and the creation of the world is not the work of an inferior imperfect god (116, 5-9), as it is the case in gnosticism. However, our writing has been influenced by hellenism and adapts itself to philosophic currents which were generally adopted up to the first ages A.D. It uses the term ἡγεμονικόν for the mind (νοῦς) (85, 1; 87, 12; 108, 24) as it is customary in the late Stoa. The λόγος, however, which, in the classical Stoa, was considered to be the ἡγεμονικόν, is narrowly linked with the νοῦς (85, 25-27; 108, 14-24). God and the νοῦς are only at a certain place (τόπος) καθ' ὑπόστασιν but not κατ' ἐπίνοιαν (99, 32; 100, 33; 116, 26). This concept calls Platonism to mind. In the same way Plotinus says: "There is also no place for it (the First Principle); for it needs no support of a foundation, as if it were not all to bear itself; the other things rest rather on it" (Enn. VI 9, 6).

These contemporary philosophic ideas have influenced the thoughts of our author, so that, sometimes, concerning the nature of God and man, he comes to an opinion that is not in conformity with the N.T. He speaks of the "divine" in man. This brings him near to immanentistic concepts as is the case in the Stoa, according to which the λόγος is the divine element in man. The author of "The Teachings of Silvanus", however, is not consistent in his system and his idea of God is not a unity.

1. Our author admonishes his pupil to have awe for the transcendent God. "My son, do not fear anyone except God alone, the Exalted One. Cast the deceitfullness of the Devil from you" (88, 9-13). God and the Devil are opposed to one another in the biblical way. "The fear of God" is a N.T. designation of the attitude of man toward God (Rom. 3, 18; II Cor. 7, 1; φόβος θεοῦ), and plays a part in the admonitions and exhortations, as they occur, for example, in the epistles of Paul. God is called the "Exalted One", which tallies with the Greek epithet ὕψιστος The LXX uses this term as a translation of עליון or מרום . Psalm 72 describes how God is exalted far above men in heaven. Ὕψιστος occurs nine times in the N.T. as a designation of God (e.g., Mark 5, 7; Luke 8, 28). God as well as the Devil are conceived as persons who influence man from outside. The pupil should turn himself away from the Devil and his "powers" and return to God and believe in him: "But return, my son, to your first father, God, and Wisdom your mother, from whom you came into being from the very first in order that you might fight against all of your enemies, the powers of the Adversary" (91, 14-20). "Cast your anxiety upon God alone" (89, 16-17), the author admonishes his pupil, a word that recalls I Petr. 5, 7, "Cast all your cares on him". Such biblical exhortations to entrust oneself to God as a person who is distinguished from man occur several times: "Entrust yourself to God alone as father and as friend" (98, 8-10). "Be pleasing to God and you will not need anyone" (98, 18-20).

However, the teacher must rebuke his pupil for having turned his back to God: "But since you cast from yourself God, the holy Father, the true Life, the Spring of Life, therefore you have obtained death as a father and have acquired ignorance as a mother" (91, 5-12). The attribute "holy" distinguishes God from man. The designation of God as "holy Father" occurs also in the N.T. (John 17, 11).

Gods transcendency is also described in a philosophical way. God transcends all places. Were God on a place, then this place would enclose him and the place would be more than God. "For do not think in your heart that God exists in a place (τόπος). If you localize the Lord of all in a place, then it is fitting for you to say that the place is more exalted than he who dwells in it. For that which contains is more exalted than that which is contained" (99, 31-100, 4). This passage further says that God is not bound to a body. The same holds true of the mind. "Furthermore, I shall speak of what is more exalted than this: the mind (νοῦς), with respect to its actual being (ὑπόστασις), is in a place, which means it is in the body; but with respect to thought (ἐπίνοια), the mind is not in a place" (99, 21-26). In Neoplatonism the First Principle and the mind are not bound to that which exists. "The origin of that which comes after it remains equal to itself. The origin remains one and does not divide itself over that which exists. Also the second, the mind, exists continuously as a light near the sun" (Plotinus, Enn. VI 9, 9). The author of "The Teachings of Silvanus" deals with this theme once more and then he says: "Consider these things about God; he is in every place; on the one hand, he is in a place. With respect to power, to be sure, he is in every place, but with respect to divinity, he is in no place" (100, 31-101, 3). Such thoughts also occur in Neoplatonism. There is a continuity between the First Principle and the sensible world as far as the former is a δύναμις The One is connected with the world through its activity (ἐνεργεία). It is δύναμις τῶν παντῶν (Plotinus, Enn. III 8, 10). The visible world and the First Principle are related to one another like the circumference of a circle and its centre and are linked by a "power" (Enn. VI 8, 18). As to its essence, however, the One is absolutely transcendent compared with the empiric world. Plotinus uses in this connection the term ἐπέκεινα. The One is even ἐπέκεινα νοῦ (Enn. V 3, 11).

God is so highly exalted that man is unable to have any concept of him. "My son, do not dare to say a word about this One, and do not confine the God of all to mental images" (102, 7-10). Also the bible witnesses of this incomparability of God. "To whom will you liken me? Who is my equal? With whom can you compare me? Where is my like?" (Isa. 46, 5; the next lines reject making an idol of God; cf. Isa. 40, 18.25).

God is not immanent in anything, but all rests in God. "Everything is in God, but God is not in anything" (101, 9-10). Cf. "For in him we live, we move, in him we exist" (Acts 17, 28).

This absolutely transcendent God is knowable through Christ only. "It is necessary to know God as he is. You cannot know God through anyone except Christ who has the image of the Father, for this image reveals the true likeness in correspondence to that which is revealed" (100, 21-29). This agrees entirely with the N.T. thought of Christ as εἰκὼν τοῦ θεοῦ (Col. 1, 15).

2. Like God, Christ is also a person, distinguished from men whom he saves. The "life in Christ" is comparable with the "existence in God" (101, 9-10). "Live (πολιτεύειν) in Christ, and you will acquire a treasure in heaven" (88, 15-17). Cf. Col. 2, 6, "Therefore, since Jesus was delivered to you as Christ and God, live your lives in union with him (ἐν αὐτῷ περιπατεῖτε)". As for "the treasure in heaven", cf., among others, Matth. 6, 20.

Christ reveals God, he is the light of the Father and he gives freely. "But Christ without being jealous receives and gives. He is the light of the Father, as he gives light without being jealous" (101, 17-20). Needless to say that the idea of Christ as the light of the world plays an important role in the Gospel of John (e.g., John 8, 12).

The author of "The Teachings of Silvanus" accepts the incarnation: "How many likenesses did Christ take on because of you? Although he was God, he was found among men as a man. He descended to the Underworld" (103, 32-104, 2). The descent on earth is described as a descent to the Underworld (descensus ad inferos). This world, in which we live, is hell, which is governed by the Adversary. Christ is truly God and truly man. "This one (Christ), being God, became man for your sake. It is this one who broke the iron bars of the Underworld" (110, 18-21).

In a writing of Wisdom it is not surprising that it is said about

Christ: "He is also God and Teacher" (110, 17-18). This is also a similarity with the N.T., where Jesus is called διδάσκαλος and the twelve his μαθηταῖ .

Christ is the Son of the Father (115, 10). He is also the mediator of creation. "Only the hand of the Lord has created all these things. For this hand of the Father is Christ and it forms all" (115, 2-6). God has created the world through the Word: "For all dwells in God, (that is) the things which have come into being through the Word which is the Son as the image of the Father" (115, 16-19). Cf. John 1, 1-3. Most of the christological statements of "The Teachings of Silvanus" entirely conform to the N.T.

3. Man is guided by two internal principles, mind (νοῦς) and reason (λόγος). The author exhorts his pupil to guard the camp of his soul against the enemies which are the passions and the desires. The most powerful weapon against these is "the mind (νοῦς) as a guiding principle (ἡγεμονικόν)" (85, 1). This term is characteristic for the Stoa, according to which reason (λόγος) is the ἡγεμονικόν . "The reasonable faculty is a part of the soul (τὸ λογιστικὸν μόριον τῆς ψυχῆς), which is also specifically called "guiding principle"; and that this is also in the heart could be demonstrated" (J. von Arnim, Stoicorum veterum fragmenta, Leipzig 1903-1924, II 839, further abbreviated as SVF). In the late Stoa the mind (νοῦς) is considered to be the guiding principle. The term νοῦς belongs rather to Platonism but, in a later stage, it occurs also in the Stoa. "Be content that in such rough water you have in yourself a certain guiding mind (νοῦς ἡγεμονικός). And if the billows carry you away, let them carry away the bit of flesh, the breath of life, and the rest; for they will not carry away the mind (νοῦς)" (M. Aurelius, Medit. XII, 14). "Silvanus" as well as the Stoa contend that man distinguishes himself from the animal by reason (e.g., Sil. 86, 1-3), and that he should govern his inferior feelings which are influenced by the flesh, the body or matter. "The Teachings of Silvanus" make a slight distinction between mind (νοῦς) and reason (λόγος). "Bring in your guide (ἡγούμενος) and your teacher. The mind (νοῦς) is the guide (ἡγούμενος), but reason (λόγος) is the teacher" (85, 24-26). Perhaps, in this case, there is talk of some subordination of reason to mind, reason handing over to man that which originates from the

mind. Mind and reason are personified. "They will bring you out of destruction and dangers" (85, 27-28). Thus it is possible to consider them to be independent entities, more or less separated from man. Personification occurs also in the following passage: "Protect yourself lest you be delivered into the hands of your enemies (i.e., passions and desires). Entrust yourself to this pair of friends, reason and mind; and no one will be victorious over you" (86, 11-16). Man himself is able to vanquish the influence of the flesh by his spiritual faculties. Mind and reason are called symbolically the helmsman and the rider of man, that is to say it is they that guide the soul. "The wretched man ... will die because he does not have the mind, the helmsman. But he is like a ship which the wind tosses to and fro and like a loose horse which has no rider (ἡνίοχος). For this man needed the rider (ἡνίοχος) which is reason" (90, 9-18). The imagery can be traced back to Plato according to whom man is like a charioteer who drives two horses, one tractable, the other intractable (Phaedr. 253 c-254 b).

"Silvanus", time and again, speaks of "the divine" in man; "those who dwell within you, namely, the guardians of the divinity and the teaching" (87, 2-4). As it appears from the context, mind and reason are meant (86, 19-20; ἡγεμονικόν 87, 12). The author admonishes his pupil: "Do not flee from the divine (θεῖον) and the teaching which are within you" (87, 22-24). "You are prominent in every respect, and are a divine (θεῖος) reason, having become master over every power" (88, 3-5). The divine in man is localized, in this case, in the λόγος . In this way "Silvanus" comes near to the Stoa, according to which man is congenial with God through his reason. Both the highest regulating principle in the universe and the supreme spiritual faculty in man are of the same substance, viz. the divine λόγος . This conception of God is immanentistic. The creative primeval power which operates in the cosmos makes itself manifest in individuals in the form of λόγοι σπερματικοί . "Matter receives the generative principles of God (τοὺς σπερματικοὺς λόγους τοῦ θεοῦ), and contains them in itself for the ordering of the universe" (Chrysippus, SVF II 1074). The divine λόγος permeates all things and is the highest spiritual principle which man and God have in common. "The law common to all things, that is to say the right reason (ὁ ὀρθὸς λόγος), which pervades all things, and is identical with Zeus, lord and ruler of all that is" (SVF III 4). "Silvanus" speaks repeatedly of the divine in man. "Do not bring grief and trouble to the divine (θεῖον) which is within you. But you should care for it and request of it that you remain pure, and become self-controlled in your soul and body" (91, 34-92, 6).

Besides an animal nature (φύσις) (89, 3), man has also a divine element within himself and he should cause this to prevail. "Therefore, from now on, my son, return to your divine nature" (literally "divinity"; 90, 29-30). This divine nature or "divinity" is situated in man's reason: "Take for yourself the side of the divinity of reason" (91, 24-25).

Page 92 f. contains an interesting passage relating to the creation of man. Man consists of three parts: mind, soul and body. The first is "created", the second is "formed" (πλάσσειν), and the third originated from the earth. The highest element is the mind, created after the image of God and having come forth directly from the essence of God. "The created, however, is the mind, which has come into being in conformity with the image (εἰκών) of God. The divine (θεῖος) mind has substance (οὐσία) from the Divine (θεῖον)" (92, 23-27). "Man has taken shape from the substance of God" (93, 26-27). From this it is clear that the mind as well as reason are called the divine in man. Now, these faculties are also used as a designation of God. "Indeed, it is good to ask and to know who God is. Reason and Mind are male names" (102, 13-16). As a possessor of mind and reason man is in this way akin to God. These spiritual faculties are the divine in man. In arguing so, our author follows the track of the immanentistic conception of God adhered to by the Stoa. This seems to be inconsistent, compared with his Christian concept of the transcendent God.

Mind and reason are called "the divine limits" in man which separate him from animalism. When these parts of the divine prevail, he participates in the Divine in the general sense of the word. "All divine limits are those which belong to God's household. Therefore, if the divine (θεῖον) agrees with you in part in anything, know that all of the Divine (θεῖον) agrees with you. But this divine (θεῖον) is not pleased with anything evil" (115, 21-28).

"Silvanus" says to his pupil "you are a divine (θεῖος) reason (λόγος)" (88, 4). The same epithet is given to Christ. In the last part of his treatise long christological passages occur: "Know who Christ is" (110, 14). Here it is said about Christ: "The divine (θεῖος) Word (λόγος) is God, he who bears patiently with man always" (111, 5-6). The designation θεῖος λόγος belongs therefore to man as well as to Christ. On the one hand Christ is a person outside man, who helps him, on the other hand he is identical with the divine reason within man. In some cases it is difficult to decide wether "Silvanus", by the term λόγος , means human reason or the Divine Word Christ. He speaks of both of them as of a door on which man ought to knock and which is opened for him. "Do not tire of knocking on the door of reason (λόγος), and do not cease walking on the way of Christ" (103, 11-15). Here one can hesitate if λόγος be Christ, on account of the parallellism with "the way of Christ", or if the λόγος as a human faculty be meant. It is clear that man is concerned in the following passage: "Knock on yourself as upon a door, and walk upon yourself as on a straight road" (106, 30-33). Doubtless this passage deals with human self-redemption by causing the rational principles to prevail within man himself. However, Christ is meant as divine Wisdom in the following lines: "And if you knock with this one (i.e., "Wisdom" as a designation of Christ), you knock on hidden treasures. For since he (i.e., Christ) is Wisdom, he makes the foolish man wise" (107, 1-4). "Open the door for yourself that you may know what is (or "the One who exists", i.e., God). Knock on yourself that the Word (Λόγος) may open for you. For he is the Ruler of Faith" (117, 5-10). Who knocks on the door of his own reason (λόγος), to him Christ, the Word (Λόγος) of God, opens. Our author, time and again, switches from human reason (λόγος) to the Word (Λόγος) of God.

The mind is called "the guide" (ἡγούμενος) and reason "the teacher" (85, 25-26). Here, human principles are concerned. But also Christ is named "Teacher" (91, 1; 96, 32; 110, 18). On the one hand the mind is spoken of as a lamp, an internal light, which illumines man (99, 17; 106, 14: "Light the light within you"). On the other hand we also find the biblical imagery of Christ as the heavenly Light: "For he (Christ) is also the light of the Eternal Light" (113, 6-7). As a light, Christ is the one who reveals the Father to man.

In his moral doctrine our author recalls the Stoa. Man sould cause his divine principles (νοῦς, λόγος) to prevail, and, in doing so, suppress his lower nature, his animal part, the desires and the passions. Chrysippus, the Stoic philosopher, made the following distinction between animal and human life: "For also the mute animals have as the principal power of their soul that one by which they discern foods ... not a reasonable (power) (rationabilis), it is true, but rather a natural one. But from all mortal beings, man only uses the principal good of the mind (mens), i.e. reason (ratio) ..." (SVF II 879). Reason (ratio, λόγος) is the immanent divine principle in man which distinguishes him from animals. The ethics of "Silvanus" is: "To be sure, animality will guide you into the race of the earth (i.e. life influenced by the body and matter), but the rational nature will guide you in rational (νοερόν) ways. Turn toward the rational (νοερόν) nature (φύσις) and cast from yourself the earth-begotten nature" (94, 12-18). "Live according to the mind. Do not think about things pertaining to the flesh. Acquire strength, for the mind is strong" (93, 3-6).

4. As for the relation between God and man, there are two lines of thought in "The Teachings of Silvanus" which are, at first sight, incompatible with one another: a) the Christian line: God is transcendent and nobody is able to know God, except through Christ. b) The immanentistic line: Man has within himself the divine mind or reason, and he is on the right way if he causes these principles to dominate over his animal nature. By the latter point of view, our author tries to bring a message which is acceptable for his hellenistic readers.

Now, one has the impression that "Silvanus" has tried to combine the two trends of thought in some way. His concept of the divine in man refers mainly to ethics: One ought to govern his passions by reason. Christ is needed for the knowledge of God and for redemption in the full sense of the word. Christ saves us from the powers of the Adversary and he reveals God to man.

It is necessary that God (respectively Christ) and man cooperate. Without God's aid human nature does not attain full development.

After having said that his pupil ought to entrust himself to reason and mind as two good friends, he continues: "May God dwell in your camp (i.e. the soul), may his Spirit (πνεῦμα) protect your gates, and may the mind of divinity protect the walls.

Let the holy reason become a torch in your mind, burning the pieces of wood which are entirely sin" (86, 16-23). God and the Holy Spirit are powers which give man assistance from outside. "The mind of *divinity*" and "the *holy* reason" are apparently transcendent powers that work *in* the human mind and influence it in a favourable way. We could make a comparison with I Cor. 2, 10-11, where the πνεῦμα θεοῦ has to come to man's assistance in order that he may obtain insight into God's revelation. The human heart should be illumined by Christ, the internal light of man being probably insufficient. "For just as the sun which is manifest and makes light for the eyes of the flesh so Christ illuminates every mind and the heart" (98, 24-28). Cf. Eph. 1, 18, "I pray that your inward eyes may be illumined". Besides his own reason as a "teacher", man needs also Christ as a "Teacher". "This (Christ) is your king and your father, for there is no one like him. The divine (θεῖος) teacher is with you always. He is a helper (βοηθός) and he meets you because of the good which is in you" (96, 29-97, 3). In this way there is a cooperation between Christ and man. Christ must help, but this aid, it is true, is conditional: Christ only rescues, when he finds the "good" in man, when man has permitted his mind and his reason to govern his passions. Christ's help and the human faculties, on the other hand, approach near to each other, when it is said: "One who does not have the mind sane, he does not delight in acquiring the light of Christ which is reason" (99, 1-4). Here, one has the impression that the human reason and the light of Christ are very near to each other, not to say that they are identical. In another passage, however, it is said clearly that the human mind should be illumined by the light from above: "Enlighten your mind with the light of heaven so that you may turn to the light of heaven" (103, 8-11). The human mind should look upward and have itself illumined by the light of heaven: "Do not allow your mind to stare downward, but rather let it look by means of the light at things above. For the light will always come from above. Even if it is upon the earth, let it seek to pursue the things above" (103, 1-8). This point of view has some similarity with the one of Plotinus: The soul should direct itself to the mind and the mind should look at the First Principle, then both of them will be illumined (Enn. IV 8, 3; VI 7, 31).

Christ is the true wine of which man ought to drink, if his

mind will be satiated. Christ grants his gifts through the Spirit. "For it (the true wine, Christ) marks the end of drinking, since there is in it (the power) to give joy to the soul and the mind through the Spirit (πνεῦμα) of God" (107, 31-35). As is the case in another passage (86, 18), God's Holy Spirit has to come to the aid of our mind. Cf. Rom. 8, 16, where the Spirit of God gives testimony with our spirit. As for Christ's work of redemption it is said: "And all were made new through the Holy Spirit (πνεῦμα) and the mind" (112, 25-27). It is not clear, in this case, if there be a cooperation between the Holy Spirit of God and the human mind, or if "Mind" as a name of God is intended, as is the case elsewhere (102, 15). Before drinking of Christ as the true wine, man should first of all strengthen his spiritual faculties. "But first nurture your reasoning power (λογισμός) before you drink of it" (108, 1-3). The passions are wild beasts which threaten man, but he can vanquish them. "It is possible for you through reasoning power (λογισμός) to conquer them ... . The rational man (λογικός) is he who fears God" (108, 18-19). Man should first, by his reason, control the passions, then he is open for God's gifts in Christ.

If we try now to define the point of view of the author of "The Teachings of Silvanus" more precisely, we could best characterize it as "synergistic". There is a cooperation of the human faculties with the divine powers. Mind and reason belong to man's proper nature. They are the divine within him by which he can subdue his animal nature. In doing so, he cannot succeed completely without God's help through Christ and the Holy Spirit. Behaviour as a rational man makes man susceptible of the revelation of Christ. Especially in the second half of his treatise our author stresses the indispensability of the revelation which Christ gives in order that man may know God. Besides that, however, he leaves room for the standpoint of contemporary philosophy: there is sense in letting mind and reason take the lead in man's inner life, so that he does not live as an animal but as a true man, in order to govern the passions and the desires. Christian faith is built on a foundation of true humanity.

Colophon — The author must say that, since he presented his paper to the congress under the title "The idea of God in 'The Teachings of Silvanus'", the study of this writing has advanced, so that he has had to alter some of his former interpretations. In this connection he has to mention the cooperation of Dr. M. L. Peel, associate-professor at Coe College, Cedar Rapids, Iowa, U.S.A., to whom he is greatly indebted, particularly for the English translation of the manuscript. Only the present author remains responsible for the contents of this article, of course.

DER EINE ALLMÄCHTIGE GOTT UND DAS BÖSE, DARGESTELLT AN DER FRÜHEN AŠʿARĪYA DES ISLAM

PETER ANTES

Nach Herkunft und Eigenart des Bösen zu fragen gehört wohl zum Grundbestand menschlichen Fragens überhaupt. Es ist daher begreiflich, dass jede Religion in ihren Antworten irgendwie diesem menschlichen Fragen Rechnung tragen muss. Zwei Seiten nämlich scheint der Bereich des Menschen und seines Handelns zu haben: gut und böse. Mit welchem Inhalt die Begriffe auch gefüllt werden: jedesmal handelt es sich um ein Widerspruchspaar, und menschliches Handeln kann nur unter dem Anspruch eines der beiden Glieder dieses Widerspruchspaares gesehen und begriffen werden. Alles deutet rein äusserlich auf zwei widerstreitende Prinzipien hin und nichts liegt näher als ihre Ewigkeit zu postulieren und damit die philosophische Konsequenz des Dualismus[1] zu ziehen.

Wer diese Konsequenz umgehen möchte, stösst zwangsläufig auf zahlreiche schwierige Probleme, denen er nicht ausweichen kann. So muss sich auch der Monotheismus mit der Frage nach dem Bösen auseinandersetzen. Je mächtiger der eine, einzige Gott ist, desto drängender wird die Frage nach dem Bösen. Ist dieser eine Gott noch allmächtig und Schöpfer von allem, was ist, so kann eine unabhängige Eigenexistenz des Bösen schwer angenommen werden.

Wenn wir nun im Folgenden ein Beispiel aus dem Islam wählen, so soll dies als ein Versuch gelten, Gottes Allmacht und menschliche Freiheit zu Gut und Böse philosophisch-theologisch zu durchleuchten.

Dem Zeugnis des Koran zufolge ist Gott der absolute Herr. Ihm zu dienen sind die Menschen erschaffen[2] und kein Bereich entzieht sich seinem allmächtigen Willen,[3] dem sich der Mensch

---

[1] vgl. W. Brugger, *Philosophisches Wörterbuch*, Freiburg⁹, 1962, S. 59 f.

[2] Sure 51, 56.

[3] vgl. D. Rahbar, *God of Justice, A study in the Ethical doctrine of the Qurʾān*, Leiden 1960, S. 40 ff.

bedingungslos zu unterwerfen hat.[4] "Dass der Mensch vor Gott stehe, nackt, wehrlos, und unfähig, sich zu rechtfertigen, war eine der vorherrschenden Ideen Muḥammads, die denn auch in den von ihm gebrauchten Namen Allāh's häufiger als irgend eine andere zum Ausdruck kommt."[5] Im Ganzen ist der Koran ein grossartiges Bekenntnis zu Gottes uneingeschränkter Allmacht, denn Gott "tut, was er will",[6] ja er erschafft nicht nur die Menschen, sondern auch deren Taten.[7] So ist er der unumschränkte Herr, der in die Irre führt, wen er will, und recht leitet, wen er will.[8]

Es konnte nicht ausbleiben, dass die ersten Theologen des Islam, die Muᶜtaziliten, dazu Stellung bezogen. Da sie von der Philosophie herkamen, widersprach ein solches Allmachtsverständnis ihrem Gerechtigkeitsbegriff.[9] Sie forderten vielmehr, dass der Mensch frei handelt,[10] was sicher gewisse Anhaltspunkte für eine gegenwärtige Renaissance der Muᶜtazila im Islam[11] bietet.

Im Gegensatz zur Muᶜtazila machten sich die Ašᶜariten[12] so sehr zu Verteidigern der göttlichen Allmacht, dass etwa aš-Šahrastāni den Muᶜtaziliten entgegenhalten kann: "Gott ist der Herr. Er hat das uneingeschränkte Verfügungsrecht über seinen Besitz. Er schaltet mit seinen Sklaven, wie er will, mögen sie schuldig oder unschuldig sein."[13]

Welche Bedeutung hat angesichts einer solchen Auffassung, wie sie weitgehend im orthodoxen Islam vertreten wird, das men-

---

[4] vgl. dies am Beispiel Pharaos in Sure 79, 17-26.

[5] A. J. Wensinck und J. H. Kramers, *Handwörterbuch des Islam*, Leiden 1941, S. 41; ähnlich auch L. Gardet, Artikel Allāh, in: *EI²* I, S. 408 f.

[6] Sure 11, 107(109).

[7] Sure 37, 96(94).

[8] vgl. Sure 13, 27; 14, 4; 16, 93(95); 74, 31(34); vgl. auch R. Caspar, *La foi selon le Coran*, in: *Proche Orient Chrétien* 1968, S. 23 f.

[9] vgl. dazu L. Gardet, Artikel Allāh, a.a.O. S. 412 f.; L. Gardet-M. M. Anawati, *Introduction à la théologie musulmane*, Paris 1948, S. 49; J. Goldziher, *Le dogme et la loi de l'Islam*, Paris 1958, S. 83; M. M. Sharif, *A History of Muslim Philosophy*, 1. Bd. Wiesbaden 1963, S. 201.

[10] vgl. W. Thomson, *Free Will and Predestination in early Islam*, in: The Muslim World XL (1950) I, S. 207-216, II, S 276-287.

[11] vgl. R. Caspar, *Le renouveau du Moᵒtazilisme*, in: *MIDEO* 4(1957), S. 141-201.

[12] vgl. Gardet-Anawati, *Introduction*, S. 52 ff.; W. Montgomery Watt, Artikel Ashᶜariyya, in: *EI²* I S. 696; Sharif, a.a.O. S. 224 ff.; F. M. Pareja, *Islamologia*, Roma 1951, S. 458 ff.

[13] zit. bei R. Paret, *Die Gottesvorstellung im Islam*, in: *Zeitschrift für Missionswissenschaft und Religionswissenschaft* 1950, S. 214.

schliche Tun, die gute Tat ebenso wie die Sünde? [14] Was ist das Wesen des Bösen? [15] Diese Fragen wollen wir nun anhand des Kitāb al-lumaʿ [16] al-Ašʿaris zu beantworten versuchen, um damit einen historischen Lösungsversuch zur eingangs gestellten Frage kennenzulernen.

Gleich zu Beginn seines Werkes [17] stellt al-Ašʿari unmissverständlich fest, dass Gott Schöpfer von allem ist. Zum Beweis nennt er Menschen, die ein Kind möchten, deren Wunsch jedoch allein nicht ausreicht, ein Kind zur Welt zu bringen. Gerade dieses Beispiel scheint nach al-Ašʿari zu zeigen, dass die handelnden Personen eben nicht die Werke vollbringen, die ihnen zugeschrieben werden. In allem Geschehen offenbart sich die Wirkkraft des allmächtigen Gottes, weshalb es auch nicht möglich ist, dass etwas geschieht, wenn Gott es nicht will. [18] "Gott – gepriesen sei er! – ist der Schöpfer von allem, was neu entsteht. Es ist unmöglich, dass er etwas erschafft, was er nicht will. Gott – gepriesen sei er! – hat gesagt: "Er tut (immer), was er will". [19] Und weiterhin ist nicht möglich, dass es im Herrschaftsbereich Gottes – gepriesen sei er! – etwas gibt, was er nicht will; denn, wenn es im Herrschaftsbereich Gottes – gepriesen sei er! – etwas gäbe, was er nicht will, dann wäre eines von zwei Dingen (anzunehmen), entweder müsste man Unachtsamkeit und Gleichgültigkeit behaupten, oder man müsste Schwäche, Unfähigkeit, Machtlosigkeit und Mangel am Erreichen dessen, was er will, annehmen. Da dieses für Gott – gepriesen sei er! – unmöglich ist, kann es in seinem Herrschaftsbereich nichts geben, was er nicht will." [20]

Die hier vorgelegte Gedankenführung ist für die philosophische Durchdringung der Allmachtsvorstellung höchst bezeichnend.

---

[14] vgl. zu diesem Problemkreis L. Gardet, *Dieu et la destinée de l'homme*, Paris 1967, S. 60 ff.; H. Ritter, *Das Meer der Seele. Mensch, Welt und Gott in den Geschichten des FarīduddīnʿAttār*, Leiden 1955, S. 67 ff.; P. Antes, *Prophetenwunder in der Ašʿarīya bis al-Ġazālī (Algazel)* Freiburg 1970, S. 47 ff.

[15] Es ist auffallend, dass sowohl in der 1. Auflage des *EI* als auch im Handwörterbuch des Islam und bei H. A. R. Gibb und J. H. Kramers, *Shorter Encyclopaedia of Islam*, Leiden 1961 der Begriff *aš-šarr* fehlt.

[16] R.J. McCarthy, *The Theology of al-Ashʿari*. Beyrouth 1953. Die angegebenen Ziffern beziehen sich im folgenden sowohl auf die Kapitel des Kitāb al-lumaʿ als auch deren englische Übersetzung.

[17] McCarthy 5.

[18] McCarthy 49.

[19] Sure 11, 107(109); 85, 16.

[20] McCarthy 52/53.

Allmacht wird hier mit einer gewissen Vollkommenheitsvorstellung philosophisch verknüpft. Nur diese Vollkommenheitsvorstellung nämlich ermöglicht Denkansätze, wie sie indirekt dem angeführten Zitat zugrunde liegen. Eindeutig werden hier die Grenzmöglichkeiten der Allmacht philosophisch ausgelotet und an der totalen Vollkommenheitsvorstellung gemessen. Wenn es nämlich etwas geben könnte, was Gott nicht will, so wäre Gott nicht mehr allmächtig, weil der philosophisch-theologische Allmachtsbegriff aufgrund seiner theoretischen Implikation eine andere Denkmöglichkeit nicht zulässt. [21] Einschränkungen aber kann die Allmacht zweifach erfahren: zufällig oder notwendig. Dabei würde "zufällig" bedeuten, dass Gott keine diesbezüglichen Anordnungen trifft, ja sich um diesen Bereich des Geschehens gar nicht kümmert, so dass aus "Unachtsamkeit und Gleichgültigkeit" etwas geschehen kann, was er nicht will. Eine solche Möglichkeit philosophisch einzuräumen, ist für einen Theologen nicht möglich, der die Totalität der göttlichen Allmacht vertritt. Wenn Gott allem, den Menschen und allem, was sie tun, durch seine konstante Schöpferkraft so sehr Sein verleiht, dass selbst jegliche Kausalität für diesen Allmachtsbegriff aufgegeben werden muss, [22] dann muss die Möglichkeit eines Geschehens aus "Unachtsamkeit und Gleichgültigkeit" ausscheiden. Umso mehr aber muss gleichzeitig die Möglichkeit einer "notwendigen" Einschränkung der göttlichen Allmacht entfallen. Denn könnte es etwas gegen Gottes ausdrücklichen Willen geben, so beinhalte dies, dass Gott nichts dagegen unternehmen könnte. Vielmehr sehe sich Gott dann einer unabänderlichen Faktizität gegenüber, die er hinzunehmen hätte. Al-Ašʿarī schliesst in einem solchen Fall, man müsse bei Gott "Schwäche, Unfähigkeit, Machtlosigkeit und Mangel am Erreichen dessen, was er will" annehmen. [23] Diese Vorstellung jedoch widerspricht total allem, was philosophisch unter Allmacht verstanden werden kann und scheidet grundsätzlich aus.

Das damit gewonnene Bild der totalen göttlichen Allmacht entspricht zwar — wie oben gesagt — der Intention des korani-

---

[21] vgl. zur Problematik dogmatischer Überlegungen P. Antes, a.a.O. S. 11 f.

[22] vgl. J. Obermann, *Das Problem der Kausalität bei den Arabern* II, in: *WZKM* XXX (1917/8) S. 80-82; E. Behler, *Die Ewigkeit der Welt*, 1. Teil. München/Paderborn/Wien 1965, S. 121.

[23] vgl. auch McCarthy 60 u. 67.

schen Gottesbildes, wirft aber umso dringlicher die Frage nach
dem Bösen auf. Auch die philosophischen Versuche, mit Hilfe
der Lehre von kasb bzw. iktisāb [24] und istiṭāᶜa [25] Gottes Allmacht und die menschliche Freiheit in vernünftigen Einklang zu
bringen, erwiesen sich als unzureichend. Letztlich bleibt Gott
Schöpfer von allem, [26] von Glauben wie auch Unglauben. [27] Gerade diese Problematik, ob Gott Ungehorsam und Unglauben erschafft, [28] zeigt, dass al-Ašᶜarī mit diesen negativen Begriffen
positive Eigenschaften verbindet. Unglauben ist in dieser Sicht
also nicht das Fehlen von Glauben, sondern wohl so etwas wie
ein *Glauben konträren Inhalts*. Desgleichen ist Ungehorsam ein
Gehorsam konträren Inhalts. Folglich müssen beide Eigenschaften vom Menschen erworben und, um zu sein, von Gott jeweils
erschaffen werden. Diese Auffassung von der positiven Existenz
des Bösen fordert aber nun zugleich, die ontologische Frage
nach dem Bösen zu stellen. Definiert al-Ašᶜarī auch nirgends ausdrücklich, was man unter dem Bösen zu verstehen hat, so geht
aus dem Kontext eindeutig hervor, [29] dass das Böse die positiven
Verbote Gottes im Koran – kurz das, was man unter Sünde
begreift – meint. Damit ist aber zugleich erreicht, dass – ontolo-
gisch gesprochen – nach al-Ašᶜarī Gut und Böse nicht ontolo-
gisch, also "in se" [30] gut bzw. böse ist, sondern nur aufgrund des
göttlichen Gebotes. Ist Lügen nur schlecht, weil Gott es zu etwas
Schlechtem erklärt hat? Al-Ašᶜarī antwortet darauf: "Natürlich.
Wenn er es gut geheissen hätte, wäre es gut und wenn er es
befohlen hätte, könnte man nicht widersprechen." [31]

Gut und Böse sind somit keine objektiven Qualifikationen
ontologischer Art, sondern entspringen einzig und allein Gottes
freiem Gebot. [32] Damit aber beginnt die Spekulation über die
Allmachtsvorstellung erneut das Gottesbild zu beeinflussen. Gottes Freiheit zu bestimmen, was gut und böse ist, wird ähnlich

---

[24] vgl. W. Montgomery Watt, *The Origine of Islamic Doctrine of Acquisition*, in:
JRAS 1943, S. 234-247.
[25] McCarthy 128; vgl. L. Gardet, *Dieu et la destinée de l'homme*, S. 65 ff.
[26] vgl. auch McCarthy 114/5.
[27] vgl. McCarthy 135 f.
[28] vgl. McCarthy 101 ff., 135 f.
[29] vgl. dazu McCarthy 107, 170.
[30] vgl. McCarthy: *The Theology*, S. 99, Anm. 7.
[31] McCarthy 171.
[32] Ähnlich wird auch der Tod positiv aufgefasst; vgl. Gardet, *Dieu et la destinée de
l'homme*, S. 240.

total verstanden wie früher seine Allmacht, so dass hier Freiheit
fast zur Willkür wird. Einziger Wertmassstab für Gut und Böse ist
Gottes willkürliches Gebot, nicht eine seinsmässige Wertordnung.

Folgerichtig im System zieht nun al-Ašᶜarī diese Konsequenzen auch für die Anthropologie. Gott ist absolut frei — diesmal
im objektiven Sinne verstanden —, Gläubige mit ewigen Höllen-
strafen zu belegen, ebenso wie er Ungläubige in den Himmel
eingehen lassen kann. [33] Dies wäre nicht schlecht, "von Gott her
gesehen". [34] Nur sein Wort verbürgt uns, dass er nicht so ver-
fahren wird.

Mit diesem Ansatz war zugleich garantiert, dass Offenbarung,
also in unserem Falle der Koran, eine einmalige Beweiskraft
hatte, denn nur dort und nicht in der Philosophie waren Gottes
Wille und Anordnungen niedergelegt. Nicht vernünftiges Nachsin-
nen über die Seinsordnung führen zur Erkenntnis von Gut und
Böse, so dass Gott selbst daran gebunden wäre, sondern allein das
positive Gesetz, das in der Offenbarung niedergelegt ist, ermöglicht diese Erkenntnis. Was gut und böse (Moral), was recht und
unrecht (Recht) ist, wird nicht aus einem rational aufweisbaren
metaphysischen Grund erklärt, sondern ist von Gottes absolutem
Willen abhängig und aus der Offenbarung Gottes abzulesen. Gott
erscheint dabei nicht so sehr als der alles ordnende Schöpfer,
vielmehr als der absolute Herr.

Stützt man sich aber so einseitig auf die Offenbarung, so zer-
fallen Glaube und Denken, d.h. Philosophie, in zwei bisweilen
widersprüchliche Gruppen, so dass auch die inneren Denknot-
wendigkeiten der Kausalität etwa aufgelöst werden. Vielleicht
scheint dies nicht sofort einsichtig, doch gebe ich hier die auffallenden Parallelen des Denkens von al-Ašᶜarī zu den Lehren der
Nominalisten des christlichen Mittelalters[35] zu bedenken. Es müsste in der Tat einmal untersucht werden, ob der islamische Okka-
sionalismus[36] nur, wie Brugger[37] meint, "auf einer falschen Auf-

---

[33]   McCarthy 169.

[34]   min Allāh, McCarthy 169.

[35]   vgl. J. Auer, Artikel Nominalismus, in: *Lexikon für Theologie und Kirche*, Hrsg.
v. J. Höfer u. K. Rahner. Freiburg² 1957 ff. 7. Bd. col. 1020-1023; H. A. Oberman,
The Harvest of Medieval Theology, Gabriel Biel and Late Medieval Nominalism. Cam-
bridge/Massachussets 1963.

[36]   vgl. M. Fakhry, *Islamic Occasionalism and its Critique by Averroës and Aquinas*.
London 1958.

[37]   W. Brugger, a.a.O. S. 221.

fassung von der Mitwirkung Gottes" bei den islamischen Mutakal-limūn beruht, ober ob er nicht besser aus einem ašᶜaritischen "Nominalismus" heraus interpretiert werden sollte.

Al-Ašᶜarīs Grundansatz kann systematisch durchaus ausgebaut werden zu einem möglichst einheitlichen, geschlossenen System. Theologen wie al-Bāqillānī, al-Baġdādī und al-Ǧuwaynī[38] haben dazu das Ihrige beigetragen. Manche — wie wir meinen — "nomi-nalistische" Konsequenz, die bei al-Ašᶜarī sich nur erahnen liess, kam erst im Werk dieser späteren Theologen voll zum Tragen. Gerade deshalb muss man auch immer wieder auf der Neuheit des Ansatzes von al-Ašᶜarī beharren. Mögen auch neuentdeckte und jüngst publizierte Texte der frühen Muᶜtazila punktuelle Ein-flüsse auf al-Ašᶜarī vermuten lassen, ja sogar suggerieren, so müs-sten stets diese Aussagen am Gottesbild mit allen seinen System-konsequenzen bei den einzelnen Autoren überprüft werden. Es ist nämlich wohl möglich, dass von hierher zunächst formal gleichlautende Aussagen eine sehr unterschiedliche, jeweils sy-stemimmanente Interpretation erfahren müssen.

Al-Ašᶜarīs Ansatz stellt einen erwägenswerten Versuch dar, mit der Realität des Bösen philosophisch-theologisch fertig zu werden. Doch leistet, strenggenommen, sein Versuch eigentlich nur, das Böse überhaupt aus der Welt zu beseitigen und die Frage nach Herkunft und Eigenart des Bösen mit der Beteuerung zu beantworten, dass dem Bösen keinerlei ontologische Wirklichkeit zugrunde liegt.

Zum Abschluss meiner Überlegungen möchte ich mit B. Welte sagen: "Unter allen dunklen philosophischen Problemen darf das Problem des Grundes des Bösen als das dunkelste gelten. Man muss Himmel und Erde, die höchsten und die untersten Prin-zipien bemühen, um es aufzuhellen, und man muss in der Arbeit an dieser Aufhellung ständig jenen schmalen und erhabenen Grat be-schreiten, in welchem die Wahrheit über den Menschen gegen die grössten und weltgeschichtlichen Irrtümer des Denkens steil abstürzt.

Dass es Böses gebe, davon überzeugt uns die Erfahrung täglich. Worin es aber im Grunde liegt und woher es eigentlich kommt, das wird uns sofort zum Problem, sobald wir nur ein wenig über-legen."[39]

---

[38] vgl. P. Antes, a.a.O. S. 56 ff.

[39] B. Welte, *Über das Böse.* Quaestiones Disputatae Nr. 6. Basel/Freiburg/Wien 1959, S. 9.

BELIEF IN A "HIGH GOD" IN
PRE-ISLAMIC MECCA*

W. MONTGOMERY WATT

It has been recognized by various writers from Julius Wellhausen onwards that there is evidence in the Qur ʾān that some persons in Mecca, while continuing to recognize the pagan deities and to worship them, regarded *Allāh* or God as creator of the world and a "high god" superior to the other deities. Wellhausen unfortunately linked his statements on this point with the hypothesis that *Allāh* was a kind of abstraction from local deities.[1] Wellhausen's hypothesis was rejected, but the evidence for belief in a "high god" has been more and more fully admitted as time went on, for example, by Frants Buhl,[2] Tor Andrae,[3] Rudi Paret,[4] Josef Henninger[5] and Toshihiko Izutsu.[6] The purpose of this paper is not to propound any fresh view on the question, but merely to show how extensive the Qurʿānic material is.

The first point to be made is that there are several passages where the pagans are described as acknowledging *Allāh* as creator of the heavens and the earth. Thus 29. 61-65 runs:

> If you ask them who created the heavens and the earth, and made the sun and moon subservient, they will certainly say, *Allāh*... And if you ask them who sent down water from heaven and thereby revived the earth after its death, they will certainly say, *Allāh*... And when they sail on the ship they pray to *Allāh* as sole object of devotion, but when he has brought them safe to land they "associate" (*yushrikūn—sc.* others with him).

Similarly in 39. 38/9 it is said:

> If you ask them who created the heavens and the earth, they will certainly say, *Allāh*. Say: Do you then consider that what you call on

*Also published in *Journal of Semitic Studies* 16/1 (Spring 1971).

[1] *Reste arabischen Heidentums*[2] (Berlin, 1927), pp. 217-24.

[2] *Das Leben Muhammeds* (Leipzig, 1930), p. 94.

[3] *Mohammed, the Man and his Faith*, tr. Menzel (New York, 1936), pp. 24-7.

[4] *Mohammed und der Koran* (Stuttgart, 1957), pp. 15-17.

[5] "La religion bédouine préislamique", in F. Gabrieli (ed.), *L'antica società beduina* (Rome, 1959), pp. 115-40, esp. pp. 133 f.

[6] *God and Man in the Koran* (Tokyo, 1964), pp. 97-105.

apart from God, those (female beings), are able, if God wills evil to me, to remove this evil, or, if he wills mercy for me, to hold back this mercy?

There are a number of other passages where similar questions are asked and a similar answer given. In one, 31. 25/4, there is no reference to other deities, but in others some such reference is implicit. Thus 43. 87 follows a verse which asserts that those they call on apart from God have no power of intercession. The passage 43. 9/8-15/14 concludes with a statement that those who have admitted various signs of God's power nevertheless (according to the usual interpretation) place some of God's servants on a level with him. In another passage, 23. 84/6-89/91, the opponents admit that the earth and what is in it belong to God, that he is the Lord of the seven heavens and the mighty throne, that the kingdom of all things is in his hand, and that he protects others whereas none protects against him. This last clause is almost certainly to be understood of pagan deities in the light of statements about the inability of these deities to avert the evil willed by God. (Incidentally this clause has frequently been misunderstood by European translators.)[7]

A second point is that, even though God is acknowledged as creator, some men set up "peers" (andād) or "partners" (shurakā᾽) for him. In 2. 21/19 f. men in general are called on to serve their Lord who created them and their predecessors, who placed the earth beneath them and the heaven above, who sent rain to give a provision of fruits; knowing this they are not to set up peers for God.[8] Later in the same sura (v. 165/0) it is stated that "some people take apart from God peers whom they love as they love God". Yet again it is said to unbelievers (40. 12): "when God alone is called on, you disbelieve; but if he is given partners (in yushrak bi-hi), you believe".

Other verses speak of the pagan deities acting as intermediaries between men and God, and in particular interceding with God on behalf of men. Thus, "those who take patrons (awliyā᾽) apart from God" are described as saying "we serve them only that they may bring us near to God in intimacy" (39. 3/4). Another description of the pagans is that "they serve apart from God what

---

[7] For the correct rendering see Lane, s.v.; and also R. Paret's German translation.
[8] Cf. 41. 9/8. Other references to andād: 14. 30/35; 34. 33/32; 39. 8/11.

neither harms nor benefits them, and they say, These are our intercessors (shufaʿāʾ) with God" (10. 18/19). Again it is said of the sinners on the Day of Judgement that "among their partners (shurakāʿ) they have no intercessors, and they believe no more in their partners" (30. 12/11). The phrase "their partners" here does not seem to imply that the deities were partners of their worshippers in any sense, but merely that the deities were those whom "they" alleged to be partners of God.[9] In the parable of the unbelieving town (36. 13/12-29/28) the man who exhorted his fellow-citizens to follow the messengers said: "Shall I take apart from him gods (āliha) whose intercession, if the Merciful wills evil to me, will not avail me aught and will not deliver me?" (v. 23/22). In 43. 86 it is similarly emphasized that the pagan deities have no power of intercession.[10]

The prevalence of the idea that the pagan deities intercede with the high god on behalf of their worshippers confirms the truth of the story of the "satanic verses" (added after 53. 20), and also shows more clearly the nature of the temptation to which Muḥammad partially succumbed. The story is that after the verses "Have you considered al-Lāt and al-ʿUzzā, and Manāt, the third, the other?", Satan inserted the words "these are the exalted gharānīq; their intercession is hoped for."[11] The word gharānīq, often translated "swan" or "crane", is obscure; there is something to be said for the suggestion mentioned by Lane that they were Numidian cranes, reputed to fly very high, and so the epithet was appropriate to those who interceded with the supreme God. Whatever the precise interpretation of this word, it is clear that the temptation for Muḥammad was to acknowledge the pagan goddesses as capable of interceding with God, in accordance with the belief of many of his contemporaries. The Qurʾān sometimes speaks of the deities as angels and criticizes the pagans for giving them female names (53. 27/28). A verse just before this (53. 26) speaks of many angels whose intercession is of no avail. The occurence of these ideas in close proximity to the passage into which the satanic verses were inscrted gives strong support to the view that Muḥammad's temptation was to inter-

---

[9] Cf. al-Bayḍāwī, ad. loc.; elsewhere God speaks of "my partners" (e.g. 18. 52/50).
[10] Cf. also 6. 94.
[11] Cf. Watt, Muhammad at Mecca, p. 102; Nöldeke-Schwally, I, 100 n. 4.

pret *Allāh* as the high god already acknowledged by many in Mecca.

A curious verse (6. 136/7) about the actual practice of making offerings may be noted at this point:

> They have assigned to God a portion from the grain and the cattle he has produced, and have said, "This is for God" – as they allege – "and this for our partners"; but what is for their partners does not reach God, whereas what is for God does reach their partners.

The exact interpretation of this verse is uncertain. The commentary of the Jalālayn suggests that God's portion went to the guests and the needy, whereas that for the pagan deities went to the *sadana*, the persons in charge of the shrine. This is not altogether convincing, since the giving of God's portion to the guests and the needy sounds like Islamic usage; but the difficulty may well have been that there was no specific shrine at which God's portion could be offered (though this in turn leads to difficulties about the Ka^c ba).

The material examined so far presents a fairly consistent picture of a widespread belief in pagan deities accompanied by a belief – perhaps not so widespread – in *Allāh* as a high god. An important function of the lesser deities is to intercede with the high god on behalf of men. In this aspect they are sometimes regarded as angels. In contrast to all this material, however, there are some passages where men in great danger, though presumably pagans, do not call on their deities to intercede, but appeal directly to *Allāh*.

> When evil touches the people, they call upon their Lord, coming back to him in penitence; then when he lets them experience a mercy from him, a party of them give partners to their Lord (30. 33/32; cf. 39. 8/11).
>
> When they sail on the ship, they call on *Allāh* as sole object of devotion, but when he has brought them safe to land they give partners (*yushrikūn–sc.* to him) (29. 65; already quoted).

The phrase here rendered "as sole object of devotion" is *mukhliṣīn la-hu d-dīn*, more literally "making the religion for him alone". In the context it seems to imply abandoning the pagan deities, at least for the moment. There are two other verses (10. 22/23; 31. 32/31) where this phrase occurs in connexion with prayers on a ship, although after the crisis is over the men are said to turn to evil actions, not to go back to the partner-gods. The former may be quoted for its description of a storm.

> He it is who makes you travel by land and sea; and when you are on the ships, and the ships run before a favouring wind with the voyagers and these rejoice at it, a squally wind strikes the ships and waves come at the people from every quarter and they think it is all over with them; then they call on God as the sole object of devotion, "If you save us from this, we shall indeed be grateful"; but when he has saved them, see, they act unscrupulously and unjustly in the land.

Presumably this pursuit of their own ends by fair means or foul was characteristic of the pagans.

It is possible that *Allāh* was specially invoked in storms because he was held to be in control of the sea. Whether this is so or not, however, there seems to be no doubt that in times of danger supplication was made to *Allāh* by men who normally recognized pagan deities. It further appears likely that the phrase *mukhliṣīn la-hu d-dīn*, which with variants occurs eleven times in the Quᶜrān, is contrasting monotheism with belief in a high god rather than with an undifferentiated polytheism. The same is probably true of the nine instances of the phrase ᶜ*ibādi-nā l-mukhlaṣīn* or *mukhliṣīn* and the latter reading seems preferable. [12]

Too much should not be made of the contrast between the direct appeal to the supreme God and the indirect approach to him through intermediaries. It is likely that there were several different shades of opinion among the pagans and the believers in a high god, so that the inconsistency on this point — if indeed there is one — may be authentic. What is to be emphasized is rather the extent to which there was some recognition among pagans of *Allāh* as a high god. This attitude may even have been more prevalent than strict polytheism, but our meagre sources make it impossible to be certain about this. We are justified, however, in holding that many verses are to be interpreted in terms of belief in a high god even when there has been no mention of partners in the verse or its context. An example of this would be the statement in 112. 4 that "match (*kufuʾ*) for him was there none".

---

[12]   Cf. al-Bayḍāwī on 12. 24.

Some other verses to be interpreted of belief in a high god are the following:

> Those who gave partners said, "If *Allāh* had willed, we had not worshipped aught apart from him, neither we nor our fathers, nor had we made aught forbidden apart from him" (16. 35/37).
>
> They swore by *Allāh* most solemnly, "*Allāh* will not raise up him who dies" (16. 38/40).
>
> They swore by *Allāh* most solemnly, that if a warner came to them they would follow the guidance more than any other people; but when a warner came to them they only rejected the more (35. 42/40).

It is not clear how the view that belief in a high god was widespread affects the interpretation of the phrase "the Lord of this House" in Sūrat Quraysh (106. 3). The House is the Kaᶜba, and the Qur'ān must be taken to imply that its Lord is God monotheistically conceived. The sura implies that the Lord has both provided for the Meccans and protected them; and these are functions of God according to the Qur'ānic view. It would seem that Muḥammad's contemporaries must at the least have regarded the Kaᶜba as a shrine of *Allāh*, the high god, even if other deities were worshipped there. [13] From this basis the Qur'ān went on to proclaim a strict monotheism.

It remains to look at some of the general conclusions to be drawn from all this Qur'ānic material. One salient point is that little remains of what had presumably once been a vigorous paganism. The pagan deities have ceased to be the natural forces they presented in pre-nomadic agricultural times. The peasant is aware of his dependence on the powers of life, but the nomad depends much more on himself and his human allies, though he knows that his plans are often overridden by inscrutable forces which he describes as Time or Fate (*dahr*, etc.). Thus for the nomad it was not incongruous that *Allāh* rather than the pagan deities should send rain and supply man with his *rizq* or provision. The Qur'ān implies that the chief function left to the pagan deities is that of intercession with the high god; and this may well have corresponded with the practice of their worshippers. The cases of direct appeal to *Allāh* in moments of danger are further evidence of the powerlessness of the pagan deities. On

---

[13] There is some evidence of recognition of *Allāh* at the Kaᶜba by Christians; cf. Andrae, p. 25; Izutsu, p. 104.

the other hand, by frequently mentioning numerous signs of *Allāh*'s power the Qur'ān gives a richer content to that power of creating which the pagans acknowledged.

The lack of power and function thus exhibited in the pagan deities fits in well with the view expressed in *Muhammad at Mecca* that the effective religion of the nomads was a tribal humanism. The deities were relics of an agricultural period, and of little meaning to nomads in a country where nature showed few signs of regularity. The townsmen of Mecca were perhaps more inclined to acknowledge a supreme god since they had some knowledge of the great empires surrounding them. Certainly the Qur'ān sets out from the position that there is a widespread acknowledgement of *Allāh* in some sense, and then shows how this acknowledgement leads by logical developments to a genuinely monotheistic conception of God. [14]

---

[14] This article contains the substance of a paper which was read at the 12th Congress of the International Association for the History of Religions, Stockholm, August 1970, and at the 5th Congrès International d'Arabisants et d'Islamisants, Brussels, September 1970.

THE SACRIFICE OF THE DIVINE BEING
IN GREEK POLYTHEISM

Notes for a historical-structural exegesis

ILEANA CHIRASSI-COLOMBO

As we all know Greek Religion appears already in its early historical moment, that is in the Mycenaean period, as a polytheistic religion. But we cannot infer much about the true nature and essence of this polytheism from the name of the gods recorded on the Linear B tablets which have come down to us.

So if we wish to talk about Greek Polytheism we must take into account the moment at which literary and epigraphical sources can give us more reliable information. That is we must refer to the late phase of polytheism which we define *mature* because belonging to a fully historical and late period in the long history of Greek civilization.

If we try to define it through a characterizing synthesis, we take man as a point of reference — as a matter of fact every form of religion tests better its validity on the anthropological level. Now, in front of man the most assiomatic position of Greek Polytheism can be summarized in the definite division between Human and Divine: gods-immortal, men-mortal.

We agree that this division can be found present in every type of religion and is more or less in relief in almost all polytheistic systems, but in Greek Polytheism it is much more exasperated.

In Homer, Hesiod, as well as in the Greek tragedians, men and gods face each other on parallel but not complementary planes. The world of the gods is similar to that of men but on an entirely macroscopic dimension which is the consequence of an anthropómorphism which involves psycological as well as sociological aspects.

There is, however, one point, that is death, which completely annihilates the value of this similarity and makes it frustrating to men as it separates them irretrivably from gods.

Gods live for ever in a timeless dimension, in the unlimited, in the infinite (εἰς ἀεί); men on the contrary are kept in a temporal dimension, in the limited, in the finite.

Greek Polytheism, when we meet it, is caught struggling in this polarity men — gods which, according to formal logic, can be defined as a necessary association by opposition not unlike those we find emphasized in the Pytagorical table of opposites quoted by Aristotle in his *Metaphysics* (I, 5, 986a, 22 f). This polarity has been accepted on the logical level but not on the psycological and spiritual levels. This polarity between men and gods accounts for that sense of alienation and frustration which is always present in Greek thought in the well-known *topos* of the lament about the brevity of human life and the ineluctability of death.

The categorical difference between men and gods if transformed into existential difference on the religious level, results into a logical fraction unbearable to man because, as a result of this, he has lost the concept of the real unity of himself on the psychic level.

If we make use of a series of simple logico-mathematical passages to express it, we have the following picture:

As A is not B, men cannot be gods as death is the opposite of life, that means the last opposition on the existential level: men and gods are confined to unchageable positions that is *immobility for both*.

In this frame the sacrifice and death of a god is highly impossible. But there is in Greek Polytheism a different viewpoint that tries to overcome the deadlock.

If we write the expression $A : B = B : X$ we find that the value of X is determinative for the relation between A and B. We can say that for a constant value of X, $A = B$.

So if we take $A = men$; $B = gods$; $X = death$ we can say that men and gods are equal for X constant, that is for a constant value of death. That means if we take death as a logical bridge an interchange between gods and men is possible in a permanent state of *mobility*.

The same terms can be used taking into account the value life in the expression $A : B = X : Y$ (where Y = Life); that means $A/B = X/Y$. If we take A/B as Totality (made up of men and gods) and X/Y as the Existence (death and life together) we see that at the level of Totality and Existence the polarity mengods, death-life disappears. Assuming Totality as One we may say that only the One exists. But this is a step farther, which mostly belongs to Philosophy.

On the anthropological level we may thus come to the conclusion that only if we can fix a constant value for X we shall be able to integrate the extreme polarity which keeps gods and men apart. If we give to X the value death it appears clear that only if we succeed in imposing this value also on the divine level, that is that only if we make gods die, it will be possible to overcome the impasse. The death of the gods, or better the possibility given to gods to die, does not imply the death of the *Divine*, but it only means that gods and men are able to meet and mingle so as to reestablish the existential plenitude which enables the Being to exist.

The peculiar value of X constant which allows the first correlation between the two otherwise incommensurable series men – gods, appears, however, in the Dionysiac religion as it does in other closely related religious movements. Dionysos is the immortal – mortal, the god-man, enclosing in his unity the most striking polarity in different aspects of existence. He is the son of the Olympian Zeus but according to myth he was born and reborn many times after meeting *"real"* death (as when he was rent apart by the Titans) or a *metaphorical one* (as when he is told in myth to return from the sea, the swamps, from distant countries, or from Hades).

Dionysos manifests himself in myth and ritual through death and sacrifice both as an obliged passage in which he can act and be acted on as he is the one who sacrifices and is sacrified. So in the so called *sparagmòs* in the climax of the holy orgy Dionysos is the tender kid, or the bull, or the ivy which is rent apart and at the same time he acts by taking possess of his followers, the Bacchantes, through *enthousiasmos* and *mania*.

His death and sacrifice as actualized in myth have at all times a positive and high significance. According to the ethnological and anthropological data we can find this particular positive meaning of death and sacrifice as a link, passage and initiation to something new in the religious experience of non-polytheistic preliterate peoples. We refer to the well known researches of A. Jensen about the dema-sacrifice amid the primitive planters. I don't wish to discuss here the matter of the validity of Jensen's conclusions but is unquestionable that on the ground of the data supplied by him, we may maintain that many elements which make up the dionysiac religion can be considered primitive and very archaic and to belong to a protohistorical phase of Greek culture. First of all the theme of the sacrifice of the god and some aspects of his polymorphism which identify him with a plant (ivy, vine ...) or its produce (wine).

This can be maintained even though, according to various literary and historical sources, Dionysim may appear as a later and foreign acquisition. To support the early presence of Dionysos in Greek religion, first of all we must take into account the record of a *Diwonusojo* on the Linear B tablets which gives evidence of the god's existence in the Mycenaean pantheon at least in the Bronze Age. Even if we cannot infer much from the scanty references available about his true rule, the record is still of great value from a historical point of view as it anticipates by a thousand years the first available epigraphic evidence which refers to a fully historical age already; it is represented by an inscription from Athens dating the second half of the fourth century (330 B.C., Syll 1078).

However, even if the mythical theme of the murdering of the divine Being can be considered present in Greek religion already at an early stage, the dionysiac religious movements which we find recorded more frequently in literary sources from the 7th — 6th century onward, are not simply archaic *survivals*. They must rather be considered as a *logical answer* to the immobility imposed by mature polytheism once this has reached its high phase of detachment from real human interests. It follows as a consequence, that the various mythical records of hostility connected with the spreading of the Dionysiac religion may be explained in a *metahistorical* sense. Hostility at the mythical level expresses the polar opposition established by Dionysism against polytheism. The god who appears among men taking on *mortal* form (μορφὴ βροτησία)/Eurip. Bacc. 4-5/, who appears as an animal, as a plant, "who being a god is poured in sacrifice" (as wine) (οὗτος θεοῖσι σπένδεται θεὸς γεγώς), /Eurip. Bacc. 284/ represents new functions of old cultural elements in an entirely new sense.

Dionysism and other related religious features which have a great outburst at a certain point of Greek History cannot be explained as external suggestions of imported spiritual and cultural patterns nor as an almost miraculous survival of an archaic ontology. They must be rather looked upon as functional and logical new religious movements arising from the core of Greek

Polytheism itself. A revival indispensable to set into motion again *from the inside* cultural and spiritual mobility against the threat of alienation and immobility established by a culture almost very near to its collapsing point.

All that has been said before necessarily calls for a further and more detailed analysis. But the most interesting conclusion which, in our opinion, is worth pointing out, is that if we wish to get a through understanding of a religious problem we must use all means at our disposal operating on different levels. As a matter of fact religious problems are always deeply rooted in the manifold aspects of the whole reality.

We have seen for instance that in order to get a fairly complete picture of the process and meaning of myth and ritual in Dionysiac religion it is necessary first of all to test it at a historical level. But its inner dynamic becomes clear only through an inner logico-mathematical analysis at the structural level. All this is of great significance with regard to methodology as it claims a closer cooperation between methods of research which are still unfortunately considered divergent or highly irreconciliable.

MONOTHEISMUS UND POLYTHEISMUS IN DER HATRÄISCHEN RELIGION

H.J.W. DRIJVERS

Seit 1951 die Ausgrabungen des Irakischen Amtes für Archäologie angefangen haben, sind unsere Kenntnisse von der Religion der Partherstadt Hatra, die etwa 50 km westlich des alten Assur liegt, durch das Auffinden vieler Skulpturen und 280 aramäischer Inschriften beträchtlich gewachsen. Obwohl nur ein Fünftel des gesamten gefundenen Materials bisher veröffentlicht wurde, obwohl die Ausgrabungen noch immer fortgesetzt werden, archäologische Auskünfte nur spärlich erteilt werden und wir voraussichtlich noch Jahre auf die offiziellen Berichte werden warten müssen, ist es dennoch möglich, bereits jetzt etwas mehr über die Religion dieser Stadt zu sagen, die ihre Blütezeit in den ersten zwei Jahrhunderten nach Christi Geburt erlebte.[1]

---

[1] Eine allgemeine Übersicht bietet: W. Andrae, *Hatra, nach Aufnahmen von Mitgliedern der Assur-Expedition der Deutschen Orient-Gesellschaft* I, *WVDOG* 9 (Leipzig 1908); II, *WVDOG* 21 (Leipzig 1912); für die neuere Ausgrabungen *vide*: N. al-Asil, *ILN* 10-11-1951, SS. 762-765; 17-11-1951; SS. 806-807; 18-12-1954, SS. 1115-1117; 25-12-1954, SS. 1160-1161; H. J. Lenzen, "Ausgrabungen in Hatra", *AA* 70, (1955), SS. 334-375; ab Vol. VIII (1951) gibt *Sumer* gedrängte Darstellungen der Ausgrabungen in den Forewords; *vide* weiter H. Ingholt, *Parthian Sculptures from Hatra*. Orient and Hellas in Art and Religion, Memoirs of the Connecticut Academy of Art and Sciences 12 (New Haven 1954); D. Homès-Fredericq, *Hatra et ses sculptures parthes*. Étude stylistique et iconographique (Istanbul 1963); die Inschriften hat F. Safar herausgegeben: Inscriptions of Hatra, *Sumer* 7 (1951), SS. 170-184 (Nr. 1-27); *Sumer* 8 (1952), SS. 183-195 (Nr. 28-42); *Sumer* 9 (1953), SS. 240-249 (Nr. 43-57); *Sumer* 11 (1955),SS. 3-14 (Nr. 58-78);*Sumer* 17 (1961), SS. 9-42 (Nr. 79-105); *Sumer* 18 (1962), SS. 21-64 (Nr. 106-206); *Sumer* 21 (1965), SS. 31-43 (Nr. 213-230); *Sumer* 24 (1968), SS. 3-32 (Nr. 231-280). J. Teixidor gab die Inschriften Nr. 207-212 heraus; Aramaic Inscriptions of Hatra, *Sumer* 20 (1964), SS. 77-82; A. Caquot hat die meisten Inschriften neu herausgegeben in *Syria*: Nouvelles inscriptions araméennes de Hatra I, *Syria* 29 (1952), pp. 89-118 (Nr. 1-27); II, *Syria* 30 (1953), pp. 234-244 (Nr. 28-42); III, *Syria* 32 (1955), pp. 49-58 (Nr. 43-57); IV, *Syria* 32 (1955), pp. 261-271 (Nr. 58-78); V, *Syria* 40 (1963), pp. 1-11 (Nr. 79-105); VI, *Syria* 41 (1964), pp. 251-272 (Nr. 106-206); *vide* weiter J. T. Milik, "A propos d'un atelier monétaire d'Adiabène: Natounia, "*Revue Numismatique* VIᵉ série IV (1962), pp. 51-58 (Nr. 13-27); O. Krückmann, "Die neuen Inschriften von Hatra," *AfO* 16 (1952-53), SS. 141-148 (Nr. 1-27); R. Degen, "Neue aramäische Inschriften aus Hatra" (Nr. 214-230), *WO* V, 1970, SS. 222-236; die Interpretationen von F. Altheim und R. Stiehl sind nicht immer richtig; *vide*: *AAW* II (Berlin 1965), SS. 191-204; *AAW* IV (Berlin 1967), SS. 243-305; gute

Hatra ist vermutlich in der Zeit der Seleukiden entstanden, aber von seiner ältesten Geschichte wissen wir nichts. Es war eine parthische Stadt, die die Parther in ihrem Kampf gegen die Römer unterstützte und dafür eine große Unabhängigkeit besaß. Die Stadt wurde berühmt, weil sie bis zu zweimal einer römischen Belagerung widerstand; im Jahre 117 war Trajan nicht imstande, die Stadt einzunehmen, während Septimius Severus in den Jahren 198 und 199 vor der Stadt eine Niederlage hinnehmen mußte.[2] Trajans Gegner war der König Sanatruq, unter dessen Regierung die Stadt ihre größte Blütezeit erlebte und von dem eine Anzahl Statuen gefunden wurden.[3] Die Anhänglichkeit Hatras an die Parther war so groß, daß die Stadt in den letzten Jahren ihrer Existenz ein Bündnis mit den Römern schloß, um den Kampf gegen die Sassaniden, die die parthischen Arsakiden vertrieben, anzufangen.[4] Die römische Hilfe jedoch nützte nichts: um 240 eroberte Shapur I. die Stadt und plünderte die Heiligtümer. Kurz darauf wurde die Stadt von einem Erdbeben heimgesucht, was den Entvölkerungsprozeß beschleunigte, so daß Hatra im Jahre 364, als Ammianus Marcellinus mit einem römischen Heer daran vorbeizieht, schon jahrelang verlassen ist.[5] Dieser Lauf der Dinge führt zu dem glücklichen Ergebnis, daß die Stadt nach der Partherzeit keine andere Kulturperiode mehr gekannt hat, so daß eine rein parthische Stadt unter dem Sande hervorkommt. Gebäude und Skulpturen zeigen typisch parthische Stilmerkmale. Daneben finden wir Beispiele griechischer Bildhauerskunst, meistens in der Form römischer Kopien, wie z.B. eine Statue Apollons und Poseidons und viele klassische Heraklesfiguren: waren die Parther nicht stolz auf ihren Beinamen "Philhellenen"?[6] Die

---

Lesungen und Interpretationen bietet B. Aggoula, "Remarques sur les Inscriptions hatréennes", *Berytus* 18 (1969), pp. 85-104 (Nr. 1-226); über die hatraïsche Religion schrieb A. Caquot, *Syria* 29 (1952), pp. 113-118; *idem*, "Note sur le *semeion* et les inscriptions araméennes de Hatra", *Syria* 32 (1955), pp. 59-69; J. Hoftijzer, *Religio Aramaica*. Godsdienstige verschijnselen in Aramese teksten (Leiden 1968), pp. 51-61.

[2] *cf.* J. Jordan, "Der Kampf um Hatra," *MDOG* 79 (August 1942), SS. 8-24.

[3] *cf.* A. Maricq, "Hatra de Sanatrouq," *Syria* 32 (1955), pp. 273-288 = *Classica et Orientalia* (Paris 1965), pp. 1-16; J., Teixidor, "Notes hatréennes 4: Sur l'ère en usage à Hatra," *Syria* 43 (1966), pp. 93-97; D. Homès-Fredericq, *o.c.*, no. 16, Pl.V, 2.

[4] *cf.* D. Oates, "A Note on three Latin Inscriptions from Hatra," *Sumer* 11 (1955), pp. 39-43; A. Marieq, Les dernières années de Hatra: l'alliance romaine, *Classica et Orientalia*, pp. 17-25; S. Downey, *The Excavations at Dura-Europos Final Report* III, Part I, Fasc. 1: *The Heracles Sculpture* (New Haven 1969), pp. 93 f.

[5] Ammianus Marcellinus XXV, 8, 5 = Loeb Ausgabe II, 539.

[6] *cf.* S. Fukai, "The Artifacts of Hatra and Parthian Art, "*East and West* 11,

Sprache der Stadt war das Aramäische; es wurde mit einer eigen-
en Variante der nordmesopotamischen Schriftform geschrieben.[7]
Der arabische Einfluß was sehr groß: viele Eigennamen sind arabi-
sch, auch wurden arabische Göttergestalten, u.a. Allât, in Hatra
verehrt. Hatra war ein Zentrum für die halbnomadischen Wüsten-
bẹwohner semitischer Herkunft innerhalb des Einflußgebietes der
Partherkultur.

Die Stadt was ausgezeichnet befestigt. Das Zentrum bestand
aus einem kreisförmigen Gebiet mit einem Durchmesser von
1,5 km, von einem doppelten Wall umgeben. In dessen Mitte finden wir ein ummauertes Rechteck, in dem sich einige kleinere
Tempel und die Trümmer desjenigen befinden, was von Andrae
"der große Palast" genannt wurde.[8] Der große Palast erwies sich
als das zentrale Heiligtum Hatras, der Triade geweiht. Neben diesem zentralen Heiligtum bis zum doppelten Wall lagen die Häuser
der Aristokraten, mit denen eine Anzahl Tempel verbunden sind.
Bisher sind elf freigelegt worden. Unversehens haben wir so das
Gebiet der Religion betreten; der Erörterung dieses Themas
möchte ich folgende Bemerkungen vorausschicken.

Trotz der vielen Funde sind die Quellen für die Kenntnis der
haträischen Religion gering: Statuen, Inschriften, einige Kultge-
genstände und Namen von Göttern und Göttinnen, aber wir kennen keinen einzigen Mythus und wissen nichts von Ritualien. Die
Kenntnisse etwa der babylonischen Religion sind bedeutend
größer. In Hatra sehen wir nur die Außenseite der Religion, wodurch sie aber beherrscht und zusammengehalten wurde — das
müssen wir erraten. Außerdem sind die uns erhalten gebliebenen
Äußerungen typisch aristokratisch und äußerst stereotyp: wir erfahren von Königen, Generälen, und Priestern, nicht aber vom
einfachen Mann aus dem Volke. Diesen Einschränkungen Rechnung tragend können wir trotzdem etwas mehr über die haträische Religion erfahren.

(1960), pp. 135-181; D. Homès-Fredericq, o.c.; Enciclopedia dell'arte antica, s.v. Hatra; J. B. Ward Perkins, "The Roman West and the Parthian East," Prov. British Acad.
LI (1965), pp. 175-199; D. Schlumberger, Der hellenisierte Orient. Die griechische und
nachgriechische Kunst ausserhalb des Mittelmeerraumes, Kunst der Welt (Baden-Baden
1969).

[7] cf. A. Caquot, "L'araméen de Hatra," GLECS IX (1960-63), pp. 87-89; J. Pir-
enne, "Aux Origines de la Graphie syriaque," Syria 40 (1963), pp. 123 ss.

[8] cf. W. Andrae, o.c.; H. J. Lenzen, "Gedanken über den grossen Tempel in Hatra,"
Sumer 11 (1955), SS. 93-106.

Die triade Hatras, der das zentrale Heiligtum geweiht war, besteht aus Maran (= Unser Herr), Martan (= unsere Frau) und Bar-Marên(a) (= Sohn unserer Herren); die Triade ist also eine heilige Familie. Meistens kommt sie in dieser stereotypen Reihenfolge in den Inschriften vor, namentlich in den sogen. Mementotexten.[9] Die Identität Marans ist etwas problematisch. In Inschrift 107 wird mitgeteilt, dass ein gewisser Gadi, Sohn Abigads, den Tempel des Shamash, des grossen Gottes und Wohltäters, vergrössert hat. Diesen Tempel hat Bar-Marên(a) für seinen Vater Shamash erbaut. In Inschrift 280 wird Bar-Marên(a) Sohn des Shamash genannt.[10] Hieraus könnte man folgern, dass Maran Shamash ist, der Sonnengott der Araber. In anderen Inschriften dagegen sind Maran und Shamash verschiedene Götter: Inschrift 74 nennt erst die Götter der Triade und dann andere Götter u.a. Shamash; in der vierten Zeile dieser Inschrift werden Maran und Shamash zusammen genannt als verschiedene Götter. Auch ein anderer Inschrift unterscheidet Maran und Shamash.[11] In drei Inschriften (79, 88, 155) wird Maran *nšr'* genannt = Adler. Der Adler nun ist der Vogel des Himmels und das Symbol des Himmelsgottes. In Palmyra z.B. ist der Adler das Symbol des Bêls und Ba'al-shamîns, welche Götter scharf unterschieden sind vom Sonnengott, der neben ihnen in ihren Triaden einen Platz hat als Yarhibol und Malakbel. Es ist wahrscheinlich dass Maran und Shamash ursprünglich grundverschieden sind und dass die Identifizierung erst später stattgefunden hat. Maran gehört zum Typos des semitischen Himmelsgottes, welches Symbol der Adler ist. Es ist zu bezweifeln ob der Adler in Syrien und Mesopotamien der Sonnenvogel ist, wie F. Cumont und nach ihm viele anderen behauptet haben.[12] Shamash ist der Sonnengott der Araber, die die Wüste bewohnen, und sich in Hatra niedergelassen haben. Nach aussen hin, z.B. auf ihren Münzen, gibt Hatra sich vor allem als die Stadt des Shamash: die Münzlegende lautet "Hatra von Shamash" = umfriedeter Hof von Shamash.[13]

---

[9] Bzw. Inschrift Nr. 25, 26, 29, 30, 50, 52, 53, 74, 75, 81, 82, 89, 151, 160, 173, 235.

[10] Eine richtige Lesung dieser Inschrift bietet B. Aggoula, *art. cit.*, SS. 97ss.

[11] cf. B. Aggoula, *art. cit.*, pp. 101s.; Drijvers, "Aramese inscripties uit Hatra," *Phoenix*, Bulletin van Ex Oriente Lux, 16 (1970), pp. 377 ff.

[12] H. Seyrig, "Le culte du Soleil en Syrie à l'époque romaine," *Syria* 48 (1971), pp. 337ss. und pp. 371ss. Appendice III: Le douteux aigle solaire.

[13] cf. J. Walker, "The Coins of Hatra," *Numismatic Chronicle* (1958) pp. 167-172.

Es besteht eine besondere Beziehung zwischen dem Adler auf der einen Seite und den Königen von Hatra auf der anderen; die Königskrone ist immer mit einem Adler geschmückt, König Sanatruq und der Adler sind zusammen auf dem grossen Altar im Tempel des Shamash abgebildet. [14]

Martan ist viel weniger wichtig und kommt nie allein in den Inschriften vor. Aller Wahrscheinlichkeit nach ist sie eine Mondgöttin. Denn man hat ein Relief gefunden, auf dem Bar-Marên(a) als der Sohn der Sonne und des Mondes abgebildet ist. Seine Büste erhebt sich aus der Mondsichel und hinter ihm sind dieselbe Sichel und der Sonnennimbus noch einmal abgebildet. [15]

Bar-Marên(a) ist zusammen mit seinem Vater der wichtigste Gott Hatras. Er wird als der Sohn der Sonne und des Mondes dargestellt, aber auch als Apollon, von dem große und kleine Statuen gefunden wurden. [16] Daneben erscheint er als Bacchus-Dionysos. Aus der Inschrift auf einem Bronzekopf des Dionysos (Inschrift 222) geht deutlich hervor, daß damit Bar-Marên(a) gemeint ist. [17] Wenn Bar-Marên(a) als Dionysos erscheint, können wir an eine Göttergestalt wie Dusares, den Gott der Nabatäer, denken, der oft als Dionysos abgebildet wird. [18] In Palmyra ist Apollon, die andere Erscheinungsform des Bar-Marên(a) als Nabu identifiziert worden, der babylonische Gott der Weisheit, Gott der Orakel und Erfinder der Künste und Wissenschaften, zugleich aber Spender der Fruchtbarkeit. [19] Bar-Marên(a) verkörpert so alle Aspekte der menschlichen Kultur und der Fruchtbarkeit in der Natur: er ist zugleich Apollon und Dionysos als Verschmelzung der Gegensätze zu einer höheren Einheit.

Die Triade ist also ein typisches Beispiel eines uranischen Hochgottes, eines Repräsentanten des allwissenden und allmächtigen Himmels, neben welchem sich einige Aspekte seines Wesens verselbständigt haben, namentlich in der Gestalt Bar-Marên(a),

---

[14]   cf. H. J. Lenzen, "Der Altar auf der Westseite des sogenannten Feuerheiligtums in Hatra," *Festschrift A. Moortgat* (Berlin 1964), SS. 136-141.

[15]   cf. *Sumer* 23, 1967, p.d und Abb. 5 C.

[16]   cf. *Sumer* 23, 1967, p.d und Abb. 6.

[17]   Inschrift Nr. 222: Der Herr Š ᶜdw, der Sohn ... des ... für Brmryn (Übersetzung von R. Degen) "Eine Abbildung des Dionysoskopfes," in *Sumer* 23 (1967), Abb. 7.

[18]   cf. *Wörterbuch der Mythologie* I, S. 433, *s.v.* Dionysos und Dusares; R. Dussaud, *La pénétration des Arabes en Syrie avant l'Islam* (Paris 1955), pp. 56-58.

[19]   cf. J. Février, *La religion du Palmyréniens*, p. 97; du Mesnil du Buisson. *o.c.*, pp. 285ss.

einer Abspaltung des uranischen Hochgottes, der seiner Weisheit und Macht auf Erden in der menschlichen Kultur Gestalt verleiht. Daneben verblaßt die Gestalt der Mondgöttin Martan einigermaßen.

Solche Triaden finden wir öfter im syrisch-mesopotamischen Raum. Besonders die Triade von Baalbek-Heliopolis zeigt einige Übereinstimmung mit derjenigen Hatras. In Heliopolis wurden Jupiter/Hadad, Venus/Atargatis und Hermes/Dionysos verehrt. [20] Auch hier sehen wir also einen uranischen Hochgott, der zusammen mit einer Göttin einen Sohn erzeugt, der Fruchtbarkeit und Weisheit personifiziert. Für diesen ganzen Vorstellungskomplex möchte ich auf Widengrens *Religionsphänomenologie*, SS. 113 ff., hinweisen.

In historischer Hinsicht ist es wahrscheinlich, dass die Triade von Hatra erst später, am Anfang unserer Zeitrechnung, entstanden ist; darauf weisen die Unstimmigkeiten hin. Vielleicht hat die Triade von Baalbek-Heliopolis darauf Einfluss ausgeübt. Jedenfalls haben Maran und Bar-Marên(a) Züge bewahrt von alt-semitischen Gottheiten, wobei wiederum zu denken ist an die Götter von Baalbek-Heliopolis: Hadad, der Himmelsgott, und Hermes-Bacchus, der Gott der Vegetation. [21] Daneben ist Martan eine blasse Erscheinung, eine theologische Konstruktion. In den haträischen Inschriften ist Allât die wichtigste Göttin, neben welcher Martan fast keine Funktion hat.

Die besondere Beziehung zwischen den Königen von Hatra und Maran, der manchmal sogar Maran Nšr ꜣ (= Unser Herr Adler) genannt wird, wie in Inschrift 79, verdient im besonderen unsere Aufmerksamkeit. Vielleicht deutet sie darauf hin, daß die Macht des Hochgottes in Hatra und seiner Umgebung von dem König ausgeübt wird. Dann würde hier eine alte mesopotamische Vorstellung weiterleben. Soviel ist deutlich, daß die zentrale Position der Triade und deren erster Person der zentralen Macht der haträischen Könige entspricht, die zu einer bestimmten Zeit in der Stadtgeschichte als primus inter pares aufgestiegen sind.

Neben der Triade finden wir allerlei andere Götter und Göttin-

---

[20] *cf.* H. Seyrig, "La triade Héliopolitaine et les temples de Baalbek," *Syria* (1929), pp. 314-356; *idem*, "Bas-relief de la triade de Baalbek trouvé à Fneidiq," *BMB* 12 (1955), pp. 25-28.

[21] *cf.* H. Seyrig, "Bêl de Palmyre," *Syria* 48 (1971), pp. 85ss. und p. 113s: Palmyre et Baalbek.

nen verschiedener Herkunft in Hatra. In den Votivinschriften und den Mementotexten werden noch erwähnt: Baᶜ al-Shamîn, Nergal, Allât, Atargatis Nanai, während die theophoren Elemente in den Eigennamen noch auf viele andere Götter hinweisen. [22] Besonders Baᶜ al-Shamîn verdient in diesem Zusammenhang unsere Aufmerksamkeit. Er wird in den Inschriften "Gott" genannt, oder "großer Gott", "König" und sogar "Schöpfer der Erde". [23] Sein Heiligtum grenzte an dasjenige der Triade, er bleibt aber doch in deren Schatten, obwohl er sehr volkstümlich war. Etwas Ähnliches sehen wir auch in Palmyra, wo Baᶜ al-Shamîn sich großer Beliebtheit erfreute, einen wichtigen Tempel hatte, aber neben der Triade stand. [24] Abgesehen von der Frage, wo die Herkunft dieses Gottes zu suchen sei — im westsemitischen Gebiet oder bei den Protoaramäern, z.B. in Mari —, soll festgestellt werden, daß monotheistische Tendenzen in der Verehrung und den Epitheta dieses Gottes zum Ausdruck gekommen sind. Auffällig ist, daß er in einer Anzahl Inschriften als einziger Gott erwähnt wird, [25] während in Inschrift 23 neben ihm alle Götter genannt werden, deren Namen nicht erwähnt werden, im Gegensatz zu den Inschriften, in denen die Triade vorhergeht. Baᶜ al-Shamîn ist mit Recht "der Herr" und umfaßt alle anderen Götter. In einer Stadt wie Hatra, in der vielerlei Einflüsse verschmelzen, konnte diese Vorstellung neben derjenigen der Triade bestehen. Sowohl Maran wie Baᶜ al-Shamîn gehören zum Typus des Hochgottes. Maran steht an der Spitze einer Triade, die in ihrer Gesamtheit alle Aspekte des Göttlichen in den verschiedenen Gestalten jener Triade umfaßt. Baᶜ al-Shamîn dagegen umfaßt alle Aspekte des Göttlichen in sich selbst, so daß wir in Bezug auf ihn von einem inklusiven Monotheismus sprechen können.

Es ist sehr wahrscheinlich, dass das Nebeneinander der Triade

---

[22] Die Personennamen in den Inschriften aus Hatra verdienen eine eigene Untersuchung; cf. A. Caquot: "Les noms propres sont des formules de dévotion, des documents sur la piété." "Sur l'onomastique religieuse de Palmyre," *Syria* 39 (1962), p. 255.

[23] Inschrift Nr. 16, 17, 23, 24, 25, 29, 30, 49; cf. Caquot, *Syria* 29 (1952), pp. 116s.; cf. R. du Mesnil du Buisson, "De Shadrafa, Dieu de Palmyre, à Baᶜal Shamîm, dieu de Hatra, aux IIe et IIIe siècles après J.-C.," *MUSJ* 38 (1962), pp. 143-160.

[24] cf. P. Collart, "Aspects du culte de Baalshamîn à Palmyre," *Mélanges offerts à Kazimierz Michailowski* (Warschau 1966), pp. 325-337.

[25] Inschrift Nr. 16, 17; cf. du Mesnil du Buisson, *art. cit.*, p. 160: "L'extension du culte de Baᶜal Shamîm correspond à un acheminement vers le monothéisme."

und Baᶜal-Shamîns in Hatra denselben Grund hat als das Neben-
einander Bêls und Baᶜal-Shamîns in Palmyra. Dort is Baᶜal-
Shamîn Stammesgott der Benê Maziyan, einer der vier Stämme
Palmyras. Sein Heiligtum lag ursprünglich ausserhalb der Stadt
und kam erst während des zweiten Jahrhunderts A.D. durch die
Ausbreitung der Stadt innerhalb der Stadt. Baᶜal-Shamîn war ein
Fremder in Palmyra.[26] Genau dasselbe Verhältnis zwischen
Maran und Baᶜal-Shamîn tritt in Hatra zutage und die Lage des
Baᶜal-Shamîn-Tempels, ausserhalb des ummauerten Zentrums der
Stadt, deutet auf dasselbe hin. War dieser Tempel auch ein Stam·
mesheiligtum?

Die Mannigfaltigkeit des Göttlichen kommt auch noch auf andere Weise zum Ausdruck, und zwar in den anderen Göttern, die
alle einen eigenen Tempel außerhalb des zentralen Heiligtums
besaßen. Diese Tempel sind meistens mit den Wohnhäusern der
haträischen Aristokratie verbunden. Sie nehmen einen unverhält-
nismäßig großen Teil des bebauten Areals der Stadt ein. In diesen
Tempeln wurden zahllose Altäre gefunden, die meistens als Votiv-
geschenke an die Seitenwand des Tempels gestellt wurden,[27] und
viele Statuen von Göttern, Göttinnen, Generälen der haträischen
Armee, von Königen und Priestern. Zahllose Inschriften erwähnen die Namen der Personen, die die Statuen weihten für das
eigene Heil oder das Wohl anderer Menschen, die ihnen teuer
waren, oder die nur wollten, daß man ihrer vor dem Antlitz der
Götter gedachte. Auch kommt es vor, daß Personen eine Statue
z.B. des Königs Sanatruq (Inschrift 79) weihen und damit den
Wunsch verbinden, daß es ihnen unter seinem Nachfolger wohl
ergehen möge. Wir lernen hier ein religiös-politisches Establishment kennen, das damit beschäftigt ist, in seinen Bildern und
Inschriften den Status derjenigen, die ihm angehören, zu er-
höhen. Denn die Errichtung der Statue einer Person in einem
Tempel erhöht sowohl den Status des Spenders als des Darge-
stellten, so daß die Inschriften gleichsam die Schnittpunkte vieler
sozialer Bezüge zwischen Personen und Personengruppen darstellen.

---

[26] cf. D. Schlumberger, "Les quatre tribus de Palmyre," *Syria* 48 (1971),
pp. 121ss; Seyrig, "Bêl de Palmyre," pp. 94ss.; P. Collart-J. Vicari, Le *Sanctuaire de
Baalshamin à Palmyre* I, *Bibliotheca Helvetica Romana* X, I (Rome 1969),
pp. 201-246; Drijvers, *Baᶜal Shamîn, de Heer van de Hemel.* Zijn plaats in het pantheon van Palmyra (Assen 1971), wo alle einschlägige Literatur zu finden ist.
[27] cf. J. Teixidor, "The altars found at Hatra," *Sumer* 21 (1965), pp. 85-92.

Der Gedanke scheint erwägenswert, daß die haträische Aristokratie die verschiedenen Tempel, in denen sie das Priesteramt
ausübte und aus denen sie ihre Einkünfte bezog, besonders be-
treute. Bemerkenswert ist z.B., daß das Amt eines *rabbyt* ' (=
Verwalter) sowohl politische wie religiöse Aspekte aufweist.
Einerseits wird z.B. in Inschrift 223 von einem *rbbyt* ' der Araber
gesprochen, anderseits von einem *rbbyt* ' des Bar-Marên(a)
(*Statue des Afrāhaṭ, des Verwalters der Araber* [oder: *von Arab*],
*die für ihn aufstellte ꜥqb, der Verwalter des Brmryn, der Sohn
des Smŝy, des Verwalters, für das Leben des ꜥbdsmy, des Königs,
seines Herrn, und für das Leben seiner Söhne.*) [28]

Der finanzielle Aspekt dieses Kultus geht aus den jüngst veröffentlichten Inschriften hervor, von denen mehrere Geldspenden
für die Tempel erwähnen, [29] sowie aus den vielen aufgefundenen
Opferstöcken. [30] Eine der wenigen in Doura-Europos gefundenen
haträischen Inschriften erwähnt ein Geschenk von 100 Denaren
für den Gott Shamash. [31]

Die Hypothese scheint nicht allzu gewagt, daß König und Aristokratie ein großes religiöses Zentrum für die Steppenbewohner
betrieben, eine Art vormuslimisches Mekka. Die Triade neben und
über den anderen Göttern entspricht genau den Königen Hatras
in ihrer Stellung neben und über den Aristokraten. Die Zusam-
mensetzung des gesamten Pantheons war so gemischt, daß sie mit
der politischen und kulturellen Situation in Hatra übereinstimmte:
einer hellenistischen Partherstadt in einem semitischen Gebiet
mit einer Kultur von ehrwürdigem Alter. Hier trifft man den
griechischen Herakles neben dem arabischen Allât in der Gestalt
Athenes, den babylonischen Nergal neben Maran, dem Sonnengott der Steppenbewohner. [32]

Stießen wir also einerseits auf monotheistische Tendenzen in
der Religion Hatras und auf zentralisierende Tendenzen in der
Verehrung der Triade, anderseits gibt es einen bunten Poly-

---

[28] *cf.* R. Degen, *art. cit.*, S. 228; S. Downey, *The Heracles Sculpture*, p. 86: "the
holder of a sort of standard of a group or tribe".

[29] Inschrift Nr. 241, 242, 243, 244.

[30] *cf.* S. Downey, "Cult Banks from Hatra," *Berytus* 16 (1966), pp. 97-109.

[31] R. du Mesnil du Buisson, *Inventaire des inscriptions palmyréniennes de Doura-
Europos* (Paris 1938), pp. 38s.; *idem, Syria* 19 (1938), p. 383; *cf.* A. Caquot, *Syria* 30
(1954), pp. 244ss.

[32] *cf.* S. Downey, *The Heracles Sculpture*, pp. 83-96; für Allât D. Homès-Fredericq, *o.c.*, p. 57 und Abb. VII, 2.

theismus, in der politischen und kulturellen Situation der Stadt funktionierend, die eine deutliche Zentrumsfunktion für vielerlei verschiedene Bevölkerungsgruppen erfüllte. Nach außen hin stellte sich die Stadt als Hatra von Shamash dar und zeigte eine solide Einheit; im Inneren war Hatra gleichsam ein buntes Mosaik. Hochgottglaube mit monotheistischen Tendenzen und Polytheismus haben so auch politisch-soziale Aspekte: Einheit und Vielheit in ihrer gegenseitigen Spannung wurden so gestaltet unter der buntgemischten Bevölkerung der mesopotamischen Steppe.

MONOTHEISM IN THE BHAGAVADGĪTĀ:
A STYLISTIC CLUE

NORVIN HEIN

The nature of the personal theology of the author of the Bhagavadgītā is still a debated matter. Orthodox Hindus assume that he was committed to one of the Hindu systems of thought, and debate the question of which system he supports. No academic analysis of the Gītā has been able to convince the Advaitin, for instance, that this scripture does not belong particularly to him. As long as this attractive poem remains the most widely-read of all Hindu scriptures and one of the three fundamental sources for all branches of Vedanta, there will continue to be Advaita understandings of the Gītā, and readers who see its worship of the personal Lord as only a practical means for achieving knowledge of the non-personal Brahman, the sole Reality for those who really know.

While Hindus have been stiff in insisting that there is only one systematic philosophy in the Gītā, the tendentiousness of western scholars has taken the form of an insistence that the Gītā's systems are many — or perhaps none. Fifty years ago it was fashionable to believe that the thought of the Gītā is heterogeneous. Its diverse teachings were considered to be irreconcilable, the outcome of massive interpolation. More recent study has convinced us that the great preponderance, at least, of the Gītā's material is the product of a single mind. But that mind puzzles us with its pronounced eclecticism, and we wonder whether the author made any serious attempt to bring his borrowings into subjection to his own view.

The poet was obviously a person of generous pan-Hindu feeling, for whom the reconciliation of the diverse tendencies in the brahmanical faith was a very great desideratum. He took up and used elements of the Vedic ritualism, aspects of an old tribal religion, concepts from early Vedanta and Sāṃkhya thought, and materials from other sources. He turns his appreciative attention now to the puruṣa doctrine of the Sāṃkhya, and again to monotheistic concepts or to monistic cosmological ideas drawn from the Upaniṣads, and it is difficult to see significant difference in the kind of acceptance that he extends to each. It is possible to see the author as a mere oecumenical creed-splicer whose desire to accommodate all branches of Hindu thought took such precedence over the demands of logic and personal convinction that he produced an agglomerate that is devoid of unity or system. Professor Franklin Edgerton in his well-known interpretive study judges that the Bhagavadgītā presents a system of thought only in the limited sense that the writer shows a favoritism toward certain doctrines and gives greater prominence to certain trends of thought than to their rivals.[1]

The crux of the difficulty is the fact that the author, though a man of great literary talent, is not an expert in lucid development of religious doctrine. He draws in ideas from various older sources and uses them boldly, but at vital points the threads with which he binds them together are hardly discernible or seem to be missing altogether. He may have systematized his materials in his own mind, but he has not revealed the outlines of the process in any unmistakable way. When they try to recover the unifying framework of the Gītā's thought, interpreters are driven to desperate expedients. They make the most of the author's own meager hints on the relation between the strains of his teaching. They speculate on the relation between ideas that rational necessity would require. But when they have made the most of their various devices they find themselves still helplessly at odds with other interpreters who start with other suppositions or have sectarian positions to defend.

In the quest for the elusive personal convictions of the author of the Bhagavadgītā, this paper will attempt to employ a new resource. It is an insight into a stylistic peculiarity in the pattern of his thinking and writing. I call it the phenomenon of the modifying addendum. It is a habitual procedure in thinking whereby he begins his consideration of a topic by setting forth an old and well-accepted religious idea with apparent approval. By a slight verbal addition he then gives the traditional teaching a twist of interpretation that for him sets it precisely right. Though he shows a genuine respect for the thinking of the past, and wishes to offend as little as possible, he reveals that he has an

---

[1] Franklin Edgerton, *The Bhagavad Gītā* (N.Y., Harper Torchbooks, 1964), pp. 106-109.

outlook of his own. He seldom winds up discussion of a matter without asserting his own conviction in a well-placed word or two. These modifying addenda are the most personal material in the Bhagavadgītā and the surest clue to the ideas that overrule and unify the whole. They are used by the author in his adaptation of many doctrines and are found throughout the Bhagavadgītā. Since our interest is in the question of whether the ultimate cosmological conceptions of the work are monotheistic or monistic, we shall limit our attention to those modifying addenda that occur in discussions of that controversial matter alone.

The question of the position of monotheism in the Bhagavadgītā is the question of the relation between its conception of Brahman and its many personal designations for divinity: Iśa, Iśvara, Bhagavān, Kṛṣṇa, Vāsudeva, and the first-person pronouns that replace these divine names in direct address.

The Gītā uses the word Brahman often and with high acceptance. The author draws the term surely from the tradition of the older Upaniṣads, many of which he knows and quotes.[2] The word in the Upaniṣads is of course almost always neuter in gender and non-personal in its characterization of divinity. For the Upaniṣad thinkers the realization of Brahman entailed the supersession of individual existence. We shall see that the Gītā writer, too, assumes that his use of this word, unmodified, will convey this impersonal conception of the Divine Being. The monistic implication of the term Brahman is so well-established that some interpreters can scarcely believe that an ardent monotheist would use it. They take its appearance in the Bhagavadgītā as sufficient evidence that the author was not a theist. Before joining them in that conclusion, we must notice that the word is often accompanied in the text by modifying addenda, and study their effect upon its meaning. A careful consideration of the word with its modifiers will reveal what the final theology of the author was.

The first occurrence of the term with such rectifications is in Bhagavadītā 6:27, where modifying addenda follow in verses 29 and 30.

> praśāntamanasaṃ hy enaṃ
> yoginaṃ sukham uttamam

---

[2] C.O. Haas, "Recurrent and Parallel Passages in the Principal Upanishads and the Bhagavadgita", in Robert Ernest Hume, *The Thirteen Principal Upanishads*, 2nd rev. ed. (Bombay, Oxford U. Press), pp. 560-562.

upaiti śāntarajasam
        brahmabhūtam akalmaṣam. 6:27

To that tranquil-minded
        yogī, the highest bliss
approaches — to him whose passions are stilled,
        stainless, who has become Brahman.

These words would be entirely suitable for expressing a traditional monistic view that is quite impersonal in its conception of Brahman. But the verse that follows gives a distinctive development to the meaning at a critical point:

yuñjann evaṃ sadā 'tmānaṃ
        yogī vigatakalmaṣaḥ
sukhena brahmasaṃsparśam
        atyantaṃ sukham aśnute. 6:28

Disciplining himself always thus
        the yogī rid of stain
does easily to contact with Brahman,
        to endless bliss, attain.

The function of verse 28 is nothing more than the reinterpretation of the term *brahmabhūtam* of verse 27d. Otherwise, it merely repeats the concepts of that verse with minimum change: again in 6:28ab it is a yogī that is being discussed, and he is stainless (*vigatakalmaṣaḥ*, 28b, cf. *akalmaṣam*, 27d), and he gets supreme or endless bliss (*atyantam sukham*, 28d, cf. *sukham uttamam*, 27b). Nothing is really different save the substitution — in the same grammatical case to stress the parallelism — for *brahmabhūtam*, "become Brahman", in 6:27d, of *brahmasaṃsparśam*, "contact with Brahman", in 6:28c. The writer's only purpose in adding this new verse was to apply a modifying gloss at this point where his earlier more conventional expression had left him unsatisfied. The modifying addendum *brahmasaṃsparśam* does not withdraw *brahmabhūtam's* promise that the persevering yogī will become one with Brahman; it merely adds that the unity must be understood in the sense of contiguity and continuity, not absorption. His final conception of the situation of the liberated involves contact (*saṃsparśam*) between ātman and Brahman, not the obliteration of their identifying boundaries. Incorporation with the Brahman will not destroy the integrity of the souls of men.

6:29f. completes this modification of the traditional meaning of Brahman by giving assurance that the Lord, too, will maintain a personal identity within the unity known to the perfected seer:

yo mām paśyati sarvatra
    sarvaṃ ca mayi paśyati
tasyā 'ham na praṇaśyāmi
    sa ca me na praṇaśyāmi. 6:30

He who sees Me everywhere
    and sees all in Me,
for him I am not lost,
    and he is not lost in Me.

By these adaptive devices the writer of the Gītā brings the central conception of the Upaniṣads into subjection to his own ruling ideas, which are clearly monotheistic.

Again in Canto Eight several passages deal in a similar manner with the proper understanding of Brahman. The leading question of the chapter is stated in its first verse: "What is that Brahman? *kiṃ tad brahma*", (8:1a). Verse 3a begins the answer by defining Brahman as the Supreme *Akṣara* — a term that means both the Indissoluble (i.e. the metaphysical Ultimate) and the Syllable (i.e. the sacred syllable *Om*). The Upaniṣads often confide that this syllable symbolizes the Brahman and is mystically identical with It.[3] Bhagavadgītā 8:9—14 is continuing a well-known earlier tradition, therefore, when it recommends the seeking of final beatitude through lifelong reflection on this irreducible character along with the imperishable Absolute that it symbolizes and captures. After certain standard yogic preliminary disciplines that include restraint of the senses and control of the breath (8:9—12), positive meditation (*yogadhāraṇa*, 12d) is to be fixed on the sacred syllable, and comments are made on its meaning and efficacy:

om ity ekākṣaraṃ brahma
    vyāharan mām anusmaran
yah prayāti tyajan dehaṃ
    sa yāti paramāṃ gatiṃ. 8:13

ananyacetāḥ satataṃ
    yo mām smarati nityaśaḥ

---

[3] Hume, *op. cit.*, index s.v. "*om*".

tasyā 'haṃ sulabhaḥ pārtha
    nityayuktasya yoginaḥ. 8:14

He who, the one-syllabled Brahman *"Om"*
    uttering and meditating on Me
goes forth when leaving the body.
    he goes to the highest condition. 8:13

He who, thinking always on no other
    keeps Me in mind habitually,
I am easily gained by him, O Pārtha —
    by that habitually — disciplined yogī. 8:14

Let us compare this meditational instruction with an earlier teaching on the yogic use of the syllable *om* that is found in Maitri Upaniṣad 6:21–22. There, the mystic syllable is the "sound-Brahman" by which meditators ascend to union with a higher, non-sound Brahman in which human individualities disappear as the nectars of many flowers lose themselves in honey. The author of the Gītā, reacting to this or a similar impersonalistic understanding of *om*, interposes after 8:13a several modifying addenda that describe how truly wise users of this phonic symbol of the Brahman will conceive its meaning. He is saying that one must realize, while pronouncing this one-syllabled Brahman, that its final reference is no neuter thing but the personal Lord. One must aspire to be found at the hour of one's death not only uttering the sound *"Om"* but also, in the same act, "meditating on Me, *mām anusmaran*," 13b, and thinking continually and exclusively on the Lord, 14ab. One who does this will attain a *summum bonum* that is not dissolution in an impersonal essence but the gaining of Me, the Lord: *tasyā 'haṃ sulabhaḥ*, 14c.

Verses 8:21–22 continue and complete this monotheistic reconception of the nature of *Akṣara*, the Imperishable, which 8:3a had already identified as the Brahman. In 8:21bc it is now called also the highest condition, *paramāṃ gatim*, and the end of all rebirth. So far the words of this passage are strictly traditional. But verse 21d then captures and converts the doctrine with the dramatic addendum, *tad dhāma paramaṃ mama*, "That highest station is Mine!"[4] The author means that one who attains the

---

[4] The concept behind these words is paralleled and confirmed by the *madbhāvam*, "My estate", of 8:5c.

Akṣara by meditational use of *akṣara* will not attain a mere impersonal Absolute but the highest ontological expression of the Lord. The efficacy of the verbal symbol depends upon the user's awareness of its personal reference. Verse 22ab, a further addendum, next extends the reconception from the realm of ideas into the area of feeling and religious practice by adding that this highest station, this supreme Spirit (*puruṣa*) is "to be obtained, however, by undivided devotion, *bhaktyā labhyas tv ananyayā*". The author's own position in theology and religious practice is quite clear.

Finally, in 13:12c, we have a dramatic example of the writer's subordinating the concept of Brahman to the concept of the Lord by means of a modifying addendum. But the passage involves a textual problem that has been thought to be insoluble. Controversy over the reading and the meaning of the line is at least as old as the tension between the commentators Śaṃkara and Rāmānuja. To justify our claim that there is a decisive theistic addendum in this line, we shall have to prove first that Rāmānuja's reading of the text is the original and correct one.

The three words of line 13:12c are the whole target of our interest, but we shall not even be able to divide and read those words correctly until we have studied the entirety of verses 12—14. The new critical edition of the Mahābhārata renders 12c in a non-committal form that allows us to defer judgment on its reading and its meaning.

> jneyaṃ yat tat pravakṣyāmi
> > yaj jnātvā 'mṛtam aśnute
> anādimatparaṃ brahma
> > na sat tan nā 'sad ucyate. 13:12

> sarvataḥpānipādaṃ tat
> > sarvatokṣiśiromukham
> sarvataḥśrutimal loke
> > sarvam āvṛtya tiṣṭhati. 13:13

> sarvendriyaguṇābhāsaṃ
> > sarvendriyavivarjitam
> asaktaṃ sarvabhṛc cai 'va
> > nirguṇaṃ guṇabhoktṛ ca. 13:14

Taking up the work of translation, the first two lines give us no difficulty:

> What the object of knowledge is, that I shall declare, knowing which,
>   one attains freedom from death. 13:12ab

Lines 12cd continue the description of the necessary object of knowledge. The term *anādimatparam* is puzzling, but it is at least clear that what one must know for one's salvation is:

> the *anādimatparam* Brahman:
>   it is called neither being nor non-being. 13:12cd

Ignoring the perplexing *anādimatparam* for the present, we can push on into verses 13 and 14 and find there a conventional uncomplicated description of the characteristics of the Brahman just mentioned:

> It has hands and feet on all sides,
>   on all sides eyes heads and mouths,
> on all sides hearing; in the world
>   it abides, enveloping all, 13:13

> having the luminosity that is the property of all senses
>   yet free of all the senses,
> unattached and yet sustaining all,
>   devoid of the Strands yet the Experiencer of them. 13:14

The above is substantially a quotation from the Śvetāśvatara Upaniṣad, a work that the author of the Gītā knows well and quotes often.[5] In 13:13—14ab he is using, verbatim, Śvet. Up. 3:16—17ab. But he has broken Śvet. Up. 3:17 in Bhagavadgītā 13:14cd. The lines that he has dropped are as follows:

> sarvasya prabhum īśānam
>   sarvasya śaranam bṛhat. (Śvet. Up. 3:17cf.)

> The Lord and Ruler of all,
>   of all the great Refuge.

At first sight we see no reason why these two lines should have been looked on with disfavor. They would have continued an alliterative scheme that the author of the Gītā has maintained less perfectly in his substitution. The substituted ideas are commonplace and do not suggest that the author gave them priority

---

[5] Haas, "Recurrent and Parallel Passages", in Hume, *op. cit.*, pp. 548-551.

because of any urgency in their message. There is a mystery, then, in the motive for carrying out this omission and insertion of materials. The consideration that moved the author is not apparent in the content of the lines themselves. We shall seek a wider perspective and then return to this question.

Now we shall face the difficulties in Bhagavadgītā 13:12c's *anādimatparaṃ brahma*, and in particular the problem of how to render *anādimatparam*. Its lack of spacing proves nothing; we know that copyists of Sanskrit manuscripts felt no obligation to separate the individual words of their texts with spaces. They separated words or joined them according to orthographic or other convenience. Convenience rather than rational considerations caused the scribes of the Bhagavadgītā to create the cluster *anādimatparam*, for it makes no sense as it stands. To obtain any meaning from it, one is forced to divide it. But two divisions are possible, and two meanings. Which did the author intend to designate as the necessary object of knowledge for all salvation seekers? *anādi matparaṃ brahma*, "the beginningless Brahman subserving Me"? or, *anādimat paraṃ brahma*, "the beginningless supreme Brahman"? If the latter, there is no trace of monotheism in the passage: *-mat* is an adverbial suffix not a personal pronoun, and the neuter Brahman stands supreme. But if the first reading is the original one, the author is revealed as a theist who conceives the Brahman as existing only for the ends of the Lord.

Both word-divisions are legitimate. Śaṃkara adopts the second reading, Rāmānuja the first. Most commentators have preserved the chamelion-like nature of the line by keeping the cluster intact, and have interpreted it according to the doctrinal assumptions of their various sects. R.C. Zaehner in his recent commentary prefers to believe that the ambivalence of meaning was intended by the author himself, who with sly humor planted a puzzle here for each reader to interpret according to his own spiritual advancement.[6] Such devices are well known, of course, in Indian religious pedagogy. The author of the Gītā seems too earnest in his convictions to be capable of such joking, but this subjective impression is insufficient to refute the view of Professor Zaehner.

It would be easy to surrender hope that any evidence available

---

[6]   R.C. Zaehner, *The Bhagavad-gītā* (Oxford, Clarendon Press, 1969), pp. 338 f.

will ever establish the historical meaning of this line. One could point out that *matpara* occurs again in the Bhagavadgītā in 2:61b and is shown thereby to belong to the author's living vocabulaty, whereas there is no such certainty about the status of the alternative, *anādimat*. But a writer cannot be denied the right to use *anādimat* or any other word only once. One can argue that the theistic idea underlying the word *matparam* is paralleled in 14:27a's *brahmano hi pratisthā 'ham*, "For I am the foundation of Brahman" – as Edgerton has pointed out.[7] But Advaita commentators have been quite capable of resisting the force of that line,[8] and will surely continue to deny that it is theistic itself or supports theistic interpretation of 13:12c.

The new consideration that we shall bring to this problem is an explanation of why, in quoting Śvetāśvatara Upaniṣad 3:16–18, the author was forced to reject the last two lines, "the Lord and Ruler of all, of all the great Refuge". The reason is not apparent in any obvious offensiveness of the dropped words nor in any special timeliness of the message of their substitutes. We begin to understand when we consider how the entire passage would have read if the author had tried to preserve these lines in connection with either of the possible readings of Bhagavadgītā 13:12c. If he had been thinking and speaking in monistic terms, he would have had no reason for breaking off his quotation of the Upaniṣadic verse: he could proceed without shock or contradiction from "the beginningless supreme Brahman" to "the Lord and Ruler of all, of all the great Refuge". Lord, Ruler and Refuge are common enough as designations of the Brahman in the Upaniṣad tradition.[9] But what problem of consistency would he have faced if, after uttering line 12c with theistic intent and form, he had adjoined Śvet. Up. 3:17cd to it? If the author had just meant and said in 13:12c that the necessary object of knowledge was "the beginningless Brahman *subserving Me*", he could not in the next verse but one allow himself to call that same subordinated Brahman "the Lord and Ruler of all". That is why he dropped these

---

[7] Franklin Edgerton, *The Bhagavad Gita* (N.Y., Harper Torchbooks, 1964), p. 99 note 5.

[8] Summarized in W. Douglas P. Hill, *The Bhagavadgītā* (Oxford University Press, 2nd abridged ed. 1953), p. 184n.

[9] Paul Deussen, *The Philosophy of the Upanishads* (Edinburgh, T & T. Clark, 1906), pp. 206 ff.

words and substituted the rather ordinary ideas that now stand in 13:14cd. The word division, *anādi matparaṃ brahma*, represents the intention of the author and the original reading of the line.

And the line, thus authenticated, amends the familiar word Brahman with the addendum *matparam*, "subserving Me". A tiny insertion, it is one of the most powerful demonstrations that the Bhagavadgītā's author was a monotheist. The personal God was not, for him, a subordinate aspect or mere appearance of the neuter Absolute. The Lord, for him, was the Ultimate Being, and the lofty Brahman was that aspect of God through which He supported the being of all creatures and took them to Himself.

The author of the Gītā was not without convictions nor timid in expressing them. Despite his polite appreciation for other outlooks than his own, monotheism is the final truth in all his thinking and the center toward which he bends the concepts of all the traditions on which his reflection plays. We have not been able, of course, to educe from the Gītā a hidden systematic theology. Edgerton's judgment that it contains no coherent structure of metaphysics remains true as a comment on what the author has actually written. His mind, however, is not incoherent but rather incompletely expressed. The accomplishment of the writer as a constructive thinker is limited by the fact that his interests are historical and promotional. He is concerned with the gap between the old prestigeous orthodoxies and the Vaiṣṇava faith for which he seeks legitimacy and universal acceptance. Therefore he does not weave his thought outward systematically from its own center but works on the perimeter of old systems. His thought ranges back and forth between established doctrines and his own convictions, establishing ties and quietly subordinating the old to the new by modifying addenda. He moves on leaving the relation between ideas clearly indicated but minimally expressed.

In this study we have been interested primarily in *what* the author of the Bhagavadgītā thought. We have in passing received insights into *how* he thought that should be useful in studies of other aspects of his doctrine.

Postcsript, May 1975

My more recent studies of *brahman* in the Bhagavadgītā make the above understandings incomplete and sometimes unsatisfactory. Adequate revision is not possible at the page-proof stage. With Brill's kind permission, the materials will be reworked soon in a longer publication. N.H.

LE MYTHE DANS LE POLYTHÉISME ROMAIN

Traditions relatives à la fondation
du temple capitolin *

GIULIA PICCALUGA

Le sujet de la présente communication paraîtra peut-être à première vue se situer un peu en marge du thème de ce congrès: l'examen des traditions relatives à la fondation du temple capitolin semblerait en effet mener plutôt à une problèmatique dont les composants fondamentaux sont la délimitation de la position du mythe dans la religion romaine et la nécessité de mettre en valeur un matériel mythique trop longtemps négligé. Mais c'est justement le fait d'avoir à nous occuper de mythes, c'est-à-dire, d'histoires sacrées, objet d'un type particulier de croyance absolue et sans alternative aux êtres extra-humains qui en sont les acteurs, qui nous ramène à ce thème.

On pourra constater au cours de cette communication le rôle joué par cette croyance sous ses divers aspects et dans ses réalisations successives au sein du polythéisme romain.

Chez les spécialistes de la religion romaine l'opinion est de plus en plus répandue selon laquelle la thèse d'une démythisation consciente qui se serait produite au sein de ce milieu religieux — thèse avancée voici plus de trente ans par C. Koch — si elle a bien amené une réévalutation d'une civilisation considérée pendant si longtemps comme constitutionnellement incapable d'élaborer une mythologie, a par ailleurs définitivement anèanti toute tentative d'utilisation et de revalorisation de la tradition romaine.

Il n'a pas, en effet, été tenu compte de ce que l'élimination des mythes relatifs à les divinitées n'exclut pas nécessairement l'existence de tout un patrimoine mythologique dont l'importance et les caractéristiques devraient être mises en lumière par une métho-

---

* Je traite longuement ce sujet dans *Terminus. I segni di confine nella religione romana*, Roma 1974, 201-209. Nous renvoyons à cet ouvrage pour tous éclaircissements ainsi que pour la documentation, d'ailleurs facile à trouver dans les manuels et les encyclopédies spécialisées.

dologie moderne, libre de tout préjugé scientifique quel qu'il soit, par l'étude comparée des religions ainsi que par l'adoption d'un concept plus large du "mythe".

En ce qui concerne, enfin, l'absence véritable — mais partielle! — de mythes divins, elle devrait être étudiée dans le contexte de ses rapports avec le processus de formation du polythéisme romain. Ce n'est qu'ainsi, en effet, que l'on pourrait remettre en évidence la façon savante dont celui-ci utilise sur le plan mythique certains motifs que l'on pourrait, à première vue, trop facilement qualifier de "légendaires" ou de "pseudo-historiques"; de cette façon on soulignerait également la substitution fréquente — mais toujours sur le plan du mythe! — d'éléments mythiques par des faits cultuels. L'analyse des traditions relatives à la fondation du temple capitolin essaiera justement de démontrer comment une religion qui a volontairement renoncé à un certain type de mythes fondés sur les aventures d'acteurs divins, le remplace souvent et à tous effets, par un genre de récits relatifs aux vicissitudes du culte de ces dieux à l'époque des origines.

A propos de la fondation du temple de Iuppiter Capitolinus il existe, on le sait, trois récits distincts. Ces récits se réfèrent à trois moments précis de sa construction: le déblaiement de l'emplacement choisi, le creusement des fondations, la décoration du fronton. Nous les examinerons à présent attentivement dans tous leurs détails et dans leurs variantes.

Le premier récit part de la prétendue inexistence à Rome de tout temple dédié à Iuppiter. C'est Tarquinius Priscus qui, à l'occasion d'une victoire, en promet l'édification et c'est à son fils que reviendra le soin d'en entreprendre les travaux. La divinité elle-même indique le lieu qui lui convient. Mais l'emplacement sur lequel devra s'élever le temple est couvert de constructions et d'édifices sacrés de toutes sortes, promis à différents dieux par Titus Tatius lors de sa guerre contre Romulus et consacrés à la fin des hostilités. Pour déblayer rituellement le terrain, il faudra donc en évoquer les "titulaires" et en transférer le siège par la célébration de sacrifices et l'interprétation des *auguria*. Les intéressés émigrent tous volontiers, à l'exception de Terminus — et, selon quelques variantes isolées dont nous ne nous occuperons par la suite afin de ne pas trop élargir les limites de notre étude, Iuventus et Mars —; c'est impossible pour les augures de le délo-

ger: l'intéressé se refuse catégoriquement à céder le pas au roi
Iuppiter. Un sacrifice destiné à révéler le sens de la contestation
est célébré; en voici le résultat: l'inamovibilité de Terminus doit
être entendue comme un auspice éminemment favorable car il
promet la stabilité et l'immobilité éternelles de toute chose et, en
particulier, des *termini Urbis* qui marquent les confins du territoire appartenant à Rome. Si Terminus, justement, demeure à
côté de Iuppiter, la cité sera assurée d'exercer une domination
éternelle sacralement garantie. A la suite de cette réponse, les
mesures suivantes seront donc prises: l'autel ou le *sacellum* de
Terminus ou, selon certaines variantes, la pierre qui le représente
sera inclus dans le temple capitolin où il restera auprès de Iuppiter; en outre, Terminus étant accoutumé de recevoir des sacrifices
à ciel ouvert, il faudra adapter aux exigences de ce dieu la nouvelle construction dont, justement, le toit présentera une ouverture pour lui permettre de voir le ciel. A partir de ce moment
Terminus ne bougera plus et restera là où il était; il sera invoqué
publiquement en tant que *custos finium*, gardien des limites des
propriétés privées comme du territoire public; puisque il n'a pas
cédé le pas, même devant Iuppiter, il ne pourra pas être déplacé.

Le second récit débute lors du creusement des fondations du
temple. Les ouvriers trouvent, profondément enfouie, une tête
humaine — selon certaines variantes, tout le reste du corps s'y
trouvait également —; cette tête, qui semble avoir été détachée du
buste à l'instant même, car les traits sont intacts et le sang coule
du cou tranché, porte en outre, gravés, des caractères étrusques.
Il s'agirait de la tête d'un certain roi Olus, ou Aulus, Vulcentanus,
dont on ne sait rien et qui aurait été exilé, on ne sait pour quelles
raisons, de sa patrie; tué par un esclave il aurait été condanné à
être enseveli en terre étrangère. Devant un tel prodige le dernier
des Tarquinii ordonne que les travaux soient immédiatement sus-
pendus et que les experts soient interrogés. Mais, les aruspices
locaux ne sachant comment interpréter les faits suggèrent que
l'on consulte un devin étrusque particulièrement renommé à
l'époque, Olenus Calenus. Sur l'ordre du souverain, une déléga-
tion de citoyens d'élite part pour l'Etrurie. Mais le devin est mo-
mentanément occupé; accueillis par son jeune fils, Argus, auquel
ils exposent le motif de leur visite, les ambassadeurs reçoivent de
leur interlocuteur un précieux avertissement. Le devin tracera un
contour sur le sol à l'aide de son bâton en leur disant: "voilà la

colline Tarpéienne, voici son côté oriental, son côté occidental, voici le nord, voici enfin le sud", puis, indiquant telle ou telle portion de cercle il demandera si c'est là que la tête a été trouvée; les délégués devront se garder de donner une réponse directe et se borner à répéter que le prodige s'est vérifié à Rome, sur la colline Tarpéienne, sinon le devin transférera aussitôt le miracle en Etrurie. Aussitôt dit, aussitôt fait; aux questions que leur pose Olenus Calenus, les Romains ne répondent pas, se contentant de répéter que la tête a été trouvée à Rome et à demander que le prodige ne soit pas transféré ailleurs. A la fin, le devin se rend et donne sa réponse: le prodige est merveilleux et annonce de très heureux événements. Les Romains deviendront, en effet, très puissants car le lieu où a été trouvée la tête, c'est-à-dire, la colline Tarpéienne sur laquelle s'élèvera le temple de Iuppiter Optimus Maximus, sera à la tête de l'Italie et de tous les peuples et le restera jusqu'à la dissolution de l'univers. C'est, justement, parce qu'il voulait donner à sa patrie cette possibilité de dominer le monde qu'il questionnait de la sorte; il demande ensuite qui les a induits à cette prudente attitude et, apprenant que c'est un jeune homme, il saute à cheval, rejoint Argus et le tue à l'endroit qui prendra, de ce fait, le nom d'Argiletum. De son côté, la colline où la tête (en latin *caput*) d'Olus avait été trouvée et où devait être édifié le temple de Iuppiter est appelée depuis lors "Capitolium", c'est-à-dire, "tête d'Olus".

La dernière des trois légendes qui nous intéressent s'ouvre sur une scène quelque peu différente. Les Tarquinii, chassés de Rome, s'allient aux Etrusques dans une guerre de restauration. Le régime républicain est désormais instauré dans la ville. Le temple de Iuppiter a, depuis longtemps, été construit mais il manque encore à son achèvement les ornements du fronton. Le dernier souverain, quand il était encore sur le trône, soit qu'il fut induit par quelque présage, soit par inspiration personnelle, avait pensé y placer des quadriges en terre cuite et, à cette fin, en avait commandé la fabrication à des artistes renommés de Véies; peu après, il fut renversé de son trône. Entre temps, les quadriges ayant été modelés et mis au four, au lieu de se consolider et de diminuer de volume par suite de l'évaporation, ils se mettent à gonfler et à croître au point que, pour les tirer du four, il faut en démolir les murs. Les aruspices interprètent très favorablement ce prodige: le peuple chez lequel seront ces quadriges sera heureux et plus puissant que tout autre. Raison pour laquelle lorsque les Romains réclament la livraison de leur commande, Véies répond par un refus catégorique: les quadriges appartiennent aux Tarquinii et non à ceux qui les ont chassés. D'après une variante unique, une guerre aurait été nécessaire pour que les quadriges fassent retour à leurs légitimes propriétaires. Selon d'autres variantes, l'histoire a une suite. Quelques jours après le refus, des courses de chars avaient lieu à Véies en présence du peuple; tandis que le vainqueur couronné et décoré de la palme sort du cirque sur son char, voici que les chevaux, ombrageux sans raison apparente, échappent au contrôle de l'aurige et se dirigent vers Rome sans qu'on parvienne à les arrêter. Arrivés au Capitole, après avoir accompli une triple *lustratio* autour du temple de Iuppiter, ils jettent à terre l'aurige; celui-ci mourra ainsi près de la porte qui lui devra le nom de Ratumena. Mais *lustrare* le Capitole trois fois de suite après une victoire dans le cirque était, alors, habituellement considéré comme l'augure le plus favorable qui soit. Aussi, les habitants de Véies, frappés en même temps qu'effrayés par ce fait prodigieux, font-ils savoir aux Romains qu'ils peuvent venir prendre livraison des quadriges en terre cuite.

Voilà les trois récits. Ils sont généralement négligés, ou qui pis est, qualifiés par les savants, à quelques rares exceptions près, du terme méprisant de "mythes étiologiques" comme s'ils avaient été créés après coup, artificiellement, pour "expliquer" certaines caractéristiques du temple capitolin (la présence du dieu Terminus à l'intérieur, les quadriges sur le fronton), ou l'étymologie du mot "Capitole". Nous essaierons, à présent, de montrer, en analysant la structure et le contenu dans leurs moindres détails, que nous nous trouvons en présence de mythes authentiques, faisant partie intégrante d'une tradition visant à fonder dans ses différents aspects une réalité précise.

Remarquons tout d'abord, qu'ils sont fréquemment rapprochés; la chronique relative à la construction du temple capitolin enregistre souvent, immédiatement après l'épisode de l'inamovibilité du dieu Terminus, celui de la découverte de la tête. Et les deux faits sont rappelés ensemble dans le discours que Camillus prononce afin d'éviter le transfert de siège à Véies, pour amener les Romains à renoncer à leur projet. De même, le prodigieux "levage" des quadriges d'argile et la découverte d'une tête humaine dans les fondations du temple sont tous deux englobés sous la même définition de "splendide et heureux augure".

Il y a lieu de se demander pourquoi ils étaient ainsi rapprochés alors qu'ils n'ont qu'un seul point commun (le fait qu'ils ont trait à la fondation du temple capitolin) et qu'il s'agit par ailleurs de récits forts différents.

Différent est, d'abord, le lieu où se déroulent leurs actions respectives: c'est à Rome que se situe le récit qui a le dieu Terminus par acteur, tandis que la tentative manquée de transférer le bénéfice du prodige de la découverte de la tête a lieu dans un endroit, non précisé, de l'Etrurie; quant à la croissance prodigieuse des quadriges d'argile, c'est toujours en Etrurie, mais à Véies cette fois, qu'elle se produit.

L'époque à laquelle se déroulent les trois récits est également différente: les deux premiers sous le règne de Tarquinius, le troisième, relatif à la dispute entre Rome et Véies pour la possession des ornements du fronton, sous la République.

Les personnages de ces trois récits ne sont pas non plus les mêmes: le premier a pour acteurs des divinités, des souverains, des augures; le second, encore des rois et des prêtres, mais aussi un aruspice étranger, son fils et un certain Olus — bien que celui-ci n'y mette que sa tête! —; au troisième, nous voyons, enfin, participer un aurige vainqueur, des céramistes et le peuple de Véies tout entier ainsi que les quadriges d'argile.

Enfin, le contenu de récits est toujours différent: nous avons d'abord l'opposition statique du dieu Terminus à quoi se ramène tout l'épisode; ensuite la tentative manquée de transférer rituellement de Rome à l'Etrurie au moyen d'un artifice un auspice favorable; et, enfin, l'action mouvementée dont le premier temps est constitué par le singulier prodige qui a eu lieu dans le four tandis que la seconde phase est représentée par la course effrénée du char de Ratumena vers Rome. En outre, un dernier prétexte de différenciation paraît être constitué par la présence, dans l'épisode de la tête et dans celui des quadriges, de l'élément tragique: la découverte de la tête d'un homme assasiné encore ruisselante de sang, le meurtre d'Argus, la mort accidentelle de Ratumena. Cet élément tragique fait entièrement défaut dans l'histoire de Terminus; enfin, toujours dans le récit relatif à l'opposition de Terminus à Iuppiter — et contrairement à ce qui se produit pour les deux autres récits — on ignore jusqu'au dernier moment le lieu où se produira effectivement le prodige.

Toutefois, et en dépit de ces considérations, sommes-nous véritablement certains que ces trois récits sont aussi différents qu'ils le paraissent? A regarder de plus près, ils présentent, en effet, à côté des éléments qui les distinguent, des analogies précises.

La première de ces analogies semble être constituée par le fond sur lequel se déroulent ces aventures. Bien que, comme nous l'avons vu, deux entre elles aient lieu en Etrurie tandis que l'histoire de Terminus se passe exclusivement à Rome, c'est toujours à cette dernière ville qu'aboutissent également les deux autres. En effet, même si cette sorte de jeu entre l'ambassade romaine et Olenus Calenus, l'un essayant de prendre ses adversaires au piège et ceux-ci déjoutant ses feintes, se passe dans une région non précisée de l'Etrurie, la tête qui est à l'origine de cette histoire a été trouvée à Rome; et c'est encore de cette ville qu'est partie la commande des quadriges aux artistes de Véies; c'est à Rome que ces quadriges reviendront, réellement et symboliquement, avec la course effrénée du char de Ratumena.

Les trois époques où les différentes histoires se situent ont également, à côté des différences que nous avons soulignées, une caracteristique commune: toutes trois s'inscrivent, en effet, dans un temps mythique nettement séparé de la réalité actuelle: ou bien le temple de Iuppiter n'existe pas ou bien il n'est pas encore ouvert au culte parce qu'incomplet, ce qui serait inconcevable dans le temps historique; il est par ailleurs possible que se vérifient des faits impensables dans la vie de tous les jours; comme, par exemple, qu'un dieu refuse de laisser transférer le lieu de son culte et se rebelle à Iuppiter, que l'on découvre dans les profondeurs du sol une tête ruisselante de sang et portant une inscription étrusque, que des quadriges d'argile croissent démesurément en cours de cuisson; de son côté, la puissance romaine est encore *in fieri*, continuellement en crise à cause de cet antagonisme avec les Etrusques, impensable dans une réalité qui voit désormais Rome maîtresse de l'Italie et d'une très grande partie du monde connu; il s'agit, enfin, d'une époque dont les acteurs sont les Tarquinii et qui, de ce fait même, apparaît comme essentiellement autre à une mentalité fondamentalement républicaine pour laquelle un Tarquinius n'est plus, désormais, qu'un lointain souvenir perdu dans les brumes d'un passé légendaire.

Il convien de souligner que les personnages des trois récits ont également des éléments communs. Remarquons, tout d'abord, que les acteurs de ces aventures sont tous, à des titres divers, en rapport avec l'Etrurie: Les Tarquinii en sont issus; une ambassade y est envoyée pour consulter Olenus Calenus; le prodige des quadriges se produit à Véies. Ajoutons à cela que les personnages ne sont pas des individus communs, anonymes, mais qu'ils semblent posséder une distinction particulière: les citoyens d'élite qui sont envoyés auprès du devin étrusque, le vainqueur des jeux du cirque, d'illustres céramistes, des augures et des aruspices, des souverains et jusqu'à des dieux. Les trois récits se rattachent au second des Tarquinii; dans tous trois interviennet les prêtres chargés d'expliquer le prodige; tous trois concernent de quelque manière Iuppiter Optimus Maximus et ce, non seulement indirectement à cause du lieu qui lie les trois récits à son temple, mais d'une manière spécifique, car c'est à lui que Terminus s'oppose, c'est dans les fondations de son temple que la tête a été retrouvée, c'est pour orner le fronton qu'il faut que soient restitués les quadriges.

Et enfin, il est possible de trouver des affinités jusque dans le contenu de ces trois histoires. Tout d'abord, dans chacune d'elles nous sommes en présence d'un conflit: conflit entre Terminus et Iuppiter, conflit entre Olenus Calenus d'une part et le fils de ce dernier et les Romains de l'autre, conflit enfin entre les habitants de Véies et les Romains. De même, dans les trois cas, nous avons à faire à un transfert: catégoriquement refusé par Terminus, transfert manqué par Olenus Calenus pour faire bénéficier l'Etrurie du prodige de la tête, transfert enfin réalisé des quadriges, bien que de Véies vers Rome et non pas l'inverse. Il y a lieu, par ailleurs, de souligner dans tous ces épisodes un intérêt constant de la communauté tout entière aux événements en question: le souverain et les prêtres s'occupent de Terminus qui ne veut pas s'en aller; toujours le roi, des prêtres et une ambassade composée de citoyens d'élite s'emploient à interpréter la découverte de la tête; les aruspices et les habitants de Véies prennent part à la tentative de revendication des quadriges dont la fabrication fut, du reste, ordonnée par le roi. Enfin, ces trois récits trouvent leur dénominateur commun dans l'institution de certains aspects de la réalité. Mais quelle est la réalité qu'ils instituent? C'est là un point sur lequel il y a lieu de s'étendre un peu plus longuement.

Une première analyse des données permet d'indiquer rapidement quels sont les éléments de l'existence actuelle qui apparaissent en fonction des événements racontés: à la suite de la découverte de la tête et du meurtre du fils d'Olenus Calenus, Argus, la colline Tarpéienne prendra le nom de Capitolium et une localité romaine s'appellera désormais Argiletum; un fait analogue se produit pour la porte Ratumena, ainsi nommée après que l'aurige étrusque a été renversé à proximité par son quadrige; enfin, à la suite de l'entêtement d'un dieu et de l'imprévisible réaction au feu des quadriges d'argile, le temple capitolin finira par présenter des caracteristiques tout à fait particulières: l'autel de Terminus à l'intérieur, le toit partiellement percé, le fronton orné d'une certaine façon.

Mais la nouvelle réalité ne s'épuise pas ici. Un aspect ultérieur des plus importants s'en trouve immédiatement éclairé si nous réfléchissons à la façon dont sont respectivement interprétes les prodiges en question. La ville qui possédera les quadriges en terre cuite, disent les experts étrusques, aura le pouvoir et le bonheur; le lieu où a été trouvée la tête humaine, explique Olenus Calenus, sera puissant et se trouvera à la tête de l'Italie et de tous les peuples et cela à jamais, ou, mieux, jusqu'à la dissolution de l'univers, car cette découverte est considérée comme un prodige, signe d'inamovible et inébranlable perpétuité; dans le cas de Terminus, le fait que ce dieu ait refusé de se déplacer pour céder le pas à Iuppiter, sa "stabilité" entêtée et cohérente, implique selon les interprètes de la volonté divine, une égale "stabilité" de la puissance romaine, stabilité qui se manifestera sur plusieurs plans: de même que Terminus ne bouge pas — même devant Iuppiter! — il ne bougera jamais plus et inamovible sera la borne qui sépare les propriétés privées, inamovibles seront les bornes qui marquent les frontières entre le territoire de l'Etat et les peuples étrangers, inamovible sera toute chose pour l'éternité. Mais pour que ce tableau de la nouvelle réalité soit encore plus complet, il est un détail que nous avons, à dessein, laissé jusqu'à présent dans l'ombre, mais qu'il ne faut pas négliger: les mythes en question ne fondent pas seulement, en effet, des aspects extérieurs de l'existence ou la pérennité et la stabilité de la puissance romaine, ou le temple de Iuppiter auquel elle est si indissolublement liée, mais ils "fondent", aussi et surtout, les dieux eux-mêmes.

Dans les mythes que nous venons de voir, Iuppiter, toujours en cause, l'est cependant sous une forme particulière; il apparaît non pas comme un personnage actif normal, comme un Tarquinius ou un Olenus Calenus, ou par exemple comme telle ou telle divinité dans un mythe grec; il agit indirectement, impersonnellement ou, plutôt, ce n'est pas de lui qu'il s'agit, mais de son temple. Il en est de même pour Terminus qui ne figure qu'en tant que possesseur du lieu de son culte. Ceci serait dû à ce que les travaux les plus récents définissent comme les caractéristiques particulières de la religion romaine: d'une part, le degré de réalisation auquel parait s'être arrêté le processus polythéiste, dont les figures divines, contrairement à celles du polythéisme grec, n'ont jamais été dotées de personnalité et de plasticité; d'autre part la démythisation qui semblerait avoir éliminé presque entièrement les mythes divins, du moins ceux du type que l'on rencontre généralement dans les mythologies des religions polythéistes. Mais, même ainsi, même s'il ne s'agit que des vicissitudes cultuelles de ces divinités on n'en a pas moins constaté qu'elles sont transposées sur un plan mythique; il paraît donc légitime à tous égards de considérer ce genre de récits comme de véritables mythes divins. Ce qui signifie qu'ils devraient être, malgré tout, en mesure de caractériser sous leurs différents aspects, les figures divines dont ils traitent, offrant ainsi un tableau plastique de leur "personnalité", les fondant justement telles qu'elles sont.

Mais quel type de personnalité peut-on tirer, pour les dieux en question, du matériel mythique que nous venons d'étudier? La réponse à cette question est, au prime abord, quelque peu décevante. Et le tableau que nous en avons est tel qu'il nous induirait à douter que les Romains, pour lesquels Iuppiter avait sans conteste, dans le panthéon, une position prédominante, y pussent prêter foi ou, pis encore, l'accepter sans discussions. Les résultats de notre analyse nous montrent, d'une part, un contestataire qui n'est pas autre chose qu'une pierre accrochée au Capitole, absolument inamovible; d'autre part, un Iuppiter qui n'a pas encore de culte — et qui, en langage mythique, n'existe donc pas encore — mais qui, cependant, se présente comme roi et, malgré cela ne parvient pas à l'emporter sur son antagoniste et doit se résigner à voir construire autour de ce dernier son propre temple. A celui-ci, par ailleurs, la présence inébranlable de Terminus assurera la pérennité et en fera le symbole par excellence d'un pouvoir inébranlable et à jamais stable. En fin de compte c'est lui qui semblerait sortir avantagé de la lutte, tandis que Iuppiter serait incontestablement humilié. Mais d'autre part, cette "humiliation" est indispensable pour que le Capitole soit inébranlable, pour que Rome conserve toujours sa puissance, pour que les frontières soient stables. Iuppiter devrait donc céder devant Terminus pour que soit garantie cette "stabilité" condition première de la société romaine dans la réalité historique.

C'est là, toutefois, une première impression. En fait, dans le polythéisme romain, l'existence et l'importance du dieu Terminus ne minaient nullement la suprématie de Iuppiter; au contraire, les deux divinités apparaissent comme un précieux équilibre de sphères d'action unies par un rapport de complémentarité.

Considérons, en effet, de plus près les liens qui, dans la religion romaine, unissent Iuppiter et Terminus.

Ces liens existent, comme on le sait généralement, sur le plan du culte: Terminus est placé dans le temple capitolin et c'est là qu'il reçoit son culte; les bornes-frontières (*termini*) sont consacrées à Iuppiter.

Mais ces deux dieux sont également liés sur le plan mythique. Il convient, en effet, de réfléchir au fait que, dans ce domaine du mythe, Terminus n'entre pas en scène pour la première fois lors de la fondation du temple capitolin; nous avons déjà vu qu'un autel ou un *sacellum* lui avait été promis sur la colline Tarpéienne par Titus Tatius, dès l'époque de la guerre contre les Sabins pour être édifié après la stipulation de la paix. Mais le dieu, spécifiquement entendu comme borne (*terminus*), bien qu'étant l'objet d'un culte, a à son actif d'autres mythes de fondation. Une tradition raconte que ce fut Numa — *flamen dialis* et étroitement lié à Iuppiter pour différentes raisons — qui introduisit chez les Romains l'usage de délimiter les propriétés privées ainsi que le territoire de l'état, afin de les inciter à un genre de vie moins belliqueux et essentiellement agricole. Avant lui il n'aurait pas existé de bornes car Romulus y aurait vu comme un frein à la puissance d'expansion de la ville. Une autre tradition, représentée par un texte d'origine prétendument étrusque et par tout un courant littéraire de l'époque d'Auguste raconte, au contraire, que l'usage des bornes fut instauré par Iuppiter lui-même après la séparation de la mer et du ciel et la revendication de L'Etrurie par le dieu, afin d'éviter les inconvénients que provoquent habituellement la cupidité et l'avidité des hommes: le déplacement abusif des limites et l'appropriation indue du terrain d'autrui. Auparavant, avant que les éléments du cosmos ne soient distincts, que Iuppiter ne se soit adjugé son propre territoire, que les *termini* ne délimitent les propriétés, l'existence aurait été caractérisée par l'atmosphère chaotique, paradisiaque, illimitée et par cela même, au fond, essentiellement négative du royaume de Saturne. La terre aurait alors produit toute chose spontanément, il n'aurait pas été nécessaire de la travailler ni de marquer les lisières des champs par des bornes; quand à Saturne se substituera Iuppiter, le premier acte du nouveau souverain sera l'institution des *termini*. Dorénavant, chaque chose aura ses limites.

Chacune de ces traditions présente, il est aisé de le constater, la même structure; Terminus et son institution — ou, selon les cas, l'institution de son culte — marquent constamment le passage du temps du mythe à celui de la réalité actuelle: de la guerre contre les Sabins à l'alliance, désormais consolidée avec ce peuple; d'une existence belliqueuse et ignorant le travail des champs aux pratiques agricoles et à la vie policée; du chaos des éléments indifférenciés à un univers ordonné; du royaume idylliaque et illimité de Saturne à la domination délimitée de Iuppiter. Or, c'est justement cette délimitation de la sphère d'action et de pouvoir de Iuppiter, jusqu'ici à peine esquissée dans l'attribution à ce dieu de l'institution des *termini*, qui est définitivement sanctionnée par le mythe qui voit dans le dieu Terminus le signe de la limite inamovible devant celui qui est, cependant, son roi; par ce même mythe qui "fonde" Iuppiter en tant que titulaire du culte capitolin, seigneur d'un temple qui est un symbole de pérennité inébranlable et à l'intérieur duquel, en garantie justement de cette pérennité, il sera pour toujours vaincu par son antagoniste. Le Iuppiter qui institue les *termini* pour que les limites ne soient ni déplacées ni modifiées est le même qui "cede" devant l'inamovibilité de Terminus; et celui-ci, a son tour, est institué par Iuppiter pour qu'il ne "céde" devant personne, pas même devant le roi des dieux; la stabilité entêtée de l'un ne fait que confirmer la souveraine suprématie de l'autre, et vice-versa. Iuppiter et Terminus ont ainsi acquis leurs physionomies définitives: l'un, souverain d'une réalité ordonnée délimitée, qui, de ce fait, ne peut être soumis à des déplacements; l'autre, pierre à jamais fichée dans le sol, garant, de par sa fixité, de la stabilité de toute chose et, d'abord, de la personnalité souveraine de Iuppiter.

Dans d'autres religions théistes, ce rapport aurait probablement pris la forme d'une lutte cosmogonique ayant pour conséquence le partage des pouvoirs; de par sa structure particulière, le polythéisme romain — à propos duquel le mot "demythisation" devrait être employé avec une prudence de plus en plus grande — l'envisage, au contraire, sur le plan des traditions cultuelles.

ALL SAINTS CULT IN MEXICO

ANNA-BRITTA HELLBOM

Two religious phenomena struck my attention during my visit to Mexico in the beginning of the 1960ies. They both captured me for the same reasons, namely, on the one hand, that these beliefs were held by almost the whole population and, on the other, the fervence by which they held them, albeit certain differences of expression.

The explanation of this almost total unanimity is without doubt to be sought in the simplicity of the beliefs and their profound human significance which creates a feeling of (particularly) close relationship between the performer of the cult and its object.

The two religious phenomena I am referring to are the preeminence of the Holy Virgin to the persons of Trinity, in the minds of the faithful, and the other, the total adherence to the cult of the dead, by all categories of people regardless of faith.

The feasts of St. Mary and All Saints' Day, therefore, seems to me to be the most important of the popular feasts.

Compared to these, the purely *religious* celebrations, like Christmas, Easter and Whitsuntide which are imposed by the clergy hierachically, seem not so close to the people's heart.

The *national* feast days, commemorating great events in the history of the nation are prescribed by the government and always follow the same pattern, chiefly through a tradition upheld in the schools.

Village or local feasts where people gather in boisterous joy in honour of the village patron saint, are nowadays being threatened by commercial exploitation flooding the country with cheap goods and the feastplaces with "modern" paraphernalia.

Only Mary and the dead are spontaneously honoured by the individual, in spite of official preferences and possibly also social pressure.

Various authors (among others Wolf and Bushnell) have maintained that the overwhelming popularity of the Virgin, especially the Virgin of Guadalupe, with believers of all social categories albeit a varying degree of piety, depends on the easily grasped idea of the Mother figure. In particular the Guadalupe Virgin whose legend and rôle as guardian of the Indians and the poor makes her their very own Motherfigure (there is a direct continuity from the Spanish Nuestra madre to the Mexican Madrecita and the Indian Mother Godness Tonantzin, of Ethnos 29: 58-72 (1964), Hellbom, Anna-Britta: Las apariciones de la Virgen de Guadalupe en Mexico y en Espana), thus strengthening in my opinion the concerned individual's selfidentification, whether alone or as a member of a collective.

As I have found these explanations plausible, i.e. simplicity, ego-identification and feeling of close relationship, I will try to apply it in part also to the other salient feature of the spiritual life of the country, namely the all-embracing observance of the cult of the Dead.

As each human being has had a mother and thus easily grasps the Symbolics of the Mother of God, so each human being has a close relative or friend who is dead and whose memory urges him to take part in the cult of the Dead, either partially or in the whole of it, alone or in the congregation, as the case may be.

Moreover, in a similar way that the Cult of Mary may afford an extra cause for identification to all mothers, thus stimulating their religious feelings, so the Cult of the Dead appeals to every living being, thus stimulating him to active participation. Not all people become mother, not even all women, but we shall all die.

The cult comprises the following parts, treated in detail in the exposé
(1) Preparations in the home.
(2) The offering tables and their symbolics.
(3) Visits to the graves.
(4) After-celebrations.
(5) Legends.

1. *Preparations in the home*

A proper celebration of the Dead entails much work and great expenses.

The most important part of the preparations is the baking of the bread, in which the whole family takes part. The pater familias himself bakes the bread in the vaulted "cupola oven" in the courtyard that is nowadays chiefly used for this purpose and on other solemn occasions. *The panes de muertos* — bread of the dead — are baked of wheat dough in a number of traditional forms: "muertecios" (dead) and *conejos* (rabbits). The dead are represented with their hands across the breast, sometimes with two heads, sometimes only a femur or other part of the body furnishes the motive. Human hearts are rendered both in pre-Spanish and European symbolic forms. For the rest, individual imagination is allowed full freedom and the results may be rather surprising. I myself was presented with a "dead's heart" with my initials and another bread "rosca", showing the volcano Popo-capetl and the inscription *"Recuerdo de Chiconcuac"* in white sugarglaze.

Another important part of the preparations are the visits to the market, where all the edibles for the feast are purchased including fruit and flowers and, last but not least, the sweets in the form of *"calaveras"* i.e. skulls and other death's emblems made of candy. These more sophisticated accessoires are increasingly gaining ground in the villages and with it goes the custom of gifts in the form of death's heads of sugar with the receiver's name in sugar glaze on its forehead.

Then comes the preparation of the food for the meals and the offering table. Traditional items are chicken with rice and *mole*, chili sauce, *chuales* which is cornpaste stuffed with amaranth-seeds and wrapped in husks, *tamales* that is steam-cooked "pies" with different stuffings, and of course, *tortillas* those large pan-cakes of corn-meal, in hugh quantities. Often professional *tortil-leras*, cornbakers, are hired to provide for the need of corn bread during the many holidays.

2. *The offering Tables and their Symbolics*

All Saints' Day, *"Todos los Santos"*, is celebrated in Mexico during several consecutive days, beginning with the 30th of October. Each age group of the dead have their own special day with offerings on the house-altar in accordance with the age and living conditions of the deceased. The offerings consisting of food, drink, death's bread, fruit, tobacco and incense, flowers and candles, are placed on the altar or offering table in portions assigned to each of the dead persons.

The 30th of october is called *Día del Limbo* and is consecrated to the infants who died unbaptized. According to Catholic belief all pre-Christian just men and unbaptized infants are confined to a region on the border of hell, Limbo. There also belong stillborn and miscarriges. At their place on the offering table are placed only flowers, candles and a glass of water, one for each infant. There are often many glasses on the altar.

The 31st of october is the dead children's day. Those are the small children who died innocent except for the original sin, and thus have not to go through Purgatory on their way to Heaven. They immediately become *"angelitos"*, "little angels". For them is offered a bowl of *atole* (maize gruel), fruit, death's bread often in the form of rabbits, incense, flowers, and sometimes a toy which belonged to the dead child.

The 1st of November finally, is the *Día de los Muertos*, i.e. the day of the adult dead. To them is offered all that one knows they liked in life. Chicken, a bowl of rice, another with *mole, tortillas, pulque* (wine of agave) *mezcal* (spirit of agave), cigarettes, cigars, heaps of fruit, bananas, oranges, sugar cane, pine apples, and of course death's bread, candles and much flowers.

During these days the spirits of the dead are believed to visit their home and partake of the offerings. These naturally remain untouched, but the dead profit by their essence and scent and leave the rest to the living.

3. *Visits to the Graves*

The 1st of November one also visit the graves of ones dead. The graves do not seem to be regularly kept in order, but today they are swept and tidied and finally adorned with incense burner, candles and heaps of flowers. The customary flower is the orange-yellow *Tagetes* (Marygold), which besides representing the Aztec colour of Death still bears its Aztec name; *cempasuchil* (originally *cempohuallixochitl* = profuse flower). In later years red and white Gladiolus has begun to compete with the traditional death's flower.

After only a couple of hours the torrid and dusty church yard has changed into a field of flowers gleaming in yellow, green, white and red. Soon a thin weil of incense from the black burners spreads over the scene while the candle lights flicker from graves and paths. Those who have their near and dear buried at distant places, lay their flowers and lights, their candles on the floor of the church.

All that is offered to the dead must be new and unsullied. Even the broom used to sweep the grave and the basket to carry the flowers must be new, the incense burner must not have been used before, and the flowers must be fresh — at least as long as the burning sun permits.

In the evening the children run about swinging *"calaveras"*, i.e. calabashes cut out to resemble death's heads with a lit candle inside. They beg for gifts singing:

Salgan, salgan, salgan, ánimas en pena!
Qué el Rosario Santo rompa sus cadenas!

4. *Concluding (After-celebrations)*

The 2nd November, called the *Día de los Responsos*, Mass is celebrated with prayers for the dead.

On the 3rd of November one can resume relationship with relatives and friends. This is the *Día de levantar las ofrendas*, i.e. the day when one can begin to eat of the delicacies on the offering table. This is the day for visits to friends and exchange of offerings, such as death's bread and fruit, for invitations to meals and many visits. This period of sociability with more or less obligatory exchange of gifts may be extended over several weeks, especially when friends and relatives live far away. As an exhausted house wife said to me: *"Toda la semana andan corriendo los conejos!"*

5. *Legends*

Encarnacion *Valdes*, 1855?
S. Miguel Chiconcuac
1.XI.62:

Dos *cuentos de los Animitas*
"En la tienda de Laredo había antes pulquería. Tres muchachas la teníen. Vivían del pulque.

Un tlachiquero se enojó porque po le dieron su tortillita, ni su comedita, ni su pulquito.

En los Santos se fué, diciendo que no creyó en que vinieron los animitas, los muertos. Un hombre le dijo: "Quieres ver a los animitas? Agarre un perrito y con su chinguiña te tocas los ojos y asi verás a los muertos!"

Lo hizo y se subió por la noche en la desván enfrente de la iglesia y a las 12? se abrió la puerta de la iglesia al repicar todo el tiempo la campana y salió una procesión como en la fiesta.

Dieron los animitas una vuelta y al alcanzar la casa se abrió la puerta y entraron.

Dijo el patrón: "Tenemos que comer pronto, pronto, porque si no nos van a cerrar la puerta de la iglesia y nos quedamos fuera!" Comieron y bebieron pronto y se fueron, llevándose los restos de la comida.

Y después de entrar en la iglesia cerraron la puerta.

El tlachiquero bajó de la azotea (?) y al ver que estaba todavía la comida, se puso a comer.

Después salió al campo a raspar, pero a las 3 de la tarde se murió.

Le ganaron los muertos y se le llevaron."

"Otro señor no creyó. Dijo que los muertos ya estaban muertos y se fué al monte por leña.

Al llegar allí se le agarró alguién y le ataron con los brazos cruzados a un palo y allí se quedó.

En la Día de los Muertos, la Víspera de los Muertos, vió una procesión de niños bajar muy bien vestidos como para fiesta y pasan y pasan y pasan y pasan y pasan.

Al día siguiente vió otra procesión de adultos — y pasan y pasan y pasan y pasan y pasan — llevando algunos frutas, otros panes o tamales, otros nada, y los últimos eran sus padres de él: la madrecita con una cazuelita en la mano y el padre con una cera y nada más.

Le dió lástima y pasados los Días de los Santos le dejaron libre, pero a los poos días se murió."

Ricardo Flores, 1905?
S. Miguel Chiconcuac
21.X.62:

Tres *cuentos del Día de los Santos*
que le contaron cuando niño
"Una viuda se casó con un jóven. En el día de los Santos no quiso el marido darle nada para comprar cosas para la mesa de los muertos. Dijo: "No, no quiero darte nada; porque lo quieres sólo para ver otra vez a tu primer esposo." —

El día mismo de los Santos el marido su fué al monte para leñas. Al pasar un gran árbol, se subió en él. Entonces se abrió el árbol, se metió dentro de él y se cerró otra vez el árbol. Allí estuvo encerrado por tres días hasta que pasaron los Santos. Entonces se abrió el árbol otra vez y le dejó libre."

"Un señor no quiso entregar nada a su señora para que comprara cosas para ofrendas a los muertos el día de los Santos. La señora lloró, pero no le dió nada para los gastos. Se fué el esposo, y la señora en vez de velas, encendió unos ocotes para sus difuntos. Por la noche el señor tuvo una visión: vió una procesión de personas que andaban en fila y todos llevaban velas encendidas en las manos — menos los padres de él y los de su señora. Llevaban sólo ocotes."

"Un señor no quiso dar dinero a su esposa para los gastos del Día de los Santos. "Yo no creo en ello y no quiero dar nada."
Por la noche tuvo una visión de una procesión de gente, unas nada más que sombras, que iban entrando en las casas y saliendo con muchas cosas. Sólo en la de él salieron sin nada!"

As I said before, what I found characteristic in the celebrations of the memory of the dead was that each individual engages himself personally in them. This entails that everybody participates in everything. They are not just spectators of something that others have organized, like dances, processions, Masses, etc. Everybody brings flowers to the church yard, everybody helps with the baking of the bread, everybody has visits to pay — everybody takes an active part in the events. This is surely what makes the celebration of All Saints' Days absorb the life of the individual to such a degree. This is also why the tradition is so strong, observed by everybody, whether faithful or not.

THE STRUCTURE OF THEISTIC BELIEFS AMONG
NORTH AMERICAN PLAINS INDIANS*

ÅKE HULTKRANTZ

For a long time the religio-scientific debate has paid particular attention to certain theistic concepts of the North American Indians, such as the Algonkin *Manitou*, the Siouan *Wakanda* and some Central Californian creator ideas.[1] The reason for this interest was originally the desire to find out whether a concept such as a single high god existed among so-called primitive peoples, and if it was represented by the notions mentioned — an alternative which was impossible for the evolutionists to accept but a matter of course to the defenders of primeval monotheism. The gap between these two views has nowadays been overbridged, for overwhelming materials from different "primitive" peoples, including the North American Indians, have demonstrated the presence of a high god who, however, does not stand alone.

The conclusion we can draw is that theistic beliefs among the real "primitive" peoples, hunters and collectors, rarely fit such labels as monotheism or polytheism. Polytheism is, as for instance Swanson and Pallis have stressed, the religious belief-pattern in an advanced society like that of, say, the Near Eastern city-states or the New World florescent and classic kingdoms.[2] Monotheism is, to quote Pettazzoni, the reaction to polytheism (in an advanced society), as we can see from the monotheistic systems created by Achn-aton of Egypt, Nezahualcoyotl of Texcoco (Mexico) or Mohammed from Mecca.[3] Hunters and collectors do not share such religious systems, the products of priest

---

* Also published in *Temenos*, Vol. 7 (1971), pp. 137-144.

[1] See the survey in Hultkrantz, *Les Religions des Indiens primitifs de l'Amérique* (Stockholm Studies in Comparative Religion, vol. 4, 1963), pp. 16 f., 18 f., 24 ff.

[2] G. E. Swanson, *The Birth of the Gods: The Origin of Primitive Beliefs* (Ann Arbor 1960), pp. 82 ff.; S. A. Pallis, *Religionsvidenskab* (Videnskaben i Dag, ed. by F. Brandt and K. Linderstrøm-Lang, Copenhagen 1944), p. 415.

[3] R. Pettazzoni, *Essays on the History of Religions* (Studies in the History of Religions, vol. I, Leiden 1954), p. 9. The monotheistic exclusivity of the early Hebrews constitutes, in my opinion, a remarkable case apart, although Pettazzoni did not see the matter thus.

speculation, dynastic ambitions and historical impact. They evince rather an unqualified "theism" where different vaguely delimited concepts exist side by side. Very common is a pattern characterized by a belief in a high god and a host of lesser spirits.

This is a pattern which is known from Africa, for example from the Nuer,[4] and from Siberia and North America. It occurs among several Plains Indian tribes, such as the Shoshoni and the Dakota (Sioux). In the following we shall study the structure of this theism in these two tribes in order to illuminate the relations which exist — or at least may exist — between the high god and the spirits. These relations have been variously interpreted by the scholars, particularly concerning the Dakota.[5] Some have conceived a vertical structure where the spirits are subordinated under the high god, others a horizontal structure where the spirits co-operate with the high god on an almost equal level, or where together they constitute the divine essence of a high god. The theistic structure is thus rather disputed among scholars.

Let us first consider the Plains Shoshoni, or Wind River Shoshoni as they are called today after their reservation in western Wyoming. I draw here upon my own field-material gathered during repeated visits to these Shoshoni in the 1940's and 1950's. The Plains Shoshoni believe in an undetermined number of spirits and a Supreme Being, *Tam Apö*. The spirits are mostly conceived in animal disguise, a heritage of the long hunting existence.[6] If we disregard those spirits which only fulfil a part in mythology, such as the trickster (culture hero) and certain primeval animal characters,[7] we receive the following series of believed-in spirits and divinities in Shoshoni religion:

---

[4] Cf. E. E. Evans-Pritchard, *Nuer Religion* (Oxford 1956). It should be noted, however, that Evans-Pritchard tries to prove (less convincingly, I think) that the lesser spirits are just different aspects of the Supreme Being, corresponding to different social structures. He seems to confuse the observer's and the native's points of view. For the alternation between monotheism and polytheism in African religions, with particular attention to Lienhardt's interpretations of the Dinka concepts of God, see O. Pettersson, "Monotheism or Polytheism? A Study of the Ideas about Supreme Beings in African Religion" (*Temenos*, vol. 2, 1966), pp. 48 ff.

[5] See Hultkrantz, "North American Indian Religion in the History of Research: A General Survey", Pt. III (*History of Religions*, vol. 7:1, 1967), pp. 14 ff.

[6] Cf. Hultkrantz, "Attitudes to Animals in Shoshoni Indian Religion" (*Studies in Comparative Religion*, vol. 4:2, 1970), pp. 70 ff.

[7] Hultkrantz, "Religion und Mythologie der Prärie-Schoschonen" (*Akten des 34. Internationalen Amerikanistenkongresses*, Wien 1960), pp. 546 ff.

(1) *Tam Apö* ("Our Father"), Supreme Being, sustainer of the Universe, the utmost resource of all things. He is represented by the Sun and (perhaps) the Moon.

(2) Thunder, lightning and wind spirits, all very powerful.

(3) Spirits of nature which are and give *puha* or supernatural power, both to the medicine-men and to young men and warriors who seek this power at rock-drawings. These spirits almost always appear as animals and birds.

(4) *Tam mbia*, Mother Earth, who makes the earth green and gives her human children plants and water.

(5) Divers uncanny spirits, such as the water-buffaloes, the man-eating ogre (*pa:ndzoaBits*), the disease-giving dwarf (*ninïmbi*) and the wandering ghost (*dzoap*). These are avoided as far as possible.

(6) The spirits of the dead in the land of the dead. They can be approached only by outstanding, very gifted medicine-men who put themselves in a trance and travel in non-physical form to the realm of the dead. Such medicine-men do not exist any longer. Also severely sick men who have arrived in a coma sometimes enter this realm.

Admittedly, this formal division of the spirits does not correspond to any general Shoshoni opinion, it is entirely the construct of the observer. Some exceptional medicine-men do, indeed, try to discern a scheme of the spirits according to rank. However, their interest as medicine-men is only to arrange the *puha*, and these may of course be grouped in order with such spirits as the mighty buffalo and the clean eagle at the apex.[8] Nevertheless, the model offered here represents the actual categories of spiritual beings and would, I think, scarcely be disputed by the Shoshoni Indians.

If now we except the two last-mentioned groups of spirits, the uncanny spirits (5) and the dead (6), all categories perform some function in the lives of the Shoshoni. The main functions correspond to specific situations. Thus, the *puha* are approached when a person's mental or physical capacity needs to be improved, that is, when he needs luck in hunting, in war, in love, in overcoming his own or somebody else's sickness. The Supreme Being is prayed to in situations of utmost need or, collectively, in the

---

[8] Hultkrantz, "Configurations of Religious Belief among the Wind River Shoshoni" (*Ethnos*, vol. 21:3-4, 1956), p. 200.

yearly Sun Dance. The Earth Mother is marginally appealed to at the Sun Dance and in some other connections and figures more pronouncedly in the newly acquired Peyote cult. The spirits of the atmosphere (thunder etc.) are partly included in the *puha* complex but play a more independent role as providers of rain, thunder and wind. When the elements of Nature are adverse to man these spirits have to be propitiated.

This is all what we could expect. However, keeping Max Müller's idea of *kathenotheism* in mind we can observe that just as a situation is complete in itself the spiritual agencies which operate within its confines constitute the whole supernatural world — at that moment. This is at least the case with the Shoshoni. When prayers are directed at the rock-drawings they concern only the *puha*, never the Supreme Being. He does not exist in this connection, although at least some Shoshoni thinkers consider that theoretically the powers of the spirits derive from him. On the other hand, when *Tam Apö* is called upon in situations of great need and distress the spirits do not enter the picture; they are lesser powers, and there is no reason why they should appear on the scene. We have here a system of what I have called alternating configurations of religious belief.[9] What is important to observe in this connection is that the Supreme Being and the *puha* spirits belong to different belief structures which usually alternate with each other. God and the spirits are theoretically co-existing, but in practice they substitute each other. As to thunder, lightning and wind spirits they appear without associations to God; but God can assume the functions which these spirits express and thus supplant them. This happens, however, very rarely. It is perhaps less surprising that different sets of spirits operate in alternating configurations, for instance, the guardian spirits and the "uncanny" spirits.

These belief structures certainly reflect, in their very organisation, the ancient social and political structure of the tribe: the prevalent socio-political pattern was in the old days one of a half-independent band-organisation interacting with an emergent centralized authority (Chief Washakie). At the same time these structures corresponded to specific cultural, social and ecological situations which challenged the balance of man and released cul-

---

[9] Hultkrantz, "Configurations of Religious Belief etc.," pp. 194 ff.

turally determined responses in him: the desire for success in hunting or on the warpath induced him to guardian spirit quests at rock-drawings, the longing for safety in thunderstorms made him appeal to the thunderers, and the immediate need for escape from great danger forced him to call on the high god himself for help. The social and political and partly also the ecological motivations have disappeared with the breakdown of traditional Plains culture at the end of the last century, but the religious patterns are largely intact even today.

We now turn to the Teton Dakota, a branch of the great Sioux nation, residing nowadays in the Dakotas but earlier nomadizing from the Missouri River to the Bighorn Mountains. There are several, although sometimes very conflicting sources to their religion. [10] It is today quite difficult to create a true picture of traditional western Dakota religion. Says Ella Deloria, herself a Dakota by birth, "The Dakota people of the past were not asked to analyze for posterity their beliefs about God. We cannot really know, therefore, in so many words by them uttered, exactly what they believed and how they expressed that belief." [11] If, however, we rely on the information we have the Dakota supernatural beings may be classified as follows. [12]

(1) *Wakan Tanka* ("Great Holy"), also called *Taku Wakan* ("Something Holy") or *Taku Skanskan* ("Something in Movement") is the Supreme Being. Although Gideon Pond, and after him Dorsey, did not find the idea of a Supreme Being represented among the (eastern) Dakota, [13] both Lynd and Densmore and the later writers testify to its existence and pre-Christian

---

[10] My analysis is founded on the following works: J. O. Dorsey, *A Study of Siouan Cults* (11th Annual Report of the Bureau of Ethnology, Washington 1894); J. R. Walker, *The Sun Dance and Other Ceremonies of the Oglala Division of the Teton Dakota* (Anthropological Papers of the American Museum of Natural History, vol. 16:2, New York 1917); F. Densmore, *Teton Sioux Music* (Bureau of American Ethnology, Bulletin 61, Washington 1918); E. Deloria, *Speaking of Indians* (New York 1944); and J. E. Brown, *The Sacred Pipe: Black Elk's Account of the Seven Rites of the Oglala Sioux* (Norman, Okla., 1953). Additional material, referring to the Eastern Dakota, has been taken from J. W. Lynd, *The Religion of the Dakotas* (Collections of the Minnesota Historical Society, vol. II, St. Paul 1889), and from the Pond brothers, missionaries in Minnesota: G. H. Pond, *Dakota Superstitions* (Minnesota Historical Collections, vol. 2:3, St. Paul 1889), and S. W. Pond, *The Dakotas or Sioux in Minnesota as they were in 1834* (Collections of the Minnesota Historical Society, vol. XII, St. Paul 1908).

[11] Deloria, *op. cit.*, p. 49.

[12] Another classification in Dorsey, *op. cit.*, p. 434.

[13] G. H. Pond, *op. cit.*, p. 217; Dorsey, *op. cit*, pp. 431 f.

origin.[14] It is significant that whereas Gideon Pond interprets
Taku Wakan as a collective name for the gods,[15] Samuel Pond
says it "had such a meaning in the minds of the Indians that none
of us hesitated to use it when speaking of the providence of
God."[16] It is obvious that the concept of the high god was
difficult to grasp for foreigners, certainly partly due — as Deloria
points out — to the structure of the Dakota language. Densmore who also stresses the difficulty to formulate "the exact
significance of the term in the mind of the Sioux"[17] quotes one
of her informants, Chased-by-Bears, who, speaking about prayers
to *Wakan Tanka*, says: "... we are sure that he hears us, and yet it
is hard to explain what we believe about this ... We believe that
he is everywhere, yet he is to us as the spirits of our [dead]
friends, whose voices we can not hear."[18] Personal and impersonal aspects seem to be interchangeable in this concept of God.

Like the Shoshoni the Teton Dakota believed that the Sun
represented the high god.[19] (The Moon, on the other hand, was
supposed to be a goddess.) The name *Taku Skanskan* indicates
that the high god was also identical with the sky.

(2) The divinities of the atmosphere, including *wakinyan* (the
thunderbirds), the four winds and the whirlwind.

(3) The rulers of the animal species, which among the Dakota
means the master spirit of the buffalo and, perhaps, the bear.[20]

(4) The guardian spirits which revealed themselves in visions —
the culmination of the vision quest — and generally manifested
themselves through natural phenomena, such as birds and animals. "They are not themselves Wakan [holy, or supernatural],
but the Wakan is in all things."[21] Other natural objects became
wakan by being coloured red and prayed to, for instance, rocks

---

[14] Lynd, *op. cit.*, pp. 151, 152 note; Densmore, *op. cit.*, p. 85 note 2. Also an
early writer like Riggs postulates that *Wakan Tanka* should be translated as "Great
Spirit". See S. R. Riggs, *Dakota Grammar, Texts, and Ethnography* (Contributions to
North American Ethnology, vol. IX, Washington 1893), pp. 105 ff., 108.

[15] G. H. Pond, *op. cit.*, pp. 217, 251.

[16] S. W. Pond, *op. cit.*, pp. 424 f.

[17] Densmore, *op. cit.*, p. 85 note 2.

[18] Densmore, *op. cit.*, p. 96.

[19] Densmore, *op. cit.*, p. 86.

[20] Joseph Epes Brown is at present investigating these concepts as part of his
doctor's thesis in comparative religion at the University of Stockholm.

[21] Deloria, *op. cit.*, p. 52.

and trees. The rock, *inyan,* was supposed to be the oldest manifestation of the Divine. [22]

(5) The Earth Mother, *Maka,* patron of chastity and children, and "The Beautiful One" or *Wohpe,* who is also the buffalo-woman who entrusted the sacred pipe to the Dakota. [23]

(6) Dangerous spirits of different kinds, such as the horned water monsters (*miniwatu,* among the Eastern Dakota *unktehi*) which are at war with the thunderbirds, man-eating giants, elves (deer women) who lead people astray and various goblins.

(7) The spirits of the dead in the land of the dead.

Finally there were principally mythological persons who were supposed to be capricious, such as the culture hero and trickster *Iktomi* ("Spider"), the wizard *Waziya* and the latter's two-faced daughter. With few exceptions these beings do not seem to have figured in ordinary religious beliefs and cult practices.

The above categorization is the author's and is not entirely exhaustive. It gives, however, a general idea of the range of supernatural beings among the Teton Dakota. Furthermore, it reflects, as far as I can see, the ideas on the subject which are held by the *common* man. The same tendency to compartmentalization that we observed among the Plains Shoshoni seems to be present here, but the deficiency of our sources does not allow us to draw decisive conclusions. What we definitely do know is however that there is the same characteristic interplay between the high god and the spirits as exists among the Shoshoni.

This interplay is facilitated by a most inclusive concept of God. "*Wakan Tanka,* you are everything, and yet above everything," says Black Elk, the Oglala Sioux medicine-man. [24] And Red Bird assures us, "We believed that there is a mysterious power greater than all others, which is represented by nature, one form of representation being the sun." [25] Deloria even equates *Wakan Tanka* and *wakan,* thereby subsuming our above cate-

---

[22]   Cf. Lynd, *op. cit.*, pp. 168 f.; Walker, *op. cit.*, p. 82.

[23]   Brown, *op. cit.*, pp. 3 ff.; G. A. Dorsey, *Legend of the Teton Sioux Medicine Pipe* (Journal of American Folklore, vol. 19, 1906), pp. 326 ff. *Wohpe* is exclusively the medicine-men's name for this divinity.

[24]   Brown, *op. cit.*, p. 13. A Swedish scholar has tried to penetrate the consequences of the Dakota high-god concept for their view of the relation between God and his creation: See K. Almqvist, *Les Trois cercles de l'existence* (Études traditionnelles, no. 393, 1966), pp. 25 ff.

[25]   Densmore, *op. cit.*, p. 86.

gories (2)–(4) under the first-mentioned concept. [26] This expansion of the main theistic concept explains why Gideon Pond could mistake *Taku Wakan* for meaning "the gods". The traditional material at our disposal shows that the high god is called upon when the unifying force of the Universe is implied, and individual spirits when special supernatural actions are inferred. Unity and diversity in religious theism are thus expressed in a simple way. The consciousness of the inclusive character of *Wakan Tanka* represents an epistomological conclusion of this world view.

These alternating structures of theistic beliefs also reflect, as among the Shoshoni, socio-political patterns and ecological conditions. What has been said above concerning the Plains Shoshoni in this respect also holds good for the Teton Dakota.

It was pointed out that among the Shoshoni certain "religious formulators", as Radin called them, tried to arrange the spirits into a ranking system. A similar development has taken place among the Teton Dakota, but resulted here in a more elaborate theological system. In other words, we find among the Teton Dakota an esoteric tradition administered by medicine-men who spoke a secret, old-fashioned language. [27] In this shamanistic speculation *Wakan Tanka* is identified with all the positive spirits, categories (1)–(5), and with certain soul concepts as well. They are united in a system based on the sacred number four and with the implication that four may be reduced to one. Thus, according to Walker's informants, *Wakan Tanka* is one, but consists nevertheless of four, the Chief God, the Great Spirit, the Creator God and the Executive God; and each of these comprises four individuals, the Chief God for instance the Sun, the Moon, the Buffalo and the Spirit (= free-soul). Vertical and horizontal combinations of four cross each other and may all be reduced to one, *Wakan Tanka*. [28] In this way the gap between extant belief structures is

---

[26]   Deloria, *op. cit.*, p. 51.

[27]   On this secret language, see Walker, *op. cit.*, pp. 56, 78 f., and Densmore, *op. cit.*, p. 120 note 1. The secrecy may have to do with the tabooed nature of certain religious concepts, such as *Wakan Tanka*. See Densmore, *op. cit.*, p. 85 note 2. Certainly, Lynd states that prayers were never directed to *Wakan Tanka*, who — after having created the world — had lost interest in his creation (Lynd, *op. cit.*, p. 151). This, then, would indicate that he was a *deus otiosus* rather than a tabooed concept. However, Lynd seems to have overstated the case, as Dakota prayer texts clearly show.

[28]   Walker, *op. cit.*, pp. 78 ff., 152 ff.

partially bridged. It is important to note, however, that this theological system is not part of the creed of common man.

Similar structures of theistic beliefs as the ones here outlined as part of the religion of common man in some Plains societies may be identified in other American Indian groups as well, for instance, among the Ojibway (Chippewa) of the Northern Woodland. [29] It may on the whole be said that many so-called primitive religions are characterized by such alternating structures. Where shamanistic speculation has not arranged the high god and the spirits in a hierarchical order the relation between them is one of alternation and interplay. The reasons for this may be sought in the demands of the cultural, ecological and psychological situations and in the experience of cosmos as one and united or pluralistic and divided.

---

[29] In his stimulating account from 1855, the German explorer Kohl says that the word for the Great Spirit, *Kitsche Manitou*, sometimes ("zuweilen") was no *nomen proprium* of a single being but an appellation of a whole class of great spirits: J. G. Kohl, *Kitschi-Gami oder Erzählungen vom Obern See* (Bremen 1859), vol. I, p. 86.

GOTTESHÜTER UND VERBORGENE HEILBRINGER

GÜNTER LANCZKOWSKI

In seinem Roman "Die Dämonen" lässt Dostojewski den
Piotr Werchowenski einen perfiden Vorschlag machen, der die
politisch gezielte Erfindung einer Legende zum Inhalt hat. Werchowenski verkündet seine Absicht mit den Worten: "Wir verbreiten Legenden über den Zarewitsch Iwan. Wir sagen zuerst,
dass er sich 'verbirgt' ... Er ist da — aber noch hat ihn niemand
gesehen. Was für eine Legende wir verbreiten werden! Er ist da,
aber keiner hat ihn gesehen; er verbirgt sich ... Die Hauptsache ist
dabei die Legende: Er bringt die neue Wahrheit und — 'verbirgt'
sich."

Die Hoffnung auf Verschwörung und Revolution, die Werchowenski mit dieser erdichteten Legende verbindet, die Be-
nutzung dieses Gerüchtes zur Erreichung politischer Ziele wirkt
deshalb in hohem Grade überzeugend, weil das Motiv, auf den
Zarewitsch Iwan übertragen, an sich echt ist, weil es — wie bekannt — sehr weit verbreitet und offensichtlich zeitlich nicht
begrenzt, mit dem Fortleben und der einstigen Rückkehr verschiedenster Persönlichkeiten verbunden wurde. Man hat, abge-
leitet von der Legende Friedrich Barbarossas, vom "Kyffhäuser-
motiv" gesprochen,[1] vom "héros revenant" und vom "entrück-
ten Helden".[2] Die Bezeichnung "verborgener Heilbringer" dürfte
der Sicht derer, die in der Erwartung seiner Rückkehr stehen, am
angemessensten erscheinen.

Es versteht sich, dass im Rahmen eines Referats das höchst
umfangreiche Material nicht erschöpfend herangezogen werden
kann und sachlich nur einige vorläufige Fragen gestellt werden
sollen. Diese betreffen zunächst den aktuellen Anlass der Legendenbildung und die Frage nach ihrer religiösen Voraussetzung,
die sich dem Zentralthema dieses Kongresses einordnet, weil sie

---

[1] Amil Abegg, *Der Messiasglaube in Indien und Iran* (Berlin und Leipzig 1928) S.
111.

[2] Axel Olrik, *Ragnarök: Die Sagen vom Weltuntergang* (Berlin und Leipzig 1922),
S. 351 ff.'

dem Gottesverhältnis des verborgenen Heilbringers gilt. Ferner ist nach dem Typus religiöser Autorität zu fragen, dem der verborgene Heilbringer zuzurechnen ist,[3] und nach dem Geschichtsbild, in dem diese Vorstellung erscheint und sinnvoll ist.

Als auslösendes Moment der Legendenbildung erscheint, allgemein gesagt, ein ungewöhnlicher Weggang des verborgenen Heilbringers aus seiner natürlichen Umgebung. Einige Beispiele mögen demonstrieren, dass sich dieses Moment spezifizieren lässt.

Einmal umfasst es den unnatürlichen Tod, der bis in unsere Gegenwart als auslösendes Faktum der Legendenbildung wirkte. Im Jahre 1961 wurde der gestürzte türkische Ministerpräsident Menderes hingerichtet. Sehr bald danach entstand unter den anatolischen Bauern der Glaube an sein Fortleben. Er werde einst, auf einem Schimmel reitend, aus der Verborgenheit auftauchen und zu seinem Volke zurückkehren.[4]

Die tödliche Verwundung im Kampf ist häufiger Anlass der Legendenbildung. In Europa findet sie sich früh im keltischen Bereich. König Artus, schwer verwundet, wird ins Reich der Feen entrückt, und der Glaube an Weiterleben und Wiederkehr des Königs ist im Volk so stark verwurzelt, dass der Chronist Alanus berichten kann, in der Bretagne wäre gesteinigt worden, wer behauptet hätte, Artus sei wie ein anderer Mensch gestorben.[5]

Csaba, der jüngste Sohn Attilas, unterstützt Dietrich von Bern und fällt in der sogenannten Krimhildenschlacht. In Ungarn wird seine Rückkehr bis ins 13. Jahrhundert als sicher erwartet; später verliert die Vorstellung an Kraft.[6]

Bei Friedrich Barbarossa, der schlafend und auf seine Wiederkunft wartend in dem von Raben umkreisten Kyffhäuser gedacht wird, verbindet sich das Moment des ungewöhnlichen mit dem des Todes fern der Heimat. Welche legendenbildende Kraft auch dieses zweite Faktum entfalten kann, zeigt ein religionsgeschichtliches Kuriosum. Die Tana Bhagat Bewegung, eine religiöse Neustiftung, erwartet für ihre Anhänger, dravidischsprachige Eingeborene Bihars, den Anbruch einer glücklichen Zeit mit der An-

---

[3] Im Sinne von Joachim Wach, *Religionssoziologie* (Tübingen 1951), S. 375 ff.

[4] "Die Zeit" vom 15.10.1965; "Der Spiegel", Jg. 1961, Nr. 40.

[5] *Alani ab Insulis Prophetia Anglicana* (Frankfurt 1603), S. 19 f.; Ignaz von Döllinger, *Kleinere Schriften* (Stuttgart 1890), S. 467.

[6] Michael de Ferdinandy, "Die Mythologie der Ungarn," in *Wörterbuch der Mythologie*, hrsg. von H. W. Haussig, I. Abt., Teil II (Stuttgart o.J.), S. 225 f.

kunft des im niederländischen Exil verstorbenen Kaiser Wilhelms II.[7]

Mit dem Tod in der Fremde hat das bewusste Verschweigen der Todesnachricht ihr erst späteres Bekanntwerden gemeinsam. Tschingis Khan verordnete, dass sein Tod geheimzuhalten sei, und im mongolischen Volke bildete sich die Vorstellung, dass er mit seinen Reitern wiederkommen werde.[8] Andrej Bjelyj hat diese Vorstellung in seinen Roman "Petersburg " aufgenommen mit den Sätzen:[9] "Doch hört nur das Stampfen von Schritten. Aus den Steppen des Urals kommt es ... Horcht! Tönt nicht ein Stampfen aus der Ferne? Das sind die eisernen Reiter des Tschingis Khan."

Jedoch wirkt nicht allein der ungewöhnliche oder verschwiegene Tod legendenbildend, sondern auch die Abreise des Lebenden aus seiner Umwelt, die dieser verbindet mit Hinweisen auf seine einstige Rückkehr.

Väinämöinen, den Elias Lönnrot zu einer Zentralfigur seines Kalevala erhob, dürfte wohl auf einer historischen Gestalt beruhen. Von seinem Weggang aus Finnland berichtet das Epos im 50. Gesang:[10]

> "Setzte selber sich ans Steuer, fuhr hinaus aufs offne Wasser,
> Sagte noch bei seinem Abschied, sprach noch so bei seiner Abfahrt:
> 'Mag doch eine Frist verfliessen, mögen Tage gehn und kommen,
> Dann bedarf man meiner wieder, wird mich suchen, mich ersehnen ...' "

Sehr ähnliche Aussagen vermitteln aztekische Texte über Quetzalcoatl, dessen Historizität zeitweise bezweifelt wurde, den jedoch literarische Quellen und archäologische Funde heute als toltekischen Herrscher an der Wende des 10. zum 11. nachchristlichen Jahrhundert erweisen. Sein Verlassen des mexikanischen Bodens überliefert Sahagún:[11] "Nachdem er an das Ufer des Meeres gekommen war, macht er die Schlangenbahre. Nachdem er sie

---

[7] Stephen Fuchs, *Rebellious Prophets*: A Study of Messianic Movements in Indian Religions (London 1965), S. 39.

[8] Michael Prawdin, *Tschingis-Chan und sein Erbe* (Stuttgart und Berlin 1938), S. 223; 508.

[9] Andrej Bjelyj, *Petersburg* (München 1919), S. 423.

[10] *Kalevala*, 50. Gesang, Vers 487-494; nach der Übersetzung von Lore und Hans Fromm, *Kalevala* [Textband] (Darmstadt 1967), S. 325.

[11] Eduard Seler, *Einige Kapitel aus dem Geschichtswerk des Fray Bernardino de Sahagún* (Stuttgart 1927), S. 292.

fertiggestellt, setzt er sich darauf; und das galt nun gleichsam als sein Schiff. Darauf ging er, wurde von dem Wasser fortgeführt ...” Mit dieser Abreise verbindet sich die Erwartung der Wiederkunft Quetzalcoatls, die bis in die Tage der Conquista lebendig blieb und zu tragischer Verwechslung mit Cortés führte. Der aztekische Historiker Chimalpahin berichtet: [12]

> “In der folgenden Weise sprechen
> die alten Männer der fernen Zeit:
> Er selbst lebt und ist,
> der bis jetzt nicht stirbt,
> und wiederum wird er zurückkehren,
> der zu herrschen kommt.”

Integrierender Bestandteil der Legendenbildung ist hier offensichtlich der persöhnliche Entschluss zum Verlassen der bisherigen Umwelt. Auffällig und bemerkenswert ist, dass er dort, wo er an sich fehlt, nachträglich in die Vita des geheimnisvoll Weiterlebenden hineinprojiziert werden kann. Miki Nakayama, die Stifterin der japanischen Tenrikyō, deren Weiterleben in ihrem Tempel in Tenri City angenommen wird, starb im Januar 1887 eines natürlichen Todes im Alter von 90 Jahren, obwohl ihr — wie allen Menschen einer erwarteten glücklichen Zeit — ein Lebensalter von 115 Jahren beschieden sein sollte. In ihrer Gemeinde aber bildete sich die Ansicht, sie habe ihr Leben für das Heil der Menschen freiwillig verkürzt. [13]

Das irgendwie ungewöhnliche Verlassen der natürlichen Lebenswelt fungiert als auslösendes Moment der Legende vom verborgenen Heilbringer nur dann, wenn dieser bereits bestimmte Qualitäten aufwies, die religiöser Art sind und in einem besonderen Gottesverhältnis bestehen. Die Viten genuin religiöser Gestalten geben hierüber am ehesten Aufschluss, und rückgreifend kann dann gefragt werden, ob ihre Charakteristika auch für die verborgenen Herrschergestalten gelten.

Generell ist festzustellen, dass der Gott, zu dem der verborgene Heilbringer ein besonderes Verhältnis besass, entweder an sich monotheistisch verstanden oder doch vom verborgenen Heilbringer selbst als die Gottheit katexochen verehrt wurde, mithin

---

[12] Walter Lehmann und Gerdt Kutscher, *Chimalpahin: Das Memorial breve* (Stuttgart 1958), S. 128.
[13] Henry van Straelen, *The Religion of Divine Wisdom* (Tokyo 1954), S. 40.

im Rahmen eines polytheistischen Systems subjektiver Theismus oder Henotheismus vorlag. Aber welcher Art ist das Verhältnis zu diesem einen Gott?

Miki Nakayama erhielt ihre Berufung in ihrem 41. Lebensjahr. Oyasama, die "elterliche Gottheit", offenbarte sich ihr mit den Worten: [14] "Ich bin der Schöpfer, der eigentliche, wahre Gott ... Jetzt bin ich persöhnlich in diese Welt gekommen, um die ganze Welt zu erlösen. Ich will Miki Nakayama als meinen Wohnsitz, meinen Tempel haben." Die Dogmatik der Tenrikyō unterstreicht ausdrücklich, dass die Stifterin "die göttliche Berufung erhielt, der Elterngottheit als Wohnsitz zu dienen". [15]

Offensichtlich ist die göttliche Einwohnung, die zur Identität der Stifterin mit der Elterngottheit führt, als ein allmählicher Vorgang zu verstehen, der jedenfalls erst sukzessive seine Wirkung entfaltet. Denn im Ōfudesaki, einer heiligen Schrift der Tenrikyō, sagt die elterliche Gottheit: [16] "Schon seit einiger Zeit habe ich meine Wohnung fest in ihrem Körper, aber bis jetzt verhielt ich mich in allem noch zurückhaltend."

Wenn für den menschlichen Partner dieser sakralen Beziehung in wörtlicher Übersetzung des aztekischen Begriffs *teopixqui* die Bezeichnung "Gotteshüter" vorgeschlagen werden soll, so deshalb, weil damit an das gemeinte Phänomen kein künstlich gebildeter Terminus herangetragen, vielmehr ein solcher aufgenommen wird, der unter jenen üblich war, die ihre Gotteshüter kannten und verehrten, was für die alten Mexikaner in besonders ausgeprägter Weise zutraf.

Das sukzessive Ineinandergreifen der göttlichen und menschlichen Sphäre schildert ein Text, der Quetzalcoatl betrifft. Von seinem Volke, den Tolteken, heisst es dort: [17] "Gar fromm waren sie; denn nur einem als ihrem Gotte waren sie ergeben, den sie anriefen, den sie verehrten, namens Quetzalcoatl. Ihr Priester war, ihr Gotteshüter, ebenfalls nur einer namens Quetzalcoatl. Und dieser war sehr fromm. Was Quetzalcoatl zu den Priestern sagte, das taten sie genau. Nicht sündigten sie; denn er sprach zu ihnen, er erklärte ihnen: es ist nur ein Gott namens Quetzalcoatl ... Und in jeder Weise glaubten sie an ihren Priester Quetzalcoatl.

---

[14] *Die Lehre der Tenrikyo*, hrsg. von Shōzen Nakayama (Tenri City 1958), S. 1.
[15] a.a.O., S. 48 f.
[16] Ōfudesaki VI, 59.
[17] Sahagún — Seler, S. 396.

Und sehr gehorsam waren sie, sehr dem Göttlichen hingegeben und sehr gottesfürchtig waren sie: denn alle gehorchten ihm, alle glaubten an Quetzalcoatl."

Wesentlich an diesem Texte ist, dass die anfängliche Unterscheidung zwischen dem menschlichen und dem göttlichen Träger des Namens Quetzalcoatl sukzessive aufgegeben wird. Dies geschieht zunächst mit dem Bericht über den Glauben der Tolteken an den menschlichen Quetzalcoatl. Und am Schluss des Textes wird dann überhaupt nicht mehr zwischen dem Gotteshüter und seinem Gott unterschieden.

Genau Entsprechendes wird von Huitzilopochtli, dem Stammesgott der Azteken, und von seinem Gotteshüter innerhalb einer Darstellung überliefert, die das Geschichtswerk Chimalpahins von den frühen Wanderungen der Azteken gibt. Dort heisst es: [18] "Ihr Führer war der namens Huitzilopochtli, der grosse Hüter des Dämons, der Diener des grossen Dämons, des Schreckensgottes; der sprach ganz leibhaftig mit ihm, dem zeigte sich der (Gott) Huitzilopochtli, so dass er (der Hüter des Gottes) sich später als sein Abbild an dessen Stelle setzte, (an die Stelle des) Schreckensgottes. Darum wurde er (der Gotteshüter) einfach Huitzilopochtli genannt."

Der Typus religiöser Autorität, der mit derartigen Textaussagen umschrieben ist, stellt eine Grösse sui generis dar, weil er hinsichtlich sowohl seiner religiösen Legitimation als auch seiner Funktion Elemente verschiedener Typen des heiligen Menschen aufweist und daher mit keinem von ihnen identisch ist.

Das indianische Material könnte es nahelegen, die religiöse Legitimation des Gotteshüters aus nagualistischen Vorstellungen abzuleiten. Tatsächlich bezeichnen ihn Texte mit dem Etymon des Terminus "Nagualismus" als *nahualli*, als "Verkleidung" und mystische Simultanexistenz seines Gottes. Doch trifft der Begriff "Nagualismus", will man ihn trotz seiner semantischen Wandlungen und der auf ihnen beruhenden Vielschichtigkeit überhaupt verwenden, [19] sicher nur für Teilaspekte zu, weil er nicht begrenzt ist auf den religiös ausserordentlichen Menschen und ausserdem den verborgenen Heilbringer, zu dem der Gotteshüter nach dem Verlassen seiner Umwelt wird, nicht mit einschliesst.

---

[18]   Lehmann – Kutscher, *Chimalpahin*, S. 32 f.
[19]   Zur Kritik des Begriffs vgl. G. Foster, "Nagualism in Mexico and Guatamala," in: *Acta Americana* (Mexico 1944), S. 85-103.

Es würde der Erfassung der religiösen Spezifika des Gottes-hüters auch nicht dienlich sein, ihn ohne attributive Kennzeich-nung dem generellen Begriff des "Heilbringers" zu subsumieren. Denn dieser Begriff, der seit seiner Bildung durch Kurt Breysig, einen Einzelgänger der Geschichtswissenschaft, [20] belastet war, [21] umfasst mit seiner Anwendung auf den Urmenschen und Ur-könig, den Demiurgen, eventuell gar die Dema-Gottheiten und sicher den urzeitlichen Kulturbringer [22] Gestalten anderer reli-giöser Legimitation und Funktion, von denen der Gotteshüter vor allem deshalb abzusetzen ist, weil er in jedem Falle als histo-risch greifbare Persönlichkeit erscheint.

Diese Historizität der Gestalt ist nicht die einzige Gemeinsam-keit mit den verborgenen Herrschern. Auch die herrscherliche Funktion an sich ist den Gotteshütern der Religionsgeschichte eigen, und sie bezieht sich auf deren königliche Stellung in einem Volke, einem Reich oder auf ihre hierarchische Position in einer Gemeinde.

Aber auch hinsichtlich ihrer sakralen Legimitation weisen die Gotteshüter der Religionsgeschichte mit jenen Herrschern, die als verborgene Heilbringer weiterleben, eine wesentliche Gemeinsam-keit auf. Sie besteht darin, dass die sakrale Qualität des Herr-schertums nicht wie im Alten Orient und speziell in Ägypten durch den Bezug der Identität oder Filiation zu einem Hochgott an sich gegeben ist, sondern im Verlauf des Lebens verliehen oder erworben wird. Das gilt durchaus für die Herrscher des Mittel-alters, die "vergottet und geheiligt" wurden, die *deificati et sanc-tificati* waren. [23]

---

[20] Kurt Breysig, *Die Entstehung des Gottesgedankens und der Heilbringer* (Berlin 1905).

[21] Vgl. P. Ehrenreich, "Götter und Heilbringer. Eine ethnologische Kritik," in: *Zeitschrift für Ethnologie* 38 (1906), S. 536-610; Gösta Kock, "Is 'Der Heilbringer' a God or not?" in: *Ethnos* 8 (1943), S. 61-77; ders., "Der Heilbringer: Ein Beitrag zur Aufklärung seiner religionsgeschichtlichen Voraussetzung," in *Ethnos* 21 (1956), S. 118-129. — Untersuchungen zu geographisch begrenzten Verbreitungsräumen bieten: Arie van Deursen, *Der Heilbringer*: Eine ethnologische Studie über den Heilbringer bei den nordamerikanischen Indianern (Groningen und Den Haag 1931); Harry Tegnaeus, *Le héros civilisateur* (Stockholm 1950). — Die Arbeit von Romano Guardini, *Der Heilbringer in Mythos, Offenbarung und Politik* (Stuttgart 1946), überschreitet die religionswissenschaftliche Problematik und steht im Dienste der Klärung einer geistes-geschichtlichen Situation.

[22] Vgl. Geo Widengren, *Religionsphänomenologie* (Berlin 1969), S. 89 ff.

[23] Friedrich Heiler, "Fortleben und Wandlungen des antiken Gottkönigtums im Christentum," in *The Sacral Kingship — La regalità sacra* Leiden 1959), S. 568.

Diese Form des Gottesbezuges und seines Erwerbs erscheint konstitutiv für die Gestalt des Gotteshüters, mag er in die Geschichte als genuin religiöse Gestalt oder vornehmlich als Herrscher eingegangen sein. Sie schliesst nicht aus, sondern bedingt vielmehr, dass die Gotteshüter in unterschiedlich starkem Masse Qualitäten anderer Typen religiöser Autorität akzidentell auf sich vereinigen können, solche des Priesters, des Heilers, des Kulturbringers, des Stifters oder Reformators.

Mit dem Gotteshüter und verborgenen Heilbringer verbindet sich die Legende der einmaligen Wiederkehr und nicht ein "Mythos der ewigen Wiederkehr", [24] Das zugehörige Geschichtsbild ist eindimensional und teleologisch, aber primär nicht universaleschatologisch. Es bleibt weiterer Überlegung die offene Frage gestellt, wie sich die messianischen Gestalten endzeitlicher Könige [25] zu den Gotteshütern verhalten. Für diese jedenfalls gilt, dass der Glaube an ihre einstige Erlöserfunktion [26] begrenzt bleibt: Quetzalcoatl wird wieder sein Reich von Tollan aufrichten, Tschingis Khan wird die Mongolen zu neuer Grösse führen, Holger Danske wird Dänemark befreien. [27] Eschatologische Aussagen sind hiermit nicht verbunden.

Zu dieser Gestalt des verborgenen Heilbringers wird der Gotteshüter nach dem Ausscheiden aus seiner natürlichen Umwelt. Wer Wohnung und Tempel seines Gottes war, ist den Bedingungen irdischen Lebens und Sterbens entzogen.

---

[24] Vgl. Mircea Eliade, *Der Mythos der ewigen Wiederkehr* (Düsseldorf 1953).

[25] Vgl. Hans Lietzmann, *Der Weltheiland* (Bonn 1909); Hugo Gressmann, *Der Messias* (Göttingen 1929); Hermann Güntert, *Der arische Weltkönig und Heiland*, (Halle a. S. 1923); Emil Abegg, l. c.; Wilhelm Weber, *Der Prophet und sein Gott*: Eine Studie zur vierten Ekloge Vergils (Leipzig 1925); Anton Fridrichsen, "Vergilius' fjärde eklog", in *Religion och Bibel* 3 (1944), S. 34-44.

[26] Vgl. Widengren, a.a.O., S. 92.

[27] Olrik, a.a.O., S. 393.

THE GODS OF THE LEPCHAS OF SIKKIM

HALFDAN SIIGER

In accordance with the general theme of the present congress: Belief in God, I shall try to view the religion of the Lepchas under this aspect.

In order to understand the religious problems which I shall deal with, a few historical facts will be necessary. Coming from some unknown places in Southeast Asia the Lepchas were originally intruders into the country of Sikkim which is situated in the Himalayas between India and Tibet, with Nepal to the west and Bhutan to the east. We do not know when this intrusion took place, but it seems that we have records of Lepcha settlements from about 1200 A.D. They lived as hunters, but had also some mountain agriculture and dry rice cultivation. They had priests and shamanistic priestesses, and probably their own chieftains or kings.

The arrival of a Tibetan royal family of the Minyag dynasty who occupied the country and became kings about 1600 A.D. marks a turning point in the history of the Lepchas. With this family the Ning-ma-pa or Red Sect Lamaism became the official religion of the country and some monasteries were built. With Lamaism came also legends of the Tibetan saint Padmasambhava, whom the Lepchas call *ta she thíng*. According to Lamaist traditions this saint had travelled in the country and subjugated the local supernatural beings. Up to our days the ancient Lepcha religion and Lamaism have lived side by side. There has been competition and occasional quarrels between the two religions, but nowadays a kind of cooperation seems to prevail.

From about 1835 the British Government exercised the real power in Sikkim. Important parts of the Maharajah's country became included into British India, especially such areas as Darjeeling to the west and Kalimpong to the south. In this way many Lepchas came under direct British rule. During the years some Christian missionaries settled in some Lepcha villages. However, a typical Lepcha reserve, strictly closed for all non-Lepchas, was established in the centre of Sikkim.

An important change in their occupation and way of life took place in the second half of the last century when dry rice cultivation was replaced by wet rice cultivation, a change which resulted in important religious consequences.

The present paper is based on my own experiences during expeditionary field work in 1949 and 1950 among the Lepchas, supplemented by observations provided by investigators and scholars like Mrs. de Beauvoir Stocks, Geoffrey Gorer, John Morris, René de Nebesky-Wojkowitz, Matthias Hermanns, Corneille Jest, and others.

With this indigenous Himalayan people we do not find a creed in the meaning of a formula of religious belief, but we do find a traditional totality of religious beliefs which can be extracted from their cults, cult-prayers, myths, legends, etc.

The supernatural world of the Lepchas consists of a great number of *rŭm* or gods, and a still greater, almost countless, number of *mung*, demons or devils. The daily and yearly ceremonial life of the people deals with invoking the blessings of the *rŭm* and averting the malignant influence of the *mung*. The present paper will concentrate on the main *rŭm*, their origin, character, abodes and activities as experienced by the people.

At the beginning of time the creator goddess, living at the bottom of Mount Kanchenjunga, the tallest mountain of Sikkim, created everything in the world, including a number of other gods, among whom the gods of the high mountain peaks are prominent.

Her last children were the goddess of procreation and her husband. This goddess gave birth to the progenitors of mankind, but also to many other children whose number became so great that she could not nurse them and completely neglected them. Consequently these children became jealous of their human brothers and sisters for whom their mother cared, and they turned into *mung* who since that time have constantly attacked human beings.

Halfway up Mount Kanchenjunga live the mythical *mă yel* beings. They are very limited in number, live in pairs in their huts, are small and hairy, and their women do not give birth to children. Every day they are young in the morning, middle-aged at noon, and old in the evening. Their crops are enormously big and fertile, and from there the Lepchas obtained their main crops

and the agricultural fertility. These beings take interest in the
fate of the Lepchas and have occasionally given them help in
difficult situations. According to some legends the soul of the
shamanistic priestess brings the souls of the deceased to this
place. The Lepchas of Sikkim perform regular agricultural fertility rites to the *mă yel* beings, requesting them to give abundant
harvest, whereas the modern Lepchas of Kalimpong abandoned
this custom with the introduction of wet rice cultivation.

Although the traditions are vague as to the origin of the *mă yel*
beings, they seem to agree in that respect that the *mă yel* beings
are neither *rŭm* nor human beings, but occupy a particular position in between. The conception of their abodes as a place for
the souls of the deceased and as the centre of fertility indicates
that they are ancestral beings bestowing fertility on the living
society.

On the top of Mount Kanchenjunga resides *kong chen*, the
great mountain god, and the eldest son of the great creator goddess. He is also a great god to the Lamaist, and modern moun-
taineering expeditions must commit themselves not to climb the
ten last metres of the peak, before they can obtain permission
from the Maharajah of Sikkim to begin their difficult task. In the
neighbourhood of this glorious peak are many other and minor
peaks. One of them represents the wife of *kong chen*, others his
brothers, and others again are his great retinue of followers or
soldiers. *kong chen* and his followers are of a fierce disposition,
but *kong chen* is the patron god of Sikkim, not only to the
Lepchas but also to the Lamaists. He is highly venerated, and
regular ceremonies are performed to him in the Lamaist monasteries of Sikkim. His followers are *mung* or of a *mung* like disposition, but they have been subjugated by *kong chen* and are
under his firm control. The Sikkimese Lepchas invoke him at a
great ceremony, on which occasion they sacrifice a yak and
request him to protect the Maharajah and the people from diseases, from attacks from hostile neighbouring countries, and
from a great number of dangerous *mung* of the high mountains.

It will be seen that Mount Kanchenjunga, outstanding from a
geographical point of view, to the Lepchas represents a magnifi-
cent concentration of religious powers. Divided into three mythical storeys or levels it abounds in supernatural life and activities:
at the lower level is the great primordial creator goddess, at the

middle level live the mythical *mă yel* beings, and on the top resides *kong chen* himself.

Apart from these prominent supernatural beings, the Lepchas have also many minor ones. Each family has its own lineage *rŭm*, the house has its own deity, and so have the domestic animals. The blacksmith and the warrior invoke their special gods. There is also a very old god of the hunters. Since very few men go out hunting nowadays, the worship of this god is disappearing and may, ultimately, completely die out.

Up to now I have concentrated on the second part of the general theme for the present congress: the question of god or gods. But the theme has also another part: the question of belief. This question implies the problem of confidence or trust which means that it is a problem concerning the personal and emotional attitude of the adherents of a religion towards their god or gods. This problem belongs to the psychology of religion, and we must therefore turn to the psychological relationship between the figures of the supernatural world and human beings.

According to the religion of the Lepchas the life of human beings is characterized by danger, agony and suffering, – this is obvious from the contents of myths and prayers. This unhappy state is a consequence of the behaviour of the goddess of procreation who could not care for all her children. Her neglected children, as said above, then turned into cruel *mung*, constantly revenging themselves by attacking the human children, causing them diseases and death. The psychology of the *mung* is quite simple: the experience of a fundamental careless indifference gives rise to a revengeful jealousy creating a hostility obsessed with innate cruelty against mankind. On the other hand, the human beings are completely unable to defend themselves. This permanent miserable state of human beings, characterized by hopeless weakness and innumerable sufferings, has its origin in the supernatural world, and consequently it can only be remedied by actions on the part of the same supernatural world. Therefore the Lepchas approach the benevolent supernatural beings and invoke the protective gods during the cultic performances. Protection is the predominant reappearing request of the rituals.

In the great ceremony to *kong chen*, mentioned previously,

the people give offerings to *kong chen* and meat and blood of the sacrificed yak to the *mung*. The meaning is that the *mung* by devouring this sacrifice accept it as a substitute for the lives of human beings. From a mythological point of view it will be realised that the miserable state of human beings, originally caused by the great creator goddess, the mother of *kong chen*, is in this way remedied by her mighty son.

We began by saying that we do not find a distinct creed among the Lepchas, but we do find a traditional totality of religious beliefs. We can now supplement this statement by saying that this totality is of a syncretistic character. It seems ready to adopt significant traits from other religions without losing its own character and it responds in a sensitive way to important changes in the people's way of life.

A few examples will elucidate this.

An example of adoption from another religion can be found in *ta she thíng*, the Lepcha name for the Lamaist Saint Padmasambhava.

The position of *ta she thíng* is rather ambiguous. He arrived together with Lamaism, he is a kind of religious intruder, but has become an accepted intruder. In many legends he bestows his blessings by authorizing ancient types of sacrifices and granting a kind of examption from the strict Buddhist prohibition on killing animals. He may have the air of a "culture hero", and occasionally his behaviour resembles that of a "trickster". It is interesting to observe that he seems to be the only mythological figure who sometimes appears in ludicrous situations. In some versions of the ancient mythology he appears as the primordial figure, even prior to the great creator goddess, whom he then created.

The importance of the *mǎ yel* beings is decreasing. With the disappearance of the dry rice cultivation the Lepchas of Kalimpong do not invoke them as they did before. The rituals of the Kalimpong dry rice cultivation, which my Lepcha interpreter took down, had already been obsolete for several decades. On the other hand, the introduction of wet rice cultivation was apparently not accompanied by any ceremonial activities, and the cultivators themselves do not seem to have instituted such activities. That is to say that the religious complex, formerly associated with rice cultivation, has disappeared. We may therefore conclude that this kind of agricultural fertility has lost its deep religious roots, and the Kalimpong people have no longer any immediate cultic connections with the *mă yel* beings in this respect. Furthermore, nowadays the central and important parts of the funeral ceremonies are performed by the lamas, and not by the Lepcha priests and priestesses. The ancient conducting of the soul of the deceased to the abodes of the *mă yel* beings is disappearing or has in some places disappeared completely. The connection with the abode of the *mă yel* beings as the abode of the ancestors is thereby loosened. No wonder that the *mă yel* beings according to the mythology isolate themselves within their inaccessible abodes halfway up Mount Kanchenjunga, and do not come to the assistance of the people as they formerly did. They are becoming mythical figures of a rather distant character, in that way resembling the great creator goddess to whom no ceremonies are performed.

There can be no doubt that the hunting god is rapidly disappearing out of the mythology as a god. At present he appears as a god who must fight for his rights to sacrifices, and when he does not obtain his sacrifices, – which he seldom does nowadays because very few go out hunting, – he may occasionally punish the hunters, almost like a *mung*. This human misbehaviour is of course interpreted by the supernatural being in accordance with the deep-rooted religious psychology as a kind of negligence. In the case of such a negligence the supernatural being reacts fiercely.

One occasionally meets Lepchas, especially from the southern regions in India, who talk of God as the one and supreme God of all gods. Their statements about this god are, however, so vague and indistinct, that one gets the impression that it is due to the influence of Christianity which has some missions among the Lepchas. It is also characteristic that this supreme God, when mentioned, occupies the position as the prime creator before or above the ordinary Lepcha gods, whom he does not replace in any way.

To summarize we may conclude that the traditional totality of religious beliefs among the Lepchas remains unaltered in its constitutive structure and function. Important changes in occupations are reflected in the religious life of corresponding disappearances of ceremonies associated with the ancient conditions.

Among the modern Lepchas the adoption of new ways of life does not inspire the creation of new religious activities. In that respect the Lepcha religion is no longer creative. The impressive appearances of new mythological figures from other religions are easily received and incorporated into the mythological totality without changing the fundamental structure. The Lepcha mythology is hospitable, and new figures are awarded honourable positions according to their character and the role they play in the foreign religions.

Literature

The present paper is based on my own results published in: Halfdan Siiger, *The Lepchas, Culture and Religion of a Himalayan People*, Part I (Publications of the National Museum, Ethnographical Series, vol. XI, Part I, Copenhagen, 1967); see especially pp. 190-201 (the great *kong chen* ceremony), pp. 172 ff. (the creative mother-goddess), pp. 89 ff. (the *mă yel* beings) and the corresponding texts published in: Halfdan Siiger and Jørgen Rischel, *The Lepchas. Culture and Religion of a Himalayan People*. Part II. Lepcha Ritual Texts and Commentary by Halfdan Siiger. Phonetic Transcriptions of Lepcha Ritual Texts with Introduction by Jørgen Rischel (Publications of the National Museum, Ethnographical Series, vol. XI, Part II, Copenhagen 1967). Compare also my papers: *A Cult for the God of Mount Kanchenjunga among the Lepcha of Northern Sikkim.* (Actes du IVe Congrès International des Sciences Anthropologiques et Ethnologiques. Vienne 1952, Tome II, Ethnologica pp. 185-189. Wien 1955), and: *Himalayan Mountain Cults* (Proceedings, VIIIth International Congress of Anthropological and Ethnological Sciences, 1968 Tokyo and Kyoto, vol. II, Ethnology, pp. 277-79).

Supplementary details have been taken from: Mrs. C. de Beauvoir Stocks, *Folk-lore and Customs of the Lap-chas of Sikhim*. See Index: e.g. Tashey-thing. (Journal and Proceedings of the Asiatic Society of Bengal, New Series, vol. 21, pp. 325-505, Calcutta 1927); Geoffrey Gorer, *Himalayan Village. An Account of the Lepchas of Sikkim*. With an Introduction by J.H. Hutton, London 1938, 2nd edn., revised and enlarged 1967, e.g. p. 236 ff. (the people of Mayel); pp. 223 ff. and pp. 459 ff. (the creative mother-goddess); John Morris, *Living With Lepchas. A Book about the Sikkim Himalayas*, London 1938; Fr. Matthias Hermanns, *The Indo-Tibetans. The Indo-Tibetan and Mongoloid Problem in the Southern Himalaya and North-Northeast India*, Bombay 1954, e.g. p. 44 f. (*mă yel*) and p. 82; M. Corneille Jest, *Religious Beliefs of the Lepchas in the Kalimpong District (West Bengal)*, (Journal of the Royal Asiatic Society, October 1960, pp. 124-134); R. von Nebesky-Wojkowitz and Geoffrey Gorer, *The Use of Thread-Crosses in Lepcha Lamaist Ceremonies* (Eastern Anthropologist, vol. IV. No. 2, pp. 65-87, Lucknow 1951), e.g. p. 65 ff.

As for the importance of Kanchenjunga to the Lamaist Buddhists, see e.g. René de Nebesky-Wojkowitz, *Oracles and Demons of Tibet*, The Hague 1956, pp. 216 ff.; and L. A. Waddell, *The Buddhism of Tibet or Lamaism*, 1st edn. 1894, Cambridge; 2nd edn. reprint 1939, pp. 370 f.

THE CATEGORY OF "FAITH" IN A "NEW STYLE" PHENOMENOLOGY OF RELIGION

JACQUES WAARDENBURG

This paper can only be an indirect contribution to the study of the central theme of this congress. We limit ourselves in several respects. First, we limit ourselves to the first half of the theme: the notion of "belief", or as we would rather call it, "faith", taking the "god" or "gods" of that faith at the moment for granted. Second, we restrict ourselves to the problem of the use of the concept of "faith" in the field of the scholarly study of religion. And third, we look into this matter from a phenomenological point of view, being aware that phenomenological research is only one of the different approaches in the study of religion and that other approaches may lead to other ways of using the concept of "faith", religious and otherwise.

Even after these three limitations the subject is still highly complex and it has so many aspects that we would prefer to put here some questions and to do some proposals, while taking phenomenology in its new style as a self-critical approach to the problem of meaning, instead of pretending to give a definite solution. The proposal to be put forward here is made in an *optique* or perspective whereby the concept of "faith" is defined in a phenomenological way, and whereby the assumptions and implications are left aside with which for example the German *Glaube*, the Dutch *geloof*, the French *foi* and the English "belief" are charged in ordinary religious language usage.

We will treat the subject in the following six parts:

1. Preliminary remarks
2. Faith in connection with the subjectmatter of research
3. Faith in connection with the subject carrying out research
4. Faith in connection with the relationship between subject and object of research
5. Some categories of "new style" phenomenological research
6. Faith as a category in phenomenological research

1. *Preliminary Remarks*

If we want phenomenology to be a scholarly discipline and if we want to claim a general validity for its findings, one of the most intricate problems is that of the concept of "faith". One of the reasons of this state of affairs is that "faith" itself has been a religious concept. In the monotheistic religions and specifically in Islam and Christianity the notion of faith has played a major role; in Protestantism it has been a central concept. It has been absolutized from time to time and in the West it functions basically as a theological concept which is linked to a certain notion of God and of revelation. Furthermore, for most Western people, including those who are not religious themselves, the notion of faith is indissolubly connected with a personalistic notion of man. The question then is legitimate whether this concept can be used at all in the scholarly study of religion. Many discussions on method and theory in this field go back to different positions taken by scholars with regard to this problem. But hardly anyone has yet tackled the problem of "faith" in the study of religion as the problem of redefining it as a possible *scholarly* category.

Behind the current use of the word "faith" there is a definite normative element: the idea that, somehow, we would know what "faith" is, or that we should know what it is, or that we should at least know what it ought to be. It is assumed in the West that we should reach it, or anyhow that we should not lose it. This is a theological problem and it remains as such an open question and maybe even a mystery, since "faith", religious or otherwise, — at least one's own faith — is not a thing, an object, something isolated in itself or something that can be isolated.

Our discipline has suffered already too much under such normative ideas, e.g. the idea that we would or should know what religion really is. We should not repeat making the same mistake with regard to the notion of faith. First of all one has to be very careful with one's wording. In what sense can we speak at all of the "faith" of other people, that is to say of people who are different from ourselves? And in what sense can we speak of the study of "faiths" in the plural, that is to say of those fundaments of the religious attitudes of different people that can be subsumed under one common and even general denominator? So, if already the wordings "one's own faith", "faith of other people" and "faiths" in the plural easily lead to wrong representations of something that is rather delicate, how could we then legitimately strive after a knowledge of it, and in scholarship even a knowledge that is generally valid?

One of the assumptions of the present paper is that the *scholarly* speech about faith is fundamentally different from the *believers'* speech about it. Furthermore that there is *no* reason *a priori* to throw the concept overboard. It is also assumed that a scholar who uses the concept has to be self-critically aware of the meaning, the way, the *intention* in or with which he uses the word "faith". Again, especially in contact with other people, he has to make clear that for purposes of research he uses current concepts always in a particular way which is different from the ordinary daily usage.

In this paper we take the basic problem of phenomenology to be: *how to know with reasonable certainty — or at least with reasonable probability — the significance of the data which we study for the communities or the individuals involved with them?* This new style phenomenology is basically a way of doing research on meaning. Behavior, speech, art, etc. carry such meaning with them and they should, consequently, also be object of investigation. In this view, any research with regard to faith will not deal with faith as a metaphysical entity in itself, but always with faith as it existed in a given culture, among certain people at a particular time and place, and how it manifested itself in their expressions. In most cases we have to proceed by inference from data of different kinds, but there is sometimes direct evidence for such faith, for instance when man in a certain situation has made a definite appeal on it. But even then we still should ask in each case whether this faith functioned indeed according to its intentions or whether it rather served as a cover for something else. And a general question like "the place of faith" in world history may be as fascinating as the question of "the role of love" in world history: but it can be answered only through the investigation of specific instances.

Let us conclude these preliminaries with two remarks on our notion of reason:

a) Philosophically speaking, we would hold that reason or thought does not and cannot succeed in arriving at an adequate grasp of faith itself, one of the reasons being that faith as such simply cannot be made a pure object. The closer reason is reflecting on faith, the more reason turns out to arise itself out of faith. And the "objects" to which faith refers are as such not objects or facts in the ordinary empirical sense of the word, but rather phenomena that are linked to faith and that to some extent as such can bring about a movement of faith. And this faith itself transcends the reality of empirical "objects".

b) Scholarly speaking, we would hold that the only sure way to arrive at any knowledge about faith is by means of investigating direct or indirect testimonies which are bound to concrete "expressions". Our research is able to grasp such direct and indirect testimonies as expressions only to the extent allowed by the available evidence. The major question is then: how to arrive at the meaning of such testimonies? And since as scholars we are not supposed to have direct access ourselves to the realities to which these testimonies testify, we have to proceed in our interpretation of such testimonies on the basis of their human context.

We come now to our subject proper. Time, however, permits only to present a framework, but this is enough to elucidate the terms of the problem.

2. *Faith in Connection with the Subjectmatter of Research*

One of the major questions here is whether or not a possible faith existing behind given religious expressions can be subject of inquiry, and if so, how this should be carried out.

a) Empirical research has to do with objects as facts: texts, representations, ideas, monuments, artifacts, pieces of art, directly observed speech and behavior, etc. Such facts can be investigated on their meaning taken as objects in themselves or in a context: this is particularly evident in the case of texts but it holds true also for other religious facts.

b) From a strictly empirical point of view it can be contended that such facts and meanings are not necessarily linked with a faith. They are then considered as products of imagination, intelligence, professional skill, etc.; their function is assessed according to biological, psychological, economic, social, etc. needs and necessities. The notion of faith does not enter into the picture of empirical considerations.

A strictly rational point of view confirms this basic rule that our research cannot establish any necessary link between these facts and their meanings on the one hand, and a hypothetical faith which would exist "behind" such facts and meanings on the other hand. Supposed indeed that there would be or would have been a real faith behind these facts and meanings, neither empirical nor rational research would as such have access to it.

c) Critical and self-critical scholarship will moreover observe that a number of statements and affirmations made by scholars about the faith of other people are, when it comes to the essentials, in fact more revealing for the spiritual qualities of the scholar and the climate of his milieu than that they bring to the open a faith quality existing "behind" the religious facts as such. Consequently, the existence of such a quality might be denied altogether. The least we can say here, actually, is that any possible perception of someone else's faith passes through one's own spirituality, that is the network of one's own faith, religiousness, religion, philosophy, and so on — be it positive or negative for the perception as such.

d) There appears to be a larger degree of objectivity in the reconstruction of the religious universe than in the perception of the faith of a given culture, community or person. It certainly remains a reconstruction, but this can be carried out methodically on the basis of given evidence, and any hypothesis or provisional conclusion can be verified. On the basis of a careful study of given religious facts and their meanings it will be possible in a number of cases, especially in present-day situations, if enough documentary material is available and if a critical method is applied, to reconstruct the mental universe of a given group or individual. Such a universe appears to be, basically, a field of significances (*champ de significations*) showing certain basic intentions that correspond with given needs and problems of the people concerned. Whereas with regard to a "faith" in the subject-matter only incidental perceptions are possible which are highly valuable but subjective, with regard to a religious universe there is the possibility of a reconstruction which remains largely subjected to norms of critical scholarship and which is, consequently, more objective in its results.

3. *Faith in Connection with the Subject Carrying out Research*

One of the major questions here is whether or not a faith on the side of the researcher himself should be a requirement for fruitful research.

a) There is no reason to assume that a specific religious faith of the researcher, or the absence of such a specific faith could *as such* lead to better results in the study of religion. The very fact that the presentations of some scholars who work themselves with an explicit faith show more daring misrepresentations of the material than adequate profundities, makes the critical scholar tend to prefer the work of scholars who are not explicitly religiously committed themselves. There is reason to distrust *a priori* the work of those who interpret their material according to — sometimes religiously determined or sanctioned — preconceived schemes of reference or closed systems of interpretation, or who — precisely because of limiting down all truth to one particular ultimate truth which they confess themselves in one particular way — are precluded from grasping *the truth character*, that is to say *the real significance* of the phenomena studied. Analytically speaking, the problem of the researcher who is himself explicitly religiously involved is that a number of assumptions held or statements made by him are beyond logical control; they appear to be incorrectible precisely because they are religiously motivated, held or sanctioned.

b) However, when speaking of a possible faith on the side of the researcher there is still room for great variety. It may consist of an adherence to a given set of doctrines, moral prescriptions and ritual practices of the truth of which one is convinced. It may be a particular kind of creative, or mystical, or metaphysically paradoxical way of existing. It may be the religious venture of an individual which may take a theological articulation. And so on. Again, in each case the relationship of such a faith with the research work itself, its psychological motivations, its intellectual questioning, etc., will be different; the range of research can thereby obtain a nearly complete autonomy, so that it is then the faith in this research itself which is the faith of the scholar. On the other hand, even if in a particular case a certain faith might be conducive to fruitful research in view of certain problems or phenomena, there are of course many more and also more essential requirements for such research in the field of religious meanings. In the last analysis, it is not a particular faith that would stand in the way of scholarly research on religion, but certain obnobulating mental attitudes such as stubbornness and selfrighteousness on one hand, and mystification and idealization on the other hand, which are incorrectible if they are held with religious pretensions.

c) On the other hand, it is important to note that the subjectivity of the scholar contains the very source of his interests and intentions, and that it is related to an existential realm. This latter will determine, for instance, in what kinds of things one is inclined to put any faith at all, and in what kinds of things one hardly will be able to do that. On this level it is not only a specifically religious faith but any faith on the side of the scholar that plays a role in original research work. There is some truth in the saying that a scholar should be a doubter and maybe even a sceptic; at least it secures him against uncritical assumptions and acceptances which go back upon too naive a faith. But there is also truth in the saying that, at least, he should have some faith, were it only in the direction of his own pursuits.

d) On the basis of what has just been mentioned we would like to submit that it is a methodical requirement that religious phenomena are studied by people not only of different specializations but also of different characters and backgrounds. Of course we do not mean thereby an adherence to different given philosophies or theological systems; on the contrary, what is required is an active autonomous reflection by each student. Such a reflection will result into positive fruits for scholarship provided that the people involved are willing to do justice to the facts and phenomena themselves. The phenomena studied as evidence in this way would be seen not only in their manifold aspects but also in their different meanings to different people.

4. *Faith in Connection with the Relationship between Subject and Object of Research*

One of the major questions here is whether research on religion would have basically the character of an interfaith relationship.

a) The proposition itself assumes that on the side of the researcher there is religious faith of such a kind, that he would be able not only to reconstruct the mental universe potentially contained in the materials before him but that he would also be able to perceive a religious faith behind these materials. It implies that he is both moved himself by a faith and that he is really interested in the faith of a given other person, community or culture.

b) A specific situation may occur in the study of the living religion of a given group or individual, when these make themselves their religious faith explicit with an appeal to others to adhere to it. In the study of such an appeal there is then the alternative either to study it as an object in itself, as a social or psychological datum which is meaningful in itself, or to carry out further research with a communicative attitude, a dialogue with the data, during which the researcher incidentally may have to explain himself. Of course, for the historian of religion this is a limit-case, but such a situation occurs often in the social sciences or in psychology. The response given by every researcher to this alternative is largely dependent on the extent to which he wants to involve himself.

c) After what has been said about some difficulties to perceive a faith behind given religious expressions and about some ambiguities of a faith on the side of the researcher, there is hardly need to stress the absolute necessity of *carefulness* in the study of living religion on an interfaith level. After all, the ambiguities are doubled here since two parties are involved, and if it is true that faith can only be perceived by faith, it is equally true that the chances of distortion are greater here than in the study of data as objects in themselves. Already the "choice" of the "other", and the way in which such a choice is made, has enormous consequences for the study of the "other", unless one would content himself to do laboratory experiments with religious people. Still more consequential is the kind of communication which establishes itself with the "other"; if anything is wrong here at the basis the very results of the study will become distorted.

d) Although the problem of interfaith research has become actual now through the possibility to meet people from different religious backgrounds and to live with them, as a problem it is much older and its basic *ethos* goes back to the idea that all human believers are as such confronted with one divine reality. This idea has given indeed a powerful impetus to the study of religion, since on this assumption one could do one's research in order to learn what other people had already discovered of that divine reality, and finally in order to learn about that reality itself. Among some scholars there has been the underlying notion that the study of religion will open up to the researcher himself, and consequently to his culture, the consciousness of dimensions of life and reality which have been lost in modern industrialized society.

e) In the case of direct interfaith-studies and especially with the basic *ethos* just mentioned, it is unavoidable that the other is interpreted in the light of one's own faith. The reason is ultimately the involvement of the complete personality of the researcher in this kind of interfaith research. He may be more philosophically minded, reflecting on human existence as such, or he may have ethical aims and motivations so as to ameliorate human conditions and communication. In either case his study of religion, in the last analysis, is carried out in view of something which is beyond scholarship as such. This is of course happening in the case of any faith, religion, ideology or conviction on the side of the researcher, unless he would have declared science to be an absolutely autonomous province, would have taken a puritan attitude and have resisted the intrusion of any considerations beyond scholarship itself. This would mean that he has put his faith in scholarship for scholarship's sake:

5. *Some Categories of "New Style" Phenomenological Research*

After these preliminary remarks and after this discussion on the terms of the problem of "faith" in the study of religion one might feel inclined to eliminate the notion of faith altogether from the study of religion and to restrict research in this field to empirical fact-finding and rational theory-building. The realities of faith would then simply fall outside of the range and scope of scholarly research.

Of the different special disciplines concerned with the study of religion, phenomenology as a *systematic* discipline has been from its conception quite concerned with this question of faith. One of its founders, Pierre Daniel Chantepie de la Saussaye, read a paper at the very first International Congress for the History of Religions — held by the way in Stockholm in 1897 — on the subject "Die vergleichende Religionsforschung und der religiöse Glaube": The Comparative Study of Religion and Religious

Faith.[1] It would be important to trace the way in which different phenomenologists of religion have formulated this problem of scholarship and faith, and to see what kind of solutions they have had in mind.

There is no need here to enter into the discipline of Phenomenology of Religion in its different variations which are well-known. We just want to stress the existence not only of phenomenological classifications, schemes and syntheses, but specifically of phenomenological *research* as the study of those human expressions in different times and places, which had or have a religious meaning or value to the people concerned according to what they themselves understood or understand by "religion". So we are here concerned with the study of religious meanings, that of human religiousness and that of the religious mental universes which man has made throughout history. Scholarly speaking, the gods lived in the faith of the believers, and we have no other way of knowing what these gods meant to man than by reconstructing the religious universes in which they occupied the top, the center or the basis, and then by some "subjective" perchance perception of a faith sustaining such universes. To put it briefly, our interest is to know what kind of people have believed in what kind of gods under what kind of circumstances. If the road which we must go in order to arrive at a scholarly answer to this question is a long one, we should not fail in taking it nevertheless and we should not anticipate the answer.

A distinguishing feature of this new style phenomenological research is that the meaning of the religious facts or phenomena is here not studied as a meaning which they have as objects in themselves or in their context but as a meaning which they have to people, that is to say they are studied on a level of *intentionality*. The "facts" of empirical research are here interpreted as human "expressions", that is to say as the concrete traces of human problems, ideals, dreams and aspirations. If there is enough documentary material we may reconstitute as a hypothetical probability some of the religious intentions which prevailed or prevail in a given society at a given time, and of which the religious phenomena that then occurred or occur may be

---

[1] This paper was published seperately in Freiburg im Breisgau in 1898. It was later reprinted in a volume of essays where it is easily available: P.D. Chantepie de la Saussaye, *Portretten en Kritieken* (Haarlem, F. Bohn, 1909), pp. 337-367.

considered to give evidence. Let us stress the wording "as a hypothetical probability" since phenomenological statements have to
be verified and checked constantly by factual research. In phenomenology there has been a development both on the level of
reflection and that of research. Like phenomenological *reflection*
moved over the last fifty years from metaphysics to human existence, so phenomenological *research* is developing from the
search for timeless essences to a search for timely meanings including those meanings which have a religious quality to the
people involved.

6. *Faith as a Category in Phenomenological Research*

From such a phenomenological point of view a religion can be
seen as a field of significances (*champ de significations*) underneath
which there is a network of basic intentions. But such intentions
and the subsequent significances can only be grasped through the
study of the concrete religious phenomena which convey meanings to the people involved with them.

If, phenomenologically speaking, a religion is a system of significances which has one or more absolute poles or points of
reference, it may be said too that, phenomenologically speaking,
religion originates at the moment that man expresses himself
religiously, that is to say *when this expression of his carries a
religious meaning for him*. When trying to grasp such meanings in
a scholarly way we can at least arrive at a reasonable probability
guess. In this view, *the concept of religious faith would indicate
the "happening" of a religious meaning to people*, that is to say
the perception of a religious signification and the subsequent
modification of behavior.

For strict phenomenological research, *"faith" would be a
limit-concept (Grenzbegriff) since it indicates the origin of the
(religious) meanings which are subject to investigation*. "Faith",
consequently, is here taken in a different sense than it is in
theology or in daily speech and ordinary language. Defined in
this way it is a concept open enough in order to be used fruit-
fully in phenomenological research, not as a religious but as a
scholarly concept.

PART FOUR

MINUTES, STATUTES AND MEMBERSHIP
OF THE CONGRESS

I. COMMITTEE MEMBERS IN 1965

The *Executive Committee* of the I.A.H.R., as it was constituted in 1965, had the following members:

President:	G. Widengren (Sweden)
Vice-Presidents:	M. Simon (France) T. Ishizu (Japan)
Secretary General:	C. J. Bleeker (Netherlands)
Deputy Secretary General:	L. J. R. Ort (Netherlands)
Honorary Treasurer:	H. J. van Lier (Netherlands)
Other members:	S. G. F. Brandon (Great Britain)
	A. Brelich (Italy)
	W. Harrelson (U.S.A.)
	F. Heiler (Germany)
	L. Honko (Finland)
	H. Ludin Jansen (Norway)
	T. Michels (Austria)
	G. Scholem (Israel)
	Sung Bum Yun (South Korea)
	I. Trencsényi-Waldapfel (Hungary)

The *International Committee* of the I.A.H.R. had at its last
session in 1965, apart from the officers present of the Executive
Committee, the following members:

Austria:	M. Vereno
Finland:	L. Honko, H. Ringgren
France:	A. Dupont-Sommer, J. Filliozat
Germany:	A. Antweiler, P. Gerlitz
Great Britain:	S. G. F. Brandon, E. G. Parrinder
Israel:	R. J. Z. Werblowsky
Italy:	U. Bianchi, V. Lanternari
Japan:	F. Masutani, R. Nieda
Netherlands:	K. A. H. Hidding, B. A. van Proosdij
Sweden:	H. Sundén
U.S.A.:	K. W. Morgan, W. C. Smith
V.Maag:	(I.O.O.T.S.)

II. MINUTES OF THE BUSINESS MEETINGS OF THE I.A.H.R. IN STOCKHOLM, AUGUST 16-22, 1970

A. MEETING OF THE EXECUTIVE COMMITTEE ON AUGUST 16, 1970

Present were

Officers:	G. Widengren, M. Simon, C. J. Bleeker, H. J. van Lier
Other members:	S. G. F. Brandon, A. Brelich, K. Goldammer (replacing F. Heiler), W. Harrelson, L. Honko, H. Ludin Jansen, G. Mayeda (T. Ishizu's substitute), R. J. Z. Werblowsky (G. Scholem's substitute)
Guests:	U. Bianchi (Italy), V. P. Jain (India), A. Schimmel (U.S.A.) Y. Takeuchi (Japan)

1. *Opening*

At 10.30 a.m. the President opened the meeting. Since Dr. Ort had resigned as Deputy Secretary General, it was agreed that the minutes of the business meetings during the congress should be taken by Dr. Waardenburg, who was a participant in the congress. Dr. Ort was thanked for his untiring labour over the last ten years in the service of the Association, first as Assistant Secretary General, then as Deputy Secretary General.

Since 1965 two members of the Executive Committee had died: Professors F. Heiler and I. Trencsényi-Waldapfel. The Belgian group *Théonoé* had been dissolved. Absent were Professors T. Ishizu, G. Scholem and Sung Bum Yun.

2. *Report of the Secretary General*

A "Report on the activities of the I.A.H.R. during the period September 1965-August 1970" was made by Dr. Ort and sent to the members of the Executive and International Committees. On page 2, under *Publications*, should be added to the "Supplements to Numen" already mentioned: Vol. XVIII, R. J. Zwi Werblowsky and C. J. Bleeker (eds.), *Types of redemption. Contributions to the Study Conference held at Jerusalem July 14-19, 1968*, which is in the press. The report was accepted with thanks and passed on to the International Committee.

3. *Report of the Honorary Treasurer*

A "Financial Review of the I.A.H.R. over the five years between the Claremont and Stockholm Conferences (1965-1970)" was made by Dr. van Lier and distributed at the meeting. On page 4, in the left column of "1970 until July 1st" should be added an amount of 14.524,90 (Dutch guilders, equivalent to US $ 4000,00), being alloted by C.I.P.S.H. for travel expenses in connection with the Stockholm Congress. The Treasurer stressed the need to enlarge the resources of the Association: until now the President and the Secretaries have received little reimbursement even for travelling expenses and this state of affairs cannot continue. Since all contributions to the Association are on a voluntary basis, the Treasurer and the Secretary General made an urgent appeal to the national groups, not only to pay outstanding debts, but also to contribute as much as their means allows them to do. A local treasurer should be appointed for each congress, as has been done for the present congress. The report was accepted with thanks and passed on to the International Committee.

A discussion took place on the fact that C.I.P.S.H. had declined to pay the 1969 subvention for the Bibliography, since the request by the I.A.H.R. for this subvention had not reached UNESCO before January 1st, 1970. A reminder to this effect sent by the Deputy Secretary General of C.I.P.S.H. had been addressed directly to the bibliographer, Mr. Alich, with a copy sent to the Treasurer, Dr. van Lier. In this letter it was stated that the money was available, without it being mentioned, however, that it had to be asked before the end of the year. The Treasurer of the I.A.H.R. later wrote to the Deputy Secretary General of the C.I.P.S.H., that he had not wanted to claim the money before the manuscript of the Bibliography over 1965 had been finished. At present, C.I.P.S.H. is ready to pay the 1970 subvention on the condition that the 1965 and 1966 volumes of the Bibliography will appear before the end of 1970. The Executive Committee approved an interim payment to Mr. Alich from I.A.H.R. funds, and decided that every effort should be made to ensure that the Association might still receive the yearly subvention of $ 1300,00 from C.I.P.S.H. for the years 1969 and 1970. The Secretary General paid tribute to Mr. Alich's devotion to his task over a number of years in difficult circumstances.

4. *Report and Proposals of the Subcommittee on the Statutes*

The members of the Executive and International Committees had received copy of the "Draft of Statutes for the International Association for the History of Religions (IAHR)". This was the result of the work of the Subcommittee on the Statutes, appointed in Claremont in 1965, with the task of formulating and proposing a draft of new statutes for the Association, since the old statutes, dating from 1950, were felt to need revision. The Subcommittee — Professors M. Simon, W. C. Smith (deputy for J. M. Kitagawa) and R. J. Z. Werblowsky — met in Strasbourg in March 1969 in order to work out the present draft; Professor Brandon was prevented from participating in the work, but had approved the proposed draft.

Professor Werblowsky gave a short explanation of the draft statutes. The old statutes no longer reflected the present situation and in some countries religious studies had greatly increased since 1950. A new basis was therefore needed. The Subcommittee had been guided by the following considerations:

— that the I.A.H.R. should be made more effective, without however a degradation of its congresses into business meetings;
— that a remedy should be found against the feeling of many members that the I.A.H.R. is not democratic enough;
— that therefore the position of the General Assembly had to be strengthened, but that there had to be a safeguard in that the General Assembly would be allowed to discuss points raised either by the International Committee or by the previous General Assembly;
— that the I.A.H.R. should be a slightly more loose type of association, with more rotation among the members of the Executive Committee which should not be a self-perpetuating body;
— that therefore the Executive Committee should appoint a nominating committee, which would have as its task to propose new members of the Executive Committee for election by the International Committee;
— that scholarly considerations make it necessary to abandon the old U.N. model of the I.A.H.R., whereby the Executive

Committee consisted of representatives of national groups
only;
— that, besides national, also regional groups should be created
wherever the number of scholars in some particular countries
would not be large enough to justify the creation of national
groups; such regional groups would also be represented in the
International Committee;
— that a maximum of four individual members of the International Committee be coopted by this Committee on the
recommendation of the Executive Committee;
— that the wording "academic" in the first article of the new
statutes (on the object of the I.A.H.R.) had been preferred to
"scientific". It indicates a scholarly and not an institutional
norm: so that there is no discrimination with regard to those
scholars who are not connected with a university institution.

The Secretary General then elaborated upon the six points of
comment which he formulated in the convocation for the present
meeting. For practical reasons he preferred to give the final authority in the I.A.H.R. to the International Committee rather
than to the General Assembly, which remains an amorphous
body. Consequently, the election of the Executive Committee
should be in the hands of the International Committee rather
than the General Assembly. A further matter of concern is how
the nominating committee would be able to meet, in view of the
lack of funds to cover travel expenses over distances which are
sometimes considerable.

Several other points were subsequently discussed. It was asked
to what extent the Executive Committee is able to judge the
scholarly performance of a group applying for membership. It
was asked whether the General Assembly could be made into an
actual business meeting, by means of a roster of participants
belonging to national groups and, consequently, having the right
to vote. With regard to the nominating committee, it was decided
that it should meet two days before each quinquennial congress,
while the actual election of the members of the new Executive
Committee should take place during the congress. There was no
need felt among the larger national groups to be represented by
more than two members in the International Committee.

The Subcommittee was requested to meet once more during

this congress, in order to review the proposed draft in the light of the suggestions and comments expressed by the Executive and International Committees on August 16th. The revised and final draft of the new statutes should be reported to the International Committee on Friday, August 21st, which would make a formal decision. Finally, it would be presented to the General Assembly on Saturday, August 22nd for definite approval.

5. *Election of members to the Executive Committee*

According to Article 5(a) of the Statutes, the new Executive Committee is nominated by the International Committee on the recommendation of the outgoing Executive Committee. The following new officers were proposed:

Professor M. Simon (France) as President
Professor T. Ishizu (Japan) as first Vice-President
Professor M. Eliade (U.S.A.) as second Vice-President
Professor S. G. F. Brandon (Great Britain) as Secretary General.

The latter was willing to take up his post if he had the backing of the members of the Executive Committee, and if he had Dr. E. J. Sharpe (Great Britain) as Deputy Secretary General.

Dr. van Lier (Netherlands) was re-elected as Honorary Treasurer
Professor Eliade, who was not present, was to be asked to accept
    nomination.

The following persons were proposed as members of the International Committee, in addition to the officers:

Austria:	T. Michels
Finland:	L. Honko (to be replaced by J. Pentikäinen)
Germany:	K. Goldammer
India:	H. H. Presler
Israel:	R. J. Z. Werblowsky
Italy:	A. Bausani
Netherlands:	K. A. H. Hidding
Norway:	H. Ludin Jansen
South Korea:	Sung Bum Yun
Sweden:	H. Ringgren

Professor Goldammer wished to decide in the course of the current week; Professors Bausani and Hidding, who were not present, were to be asked to accept nomination. Professors Michels, Presler and Sung Bum Yun, who were not at the congress, were re-elected or elected in their absence.

Since the new Secretary General will have to carry out a number of duties, Professor Bleeker expressed his willingness to continue to take care of the editorial work of the publications of the I.A.H.R., provided that he had the assistance of an Editorial Board. This offer was accepted by the Executive Committee.

6. *Extension of the I.A.H.R.*

The following groups had applied for membership of the I.A.H.R.:

(1) *The Religionsgeschichtliche Studiengesellschaft* (Germany). It was suggested that this group should contact the existing German national group, and that it might consider affiliation with the latter group. The decision on affiliation was postponed.

(2) *The Canadian Society for the Study of Religion* was accepted as a member.

(3) *The Council on the Study of Religion* (U.S.A.), being an umbrella organization of a number of American societies existing in the field, was accepted as a member alongside the American Society for the Study of Religion.

(4) *The Société Polonaise de Science des Religions* had been in contact with the I.A.H.R. for a period of seven years. Although no Polish delegate could be present at the congress, it was decided to accept this Polish society as a member.

(5) *The Associazione "Raffaele Pettazoni"*: following upon a statement made by the representative of the Società Italiana di Storia delle Religioni, this society was accepted as a member under Article 4(a) of the Statutes providing for membership of "societies, national or otherwise".

Australia is organising its own national group, which is however not yet in a shape to apply formally for membership. Denmark too is constituting its own society.

7. *Publications*

The Secretary General announced that the bibliography of 1966 is in the press at the moment. Professor Werblowsky's proposal to recommend the new secretariat to examine the question of the bibliography was endorsed by the Executive Committee.

The members of the Executive and International Committees were encouraged to contribute articles to *Numen*.

8. *Future activities*

For the next congress in 1975 Canada was suggested as a possibility. It was further suggested that a study conference should be held in Finland.

It was decided that the members of the new Executive Committee, together with the present officers, should convene informally at the end of the congress on Saturday morning, August 22nd, under the new President.

The meeting was closed at 1.10 p.m.

B. MEETING OF THE INTERNATIONAL COMMITTEE ON AUGUST 16, 1970

Present were:

Officers: G. Widengren, C. J. Bleeker, H. J. van Lier

Members by country:

Finland:	L. Honko, J. Pentikäinen
France:	A. Caquot
Germany:	E. Damman, K. Goldammer
Great Britain:	S. G. F. Brandon, E. G. Parrinder
India:	V. P. Jain
Israel:	R. J. Z. Werblowsky
Italy:	A. Bausani, U. Bianchi
Japan:	G. Mayeda, Y. Takeuchi
Netherlands:	K. A. H. Hidding
Norway:	A. Kragerud, H. Ludin Jansen
Sweden:	H. Sundén
U.S.A.:	W. Harrelson, J. M. Robinson

Observer: W. Klassen (Canada)

1. *Opening*

At 3.15 p.m. the President opened the meeting of the International Committee. Since Dr. Ort had resigned as Deputy Secretary General of the I.A.H.R., Dr. Waardenburg, who was a participant of the present congress, had been asked by the General Secretary take the minutes of this and other business meetings held during the congress.

2. *Report of the General Secretary*

There were no questions or remarks with regard to Dr. Ort's Report on the activities of the I.A.H.R. during the period September 1965-August 1970, sent in advance to the members of the International and Executive Committees. The report was accepted with thanks by the International Committee.

3. *Report of the Honorary Treasurer*

The Financial Review of the I.A.H.R. over the five years between the Claremont and Stockholm conferences (1965-1970), made by Dr. van Lier, was distributed at the meeting. On page 4, in the left column of "1970 until July 1st" should be added the amount of 14.524,90 (Dutch guilders, equivalent to US. $4000,00) allotted by C.I.P.S.H. for travel expenses at this congress. As the Executive Committee the same morning, the Treasurer and the General Secretary stressed that outstanding debts should be paid, and expressed the hope that members would increase their voluntary contributions.

In the following discussion the complaint was voiced that receipts were not always issued for amounts paid. Moreover, for a number of countries invoices are needed in order that payments abroad be authorised by the government: consequently, it was decided that the Treasurer should approach the national groups informally to inquire about their voluntary contribution for the current year, and that he should then send them official invoices. It was also asked that the accounts of the I.A.H.R. be audited. It was decided that Professors Hidding and Parrinder should check the accounts during this congress.

The more general question was then raised, in what way the

travelling expenses available for a congress should be allotted to participants. The General Secretary said that the funds provided by C.I.P.S.H. were meant to enable scholars from distant countries to attend the congress; in this connection special attention is given to younger scholars, and the travelling expenses of members of the Executive Committee cannot be covered. For the present congress, the sum of US.$.4000.00 was available for the purpose, distributed as follows: for participation from Latin America $.1000.00, from Japan $.750.00, from India $.250.00, from France $.1000.00. An amount of $.1000.00 was placed at the disposal of the President to help younger scholars to attend. All disbursements are at the discretion of the officers.

4. *Report and proposals of the Subcommittee on the Statutes*

The draft of the new Statutes had been sent to all members of the International and Executive Committees, and Professor Werblowsky explained the substances of it in the same wording as before the Executive Committee.

In discussion the following points were raised. The link existed in the old statutes (Article 5(a) between national groups and membership of the Executive Committee is consciously severed in the new statutes (Article 4(c). The reason for this is, that on the one hand the number of national groups is expanding considerably, and that on the other hand there are countries where more than one group exists which is a member of the Association. It was urged that at least some (e.g. not more than two) members of the Executive Committee should be chosen in their capacity of being outstanding scholars. The nominating committee should have its proposed candidates for the Executive Committee endorsed by the International Committee, and then confirmed by the General Assembly. All nominations are individual.

The question was put, how many people belonging to member groups can be reckoned as being affiliated with the Association, and also how many individual members of the I.A.H.R. could be counted, and what their contribution is. The General Secretary answered that exact figures are not available.

The discussion then turned to the role of the General Assembly in decision-making within the I.A.H.R. Professor Werblowsky, speaking for the Subcommittee, pointed out that in the past the General Assembly had in practice been composed of all those happening to attend the conference: no distinction was made between voting and attending members, and decisions were made by acclamation. For a reorganisation of the I.A.H.R. one could choose either to reconstruct the organisation of the General Assembly's handling or to consider a different Executive Committee and International Committee; the speaker himself proposed the second alternative. One of the wishes expressed was that the General Assembly should have the competence to recommend measures to the Committee or to refer things back to them, and that the people actually present should have the opportunity to indicate their views in the matter. Another wish was that the General Assembly should take place in the middle of the congress, when all participants were likely to be present.

An important question was raised concerning the people who actually attend a congress. Invitations are sent to the national groups, who are responsible for forwarding them to their members. However, in this way a number of scholars do not receive invitations; because for one reason or another they do not happen to be members of a national group. The President stated that the organisation of the national groups in many countries is unsatisfactory: the best scholars are simply not there. He advocated that the I.A.H.R. should be restructured in such a way as to include all scholars who wish to cooperate.

The Committee endorsed the decision of the Executive Committee, that the Subcommittee on the Statutes should present a final draft of the new Statutes on Friday, August 21st, reviewing the proposed draft in the light of the suggestions and comments expressed by the Executive and International Committees.

5. & 6. *Election of members of the Executive Council, Extension of I.A.H.R. membership*

The International Committee endorsed the new officers and the new members of the Executive Committee. It also endorsed the new members admitted to the I.A.H.R. by the Executive Committee earlier in the day.

7. *Publications*

The International Committee endorsed the acceptance by the Executive Committee of Professor Bleeker's willingness to continue to do the editorial work for the I.A.H.R., with the assistance of an Editorial Board. The President expressed sincere gratitude to the General Secretary for his offer. (Cf. under point 6 of the Minutes of the meeting of the Executive Committee).

8. *Future activities*

As possible host countries for the next congress in 1975, Canada and Great Britain were considered. As possible host countries for study conferences Finland and the Lebanon were considered. In the event of a study conference being organised in the Lebanon, it was considered advisable to undertake preliminary research into the suitability of Beirut for such an event. At 5.05 p.m. the meeting closed.

C. MEETING OF THE INTERNATIONAL COMMITTEE ON AUGUST 21ST, 1970

Present were:

Officers: G. Widengren, M. Simon, C. J. Bleeker, H. J. van Lier

Members by country:

Finland:	H. Biezais, J. Pentikäinen
France:	A. Caquot
Germany:	E. Dammann, K. Goldammer
Great Britain:	S. G. F. Brandon, E. G. Parrinder
India:	V. P. Jain
Israel:	R. J. Z. Werblowsky
Italy:	A. Bausani, U. Bianchi
Japan:	G. Mayeda, Y. Takeuchi
Netherlands:	M. Heerma van Voss, K. A. H. Hidding
Norway:	A. Kragerud, H. Ludin Jansen
Sweden:	A. Hultkrantz, H. Sundén
U.S.A.:	J. M. Kitagawa, J. M. Robinson

Observers: S. Bjerke (Norway)
D. Kinsley (Canada)
E. J. Sharpe (Great Britain)
C. Welch (U.S.A.)

1. *Opening*

At 3.30 p.m. the President opened this second meeting of the International Committee. The General Secretary reported that Mr. Jean d'Ormesson, Deputy Secretary General of C.I.P.S.H., had cabled that unfortunately he had been prevented from attending the congress.

2. *Further election of members of the Executive Committee*

Professor Honko asked that Professor Pentikäinen be elected in his place to the Executive Comittee. Professor Goldammer agreed to represent Germany, and Professor Klassen will represent Canada on the Executive Committee. Together with these three members, on the recommendation of the Secretary General, Professor J. Keller was elected for Poland. The Secretary General requested the recognition in advance of the successor of Professor I. Trencsényi-Waldapfel, to be appointed by the Hungarian Academy of Sciences. This was decided.

The majority of the members saw no specific reason to institute a "corresponding membership" of the I.A.H.R.

3. *Publication of the Proceedings*

The Secretary General reported that the Publishers, E. J. Brill will publish the Proceedings of the Congress in book form, i.e., 300 pages of paper in full text, plus 100 pages of abstracts. The Minutes of the business meetings and the list of participants are to be published in a less expensive form.

4. *Report of the Honorary Treasurer*

The Auditing Committee expressed its satisfaction with the accounts and the report of the Treasurer was accepted with thanks by the International Committee.

5. *Revised draft of new Statutes of the I.A.H.R.*

The revised draft of the new Statutes, as requested by the Executive and International Committeees on August 16th, was distributed to the members of the International Committee. On behalf of the Subcommittee. Professor Werblowsky gave the following comments on the revised draft:

Article 1: The term "academic" has been preferred to "scientific", but without discrimination against scholars not connected with a university institution;

Article 3: As well as national, there are also regional groups; the expression "national" does not imply that there is only one group per country. Under b(1) the speaker thinks of a possible affiliation to the I.A.H.R. by associations like, e.g. the International Anthropological Association.

The Subcommittee recommended that the new Secretariat give attention to the possibility of affiliation to the I.A.H.R. by scholarly Institutes, which cannot always be counted under the national groups.

Since there is nothing to prevent the Secretariat from conducting correspondence, the Subcommittee does not see a specific reason to create a new category of "corresponding members". But it wants to keep the question open for discussion.

Article 4: This Article explains how the three different bodies of the I.A.H.R. work. Although Professor W. C. Smith had some slight misgivings, the present revised draft, made in the light of the comments given by Executive and International Committees on the first draft, implies that the Executive Committee and the International Committee alone are representative. The General Assembly is a more accidental body, which should not have as great an authority as was proposed in the previous draft.

There should be trust in the Secretariat and the Executive Committee, that the expression "as reasonably to reflect various parts of the world ..." should be rightly implemented.

The nominating committee should submit its proposed nominations for the Executive Committee between twelve and nine months before the meeting of the International Committee. This is formulated in view of the fact that the national and regional groups should have time to put the point of election of members of the Executive Committee on the agenda of their annual meeting, to be discussed there.

The Subcommittee feels that no potential officers of the I.A.H.R., should be a member of the nominating committee, but that e.g., previous Presidents should be asked to be members.

Article 7: The Subcommittee wants to see added: "An audited report shall be submitted by the Treasurer to the International Committee at every quinquennial congress". For technical reasons this phrase did not figure in the distributed text.

The request by Dr. van Lier that the "audited report" be specified as "audited report by members of the International Committee" was not accepted. This does not imply that the report is to be audited by a registered auditor.

The different articles were discussed and voted upon separately.

Article 3: Professor Brandon wondered if an additional category of "corresponding members" would not be helpful to associations in Eastern Europe, Asia, Africa and Latin America, who want to be affiliated to the I.A.H.R. This would give them at least a certain status with regard to the Association.

Article 4: Professor Bianchi asked if the new Executive Committee elected at this congress is already constituted on the criteria of this draft. This is not the case: the next Executive Committee, to be proposed in five year's time, will be elected according to the new Statutes.

Article 8: Professor Parrinder suggested that the word "can" be altered to "may". This was decided.

With the addition made by the Subcommittee with regard to Article 7, and the change made in Article 8, the revised draft of the new Statutes of the I.A.H.R. was accepted unanimously by the International Committee.

6. *Future activities*

On the President's request that the next congress of the I.A.H.R. should be held in Manchester in 1975 in the latter part of August, Professor Brandon agreed provisionally. This arrangement was welcomed by the International Committee.

A study conference also will probably be held in Canada (Montreal or Toronto) in 1972; with another study conference in Finland (Abo Turku) in 1973; the Finnish representatives proposed as its theme: "Methodology in the Science of Religion". Both study conferences were welcomed by the International Committee.

7. *Other business*

Professor J. M. Robinson is to consult Professor M. Krause on publication matters, including the publication of the remaining Nag Hammadi texts, on which the meeting in Messina in 1966 had laid stress.

The Secretary General asked the consent of the International Committee with regard to the agenda of the meeting of the General Assembly on Saturday, August 22nd, announced as "Closing of the Congress".

Professor Brandon suggested that a minimum amount be established and a guideline be established for the annual fee of groups and individual members of the I.A.H.R., since these have remained undefined in the past. People want to fulfil their obligations without paying too much: some indication should be given as to the nature of these obligations.

The meeting was closed at 4.35 p.m.

D. INFORMAL MEETING OF THE NEW EXECUTIVE COMMITTEE ON AUGUST 22 (MORNING)

This meeting had an informal character, because the new officers will take up their functions only at the end of the meeting of the General Assembly in the afternoon.

Present were:

Officers:	M. Simon, M. Eliade, S. G. F. Brandon, E. J. Sharpe, H. J. van Lier
Other members:	A. Bausani, J. M. Kitagawa (for U.S.A.), H. Ludin Jansen, G. Mayeda (T. Ishizu's substitute), J. Pentikäinen, H. Ringgren, R. J. Z. Werblowsky
Guests:	G. Widengren, C. J. Bleeker, V. P. Jain, A. Schimmel

As the new President, Professor Simon expressed the warm gratitude of those present to Professors Widengren and Bleeker for all the services they had rendered to the Association during the 20 years they were Vice-President/President and Secretary General respectively. He proposed to send a telegram of thanks

and congratulations to Dr. Ort for the ten years he had served the
Association as its Assistant/Deputy Secretary General.

There are several points to be discussed. The first is that of the
future publications of the I.A.H.R. The new Secretary General
wished to see carefully defined the responsibility of the Editorial
Board around Professor Bleeker. The latter suggested that Professor Brandon as Secretary General had ultimate responsibility for
all publications. Professor Werblowsky suggested that ultimate
responsibility for the publications of the I.A.H.R. should rest
with the Secretariat and the Executive Committee of the
I.A.H.R. It would be, however, the new Secretariat and the Editorial Board who would determine the policy of these publications, including the bibliography. Professor Brandon agreed with
this, and this was the general feeling of the meeting. Professor
Werblowsky also suggested that the Executive Committee as such
should cease to function as the Editorial Board of *Numen*; their
names might, however, be mentioned on a separate page in each
issue.

The discussion then turned to the size and membership of the
Editorial Board. Several members were in favour of a small
Board, in order to evaluate specific articles; an expert could always be consulted. It could meet more frequently, as in the case
of the editors of "Vetus Testamentum" who are invited two or
three times a year by the Publishing House E. J. Brill: the same
might happen for the Editorial Board of the I.A.H.R. Professor
Bleeker undertook to enquire of Brill about financial support for
such meetings. As members of the Editorial Board were appointed:

C. J. Bleeker (General Editor)
S. G. F. Brandon (Deputy General Editor)
M. Eliade (Consulting Editor)
M. S. H. G. Heerma van Voss (Religions of Antiquity)
J. U. Heesterman (S. E. Asia: to be asked)
J. H. Kamstra (Buddhism)
J. M. Kitagawa (Far East)
A. Schimmel (Islam)
R. J. Z. Werblowsky (Judaism and Religions with Semitic lan-
  guages)

A special point in the discussion on publication was that of the bibliography. Professor Werblowsky suggested that what is lacking is not so much a bibliography, but rather a regular "Zeitschriftenschau", a greater number of book reviews, and a continuous series of "Stand und Aufgaben" articles for the different branches of the History of Religions. This may be incorporated into *Numen*. He recommended that a committee be appointed to report on this matter. Professor Blecker mentioned some practical problems connected with such an enterprise: for instance, how to find the people who would take such tasks upon themselves?

The periodicals which exist in the field were considered. Professor Eliade reported on *"History of Religions"*, which addresses itself especially to American scholars and which insists on the technical aspects of research. Professor Brandon reported on *"Religious Studies"*, a periodical which is of a more philosophical nature. Dr. Sharpe reported on the new British periodical *"Religion"*, which will contain, as well as articles, also reviews of current research and of recent work; there is an Editorial Board of which Professor Smart is the Chairman.

The Secretary General stated that the bibliography should continue — if Mr. Alich is willing to remain bibliographer — since UNESCO gives money for it, but that there is a problem here and that Professor Werblowsky's observations should be considered. The latter insisted again that there should be a committee to investigate the situation and to explore the possibilities. Professor Ringgren suggested cooperation with other existing bibliographies, because in several cases there is an overlapping as to subject matter. The Secretary General suggested that every national group might appoint one man responsible for bibliographical data of the country concerned, especially in local languages. The representatives of Germany, Sweden, and the U.S.A. thought this could be realised for their respective countries. Dr. Sharpe suggested that the Editorial Board might distribute a model for the bibliographical material to be submitted. In any case, the Editorial Board should meet as soon as possible.

Next, the nominating committee was appointed according to the new statutes. Although Professor Widengren was urged to become one of its members, he declined the invitation on the grounds that he wishes to concentrate on academic work. Professors Brandon, Bausani and Scholem were then appointed.

A number of practical questions called for attention. The new statutes have to be translated into French, German and Italian. On the question whether the Canadian seat in the Executive Committee should be left vacant, since it is the Canadian Society for the Study of Religion which has to propose a delegate, it was decided that the Secretariat should wait for a formal letter from the Society with regard to Professor Klassen, who has been formally nominated by the International Committee. Professor Werblowsky suggested for future nominations that in the nominations committee other continents should be represented. It was agreed that, should circumstances warrant, the President might act on behalf of the committee.

Finally it was decided that the next congress will take place in Manchester in 1975, with the theme "Man: his Nature and Destiny". Although Salzburg, Innsbruck and Aix-enProvence were mentioned as alternatives if Manchester was not possible, preference as an alternative was given to the U.S.A., and Professor Kitagawa promised that he could work this out with his American colleagues, if the need for this should arise. There will be a study conference in Canada (Montreal or Toronto) in 1972, and another in Finland (Abo) in 1973, the latter having as its theme "Methodology in the Science of Religion". The Committee was grateful for the offer of Dr. Jain to organise a third study conference in India (New Dehli or Jabalpur). This might be possible in 1976 or 1977, and to devote this study conference especially to Indian religions. Dr. Jain was advised to contact Professor Ishizu, who is responsible for congresses in the East. The Secretariat will explore the matter further, if informed by Dr. Jain that such a study conference can be arranged. Since UNESCO has funds available to support special activities in Asia, Africa and Latin America, a study conference in India might be financially possible before 1975.

This informal meeting of the new Executive Committee lasted an hour and a half, and was closed by the new President at 11.45 a.m.

E. GENERAL ASSEMBLY OF THE INTERNATIONAL ASSOCIATION
FOR THE HISTORY OF RELIGIONS
AUGUST 22ND (AFTERNOON)

The President, Professor Widengren, opened the meeting of the General Assembly, which was at the same time the closing session of the XIIth Congress of the I.A.H.R., at 1.00 p.m.

The retiring Secretary General, Professor Bleeker, then delivered his address "Looking backward and forward", the text of which is printed elsewhere. He then reported briefly on the activities of the International Committee and the Association over the period 1965-1970, with reference to Dr. Ort's report on this period. The report was accepted.

On behalf of the Subcommittee on the Statutes, Professor Werblowski read the text of the final draft of the new statutes, since there were not enough copies available to have this text distributed. In giving his comments and explanation, he referred in substances to what he had said to the International Committee on August 21st, and to the Executive Committee on August 16th. The new statutes were endorsed by the General Assembly without questions or observations.

The Secretary General then announced the names of the new officers, the members of the Executive Committee, and the new Editorial Board. He also announced the names of the four new groups which had become new members of the I.A.H.R., the places of the next conferences and the next congress, and the details of the publications of the Proceedings of this congress, as decided by the General Assembly without questions or observations.

Professor J. M. Robinson read the text of a cable to be sent to UNESCO with regard to the publication of the remaining Nag Hammadi texts, as agreed in Messina in 1966.

The President then invited a general discussion concerning the work of the Association, but no proposals or observations were made. After the communication of a few practical matters, the President expressed his gratitude to the officers and other members of the Executive Committee, who served with him over the last few years. He also expressed his satisfaction to have found a new team of officers, whom he whole-heartedly entrusted the future of the Association.

The newly elected President, Professor Simon, then thanked Professor Widengren for the services he had rendered to the Association over a period of twenty years. He expressed his gratitude for the confidence shown to him and for the honour done to his country, and his happiness at taking office with Professor Brandon as Secretary General. Hoping that, after the Swedish-Dutch combination, now the French-British one may rightly guide the Association, he concluded: Nous continuerons dans la ligne de la recherche objective, de l'étude historique et impartiale des religions; cela signifie à mes yeux, pour utilisez une formule du vocabulaire politique français, continuité et ouverture.

The meeting of the General Assembly closed at 2.30 p.m.

III. THE INTERNATIONAL ASSOCIATION FOR THE HISTORY OF RELIGIONS COMMITTEE MEMBERS AS AT AUGUST 22ND, 1970

Executive Committee

Officers:
  President: M. Simon (France)
  Vice-Presidents: T. Ishizu (Japan)
            M. Eliade (U.S.A.)
  Secretary General: S. G. F. Brandon (Great Britain)
  Deputy Secretary General: E. J. Sharpe (Great Britain)
  Honorary Treasurer: H. J. van Lier (Netherlands)

Other members:
  Austria: T. Michels
  Finland: J. Pentikäinen
  Germany: K. Goldammer
  India: H. H. Presler
  Israel: R. J. Z. Werblowsky
  Italy: A. Bausani
  Netherlands: K. A. H. Hidding
  Norway: H. Ludin Jansen
  South Korea: Sung Bum Yun
  Sweden: H. Ringgren

International Committee (as at August 21st, 1970)
Besides the Officers mentioned above:

Canada	D. Kinsley, M. Leibovici
Finland:	H. Biezais
France:	A. Caquot
Germany:	E. Dammann
Great Britain:	E. G. Parrinder
India:	V. P. Jain
Italy:	U. Bianchi
Japan:	G. Mayeda, Y. Takeuchi
Netherlands:	M. Heerma van Voss
Norway:	A. Kragerud
Sweden:	A. Hultkrantz, H. Sundén
U.S.A.:	J. M. Kitagawa, J. M. Robinson

Nominating Committee
A. Bausani (Italy)
S. G. F. Brandon (Great Britain)
G. Scholem (Israel)

Editorial Board for Publications:
C. J. Bleeker, *General Editor*
S. G. F. Brandon, *Deputy General Editor*
M. Eliade, *Consulting Editor*
M. Heerma van Voss (Netherlands)
J. C. Heesterman (Netherlands)
J. H. Kamstra (Netherlands)
J. M. Kitagawa (U.S.A.)
A. Schimmel (U.S.A.)
R. J. Z. Werblowsky (Israel)

New members of the I.A.H.R.:

Canada:	The Canadian Society for the Study of Religion
Italy:	Associazione "Raffaele Pettazoni"
Poland:	La Société Polonaise de Science des Religions
U.S.A.:	Council on the Study of Religion

STATUTES OF THE INTERNATIONAL ASSOCIATION
FOR THE HISTORY OF RELIGIONS
(IAHR)

as accepted and confirmed by the General Assembly of the IAHR at its XIIth International Congress, held in Stockholm, on August 22nd, 1970.

Article 1. The International Association for the History of Religions (abbreviated, from its English title, to IAHR), founded in September, 1950 on the occasion of the 7th International History of Religions Congress, is a world-wide organization which has as its object the promotion of the academic study of the history of religions through the international collaboration of all scholars whose research has a bearing on the subject.

Article 2. The IAHR seeks to achieve this object:

(1) by holding regular international congresses and occasional symposia and colloquia;

(2) by publishing the proceedings of such congresses and meetings;

(3) by assisting the formation of national and regional associations of historians of religions;

(4) by encouraging and sponsoring publications of general interest to the study of the history of religions: e.g. an international review, bibliographical bulletins, monograph series;

(5) by taking all appropriate steps to encourage and further the academic study of the history of religions.

Article 3. A) The IAHR is constituted by national or multi-national (regional) societies for the academic study of religions. These are such societies as are now members and such societies as apply for membership and, on recommendation of the Executive and International Committees (see below), may be admitted by the General Assembly at future International Congresses.

B) To the IAHR may be affiliated:

(1) International associations for the academic study of particular areas within the history of religions;

(2) Individual scholars for whom there is no appropriate national or regional society.

Affiliation is effected by application to the Executive and International Committees and by approval of the General Assembly.

Article 4. The work of the IAHR is carried out through (a) the General Assembly, (b) the International Committee, and (c) the Executive Committee .

A) The General Assembly of the Association meets at each international congress and is composed of all members of constituent societies of the Association present at that congress. The General Assembly may take action only on matters referred to it from the International Committee, and it may refer any matter to the International or Executive Committees for consideration and report.

B) The International Committee is composed of:

(1) Two representatives each of the constituent national and regional societies except that there shall not be more than two representatives from any one country.

(2) The Executive Committee (see below)

(3) Up to four individual members coopted by the International Committee on the recommendation of the Executive Committee.

C) The Executive Committee is composed of a President, two Vice-Presidents, a General Secretary, a Treasurer, and five other members. The officers in particular, and the members of the Executive Committee in general shall be chosen in such a way as reasonably to reflect various parts of the world where academic study of religion is pursued in its various disciplines. A Nominating Committee, appointed by the Executive Committee, shall submit nominations for the next Executive Committee to the members of the International Committee by mail not more than twelve months and not less than nine months prior to each international congress. Members of the International Committee may propose alternate nominations not less than one month prior to each international congress. The International Committee, at its meeting just preceding the General Assembly shall elect the Executive Committee and shall report this to the General Assembly for endorsement.

The members of the Executive Committee shall hold office for one quinquennial term each and be subject to re-election, but not more than two-thirds of the Committee shall be carried on from one term to the next, and no one member shall serve in the same office more than two terms.

Article 5. The Executive Committee shall meet on the occasion of each congress and at such other times as is judged necessary and possible, at the call of the President or both Vice-Presidents. In between meetings its business shall be conducted by correspondence. An account of the work of the Executive shall be submitted each year for the approval of the International Committee.

Article 6. The International Committee shall meet on the occasion of each congress, between the meeting of the Executive Committee and that of the General Assembly, and more often if necessary. It reports to the General Assembly.

Article 7. The resources of the IAHR consists of: A) annual contributions paid by the constituent societies, affiliated societies and individual members, the amount of which is assessed by the Executive Committee, and B) grants, donations and other sources of revenue. An audited report will be submitted to the International Committee at every International Congress.

Article 8. The Statutes may be modified only by the General Assembly on the recommendation of the International Committee.

MEMBERS OF THE XIITH CONGRESS OF THE I.A.H.R.

Alcén, Ragnar, Fil. kand.	Sweden
Alsdorff, Paul	BRD
Alver, Bente Gullveig, Forskningsstipendiat	Norway
Alver, Brynjulf, Universittetslektor	Norway
Anati, Emmanuel, Professor	Italy
Antes, Peter, Dipl. -Theol. Dr.	BRD
Antweiler, Anton, Professor	BRD
Arnold, Wilhelm, Professor	BRD
Baljon, J. M. S., Dr.	Netherlands
Baur, Tona, Fr.	BRD
Bausani, Alessandro, Professor	Italy
Becken, Hans-Jürgen, Cand. theol.	BRD
Berggren, Erik, Lektor, Teol. dr.	Sweden
Bergman, Jan, Docent	Sweden
Betz, Hans Dieter, Professor	USA
Bianchi, Ugo, Professor	Italy
Biezais, Haralds, Professor	Finland
Bisi, Anna Maria, Libera Docente	Italy
Bjerke, Svein, Universitetslektor	Norway
Bleeker, C. J., Professor	Netherlands
Boccassino, Renato, Professor	Italy
Bodrogi, Tibor, Dr.	Hungary
Bolle, Kees W., Assoc. professor	USA
Boozer, Jack, Professor	BRD
Bourgault, Raymond, Professor	Canada
Bouritius, Gerben J. F., Dr. phil.	Netherlands
Brandon, S. G. F., Professor	UK
Brelich, Angelo, Professor	Italy
Buri, Fritz, Dr. theol.	Switzerland
Bürkle, Horst, Professor	BRD
Bäckman, Louise, Fil. kand.	Sweden
Cain, Horst, Cand. phil.	BRD
Caquot, André, Directeur d'Études à l'École Pratique des Hautes Études	France
Carlson, Agge, Docent	Sweden
Castiglione, Lăszló, Dr.	Hungary

Chirassi-Colombo, Ileana, Professor	Italy
Cold, Eberhard, Dr.	BRD
Colpe, Carsten, Professor	BRD
Dahlquist, Allan, Teol. dr.	Sweden
Dammann, Ernst, Professor	BRD
Dandekar, R. N., Professor	India
Donini, Ambrogio, Professor	Italy
Drynjeff, Kaarina, Teol. kand.	Sweden
Drijvers, H. J. W., Assistent-professor	Netherlands
Dumoulin, Heinrich, Professor	Japan
Dupré, Wilhelm, Assoc. professor	USA
af Edholm, Erik, Fil. kand.	Sweden
Edsman, Carl-Martin, Professor	Sweden
Ejerfeldt, Lennart, Fil. lic.	Sweden
Eliade, Mircea, Professor	USA
Elitzur, Yehuda, Assoc. professor	Israel
Erlandsson, Seth, Teol. dr.	Sweden
Eschmann, Anncharlott, Dr. phil.	BRD
Fabian, Johannes, Assistant professor	USA
Feiereis, K., Dr.	DDR
Flasche, Rainer, Magister	BRD
Fujimoto, Kazuo, Litt. D.	Japan
Gaba, Christian, Dr.	Ghana
Gamberoni, Johann, Professor	Italy
Gaster, Theodor H., Professor	USA
Gerlitz, Peter, Pastor	BRD
Ghirshman, Roman, Membre de l'Académie des Inscriptions	France
Giversen, Søren, Docent	Denmark
Giuffre, Concetta, Dr.	Italy
Gnoli, Gherardo, Professor	Italy
Goldammer, Kurt, Professor	BRD
Gonda, J., Professor	Netherlands
Greschat, Hans-Jürgen, Dr.	BRD
von Grunebaum, G. E., Professor	USA
Guépin, J. P., Dr.	Netherlands
Gunn, C. Douglas, Assistant professor	USA
Gwyn Griffiths, J., Dr.	UK
Haglund, Åke, Fil. lic.	Sweden
Hansen, Holger Bernt, Cand. theol.	Denmark

Haran, Menahem, Chairman	Israel
Harrelson, Walter, Professor	USA
Hartman, Sven S., Professor	Sweden
Heeger, Robert, Teol. lic.	Sweden
Hein, Norvin, Assoc. professor	USA
Heinemann, Joseph, Dr.	Israel
Heintz, Jean-Georges, Professor	France
Hellbom, Anna-Britta, Dr.	Sweden
Hemberger, Adolf, Dozent	BRD
Henkel, O. V., Dr.	Netherlands
Henry, Marie-Louise, Professor	BRD
Hidding, K. A. H., Professor	Netherlands
Hillmann, Dorothea, Dr. phil.	BRD
Hinnells, John R.	UK
Hjärpe, Jan, Teol. kand., fil. kand.	Sweden
Hjern, Olle, Fil. kand.	Sweden
Holmgren, Biddie, Fru	Sweden
Honko, Lauri, Professor	Finland
Hultberg, Thomas K-son, Fil. kand.	Sweden
Hultgård, Anders, Teol. lic., fil. mag.	Sweden
Hultkrantz, Åke, Professor	Sweden
Hurwitz, J., M.A.	Netherlands
Jain, Vimal Prakash, Dr.	India
James, E. O., Professor	UK
Jansen, Herman Ludin, Professor	Norway
Janssen, L. F., Dr.	Netherlands
Jenson, Annemarie, Lehrerin	BRD
Johannessen, Steffen, Amanuensis	Denmark
Johansen, J. Prytz, Professor	Denmark
Johansons, Andrejs, Docent	Sweden
Jurji, Edward J., Professor	USA
Kàkosy, Làszló, Assistant professor	Hungary
Kamstra, Jac. H., Professor	Netherlands
Kanus-Credé, Helmhart, Assistant professor	BRD
Kefelian, Michel	France
Keilbach, Wilhelm, Professor	BRD
Keller, Carl-A., Professor	Switzerland
Khoury, Adel-Théodore, Professor	BRD
Kietzig, Ottfried, Dr. theol. habil.	BRD
Kinsley, David R., Assistant professor	Canada

Kippenberg, Hans G., Dr.	BRD
Kitagawa, Joseph M., Professor	USA
Ki-Yong, Rhi, Professor	Korea
Klassen, William, Professor	Canada
Klimkeit, Hans-Joachim, Dozent	BRD
Klimov, Alexis, Directeur de Recherches	Canada
Koivu, Leena, Fil. maist.	Finland
Korvin-Krasinski, Cyrill, Dr. phil.	BRD
Koskinen, Aarne A., Dr.	Finland
Krause, Martin, Professor	BRD
Krenn, Kurt, Dr.	BRD
Krüger, Heino, Cand. phil.	BRD
Kuusi, Anna-Leena, Fil. maistr.	Finland
Lademann, Gabriele, Stud. theol.	BRD
Lanczkowski, G., Professor	BRD
Leibovici, Marcel, Professor	Canada
Lewis, Hywel David, Professor	UK
Lienhard, Siegried, Professor	Sweden
Long, Charles H., Professor	USA
MacRae, George W., Professor	USA
Magne, Jean Léon, Bibiliothécaire de l'Institut d'Études Sémitiques de l'Université de Paris	France
Magni, Klas G., Fil. lic.	Sweden
Makdisi, George, Professor	USA
Mantel, Hugo, Assoc. professor	Israel
Mariscotti, Ana Maria, Liz., cand. phil.	BRD
Martin, James L., Professor	USA
Maximilien, Kari Vogt, Universitetslektor	Norway
Mayeda, Goro, Professor	Japan
Meany, William, Professor	Ireland
Mehta, J. L., Professor	India
Ménard, Jacques-E., Professor	France
Millroth, Berta, Teol. dr.	Sweden
Minkner, Konrad, Dr. phil.	BRD
Mohebbi, M. Khodayar, Professor	Iran
Nagel, B. M. J., Dr.	Netherlands
Nathhorst, Bertel, Fil. dr.	Sweden
Nelson, Bemjamin, Professor	USA
Neuland, Lena, Librarian	Sweden

Neusner, Jakob, Professor .... USA
Nielsen, Jan, Lecturer .... Denmark
Nielsen, Niels C. Jr., Professor .... USA
Ojansuu, Raila, Fil. lic. .... Finland
Organ, Troy, Professor .... USA
Ottosson, Magnus, Teol. Dr., Docent .... Sweden
Oxtoby, Willard G., Assoc. professor .... USA
Papadimas, Stylianos, Dr. theol. .... Greece
Parpola, Asko, Docent .... Denmark
Parrinder, E. G., Dr. .... UK
Parrinder, E. M., Mrs. .... UK
Pearson, Birger A., Assistant professor .... USA
Pentikäinen, Juha, Docent .... Finland
Pettersson, Thorleif, Eil. kand. .... Sweden
Pezzali, Amalia, Dr. .... Italy
Philonenko, Marc, Professor .... France
Piccaluga, Giulia, Assistente .... Italy
Piltz, Elisabeth, Fil. lic. .... Sweden
Posse, Krister, Teol. lic. .... Sweden
Pummer, Reinhard, Assistant professor .... Canada
Raju, P. T., Professor .... USA
Reif, Josef, Pater .... BRD
Reimbold, Ernst Thomas, Dr. Dr. .... BRD
Riedmar, Manfred, Cand. phil. .... BRD
Ries, Julien, Professor .... Belgium
Ringgren, Helmer, Professor .... Sweden
Robinson, James M., Professor .... USA
Rodhe, Sten, Lektor, Dr. .... Sweden
Rooth, Helena, Fil. kand. .... Sweden
Rupp, Alfred, Dr. .... BRD
Sabbatucci, Dario, Professor .... Italy
Saenz de Santa Maria, Professor .... Spain
Sakellarakis, I. A., Dr. .... BRD
Salman, D. H., Professor .... Canada
de Savignac, Jean Delioux, Professor .... Belgium
Schedl, Claus, Professor .... Austria
Schiffer, Wilhelm, Professor .... Japan
Schimmel, Annemarie, Professor .... BRD
Schlosser, Katesa, Professor .... BRD
Schmidt, Werner, Professor .... BRD

Schunck, Klaus-Dietrich, Professor	DDR
Schwarz, Eva, Dr. theol.	BRD
Schwarz, Gerhard, Assessor	BRD
Segelberg, Eric, Professor	Sweden
Seligson, Miriam, Ph. D.	Finland
Sharma, P. Sarveswara, Dr. phil.	BRD
Sharpe, Eric J., Teol. dr.	UK
Shatz-Uffenheimer, Rivka, Senior Lecturer	Israel
Sicard, S. von, Teol. dr.	Sweden
Siiger, Halfdan, Professor	Denmark
Simon, Marcel, Professor	France
Sivaraman, K., Dr.	India
Sjöberg, Åke W., Professor	USA
Slokenbergs, Maris R., M.A., teol. kand.	Sweden
Smart, Ninian, Professor	Italy
Smith, H. Daniel, Professor	USA
Smith, Wilfred Cantwell, Professor	USA
Stephenson, Gunther, Dr.	BRD
Ström, Folke, Docent	Sweden
Ström, Siv R., Fil. kand.	Sweden
Ström, Åke V., Docent	Sweden
Ståhlberg, Gustaf, Teol. kand.	Sweden
Sundén, Hjalmar, Professor	Sweden
Sundkler, Bengt, Professor	Sweden
Szolc (Scholz), Piotr Otto	BRD
Szyszman, Simon	France
Söderberg, Staffan, Amanuens	Sweden
Takeuchi, Yoshinori, Professor	Japan
Taylor, John B.	UK
Thomas, John Heywood, Rev.	UK
Tierney, James Joseph, Professor	Ireland
Tishby, Isaiah, Professor	USA
Turner, Harold W., Dr.	UK
Uffenheimer, Benjamin, Professor	Israel
Waardenburg, Jacques, Senior Researcher	Netherlands
Wagner, Siegfried, Professor	DDR
Wagtendonk, K., Dr.	Netherlands
Vallée, Gérard	BRD
Watt, W. Montgomery, Professor	UK
Weckman, George A., Assistant professor	USA

Welch, Claude, Professor	USA
te Velde, H., Dr.	Netherlands
Werblowsky, R. J. Zwi, Professor	USA
Vesci, Uma Marina, Ph. D.	India
Widengren, Geo, Professor	Sweden
Wieder, F. C., Director	Netherlands
Wiessner, Gernot, Dr. Dr.	BRD
Virkkunen, T. P., Theol. Dr.	Finland
Wissmann, Hans	BRD
Voigt, Wolfgang, Bibliotheksdirektor	BRD
van Voss, M. Heerma, Professor	Netherlands
Würtz-Jørgensen, Cand. theol.	Denmark
Yoshida, Dr.	France
Zaehner, R. C., Professor	UK
Zandee, J., Professor	Netherlands
Zerkavod, Mordechay, Professor	Israel
Åhström, Birger, Fil. kand.	Sweden
Aneer, Gudmar, Teol. kand., fil. kand	Sweden
Kleen, Erland, Ambassador	Sweden
May, L. S., Dr.	USA